JUDAISM FACES
THE TWENTIETH
CENTURY

Mordecai M. Kaplan, ca. 1934. (Courtesy Library of JTS.)

JUDAISM FACES
THE TWENTIETH
CENTURY

A Biography of

Mordecai M. Kaplan

Mel Scult

 WAYNE STATE UNIVERSITY PRESS   DETROIT

American Jewish Civilization Series
Editors
Moses Rischin
San Francisco State University
Jonathan D. Sarna
Brandeis University

BOOKS IN THIS SERIES
Jews of the American West, edited by Moses Rischin
and John Livingston, 1991
*An Ambiguous Partnership: Non-Zionists and Zionists in
America 1939–1948*, by Menahem Kaufman, 1991
Hebrew in America: Perspectives and Prospects, edited by
Alan Mintz, 1992
*A Credit to Their Community: Jewish Loan Societies
in the United States, 1880–1945*, by Shelly
Tenenbaum, 1993
*Judaism Faces the Twentieth Century: A Biography of
Mordecai M. Kaplan*, by Mel Scult, 1993

Library of Congress Cataloging-in-Publication Data

Scult, Mel.
Judaism faces the twentieth century : a biography of
Mordecai M. Kaplan / Mel Scult.
p.   cm. — (American Jewish civilization series)
Includes bibliographical references and index.
ISBN 0-8143-2279-4 (alk. paper)
1. Kaplan, Mordecai Menahem, 1881–   . 2. Rabbis —
United States — Biography.   3. Judaism — 20th century.
4. Reconstructionist Judaism.   I. Title.   II. Series.
BM755.K289S38   1993
296.8'344'092 — dc20
[B]   92-46694

Designer: Joanne E. Kinney

Jacket photos: Mordecai M. Kaplan in 1908, at the time
of his engagement. (Courtesy Hadassah K. Musher)
(front cover). Mel Scult interviewing Mordecai Kaplan.
Photograph by Peter Addelston (back cover).

To my wife, Barbara Gish,
who redeems me
To my brother Allen,
sometimes older,
sometimes younger,
but always there for me
❋

The prophet is a man who feels fiercely . . .
he rarely sings but castigates.
—Abraham Joshua Heschel, *The Prophets*

CONTENTS

The self-help literature tells us that having a game worth playing makes one's life happy and productive. For a great many years, Mordecai Kaplan has been my game. He has sustained me, and I am grateful. I would like to believe that for a brief period in his nineties I helped to sustain him. He was not excited about or even very interested in talking to me about his life, but he did enjoy the constant audience and another chance to relate his most recent formulation to a problem he had been thinking about for the previous seventy-six years. One day he said to me, "I finally found out the meaning of the *Shemah*. The central idea is to love God intellectually, emotionally, and practically. Imagine, after all this time."

His vitality was overwhelming even in his nineties. When we first met, he talked until I was worn out. Subsequent to our initial series of meetings, I told him that he could call me on the telephone day or night and I would record the conversation. Thus he could speak for eternity at any moment and, of course, enjoyed the prospect. I continued to be overwhelmed as I began my research. Kaplan was a workaholic and left a staggering paper trail. It was like quicksand; once I got in, I thought I would never get out. He kept a diary from the time he was very young. People who knew him had heard about the diary, but no one was quite aware of its length. Begun in 1913 and ending shortly before his death, the diary, written in large accountant-type tomes, comes to twenty-seven volumes. Kaplan may be remembered as one of the greatest

Jewish diarists of all time. But then there were also the letters, some ten thousand of them, his sermons, his notes, and so on. And, of course, this was only the beginning, since I did not want to write his auto-biography.

The Kaplan of the diaries, papers, and sermons is a much more complex individual than the Kaplan who emerges from his published writing. In preparing a publication and especially when formulating his ideas, a writer has to clean things up and discard the ambiguities, the doubts, and the ambivalences. In a diary, inconsistencies and question-ing are inevitable. The public self is always quite different from the private self. Still another personality appears in the sermons; the Kap-lan of the pulpit was much more spiritual and much less analytic. He struggled with the traditional model of Judaism in a way his published works do not always make clear.

If we can speak of a fifty-year-old person as young, then the younger Kaplan may be much more a man for our time than the well-known Kaplan of his later years. Our age is a time of greater sensitivity to the spiritual and the numinous — yes, even to the mystical. As a younger man, Kaplan was closer to his origins in the traditional Jewish civilization of Eastern Europe. Alienated like so many of his generation from the world of his fathers, he sought methods of adjustment to life in America. But modes of thought change slowly; in significant ways, Kaplan still lived in the world into which he was born. Our task is evi-dent: "what the historian must do is to uncover in the past what is muted, suppressed, marginalized, which bears on the urgency of the present." [1]

The over-arching category which best describes Mordecai Kaplan is "rabbi." He was an intellectual and a writer, but the title of rabbi suits him best. His mission was to bring unity to the Jewish people and to help them survive. Never satisfied with what came easily, he struggled mightily with the written word — to become a writer. Never secure in the particular form of his thought he continually reworked the formu-lation, endlessly hoping to get it right. [2]

But his insecurities ran in other directions as well. His supporters, even those closest to him, never suspected the depth of his self-doubts. He was so intimidating — how could he ever doubt himself? What impressed those who knew him well, whether as teacher or as rabbi, was his monumental anger. An early student described him as the *"maʿayan ha-mitgabber,"* an ever-rushing stream, both destructive and reconstructive." [3] The anger flowed from his very demanding nature, both with himself and with others. His students always felt it — even during his last days, when he seemed to have lost everything else, the anger remained.

Kaplan's sufferings, which were never openly displayed, may be attributed primarily to his relationship with the Jewish Theological Seminary, which was his home for much of his life. The Seminary is not just an institution; it is a state of mind and a very exacting, if loving, parent. Not a month passed when he did not think about leaving, and yet he labored there for more than fifty-seven years. This reality highlights one of Kaplan's most notable qualities — his inertia. However freely he might speak, he frequently found action arduous. The implications for his own life and for the Reconstructionist movement were enormous.

Though he has often been described as pragmatic, Kaplan was an idealist who lived in a thought-world where everything seemed possible if people only understood the right way. His thought modalities were those of the teacher (*Rav*) who needed but to deliver the message.

There was a transparent intentionality about his life. He was unfailingly devoted to solving his primary problem: how to save the Jewish people. Why he thought it was *his* problem is not certain, but his devotion to solving this problem is evident from early in his life through his declining years. His sense of mission had nothing egotistical about it. At his ninetieth birthday dinner, Abraham Heschel offered a tribute in which he captured Kaplan's essence: "Kaplan takes Judaism personally. It is a magnificent obsession with him. I have a suspicion that just as the mystics of old used to stay up at midnight worrying about the *Shekhina*, he stays up at midnight doing *Tikkun Hatzos* [a midnight vigil] and worrying about the Jewish people."[4]

ACKNOWLEDGMENTS

The Kaplan family has been enormously helpful from the beginning. Special thanks are due to Rabbi Ira Eisenstein and Judith Kaplan Eisenstein for their many insights over the years. I am indebted to Naomi Kaplan Wenner for her enthusiastic support of my work; to Hadassah Kaplan Musher, friend and fellow congregant, for her consistent help and support. I regret that Sidney Musher did not live to see the work he so ardently encouraged. I also want to thank Selma Kaplan Goldman and the late Dr. Joseph Goldman for their help.

Jonathan Sarna's informed analysis and gentle prodding led me to rework this book in significant ways. I am grateful to Moses Rischin for his abundant support. Deborah Dash Moore read the manuscript in its entirety, and her enormous editing effort has been crucial in improving my work both in content and in style. Helene Aguilar worked closely with me and read this book more times than any other person. Her patient, supportive criticism was invaluable and inspired me to seek a higher level of expression.

I am indebted to my good friend and professional colleague Emanuel S. Goldsmith, whose support sustained me and whose insights about Kaplan were always valuable. Robert Seltzer gave freely of his thoughts; for his friendship and his generosity of spirit, I am grateful. Special gratitude goes to Harold Gorvine, whose acceptance and intelligent reactions were always a source of sustenance from the very beginning of this project. The late Ludwig Nadelman's insights in the early stages of this project were enriching and opened new paths of inquiry. I am indebted to Norbert Samuelson, who read some of the philosophical material, and to Ellen Umansky, who read the material on the Seminary.

At the Reconstructionist Rabbinical College, I want to thank Mordecai Liebling, David Teutsch, Jacob Staub, and Arthur Green for all their help. Throughout the years, Jennifer Abraham and Dee Einhorn gave me important assistance.

At the Jewish Theological Seminary, I am indebted to Jules Harlow for his encouragement over the years; to Dr. Ismar Schorsch for reading parts of this manuscript that deal with the Seminary and for his continuous support of my work; to Neil Gilman for his valuable insights; and to Jack Wertheimer, Avraham Holtz, Baila Round Shargel, Menahem Schmeltzer, and Rabbi Simon Greenberg. At Brooklyn College, my friend and colleague Yaffa Eliach gave me vital aid and support. My thanks also to Sid Leiman for reading portions of this work.

To Elizabeth Archer, who helped me in the early stages of this project; to Evelyn Fachler, who struggled with typing this manuscript in its precomputer incarnation; and to Melanie Southerland, who typed much of the book, I am grateful. To Kathryn Wildfong, my editor at Wayne State University Press, my gratitude for her energy, effort, and support.

The following people also deserve my thanks: Barbara Heyman, Emily Fairey, Elinore Grumet, Judith Fixler, Francesca Brasil, the Hon. Benjamin Wm. Mehlman, Terry Toll, Adina Eshel, Gerald Schwartzbart, Julie Miller, Abe Peck, Fanny Zelcer, and Stephen Siegel.

A previous version of chapter 4 appeared in *American Jewish Archives* 38 (April 1986). A previous version of chapters 6 and 9 appeared in *The American Judaism of Mordecai Kaplan*, ed. Emanuel S. Goldsmith, Mel Scult, and Robert Seltzer (New York: New York University Press, 1990).

My brother Allen not only has given me abundant support and encouragement but always listened carefully and shared his very valuable reactions with me. Our conversations helped to generate certain key themes of this book. My wife, Barbara Gish, who identifies with me, sustains me, edits me, and redeems me, will always have my unfailing devotion and gratitude.

1

FROM MOTL TO MAURICE TO MORDECAI

O"f all that is written I love only what a man has written with his blood." Inscribed by Mordecai Kaplan on the cover page of his earliest diary, this quotation from Nietzsche aptly reflects Kaplan's own passionate mode of being. He was a man of ideas and a rationalist, yet his emotions ran deep; his piety and spirituality were essential to his being, and his concern for the Jewish people was the primary obsession of his life. Begun in the same year as the Russian pogroms, his life exemplifies and symbolizes the odyssey of the modern Jew.

Mordecai Kaplan is usually associated with his American context, with the sociological and pragmatic roots of his thought. Kaplan's Americanism, his belief in democracy, runs deep. However, he was nursed not on John Dewey or Emile Durkheim but on the rabbis. He was born into a society where God was still alive, and he was not weaned from his background until he was well into his twenties. He lived at home until he was twenty-eight, and that home was strictly traditional in the Lithuanian style.

Israel Kaplan, Mordecai's father, was born in 1848 not far from the town of Kovno, then a thriving center of Jewish life and learning. He was the second of five children and was sent at the age of twelve to the city of Vilna to study in the yeshiva there. As a young adult, he "learned" in the great yeshivas of Volozhin and Kovno and later was recognized for his achievements in the form of rabbinical ordination (*smicha*) from the best-known Lithuanian rabbis of his day. At that time

Kaplan's father, Rabbi Israel Kaplan.
(Courtesy Judith K. Eisenstein.)

Kaplan's mother, Anna Kaplan.
(Courtesy Judith K. Eisenstein.)

no one studied to be a rabbi in the same way that contemporary students take a course and pursue a degree. Studying was a sacred act in and of itself, requiring no outside goal or justification.

Legend has it that Napoleon, astonished by all the Jews he saw there, was the first to call Vilna "the Jerusalem of Lithuania." Vilna had possessed a Jewish community for centuries, although it was not until the nineteenth century that the city became the center of Talmudic learning with which we are so familiar.

The preeminence of Lithuanian Jewry in Talmudic learning may be traced back to a figure of mythical proportions. Elijah Ben Solomon Zalman, the Vilna *Gaon* ("genius"), 1720–1797, towered over Lithuanian Jewry throughout the nineteenth century. His "unrelenting intellectuality"[1] set the tone for the battle against the pietistic movement of Hasidism with its emphasis on exultation and joy. The holy war against pietism did not stop the *Gaon* from studying the many works of Jewish mysticism or from writing commentaries on them. The Gaon also studied mathematics and astronomy for the sole purpose of understanding certain legal (*halakhic*) questions more accurately. He fought against "casuistic hair-splitting" (*pilpul*) and sought to establish the correct texts of many Jewish works. Hayim of Volozhin (1749–1821), the most important disciple of the *Gaon*, established a yeshiva in Volozhin. It was a national institution which in the 1860s had between two hundred and three hundred students. Prior to this time, a yeshiva was always small and local even though it might be associated with the name of a great rabbi.

Volozhin had already achieved its status as the hub of learning when Israel Kaplan commenced his studies there in the 1860s. Many traditional Jews had begun to concentrate more on the later legal codes (e.g., *Shulhan Arukh*) which were directly related to everyday observance. In establishing the yeshiva, Rabbi Hayim was committed to a return to the sources of the tradition — the Talmud and its commentaries. He also continued the emphasis on clarity and rigor of intellectual analysis which were initiated by the *Gaon*. The yeshiva endured almost the whole of the nineteenth century (1803–1892) and was housed in a sturdy building which nonetheless was destroyed by fire. After the fire, it was rebuilt of white stone.[2]

At the head of the Volozhin yeshiva for the last forty years of its life and during the apprenticeship of Israel Kaplan was Rabbi Naphtali Zvi Judah Berlin (1817–1893), called the *Netziv*. He had married the granddaughter of Rabbi Hayim of Volozhin and continued the founder's policies and curriculum. In fact, there really was no set curriculum. Although the head of the yeshiva (the director of a yeshiva is

Yeshiva of Volozhin, where Israel Kaplan studied
as a young man. The Yeshiva building was recon-
structed after a fire in 1886. (Courtesy Yaffa Eliach
Shtetl Collection.)

called *rosh* or "head") would deliver public lectures, all young men studied alone and were responsible only to themselves. The *Netziv* encouraged his students to study the whole of the Babylonian Talmud in the
order of its arrangement, not omitting even the minor tractates. He
also devoted much attention to study of the scriptures. His commentary on the Pentateuch, *Ha'amek Davar*, appeared in 1879. Although
opposed to modernization, the *Netziv* believed that secular studies were
valuable in a very restricted way when carried out under the supervision
of a pious teacher. However, such pursuits were not to be carried out in
the yeshiva. He also supported the *Hibbat Zion* (Lovers of Zion) movement during its early years.[3] Mordecai Kaplan's father received rabbinical ordination from the *Netziv* and studied at Volozhin intermittently.
Israel Kaplan also obtained rabbinic ordination from Isaac Elhanan
Specktor of Kovno, after whom the rabbinical seminary at Yeshiva
University was named.

We know about Israel Kaplan only through the eyes of his son
Mordecai. The elder Kaplan seemed to fit perfectly the prototype of
the deeply committed, studious Lithuanian Jew who devoted himself

fully to his learning. Even after he married, he continued his life of Talmud study. He settled in the town of Sventzian, which was about twenty-five miles away, less than a day's journey from Vilna and Volozhin. After his marriage, he remained in Sventzian for a few years but could not resist the call of the yeshiva and returned to Kovno, coming home only for holiday visits. Such a pattern was not unusual among traditional Lithuanian Jews.

The Eastern European world in which Mordecai Kaplan's family lived was awash in a sea of change during the 1860s and 1870s. The Jewish enlightenment, or *Haskalah*, which began in the early years of the nineteenth century had become a powerful force among the younger men. The *Maskilim* (Enlightened Ones) maintained that the Jewish people could survive only by moving into the modern world and learning its ways. Such a process should not be understood as a move toward assimilation. Particularly in the east, the leaders of the *Haskalah* sought a synthesis of Judaism and Europeanism, often advocating the revival of Hebrew language and literature as the vehicle for the synthesis. Judah Leib Gordon's (1830–1892) poem "Awake My People," which served as a clarion call to the enlightenment, contains the famous exhortation "Be a man in the streets and a Jew at home." This verse became the slogan of the Hebrew enlightenment, but it has been widely misinterpreted. Gordon was not advocating the bifurcation of Jewish life or that Jews be ashamed of their Jewishness; rather, he was advocating the integration of the general culture, in this case Russian, with the deeply committed life of the creative Jew. The *Haskalah* movement, in supporting Gordon's idea, was advocating that Jews live in two civilizations simultaneously — an idea that became central to the philosophy of Mordecai Kaplan.[4]

One principal element in *Haskalah* ideology was the education of women. In the traditional Jewish world, women were educated in only a minimal way. The *Maskilim* advocated that women be included in all their educational reforms and receive an equal education in the schools they established. Israel Kaplan was no *Maskil*, but he sent his daughter Shprintse to the local elementary school (*heder*), which ordinarily did not enroll girls, and he was determined that she should receive a good Hebrew education. According to Mordecai Kaplan, his sister was competent in Hebrew. The elder Kaplan also may have read the works of the Hebraic enlighteners.[5]

Eastern European Jewry had a special concern for ethical issues, and Mordecai Kaplan's own ethical emphasis was rooted in the ethical (*Musar*) movement of the late nineteenth century. Israel Kaplan was described by his son as a *Musarnik*, meaning that the elder Kaplan was a follower of Israel Salanter and the *Musar* movement. Salanter (1810–1883), who was born Israel Lipkin, took his name from the town where he studied as a young man. He was among those who fought the new trend toward enlightenment and believed that Talmud study had to be supplemented by a devotion to ethical literature in order to ensure a high level of ethical behavior and discipline among traditional Jews. Salanter advocated that a separate institution called a *Musar Shtibl* (moralist conventicle) be established where young men would study *Musar* literature and pursue a strictly disciplined ethical life. He believed that understanding in and of itself was not sufficient for right action. Each person must have a clear recognition of the power of his or her evil inclination (the *Yetzer Ha-Ra*, or the id, one might say) and should be continually vigilant in gaining self control through self-criticism and meditation. This constant self-criticism would reform the person's character so that acting ethically would become second nature.[6]

The Jewish world of Lithuania thus incorporated the values that later became the major components of Mordecai Kaplan's consciousness. Lines of causation are never clear, and Kaplan did not learn these matters directly from his father. Atmosphere and zeitgeist were nonetheless significant, and the fundamental ways of seeing the world were all in place: an analytical and logical emphasis on the approach to rabbinic sources, as well as a profound commitment to the proposition that lifelong study would have a direct impact on ethical behavior. (Kaplan conceived of the Society for the Advancement of Judaism perhaps as a kind of *Musar Shtibl*. See chapters 10 and 11 herein.) Both of these trends existed within the traditional communities of Lithuanian Jewry. In addition, the countertrend of the *Haskalah* stressed the idea that the modern world was not a threat but an opportunity, and Jews needed to be prepared for it if they were going to survive as Jews. Israel Kaplan could not have remained uninfluenced by all these developments.

When Israel Kaplan was still quite young, he was selected by the Kovarsky family of Sventzian for an introduction to Haya Nehama (later called Anna). The young couple married and settled down near the bride's home. Israel Kaplan was considered a good catch because he had a fine reputation and was known as a *Harif ubaki* (brilliant and erudite person). We know much less about Haya Nehama. She came from a traditional family and was an intelligent and able woman. Her father died before she was married, and she had the primary responsibility for sustaining and preserving the family. Her son reports that she was talented in music and languages. More importantly, she supported the family while her husband "learned" in the yeshivas in and around

Vilna. They owned a small general store in Sventzian, which Anna managed.

Mordecai Kaplan (called Motl as a boy) was born on the fourteenth day of the month of Sivan 5641 (1881). He did not know the corresponding English date for his birth until many years later, when he went to the New York Public Library and looked it up in a Jewish newspaper for that day. He was born on a Friday night at 11:50; the precise time was marked by his father, who stopped the clock. Kaplan reported proudly that Maimonides' father did the same thing when his son was born.

Although Israel Kaplan traveled often to the yeshivas nearby, he also established significant relationships in the town. One of the closest was with the local rabbi, Isaac Jacob Reines. Reines (1839–1915), known primarily for his work in the founding of the Religious Zionist party, or *Mizrachi* as it is called, was about ten years older than Israel Kaplan, and the two became colleagues and good friends. Reines hoped that the Orthodox would become Zionists and that the Zionists would become Orthodox. In addition to the *Mizrachi*, his other claim to fame is the founding of a rather innovative yeshiva in Lida, a town not far from Vilna. This new kind of yeshiva had its roots in his experience in Sventzian, where he inaugurated his imaginative educational ideas. The experiment was an interesting one, and, according to Mordecai Kaplan, the new school began by meeting at the Kaplan house.

For many years, the Russian government had been trying to encourage the establishment of schools where Jews would study Russian and become more acculturated to Russian society. While many *Maskilim* were happy to join in this effort, traditional rabbis felt threatened. They believed such endeavors undermined the Torah-centered life of the Jewish people. Reines was unusual because, despite his commitment to the tradition, he accepted the need for innovation. At a meeting in St. Petersburg in 1882, he spoke to a group of his rabbinical colleagues and outlined his ideas for "reforming" yeshiva education. He was concerned with the degeneration of learning, resulting in part from the fact that young men had to leave the yeshiva prematurely. Students needed to be prepared to make a living and needed to know enough about the "new learning" (secular culture) to oppose it effectively. Both of these goals could be achieved by the introduction of secular subjects into the curriculum.[7]

Reines's ideas were viciously attacked in the Hebrew press, but there was also strong support. Among his supporters from Sventzian was Jacob Kovarsky, a relative of Anna Kaplan, who published a detailed account of the plan.[8] The school would prepare rabbis for making legal (*halahkic*) decisions and becoming community leaders. They would commence at age thirteen and would learn Talmud as well as Hebrew, Russian, German, mathematics, geography, basic science, general history, the history of Israel, and the history of the Russian people. The yeshiva would be managed in accordance with the latest "rules of hygiene" and would be properly ventilated with clean air. Reines assured the public that the quarters would be "spacious and healthy."[9]

Reines knew that even within Sventzian there were extremists who wanted to destroy the new yeshiva. He was confident, however, that it would prevail. Reines was no closet liberal. He was a traditional Jew who wanted to be realistic in arming the Jewish people so they could preserve their traditional ways yet also survive in the modern world.

He was attacked personally by individuals who spread rumors about him — that he was engaged in subversive activity and that he was misusing funds he was given. In 1883, while in Moscow seeking money for his yeshiva, Reines was imprisoned by the Russian authorities because of charges brought against him. Despite the strong opposition to Reines's ideas, Israel Kaplan invited the rabbi to launch his school in the Kaplan household. Many years later (1908), when Mordecai Kaplan came to Europe to meet with Reines for his rabbinical ordination, the old rabbi mentioned the lessons that were conducted in the Kaplan house when Mordecai was still a toddler.

Israel Kaplan supported change but was not a radical. He read Russian (there were Russian books in the house when Mordecai was a child) but was not an apostle of enlightenment and Russian culture. He wanted his daughter educated, but, so far as we know, he did not support sweeping changes in the education of women. He was cautiously tolerant of new ideas and unwittingly prepared the way for his son.

Mordecai Kaplan lived with his parents in Sventzian until he was seven years old. During these years, he received a typical traditional education both in the *heder* and in his home. It may be that Shprintse, his older sister, also taught him. She was so competent in Hebrew that she was sent to a blind Hebraist in the town to read Hebrew works to him. As a young child, Mordecai had relatively little contact with his father. Israel Kaplan was frequently away from home studying in various yeshivas.

Haya Nehama had great plans for her young son, fantasizing that one day he might attain the position of chief rabbi of the British Empire. A large picture of Sir Moses Montefiore, the British philanthropist, was prominently displayed in the house; Mordecai's mother may have thought he was also a rabbi. She bore two sons before Mordecai;

both died in infancy. So when Kaplan survived she believed it was a sign that he was destined for great things. Her conviction that young Mottel would excel obviously had a significant impact on the boy. Throughout his life, Kaplan had high expectations of himself. These demands can be traced back to a mother who was capable and intelligent yet lived in a society where women could not themselves achieve prominence, and so were invested in the success of their sons.[10] Kaplan's exaggerated sense of his responsibilities also may stem from Israel Kaplan's frequent absences. The little boy of six or seven may have felt that he had to be the man of the family.

Jewish history of the 1880s is usually explained in terms of a number of key facts. The sequence is familiar. In 1881, the czar was assassinated, the Jews were blamed, and pogroms ensued, which led in turn to a number of major developments with which the modern era in Jewish history began. These developments were the beginning of a flood of immigration to the west (primarily America), the urge to solve the "Jewish problem" through Jewish nationalism (Zionism), and the idea that the Jews could become safe only if the repressive forces of the czar and of capitalism were overthrown. There is no denying that there is truth to these assertions. It is no less true that the immigration from Russia began before the pogroms, as did the Jewish nationalist movement. The ideologies of socialism and nationalism were present within the Jewish community before the anti-Jewish riots. The pogroms served as a galvanizing agent for pressures already present in the Jewish community, but these important social forces might have erupted in any case.[11]

Mordecai Kaplan's ideology is the quintessence of modernism, and it is tempting to place him within the modern sequence of the recent Jewish past. The year of his birth, 1881, was the year of the pogroms, the year of the beginning of the modern Jew. He left his home with his parents a few years later as part of the great immigration to America. The Kaplans had contemplated a move for a number of years, but the final decision was triggered by factors other than the general historical ones. For one thing, Israel Kaplan was approaching forty and still did not have a stable position. He had been recommended by Reines and by Rabbi Isaac Elhanan Specktor for a number of rabbinical posts but obtained none of them. He was a highly principled person and this created difficulties for him. When he finally did obtain a position he became ill and could not carry out his duties. Mordecai Kaplan believed that the exodus of the family had something to do with a gentile boycott of the Jewish stores. In 1885, a fire ravaged the town of Sventzian, which led to severe hardship and economic dislocation. Thus, an offer of a position in America looked extremely good to Israel Kaplan. In 1886, he started out for America, traveling as far as Hamburg and then turning back. According to his son, he was so disgusted with the vulgarity of the masses of Jews he encountered that he decided to return to Sventzian.[12]

In July 1888, he finally succeeded in leaving and traveled to Kovno to say farewell to Rabbi Isaac Elhanan Specktor and to receive his blessing. While Israel traveled on to New York to assume a rabbinical position, Haya Nehama, Shprintse, and Motl went to Paris to stay with her two brothers. Mordecai Kaplan remembers playing under the Eiffel Tower while his mother sold homemade candies. Haya Nehama ruled the family with a heavy hand, as indeed she had to. She learned French, insisted the children do likewise, and was perceived by her son as being a strict disciplinarian.

The year in Paris was not without its problems for the seven-year-old Mottel, who was now called Maurice. The first school he attended was closed on Thursday and Sunday and met on the Sabbath. Kaplan remembered telling the teacher that his hand hurt, so that he would not have to write on the holy day. He learned to recite the Ten Commandments in French for the chief rabbi who came to visit the Jewish school he attended later on.

In early July, the family sailed for America, and Kaplan remembered one incident aboard ship very vividly. It was Bastille Day, and everyone was on deck watching fireworks. It also happened to be the Sabbath and time for prayer. Kaplan had not yet learned to "skip" in his praying, as he later put it, so that by the time he finished and arrived on deck the fireworks were over. He was furious with his mother, and the childhood anger stayed in his mind for the next eighty years.

On Sunday, July 16, 1889, Mordecai Kaplan arrived with his mother and sister at Castle Garden on the S.S. *Burgoyne*. Israel, who had not seen them for a year, met them at the ship and took them to the home of Anna's cousin. They quickly secured a place of their own at 32 Suffolk Street, where they settled into their new life.

Israel Kaplan immigrated to America as part of the entourage of Chief Rabbi Jacob Joseph. A group of New York Jews concerned about the condition of the tradition sought to strengthen the position of those dedicated to preserving Orthodox life in America. Their strategy was to bring to New York a rabbi of eminence who would unify the Orthodox and increase their self-respect. The pressures of acculturation in the "Golden Land" were immense. The very foundations of American culture seemed to undermine the primary principles to which Jews had been dedicated throughout the centuries. Jewish society had never been a democracy. Those who were wealthy wielded a considerable degree of power and had to deal only with the learned elite. The ideal of Jewish society was not democratic, nor was the reality. In America, on the other hand, the meeting hall seemed much more important than the study hall. The immigration to the United States meant a shift from a "contemplative culture centered around study to a political one where power predominated." [13]

The primary problem facing local leaders was the matter of *kashrut*. One Hebrew paper noted there were Jews who got off the boat, bought the appropriate clothes, and presented themselves as rabbis. They would then become ritual slaughterers without having the proper training and might certify meat as kosher without knowing its origin. There was a constant conflict between their Judaism and their jobs. Perhaps more importantly, it was easy for a storekeeper to present ordinary meat as kosher because there was no systematic supervision. [14]

It was the hope of a small group of men that Rabbi Jacob Joseph would solve these problems. This well-known scholar from Vilna was given a six-year contract at $2,500 a year to be *the* rabbi of the New York Jewish community. He brought with him a number of younger men, Israel Kaplan among them, who would serve on his rabbinical court and assist him in his duties.

Among the businessmen who helped raise the money to bring over the new rabbi was Judah David Eisenstein. Eisenstein was an indefatigable hebraeophile. He was also the grandfather of Ira Eisenstein, later to become Kaplan's most devoted disciple and the husband of his eldest daughter, Judith. The ubiquitous Eisenstein was a learned Jew, and well known within the Jewish community. According to his own account, he was one of the first to walk over the Brooklyn Bridge in 1883 and among the first to climb to the top of the new Statue of Liberty. He wrote frequently for the Jewish press and was the official historian of his congregation, Beth Hamedrash Ha-Godol. [15]

The chief rabbi, however, brought more chaos than order; there were troubles from the beginning. Money had to be raised to pay the rabbi and to reimburse those who financed his trip from Europe. His supporters wanted to be sure that the rabbi would not be accused of any improprieties, so they retained control of all the money collected in the rabbi's name. In 1887, they had formed themselves into the Association of American Orthodox Hebrew Congregations, which was to be responsible for importing the rabbi and supervising his activities. The whole association strategy backfired. In order to control the *kashrut* situation and to raise money, the rabbi imposed a half-cent tax on every kosher chicken, such chickens to be specially tagged so that people could be sure they were kosher. There was an outcry from local rabbis who had been there before the chief rabbi arrived and whose certifications were now brought into question if they did not cooperate with or work for the chief rabbi. The half-penny tax reminded many of the oppressive taxes that had brought the Jews so much heartache in Europe. Uptown religious Jews charged that the founders of the association were in business to make money for themselves and that the kosher tags of the chief rabbi were being attached to "choked and putrid chickens." Radical Jews referred to Jacob Joseph as the "Chief Charlatan" and were delighted that the religious Jews were in such a predicament.[16]

Israel Kaplan left the office of the chief rabbi shortly after he arrived. He wanted no part of the charges of corruption and fraud. Though no evidence suggests that Rabbi Jacob Joseph was guilty of fraud, neither was he able to extricate himself from the conflict. The unwitting victim of a complex situation, he lacked the managerial ability to extricate himself from it. Kaplan's father was disgusted with the traditional community as well as the local rabbis who criticized Rabbi Jacob Joseph.

Having heard such stories as a child, Mordecai Kaplan internalized a mistrust of Orthodox rabbis that remained with him for many years. He thought that Orthodox Jews should have acted with higher standards: "The experiences my father underwent in his relations with R. Jacob Joseph and other rabbis planted in my mind a distrust of that species of rabbi, a distrust which in all the years since has seldom proved to be unwarranted. Somehow their ethical standards never correspond to what one has a right to expect from men who are considered spiritual leaders." The question, of course, is not the accuracy of Kaplan's picture of the conflicts surrounding Rabbi Jacob Joseph, but rather his emotional reaction as an adult when he remembered these childhood events. His predisposition to be critical of the ethical standards of the Orthodox can be traced back to his father and the very painful saga of the chief rabbi.[17]

Israel Kaplan had no trouble finding a position as a ritual slaughterer on his own. His credentials were impeccable and his knowledge formidable. Family life now settled down to a routine quite different from that in the old country. In America, Israel lived at home, and Haya Nehama, now called Anna, ceased to work outside the home. In Sventzian, she had been the primary supporter of the household and presumably felt some dismay at the reduction of her status.

The young boy of eight benefited considerably from the new arrangement. In Sventzian, he saw his father rarely; in Paris, not at all. Now he saw him every day. Israel Kaplan became his teacher and taught his son on a regular basis until his last days. Mordecai was very attached to his father and admired him greatly. Their learning together strengthened and deepened the natural bonds between them, and intensified Mordecai's identity as a Jew.

The changes of his name reflect one aspect of Kaplan's evolution as a Jew. Coming to a new land required many changes. Name changing was a natural part of the Americanization process, but sometimes it betokened transformation in one's inner condition as well as responses to outside pressures. Motl, who was called Maurice while in France, was now called Max as well as Mark, and Shprintse became Sophie. But Max or Mark Kaplan was not yet Mordecai. The last stage of the naming process was more intentional and occurred a few years later, when Kaplan responded to the Spanish-American War and the resurgent nationalism of those seeking liberation from Spanish domination. The hero of the day was a young man named Emilio Aguinaldo, who led an insurrection against the Spanish to free the Philippines from foreign rule. For a brief period, he set up a republic with himself as president. These developments made a deep impression on the young Kaplan. If the Philippine people were going to assert their independence and ethnic identity, then so should he. So he changed his name to Mordecai (his original Hebrew name), even though many members of the family continued to know him as Mark.[18]

It was natural for Israel Kaplan to enroll his son in the best yeshiva he could find. A few years before Mordecai's arrival, the same people who invited the chief rabbi had organized a new Jewish school called the *Jeshivath Etz Chaiem* (hereafter called Yeshivat Etz Chaim). The establishment of this yeshiva is indicative of the developing needs of the new immigrants. Some of the traditional Eastern European Jews believed that the existing Jewish schools would make their children more American rather than more Jewish. American Jews before the Civil War had sent their children to schools run by their own congregations. As the public school system in New York City grew, many embraced the new educational opportunity. In order to further Jewish education, afternoon schools, sometimes called Hebrew Free Schools, were established during the 1870s. Some of the more religious Eastern European Jews who immigrated at this time were unhappy with the Hebrew Free Schools, which taught in English and were frequently supported by wealthy Reform Jews. They sought to establish afternoon schools that would be more traditional and would teach in the Eastern European mode. The largest of these traditional elementary schools, called Machzike Talmud Torah, had some four hundred students by 1887. But even the Machzike Talmud Torah met in the afternoon and assumed that in the morning students would attend the public school.

Yeshivat Etz Chaim was established by Jews who wanted a typical Eastern European all-day school where the language would be Yiddish and where the students would study traditional subjects.[19]

Yeshivat Etz Chaim was established in the fall of 1886 in a small private house on Canal Street. From nine in the morning until four in the afternoon, the students concentrated on Talmud, Bible, and Jewish law (in this case, the *Shulhan Arukh*). After four, they would turn to secular subjects and English-language instruction. The yeshiva raised money in a number of ways, including charity boxes, and established a Malbish Arumim Society for the specific purpose of providing the children with clothes and shoes. One of the earliest English-language teachers was the young Abraham Cahan, who went on to become a famous writer and the editor of the Yiddish-language newspaper *The Forward*. (The other English teacher was a fourteen-year-old boy.) Cahan struggled to teach his students English in a chilly atmosphere, finding the powers that be rather unresponsive to his requests for English textbooks. The "powers," on the other hand, found Cahan completely unacceptable when they learned of his socialist ideals and secular orientation. He was dismissed in July 1888, after being attacked by the supporters of the yeshiva as an "anarchist, a sinner and a beguiler."[20]

Kaplan attended the Machzike Talmud Torah and was transferred to Etz Chaim when he was about nine and a half. Etz Chaim was eventually (1915) combined with Rabbi Isaac Elchanan Theological Seminary, established in 1897, which later became the core of Yeshiva University. In his later years, Kaplan was fond of telling people that he was the oldest living graduate of Yeshiva University. He remained at Etz Chaim about three years. In the lower class, students covered half a page of Talmud a week, and in the upper class, they were able to cover two folio pages a week. The teacher was known as Rabbi Shmuel "Langenoz" ("Long Nose"), according to the children. Kaplan's study at the yeshiva together with the continual studying with his father gave him a firm grounding in the traditional sources. He was also strictly observant of Jewish law during this early period. He remembered reading the condensation of the *Shulkan Arukh* and noticing the rule that a man should not walk between two women. The next time he went out with his mother and Sophie, he insisted on walking on the side and not between them as he usually did.

The routine of the Kaplan household included study as a regular activity. Israel Kaplan would spend the mornings at the slaughterhouses he supervised. He would usually come home in the late afternoon and, after taking a nap, would devote himself to Talmudic study. One afternoon when young Mordecai was about eight years old, his father was asleep on the couch. Anna told her son to wake up his father. Mordecai nudged his father, who did not get up but just turned over and continued his nap. At that point, Mordecai said, "TaTa Li Oreph." This expression is a play on words from the Hebrew to the Yiddish which appears in the last part of the verse in Psalms 18:41 and reads in English, "Thou hast also made my enemies turn their backs to me." Israel Kaplan was so proud of his son's cleverness that he ran directly to the chief rabbi, who lived nearby, to relate the incident.

Kaplan remembered his father as "weak and unfit for strenuous labor of any kind." The father and son studied together often, with Yiddish as the language of instruction. Israel Kaplan conversed with his son in Hebrew, but he had a "poor ear" and was never able to acquire a working knowledge of English.

Israel Kaplan's influence on his son and his devotion to Mordecai's learning is striking when Kaplan's situation is compared to that of Jewish households lacking a learned father. Morris Raphael Cohen, who later became a famous philosopher, was Mordecai's childhood friend. Cohen was born in Minsk a year before Kaplan and came to America as a boy. The two knew each other in elementary school and at City College. In his autobiography, Cohen says that his intellectual life began when he first read *The Arabian Nights* in Yiddish along with the books of the Yiddish writer Mendele Mokher Sforim. With encouragement, Cohen might have continued Talmudic study. "In the first place," he wrote, "there was no incentive and little opportunity for me to continue my Hebraic and Talmudic studies. There was no suitable books in the house and no one urged me to continue such study. It was taken for granted that in a few years I would join my father in some phase of tailoring." Cohen recalls trying to study on his own but was not able to get past "the difficult places."[21]

Israel Kaplan helped his son get past the difficult places not only in Talmudic study but in other areas as well. Israel wanted his son to master the English language, and so after three years at the yeshiva, Mordecai was transferred to public school. So strong was the pressure to learn English that eventually Etz Chaim was forced to open an afternoon Hebrew department for those who had transferred to the public schools. Mordecai continued his Talmudic studies with his father and also with a local rabbi hired by the family. Kaplan noted that he started out studying with the rabbi in the evening, but after he fell asleep several times, the tutoring was switched to the morning before he left for school.[22]

Kaplan not only studied with a rabbi, he also regularly attended the big *shul* (synagogue) on Eldridge Street with his father. During the week, the two went to *shul*, where the elder Kaplan studied and lectured

Eldridge Street synagogue, Lower East Side. Kaplan attended here regularly with his father and was bar mitzvah here. (Reprinted by permission from The Lower East Side, *text by Ronald Sanders, photographs by Edmund V. Gillon, Jr., pl. 87 © 1979, Ronald Sanders and Dover Publications.)*

on the Talmud. When Mordecai Kaplan was in his forties, he chanced to visit the synagogue where he had prayed as a child and where he had celebrated his bar mitzvah. Many sad and warm memories embraced him as he stood in the synagogue that Sabbath morning and reminisced:

> There were the same lofty vaults in the ceiling, the same stained-glass windows, the same lighting fixtures, the large chandelier suspended from the center of the ceiling by a long, thin pipe which I used to be afraid would snap. On the *almemar* [pulpit], I recognized the bench which served as a container for the *talethim* and prayer books. Boys rushed up to it now and then to snatch a prayer book as of old. The box of snuff tobacco was still there, and every once in a while someone would help himself in the course of the prayers. In fact, the atmosphere was so strong with the smell of snuff tobacco that my nose was irritated. This sensation I do not recall having felt there as a boy. I also walked down to what is usually called the vestry. It was there I used to pray weekdays with Father. I looked long at the seat near the Ark where he and I used to sit and engage in Talmud discussions. I recalled the joy and the pride that would fill his heart when I would put a question to him that had been asked by some of the famous commentators.

The deep reserves of these childhood memories had a lifelong impact on his character and thought.

Kaplan commenced his career at City College when he was about fourteen. In those years, colleges were often a combination of high school and university. In 1895, Kaplan began to attend the City College of New York at its "uptown" location on Twenty-third Street. City College was not then the school with which we are familiar from the many Jewish writers of the pre–World War II period. It was not filled with Jews working their way out of the ghetto. Nor was it a hotbed of radicalism. Before 1900, City College was a school for the children of the wealthy. It had a completely traditional curriculum of Greek and Latin. Most entering students did not complete a degree; those who were determined to make money did not go to college. "Higher education all across the country was geared to giving cultural polish to men of independent means." City College was still Christian, attendance at chapel being mandatory until 1904. Education, especially higher education, was not yet the avenue of mobility it later became. The large array of courses that would prepare students to function in the growing industrial economy of the twentieth century had not yet been developed. In a later period, the colleges would train the lawyers, accountants, engineers, and architects whom business needed, but in Kaplan's time the children of the immigrants had not yet invaded higher education. Radical in his theology, Kaplan remained quite conservative in many other ways, and this conservatism can be traced back to his youth, to City College, and to the more placid days of the era before the Great War.[23]

When Kaplan was completing college, the whole system began to assume its modern shape. City College in 1901 added two years to its preparatory course, and shortly afterward admission to the college was restricted to those who had completed the preparatory course or to those who had completed high school. In addition, the late nineteenth century witnessed the introduction of the elective system and the teaching of commercial and scientific subjects.

Kaplan's college education consisted of a heavy dose of Greek and Latin with a smattering of other subjects. The curriculum included not only the ancient languages but also ancient history, mythology, art, social and political antiquities, and classical law. Students studied philosophy in the sophomore year, logic in the junior year, and psychology in the last year.

Many years later, Kaplan recalled his college experience with disgust. He felt that his adolescence was wasted on preparing texts that were neither stimulating nor interesting. Indeed, he confessed that often he had no idea of the meaning of the text and he felt that the professors seemed to show little interest in the intellectual development of their charges. Even when the texts were modern, they sometimes eluded him, as was the case with the psychology of John Dewey. "I had not the least idea what it was all about," he wrote much later. "They had a young fellow just graduated from college teach it. I dreaded his hour for fear that he would call on me. I lived in fear all that year." Nevertheless, Kaplan did well at City College. Each year, a booklet entitled "The Merit Roll" was published. Each student in each class was ranked on the basis of tests and recitations. For the year 1896–97, out of a class of 219, Morris Raphael Cohen placed fourteenth with no demerits, and Kaplan was twenty-second with eight demerits. The pressure was obviously immense, because after two years, more than half the class had dropped out.[24]

While attending City College, Kaplan also studied at the Jewish Theological Seminary. The significance of the Seminary in Kaplan's development cannot be overestimated. It functioned as his primary context throughout his life. He graduated from the Seminary at the age of twenty-one (1902) and returned seven years later as a member of the faculty. He remained there until his retirement in 1963. Throughout his life, he found his days at the Seminary burdensome but could never rouse himself sufficiently to sever his relationship with the institution. Kaplan's journal is filled with expressions of his determination to leave, but he ended up being one of the most long-lived members of the faculty.

The Seminary must be understood against the background of the split between Reform and traditional Jews and the desire of some Reform Jews to Americanize the newly arrived immigrants. The strongly congregational character of religious life in America determined the context of Jewish life. Throughout the nineteenth century, various individuals attempted to bring unity and uniformity into Jewish life. Rabbi Isaac Mayer Wise, the nineteenth-century leader of Reform Judaism, issued a new prayer book, the *Minhag America*, which, despite the opposition it aroused, represented a significant albeit failed attempt at uniformity in ritual behavior. Rabbi Isaac Leeser, the more traditional representative of the Historical School, attempted to convene a synod, but it never materialized. (The Historical School began among nineteenth-century German Jewry and represented an attempt to study the Jewish past scientifically. It constituted part of the background of Conservative Judaism.)

In the 1870s, Wise succeeded in creating an organization to unify many Reform congregations and established a rabbinical school in Cincinnati. It is no accident that both the college (Hebrew Union College) and the organization of synagogues (Union of American Hebrew Congregations) contained the word *union*. The Historical School had grown weaker with the passing of Leeser, and Wise hoped his rabbinical college might yet serve all except the most traditional Jews. The problem of unity was to haunt Mordecai Kaplan and those who fought him. Louis Finkelstein, president of the Jewish Theological Seminary in the 1940s and 1950s, strongly opposed Reconstructionism because he saw it as schismatic. Indeed, Kaplan's fervent desire to maintain the Reconstructionist movement as a school of thought was a reflection of his fear of fragmenting the Jewish community.

I. M. Wise was justified in thinking he had achieved a degree of unity, for even Rabbi Sabato Morais of Philadelphia, a vocal and relentless critic of Reform Judaism, supported the Hebrew Union College, hoping it would embrace all kinds of Jews. Although ideological differences existed in the late nineteenth century, separate institutional structures for each group were not yet the rule. Thus, cooperation was both easier and more necessary. However, in the course of the 1870s, Reform Jews became more alienated from their coreligionists. Wise and other reformers seemed almost intent on alienation, or, perhaps they felt no need to compromise since the Historical School did not offer a serious challenge. The most bitter controversy centered on the matter of kosher laws, which so many progressives considered medieval. As if to make the point in the most blatant way possible, the dinner at the first graduation of students from the Hebrew Union College in 1883 served nonkosher food. While perhaps not intended as a symbolic statement, the famous *trefah* banquet became emblematic of the difficulties of holding together the fragile coalition of Reform and more traditional Jews. It strengthened the feeling of some of the more traditional rabbis that they could no longer cooperate to support Reform institutions.[25]

The last straw came with the Pittsburgh Platform. In November 1885, Rabbi Kaufman Kohler, a New York Reform leader, convened a caucus of rabbis in Pittsburgh in order to issue a formal statement of principles that would define Judaism as they understood it. The nineteen rabbis assembled issued eight principles of faith. Perhaps the most severe break with tradition was embodied in the following statements:

> Third — . . . we accept as binding only the moral laws and maintain only such ceremonies as elevate and sanctify our lives, but reject all such as are not adapted to the views and habits of modern civilization. Fourth — we hold that all such Mosaic and rabbinical laws as regulate diet, priestly purity and dress originated in ages and under the influence of ideas altogether foreign to our present mental and spiritual state. They fail to impress the modern Jew [and] their observance in our days is apt rather to obstruct than to further modern spiritual elevation.[26]

There was a direct relationship between the issuing of these statements and the opening of the Jewish Theological Seminary fourteen months later. The leading newspaper of the Historical School raised the specter of intermarriage: "We do not want our young women and young men to find intermarriage facilitated by the removal of all doctrinal and other religious barriers." The radical nature of these principles forced many to withdraw their support from the institution that promulgated this platform. The *American Hebrew* stated the matter unequivocally: "it becomes necessary for all Jewish congregations and individuals who disapprove of the principles promulgated at Pittsburgh to provide for the training of teachers and rabbis under suitable influences."[27]

The Seminary also must be understood within the context of the pressures of acculturation on the Eastern European immigrants. Becoming an American was not a simple process. Opposing loyalties continually pulled at the immigrants. For those who wanted to maintain their ancestral traditions, there were basically two modes of reacting. One was to resist accommodation wherever possible and attempt to maintain the ties to Eastern European Jewish culture. This road was taken by the supporters of Chief Rabbi Jacob Joseph. The other possibility was to accept the fact that traditional Jewish life would inevitably change and, therefore, accommodation was the only intelligent choice. Those pursuing the accommodating stance attempted to create a viable traditional Judaism that would be fully at home in the American English-speaking context. The Seminary founders represented the leaders of the accommodating group.[28]

During the spring of 1886, a Jewish Theological Seminary Association was formed, and on January 2, 1887, a freezing Sunday afternoon, the Seminary was formally opened. The weather was so severe that week that a number of lectures in New York City had to be canceled. A large crowd nevertheless gathered to mark the occasion with uplifting speeches. A week later, the preparatory class began with only eight students ranging in age from thirteen to seventeen and including Kaplan's friend Joseph Hertz, later to become chief rabbi of the British Empire. The small size of the class did not diminish the significance of the event: "Here a new Zion has been established, a Zion of Jewish learning for the regeneration of American Judaism."[29]

The Jewish Theological Seminary of New York must be clearly differentiated from the institution Solomon Schechter headed after 1902. The Old Seminary, as it is sometimes called, enrolled much younger students. Kaplan, for example, began attending the Seminary when he was twelve and a half. He attended continuously until his graduation at the age of twenty-one. Only under Schechter did the Seminary become a graduate institution. Classes were held for the most part in the afternoon, although a few classes also were held in the early morning. Thus, for both students and faculty, it was a part-time involvement. The program began with three sessions a week of two hours each; after a month, it was expanded to five sessions of two hours each.[30]

The faculty of the Old Seminary consisted of dedicated and knowledgeable rabbis. They were, however, not great scholars. For a part-time Hebrew high school and college, perhaps great scholars were not required; nor were the students themselves well grounded in Judaic studies. The entrance examination, for example, included reading from the Pentateuch and translating the material together with some rabbinic commentaries, usually Rashi (the medieval commentator). Being more comfortable in Yiddish, Kaplan translated Rashi into his mother tongue. A youngster like Kaplan, who had spent many years at a yeshiva and studied Talmud with his father, viewed such an elementary examination with contempt.[31]

The Seminary was Kaplan's home from 1893 until 1902. For a time, he lived on the top floor of the Seminary building on Lexington at Fifty-ninth Street. In a sense, he grew up with the Seminary, so that even though it was a part-time school, it exerted full-time influence over his life and shaped his relationship with the Jewish people and the world at large. The depth of his attachment to the Seminary is reflected in his inability to leave when it made no sense for him to remain.

Although both faculty and students observed Jewish ritual in a traditional manner, the Seminary was not a traditional yeshiva with exclusive emphasis on Talmud and the legal literature related to it. Sabato Morais, one of the founders, spoke in Baltimore a year before the Seminary was established, boasting that it would produce "surpassing scripturalists . . . though they may not rank foremost among skilled Talmudists." The faculty members themselves were not trained in the Eastern European mode but were men of the emancipated west. They shared an acceptance of modern western culture together with a deep love for and dedication to Judaism and the Jewish people. Everything Jewish interested them, from the latest scholarly adventure in Europe (e.g., Schechter and the medieval manuscripts from the Old Synagogue in Cairo) to the fact that Helena, Montana, a Wild West outpost in those days, had fifty Jewish families in 1887, with thirty children attending its Sabbath School.[32]

The prime movers in the early period of the Seminary, who also helped set the context for Kaplan's adolescent years, were firmly identified with the Historical School in America and with America itself. They were Rabbi Sabato Morais, Rabbi Alexander Kohut, Rabbi Henry P. Mendes, and Rabbi Bernard Drachman. These men believed strongly in the divine origin of the Torah and that the only way to preserve the Jewish people was through the commandments (or *Mitzvot*). For them, Judaism had developed organically and naturally throughout the centuries, as indeed it would continue to do in their own time. Such development was necessary, but it must come in such a way that all of the Jews (*Klal Yisrael*) could accept it. They were also united in their opposition to Reform Judaism and its radical breaks with the past. However, both Reform leaders and the founders of the Seminary assumed that modern scientific methods would be used to study the Jewish past.[33]

The principal personalities associated with the Old Seminary were men who identified themselves with the scientific study of Judaism and

Dr. Bernard Drachman, Kaplan's teacher at pre-Schechter JTS. (Courtesy Library of JTS.)

evinced a deep appreciation for secular knowledge and culture. They expected their young charges to be educated and refined as well as observant Jews. They were committed to the Jewish people and to their integration into American society. The Seminary faculty members who came later were without doubt greater scholars, but these early pioneers were more dedicated to the goal of turning out good rabbis.

When Kaplan was twelve years old (1893), he overheard a classmate ask to be excused in order to take an examination in an afternoon school where he was studying to become a rabbi. This classmate was C. E. Hillel Kauvar, a distant relative of Kaplan's. Kaplan asked Kauvar about the school because his parents also wanted him to be a rabbi. After some preliminary investigation, Kaplan and his father went to the seminary to inquire about admission. Kaplan learned about the Seminary accidentally, but considering that Rabbi Isaac Elchanan Theological Seminary had not been organized yet, there was no other traditional school of higher Jewish learning in the United States where he could continue his studies. (Israel Kaplan had considered sending his son back to Eastern Europe for his education.)

Although Kaplan was admitted immediately, such admission was not automatic. In addition to a Hebrew background, prospective candidates also had to demonstrate sufficient knowledge of English. In the first year of operation, even though the seminary was desperate for students, five boys were denied admission until such time as their English improved.[34]

Thus, at the age of twelve and a half, Mordecai Kaplan began traveling uptown every day after school to Lexington and Fifty-ninth to attend classes at the Seminary opposite Bloomingdale's department store. The commute on the el from the Lower East Side took time and was difficult; after a year or so, Kaplan moved into the Seminary building. A number of boys from out of town and the Lower East Side lived in the top-floor dormitory. About this time, Kaplan changed from short pants to long pants and remembered admiring himself in the mirror and thinking how handsome he was.

His room was a storage room with little air or light. His roommate, Julius Greenstone, older than Kaplan, was already a Talmudic scholar before he came to the United States. He was well known to the Kaplan family; they were delighted to have him as Mordecai's roommate. Kaplan and Greenstone lived together for approximately two years. They talked endlessly and prepared their lessons together. It is likely that Greenstone's views influenced Kaplan; while still at the Seminary, Greenstone exhibited a liberal point of view. In his student sermon on "Progress and Religion," Greenstone maintained that "progress in religion means to take a broader view of life, to apply all the improvements of the age to religion."[35]

Kaplan's teachers during his first year were Drachman, who taught Bible and Hebrew grammar, and Henry Speaker (who Kaplan remembered stuttering), who also taught Bible. Speaker, later the head of Gratz College in Philadelphia, was only a student himself, and did not graduate from the Seminary until 1895 at the age of twenty-eight. Kaplan's third teacher was Joshua Jaffe, who taught Talmud to the preparatory classes. Jaffe was born in 1862; he studied at the Volozhin yeshiva, received his *Smikha* in Vilna, and later received his doctorate. Jaffe published a number of articles on rabbinic themes. He was unmarried and apparently lived at the Seminary with the students.

Greenstone's portrait of student life was vivid:

> The home of the Seminary was at 736 Lexington Avenue, then considered all the way uptown. This was indeed a home, because most of the students also lived in the dormitories on the third floor, and had their meals in the basement. Since practically all the students were undergraduates attending college in the morning, all Hebrew instruction was given in the afternoons, although Professor Jaffe often took advantage of the fact that we were all together in the morning to

Kaplan at age thirteen, about the time he entered the Jewish Theological Seminary. (Courtesy Dr. Naomi Kaplan Wenner.)

give us an hour or so before breakfast in some advanced subject. Services were held in the chapel every day, and often three times a day. The students would all walk together from 57th Street to 23rd Street, where the City College was situated. There were naturally certain cliques and factions in the student body, such as grouped themselves together for various personal reasons or because of similar characteristics, but as a rule there was a harmonious feeling among them and some friendships made there have lasted throughout life. Immediately after dinner [i.e., lunch], the Seminary courses began and lasted until supper. After supper, many would hasten for a short stroll to Central

Park, which was within one or two blocks [*sic:* it was three long blocks to the park], while others would go out to give lessons to children in the vicinity. It was not before 9 or 10 in the evening that we were able to start the work of preparing our lessons for the next day. And then what a busy place the third floor became. Each one was working in his own room, or rather in his own bed, since each room had more than one occupant, the front room having four or five beds in it. Those who were proficient in a certain subject would be besieged by the others to give them aid, which was often cheerfully and freely given. In one corner [Phineas] Israeli would assist two or three students with their Latin compositions, in another Eichler would help a student with his oration, here an upper classmate would dispense of his notes from previous years and there a skilled draughtsman would suggest some improvements in a drawing that had to be handed in the following day. We rarely went to bed before midnight and frequently there would be quarrels about the gaslight which a student wanted to use and another found it disturbing to a much-needed rest." [36]

In 1893–94, the entire student body numbered twenty-two, half of whom were in the preparatory division. According to the official report, the preparatory division, under Speaker's direction, finished Genesis, Proverbs, Ethics of the Fathers, six pages of Talmud from the Tractate Sabbath, and *Mishnah Berachot*. Some of the students did not take their learning very seriously, as Morais noted in his year-end report. "I regret, however, that the *Cuzari* [a medieval philosophical work] which ought to have commanded the profound reflection of our students was abandoned by reason of insufficient regularity in the attendance on the part of the instructed." The Seminary also had its own department of secular studies for those students who found the City College too "demanding." The Seminary at times taught Latin, Greek, German, history, English literature, algebra, geometry, physics, and advanced English. This policy continued under Schechter after 1902. [37]

Kaplan's personal life as an adolescent was quite proper, according to the stringent moral standards of the time. The Seminary had no female students, and neither did City College. The only young women in Kaplan's life were his sister, Sophie, and some cousins who immigrated from Poland when he was a teenager. It was not the custom in those years to discuss sexual matters; Kaplan sensed a prohibition against even thinking about such things. Thus, when a particular Talmudic discussion involved the concept of virginity, he didn't know what the word meant and was too embarrassed to ask during the class session. No doubt, the students shared their ignorance afterward. There was a hospital near the Seminary where they occasionally socialized with the nurses.

Kaplan never forgot these years; schoolday anecdotes were dear to him.

> I recall our wonderful dormitory and the way Greenstone used to emerge every morning from the little sky-lighted bedroom which he and I occupied; Greenstone, sour-faced and with a towel on his shoulder as he walked down two flights of stairs to wash up. That was a sight for the gods. Then I would think of the time when Bernard Ehrenreich ran to the bedroom where Elias Solomon slept and at 7:00 A.M. shouted to him that his mother was waiting for him downstairs and when the poor fellow, shocked out of his wits, dressed quickly and ran down, he found only our so-called 'Mother,' Professor Jaffe, waiting for his class.[38]

When Kaplan's parents moved uptown to Second Avenue and Fiftieth Street, a few blocks from the seminary, Kaplan again lived at home. This area on the East Side was a thriving Jewish neighborhood at the time. In addition to the Seminary on Lexington Avenue, the YMHA, which later moved to Ninety-second Street, was, in the late 1890s, located on Sixty-fifth and Lexington. The offices of B'nai B'rith were across the street from the seminary and housed a library (the Maimonides Library) which Kaplan used. There were also some synagogues in the area.[39] Kaplan resumed studying Talmud with his father, who was his most important teacher. They studied in a regular, disciplined way, and Kaplan enjoyed the paternal attention he had never received when they lived in Europe. It was also at this time that Arnold Ehrlich, a very talented Bible scholar, began to frequent the Kaplan home. In the absence of any Hebrew concordance to the Talmud, Ehrlich would visit Israel Kaplan when he wanted to find out how a particular Hebrew word was used in the Talmud. While he was there, Ehrlich would discuss his work with the Kaplan children. It was through Ehrlich that Kaplan became aware of scholars who doubted the Mosaic authorship of the Bible and theorized that the Pentateuch was written years after Moses died and existed in many versions which were edited into one document. Kaplan, young and impressionable, took the ideas he heard from Ehrlich and presented them to his fellow students at the seminary. There is no doubt that Israel Kaplan had mixed feelings about Ehrlich:

> Friday nights, after the usual stroll in the park, most of the [Seminary] students went to bed early. In later years, it became a custom for

several students to visit the home of Kaplan's parents, who lived in the neighborhood, where they were joined by the late A. B. Ehrlich, the most original Bible commentator of modern days and the most erratic of men. Conversation became very heated at times, usually turning on the question of higher criticism or some theological topic. We were always deeply impressed with the tolerance of old Rabbi Kaplan, who could join the discussion with the heretical Ehrlich.[40]

One of the major points of contention was miracles, which Kaplan began to question. He also showed his friends the many contradictions in the biblical text that Ehrlich had pointed out. Every time Ehrlich published a book, he would bring it to the house to show the Kaplans. Israel Kaplan became increasingly unhappy with Ehrlich's influence and eventually he engaged an acquaintance by the name of Joseph Sossnitz to teach young Kaplan *The Guide for the Perplexed* in order to counter Ehrlich's approach. Mordecai Kaplan once asked Sossnitz, "How can we ascribe to Moses the authorship of a text like the following: "And Moses was the humblest of all men'?" His reply was that Moses was so unselfconscious that he could write about himself in the third person. "I cannot say that the answer satisfied me," Kaplan wrote many years later.[41]

Mordecai Kaplan never overtly rebelled against his father, yet the association with Ehrlich helped set the son on the road to his separate sense of identity. The influence of Ehrlich and the Seminary were mutually reinforcing. The Seminary gave young Mordecai an opportunity to live away from home and to acquire an independent sense of himself without the need to overtly rebel. The curriculum included some lectures on archaeology by Cyrus Adler, providing Kaplan with an untraditional view of the Bible. Talking to his classmates about Ehrlich's ideas intensified Kaplan's quest for other than traditional viewpoints, and the Seminary came to replace his father as the primary source of authority early in Kaplan's development; it was also the context for his social life. It was a caretaking institution suffused with many pleasant childhood associations and at the same time a parent-like authority that stifled him. In Kaplan's later reflections, the warm, caretaking feeling of the Seminary alternates with anger at the imposition of authority.

◆

If Kaplan's home life was very rich in Jewish learning the Seminary curriculum by contrast seemed elementary. Nonetheless, it was solid and well structured. Each year, he studied a book of the Pentateuch with more medieval commentators, the Prophets, and the wisdom literature with Hebrew commentaries, Hebrew grammar, Jewish history, Talmud (with the hours increasing each year), Jewish philosophy, and rabbinic codes.

This curriculum was, of course, very different from the traditional yeshiva mode which concentrated exclusively on complicated Talmudic treatises, legal codes, and rabbinic *responsa*. Although Kaplan's father mistrusted Ehrlich's orientation and abhorred his guest's advocacy of biblical criticism, he apparently voiced no objections to the Seminary curriculum. There were, however, traditional Jews who venomously attacked the fledgling institution. Neither did Eastern European Jews relate so easily to an institution heavily supported by Sephardic rabbis. Gilbert Klaperman, who wrote a history of Yeshiva University, maintained that the Seminary did not allow its students to be publicly examined by visiting rabbis from Europe, as was the custom in the downtown yeshivas. "It was a gratuitous slight or evidence that the Seminary did not recognize the Eastern European rabbis and the people they represented."[42]

Julius Greenstone related the painful memories of his own examination, which helps us to understand the Seminary of that time:

I cannot refrain from giving here an account of my final examinations in the summer of 1900. There were three applicants for graduation, for whose examination three full days were set aside. It happened that the Central Conference of American Rabbis had its annual meeting in New York at that time and several of these rabbis came to the Seminary to see the sight. I was the first victim. Besides the teachers of the Seminary, each of whom was to examine in his subject, there were present several of the trustees and a number of Rabbis, some of the more important Reform Rabbis of the time. Each one was invited to ask questions and here was the opportunity for some of them to show how learned they were. It was most fortunate for me that Dr. J. H. Hertz was at that time visiting New York on his vacation from South Africa and he assumed the role of Chairman of the examining board, so that the questions later became a little more orderly and more systematic. The test began at nine o'clock in the morning and lasted until five in the afternoon. Let me mention one question which still lingers in my mind. A rabbi from San Francisco wanted to know what would be the law in the following case: A man died in Australia on Saturday evening and a cable dispatch sent to his son in New York, informing him of his father's death, reached here Saturday morning. Should the

son say Kaddish on Saturday, really 'before' his father passed away?
... My fellow student, who was to be examined the following day,
failed his test, and the third applicant was so frightened that he did not
come up for examination at all, so that I was the only graduate that
year. In order to save the Seminary the expense connected with a formal graduation, I was given my diploma privately."[43]

The Conservative Jews of this era placed a great deal of emphasis
on the value of English as a sign of integration into American society.
Kaplan learned to speak English without an accent, and the Seminary
atmosphere was no doubt helpful. The Seminary, at times, had a problem in securing teachers of Talmud who could teach in English. According to one Hebrew newspaper, "There were many who can and
will not and others who will and cannot." The *American Hebrew*, which
represented Conservative leadership, was quite blunt when commenting on the importance of using English as a language of instruction:
"the vernacular English preferably, German if necessary, [but not Yid-
dish] in view of the wretched jargon-German which is at this day a
badge of servile inferiority and vulgarity. To perpetuate such marks of
slavery is neither religious nor wise."[44]

One of the most interesting critics from the Orthodox side was
Judah David Eisenstein. He had little use for either extremely Orthodox Jews, who he said did not need to think but already have a ready
answer for all questions, or the radical reformers who have "no authorities at all." He believed that Conservatives were going in the same
direction as the radical reformers but at a slower pace. Eisenstein, perhaps unfairly at this early point, describes Conservative Jews as "each
one making his own *Shulhan Arukh*" (Jewish law code). He believed
that Seminary men should be scrupulous in their religious subjects, but
he made no direct criticisms of the proposed curriculum of the Seminary. Some Orthodox newspapers like *Ha-Ivri* continually hammered
away at the Seminary, charging that the Seminary professors had
"knowledge but no faith," that students accomplished little, and that
there was small difference between the Seminary and Cincinnati. As
late as 1905, Henry P. Mendes, who became a forceful supporter of
Yeshiva University, lamented that the Seminary did not have stronger
support among the Orthodox: "It seems strange that the Seminary is
not supported by the community most interested in its success, the
downtown Jews. The downtown Jews, those usually called ultra-
Orthodox, display no interest in our efforts. They don't come to us. We
must, therefore, go to them and show them that the future of traditional Judaism in America lies in this institution." The Seminary did

*JTS students and Rabbi Joshua Jaffe, 1897. Kaplan
is in the second row, second from the left. (Courtesy
Library of JTS.)*

receive the support of some of the outstanding critical scholars of the
day, as indicated by the fact that Solomon Buber, Martin Buber's grandfather, donated a complete set of his own works (13 volumes) to the
Seminary library.[45]

The purpose of the Seminary as conceived by its founders was not
to turn out rabbis and scholars in the traditional mold but rather, as
Joseph Blumenthal, the first president of the Seminary Board, explained in 1888, "to train rabbis who will be American, scholars, tolerant, temperate and courteous gentlemen, and Jews with a knowledge of
Jewish law and literature, and with the firm purpose of acknowledging
and vindicating the validity of that law." A few years later, Blumenthal
underscored the goal of integration when he called for the rabbis to
bring "culture, refinement and civilization" to the new immigrants
from Eastern Europe. In line with this objective, the Seminary organized a literary society which regularly sponsored debates on topics of
general interest as well as Jewish subjects and arranged lectures, decla-
mations, and orations. Mordecai Kaplan participated in these sessions,
delivering in 1899 an oration on the "Rights of the Minority." That

same night, there was a debate regarding the works of Israel Zangwill, a well-known Jewish writer. On one occasion, Kaplan held forth in Hebrew on "The Soliloquy of Saul at Gilboa." Most of the audience did not understand him, according to the *American Hebrew*, but nonetheless, "his intonation, expression of gesture made the contents clear to his hearers," the newspaper noted. During his last year at the Seminary, Kaplan was elected treasurer of the Jewish Theological Seminary Literary Society.[46]

Kaplan, renowned for his oratorical abilities, had many opportunities to speak during his years at the seminary. His first student sermon was entitled "Judaism: A Religion of Faith" and was delivered in April 1901 during the same week when Buffalo Bill's Wild West and Rough Riders opened at Madison Square Garden and Ethel Barrymore appeared in a play entitled "Captain Jinks of the Horse Marines." Kaplan attained considerable stature among his fellow students, for he was chosen to speak on their behalf at a memorial service for Joseph Blumenthal, the president of the board.[47]

Delivering a sermon before fellow students was no easy task. "The sermons were usually quite long and some of them rather soporific, although this did not prevent Dr. Drachman, the teacher in Homiletics, from criticizing them. The formal criticism on the part of the teachers and trustees was followed by the informal and friendly criticisms of the students at the supper table and later in the rooms." Kaplan remembered his own student sermons as a painful experience:

> I shall never forget the ordeal I went through when, as a student of about twenty, I tried to deliver a memorized sermon before the students on a Sabbath afternoon. When I got to the middle of the sermon, I completely forgot what I had to say, and being unable to go on, I went down from the pulpit. It was as a result of that bitter experience that I made up my mind to learn to speak extemporaneously. . . . To this day [1929] I need a full outline before me, if I want to be free of a sense of anxiety before I get up to speak, although some of my most powerful sermons have been those which were delivered without the aid of notes, and which I had to mull over in my mind until I rose to speak. But the energy and the time that go into the latter kind of sermon are too large a price to pay for the more effective delivery.

The student sermon is one of Kaplan's earliest creative efforts still extant. Kaplan gave the same sermon at a number of local synagogues on the Sabbath before Passover and during the holiday.[48] In many ways quite traditional, it reveals directions of thought that were to be developed in Kaplan's maturity. The nature of faith was the core issue — the trust the Israelites exhibited in following God's commands during the Exodus. Kaplan then defined and analyzed faith, how it functions, and how it serves the individual.

Other sources indicate that at a rather early age, Kaplan began to doubt the existence of the miracles mentioned in the Hebrew scriptures.[49] At the beginning of the sermon, the young Kaplan struggles to be true to his beliefs and at the same time remain faithful to the tradition: "From a slave of Pharaoh to a child of God, this was the miraculous change compared with which all other miracles dwindle into insignificance. Thus their reliance upon God and their faith in him rendered Israel worthy of redemption." Kaplan's naturalistic tendency was evident, for he saw the greatest miracles in the transformation of human beings rather than in any mechanical suspension of the laws of nature. He went on to discuss faith in God and defined it in terms of dependence: "It is the consciousness of complete helplessness but for the supporting hand of the Almighty." Faith, Kaplan continued, will help the individual triumph over sin, for without it we go from "transgression to sin, from sin to wickedness . . . sinking ever deeper till there is no chance of escape."

Kaplan described the plight of the individual confronting death. Faith would allow the individual to confront this crisis with greater strength:

How bitter those last moments when we have to part with everything dear to us, with wealth which took a lifetime of toil and labor to gather, with happiness which it cost the life blood to build up, in the circle of friends and relations among whom we moved, to leave all this and die. But on the other hand, how serene, how hopeful is he who reposeth in faith, who rests assured that this world is only the *'Prozdor,'* the corridor or ante-chamber to a larger life, a grander life, a life that is not limited by the senses.

We can discern a direction here, for Kaplan was already thinking in terms of function, even though his language and metaphors were completely traditional. His increasing intellectual sophistication and his doubts about religion were directly related to his exposure to the world of philosophy and the social sciences. Beginning in 1900, during his last years at the Seminary, he embarked on a graduate degree that would lead him farther and farther away from his traditional background.

2

BEGINNINGS:

Graduate School and the First Pulpit

The context of Mordecai Kaplan's intellectual quest during the first decade of the twentieth century was his graduate work.[1] Upon graduating from City College in 1900, he immediately registered in a master's program at Columbia University. Columbia was small in those days, having a combined student body of 2,600. It was just in the process of becoming a university in the twentieth-century sense. The Graduate Faculty of Philosophy, for example, had been organized in 1890, the Faculty of Pure Science in 1892, and the School of Engineering in 1896.[2] Compulsory chapel had been abolished in 1891, and in the late 1890s, the word *university* was being used for the first time. The title Columbia University did not become legal until 1912.[3] In the late nineteenth century, the students called themselves "forty-niners" because the college was located on Forty-ninth Street and Madison Avenue. In 1897, land was purchased at Morningside Heights, and gradually classes were shifted uptown. The site included an institution called the Bloomingdale Insane Asylum, which Columbia used for classrooms. One of the guards from Bloomingdale's stayed on and consistently referred to the students as "inmates."[4]

When Kaplan began his graduate work in 1900, the president of Columbia was Seth Low, who subsequently ran for mayor of New York City and assumed that office in 1902. Nicholas Murray Butler, referred to by Theodore Roosevelt as "Nicholas the Miraculous," became president in 1902. Butler, who was brought up in Paterson, New Jersey, taught philosophy and was a primary force in organizing Teachers' College during the 1890s. He went on to become one of the leading personalities in American education and was responsible for raising fifteen million dollars toward Columbia's endowment between 1901 and 1911.[5] Butler, a young man who had not yet turned forty in 1900, was Mordecai Kaplan's philosophy instructor in his first term at Columbia.[6]

Kaplan enrolled in courses in philosophy, sociology, education, English, German, and mechanics. Some of his teachers are well known. In February 1903, for example, he took a course in political and social ethics with Felix Adler, the prominent founder of the Ethical Culture Society.[7] Adler became a major influence in Kaplan's life despite the fact that Kaplan looked upon his teacher with disdain because Adler had rejected the Jewish religion. Kaplan was attracted to the philosophy of ethical culture nonetheless.

During this period, Kaplan was living at home at 411 East Fifty-second Street and attending the Jewish Theological Seminary, also located in Midtown. After graduation from the Seminary in 1902, he assumed his first rabbinical position with Kehilath Jeshurun, which he held until 1909. He thus began a lifelong pattern in which he functioned as a rabbi and pursued scholarly activities at the same time. During the first decade of this century, he was tormented by the conflict between his life as a rabbi and the ideas he was learning in graduate school.

Three intellectual movements were of primary importance in shaping Kaplan's mind. First, there was the ferment in the wake of the Darwinian revolution. Most contemporary writers were concerned with evolution and its impact on religion, on ethics, and on the understanding of human nature. The second intellectual area, very much related to the first and yet distinct, was the development of the social sciences, particularly anthropology and sociology. There were noted sociologists in the nineteenth century, but it was only in the early twentieth century that sociology became a standard discipline in colleges and universities. The sociological cast of Kaplan's mind is well known and is related to his earliest studies at the turn of the century. The third area, and one of equal importance, is philosophy. Kaplan was particularly concerned with ethical questions, as evidenced by his master's thesis on the ethical philosopher Henry Sidgwick.[8] Through his studies, he was introduced to the history of philosophy and devoted himself particularly to the study of Spinoza, Kant, and the major philosophers of the nineteenth century. He also read William James and Friedrich Nietzsche, both of whom were popular when Kaplan was in graduate school. Even at this early point, he was open-minded; though he was strictly Orthodox in his behavior, he had no trouble relating to the teachings of Spinoza, who had been excommunicated by the Jewish community. "Spinoza is as Jewish as Maimonides," he wrote in 1906, "and if he were alive today he would not be banished from the Jewish community."[9] In 1945, when Kaplan himself was excommunicated, he received a letter of support from a descendant of Spinoza.

The nineteenth century witnessed tremendous growth in science, in both its theoretical and applied forms. Darwin's work was accepted by so many scientists because the belief in evolution had already become widespread among scientists and intellectuals before 1859, the year *Origin of the Species* appeared. If the notion of reason dominated the eighteenth century, in the nineteenth century people believed change and evolution were the keys to understanding both the natural and the human world.

The concepts of progress, growth, and development had, of course, been central to the Enlightenment. The Romantic movement, which rejected so much of Enlightenment thought, retained a keen historical sense. In the nineteenth century the study of origins became scientific, and great national historians flourished all over Europe. Thus, in philosophy, science, and history, the concept of evolution stood at the center of the human approach to the world.

In the latter part of the nineteenth century, Darwin's work intensified and exacerbated the conflicts over the concept of evolution. Among those who took up the standard, applying evolutionary theory over a wide range of fields, Herbert Spencer stands out as one of the most prominent.[10] Spencer was a primary force in molding Kaplan's thought. For his courses in sociology, he immersed himself in Spencer's work and remembered being struck by the fact that he was studying an author who was still alive.[11]

Spencer viewed evolution as a universal phenomenon. In all fields and on all levels, change occurred from the simple to the complex by successive differentiation. However, a belief in such evolutionary change did not necessarily imply a belief that the strong were destined to triumph. Spencer, like many other social Darwinists, was strongly committed to the view that social development necessitates a check on violent instincts; as he himself put it, "any rational comprehensive view of evolution involves that, in the course of social evolution, the human mind is disciplined . . . into a check upon that part of the cosmic process which consists in the unqualified struggle for existence."[12]

Although some may consider Spencer a proto-sociologist, he considered himself a moral philosopher. After the traditional ground had crumbled, it was necessary to create some solid foundation for morality by an appeal directly or through analogy to the world of science. The major ethical issue for Spencer was the perennial problem of how to advance people from knowing what is right to doing what is right. He told his readers that a more ideal kind of behavior and social system were inevitably evolving — were a historical necessity — and he urged them to be part of this ethical wave of the future. Spencer was pragmatic, in the sense that he tried to show that moral action, both individually and socially, actually works. He maintained that higher development in humans was moral development and that it was only through moral action that human beings as a collectivity could survive.[13] Spencer influenced Kaplan through his own works and indirectly through his effects on other thinkers such as the Zionist philosopher Ahad Ha-Am and the sociologist Emile Durkheim.[14]

Kaplan accepted evolution and its implications as a fact of life. For Kaplan, to be modern was to think in terms of development. The implications are far-reaching. He did not hesitate to accept fully the import of biological and social evolution when he approached the Bible and the study of religion. He argued consistently and rigorously for the use of traditional notions in a form harmonious with scientific knowledge.

Even though Kaplan majored in philosophy while he was at Columbia, he took more courses in sociology with Franklin Giddings than with anyone else. It was Giddings, the sociologist, who signed Kaplan's application to be admitted to candidacy for the degree of Doctor of Philosophy. Kaplan never received his doctorate, although he worked on a number of different projects that could have become dissertations. At the same time as Kaplan was submitting his application for doctoral candidacy, he records a conversation with Professor Israel Friedlaender of the Jewish Theological Seminary, which suggests the dissertation topic he had in mind: "I saw Professor Friedlaender this morning with regard to the subject of my essay and after settling with him that the subject should be nationalism and religion, we spoke about things in general." Kaplan and Friedlaender were close in age (Kaplan was five years younger) as well as philosophy; they served together on the faculty of the seminary and on the Education Committee of the New York Jewish Community (Kehillah).[15]

Giddings, Kaplan's professor of sociology, was born in Connecticut in 1855, graduated from Union College in 1877, and worked for a number of years as a journalist before he began lecturing at Bryn Mawr College in 1888. He came to Columbia in 1894 and established himself as a primary force in the burgeoning field of sociology. He was a loyal follower of Spencer and advocated his theories after others ceased to be interested.[16]

The relationship between group life and the nature of religion was a basic concern of Kaplan, and it is the work of Giddings which provided him with the basis for understanding this connection. The cornerstone of Giddings's system was the notion of like-mindedness. This concept, according to Giddings (and others as well), allows us to understand how societies form, how they function, and how they develop. This concept of the social mind became the foundation of the notion of collective consciousness in Kaplan's system.[17]

A human society, according to Giddings, consists of like-minded individuals, whom he called *socii*, who would know and enjoy their like-mindedness and therefore be able to work together for common ends.[18] He used the expression *social mind* in referring to the assumptions and attitudes which the members of a collectivity shared with one another. The social mind should not be thought of as some supra-individual entity. Giddings made this perfectly clear: "the social mind is nothing more or less than that simultaneous like-responsiveness of like minds to the same stimulus."[19] The social mind, although not an entity, may yet be described as a force or a form of energy. The concerted behaviors one sees in the panic reaction of a crowd are a clear example of the force that can be exerted by the social mind. Giddings believed in a rather naïve fashion that rational thinking could restrain the wilder manifestations of the social mind: "The only restraint that can hold in check the tendency to impulsive social action, is deliberation, and critical comprehensive thinking."[20] The problem, of course, is *how* to increase the rational while suppressing the impulsive. Kaplan was to follow his teacher closely in believing in the power of the rational faculties to direct behavior.

Giddings had a primitive understanding of the concept of religion and defined it in a limited way.[21] While he learned a great deal from his teacher and mentor, Kaplan did not derive his theories on religion from Giddings. The Columbia professor helped him along the road to becoming a sociologist, but it was Kaplan himself who took what he learned and applied it to religion. Kaplan emerges as an original theorist of the first rank with regard to the sociological understanding of religion in general.

Most students of Kaplan believe that his thinking derived mainly from Emile Durkheim. But it seems quite clear that the work of Durkheim was not important in molding Kaplan's young mind. In Durkheim's system, there is no place for a god that is not completely identified with the collective mind. Kaplan struggled all his life to articulate the transcendent reality of the divine. Durkheim's work confirmed much of Kaplan's direction but did not determine it. The great sociologist's major study on religion was published in 1912, by which time the major thrust of Kaplan's thought was already clear. Although late in his career Kaplan assigned a major place to Durkheim, at an earlier point (the late 1930s) he reported that Durkheim's influence over him was minor. Kaplan thus misremembered on the question of Durkheim's influence, and students of Kaplan have been misled ever since.[22]

Although Giddings did not deal extensively with religion, he dealt with customs, traditions, and folkways. He exhibited a very fine sense of the power of the social mind: "It [meaning society, the social mind, or what we could call the social consensus] makes a man accept what he cannot understand, and obey what he does not believe."[23] Public opinion and the social consensus existing over the generations become tradition. Giddings believed that we need to distinguish between knowledge which we can prove by some empirical method and simple beliefs which we may hold to be true but for which we have no adequate evidence. Traditions for Giddings were associated more with the "emotional and imaginative" than with the "intellectual and contemplative." There are two primary laws that govern traditions: "First — tradition is authoritative and coercive in proportion to its antiquity. . . . Second — tradition is authoritative and coercive in proportion as its subject matter consists of belief rather than of critically established knowledge."[24]

How did the young Kaplan react to these ideas, living at home with his Orthodox family and teaching a class in Mishna every morning at the congregation where he was rabbi? His religious conflicts were directly related to his studies, because sociology took the tradition and brought it down from the mountain.

Giddings, writing in 1896 just a few years before Kaplan entered his class, was supremely optimistic about the direction in which the world was developing. The first world war and the horrors of the twentieth century were still a long way off:

[The] western nations are now a world community of powerful, unified, independent states in which the great major work of political and social organization is accomplished, and in which liberty is guaranteed by law. Savagery and barbarism without are no longer formidable, and, while international wars are always possible, and from time to time are actual, the normal state of international affairs is one of peace. Energy is expending itself, therefore, in new directions. These nations have entered upon a third stage of civilization, the economic and the ethical. They are absorbing themselves in industry, in amassing wealth and in discovering its uses, in popular education, and, more and more, in the task of realizing the life possibilities of the masses of people.[25]

Giddings expresses many of the fundamental assumptions of the age, which in a somewhat special form become characteristic of Kaplan's thought. The confidence in science and technology, the optimism about the future, and the general sense that the present was a rather high stage in the evolutionary process are found in Felix Adler, in Herbert Spencer, and in other thinkers to whom Kaplan was exposed at the university. Kaplan is sometimes reproached for uncritically accepting the modern age, for having no sense of the tragic aspects of technological and scientific developments. The explanation for his attitude lies partially in the university world he inhabited between 1900 and 1909. It is important to remember that Kaplan lived a very long time and was active and vigorous for many years. In 1918, Kaplan was already thirty-seven years old; he never really lost the optimism of the prewar world. As one writer astutely remarked of George Bernard Shaw, "It is the fate of those who live very long lives to be remembered in their latest phase."

◆

Even after his graduation from the Seminary in 1902, Kaplan remained tied to and affected by the institution. The Seminary was in transition, and so was Kaplan, and the two transitions intersected in a number of significant ways.

In a sense, the institution in which Kaplan spent nine years ceased to exist in 1902. The Old Seminary had financial problems, and after the death of its first president, Sabato Morais, in 1897, there was a significant lack of leadership. These problems were solved in 1902 by the infusion of new funds and the arrival of Solomon Schechter, the most prominent Jewish scholar in the western world. Schechter and the new Seminary were to play a major role in Kaplan's life.

Schechter, who eventually brought Kaplan to the Seminary to head the Teachers' Institute, was renowned among Jewish leaders in America even before he made his great discoveries of medieval documents in the old Cairo synagogue. As early as 1890, Morais attempted to get Schechter to leave Cambridge University and join the faculty of the seminary. Throughout the 1890s, Seminary leaders wooed Schechter without success. In 1895, he sailed to Philadelphia to give a series of lectures on aspects of rabbinic theology. He was greeted with great fanfare in the Anglo-Jewish press.[26] Still, it took another six years before

*Solomon Schechter and Rabbi Herman Abromowitz
in Atlantic City, 1906. (Courtesy Library of JTS.)*

Schechter accepted a position with the Seminary, as the head of a totally reorganized institution. During this period, Schechter's name was constantly before the American Jewish community because of his discovery of the medieval manuscripts in Cairo. He eventually purchased the manuscripts and brought the treasure to Cambridge. The *Geniza*, as it came to be known, has been a continual source of new and significant revelations.[27]

In April 1902, Schechter came to America, infusing the Seminary with a new sense of vitality and vigor: "The arrival of Schechter . . . was widely hailed as the beginning of a new era in American-Jewish religious life and scholarship. No single individual has contributed more to the furtherance of Jewish learning and perhaps no one else has had greater influence on the course and direction of religious life."[28]

Two and a half months after Schechter's arrival on July 1, 1902, at the Seminary's commencement exercises held at the YMHA on Lexington Avenue and Ninety-second Street, Mordecai Menahem Ben Yisrael Kaplan, age twenty-one, became a rabbi. There were eight graduates, including Charles H. Kauvar, Kaplan's distant relative, who had initially introduced him to the Seminary and was the valedictorian of his class. It was reported in the Yiddish press that during the graduation, "the professors of the school sat with uncovered heads . . . and Professor Abraham Joshua Jaffe, who delivered a major address in Hebrew was also bare headed and mentioned the name of God without covering his head."[29] The *American Hebrew*, reflecting the attitudes of many associated with the Old Seminary, noted with no little pique that "the head of the new faculty, Dr. Solomon Schechter was not present at the graduating exercises nor at the public examinations held at the Seminary buildings last week. He is summering in Tannersville, Greene County."[30] Schechter obviously wanted to distance himself from the Old Seminary which did not measure up to his standards.

An essential facet of the Seminary's reorganization was the stipulation that Cyrus Adler become chairman of the board. In this capacity, he turned to some of the graduates of the class of 1902 and asked them to stay on and postpone receiving their degrees for two years. Apparently he wanted a large graduating class that would reflect well on Schechter. Kaplan was one of the graduates Adler tried to pressure. Kaplan rejected Adler's plan and proposed a compromise in which a special postgraduate course would be organized for those who stayed on after graduation. In November 1903, as the most outstanding student of the senior class, Kaplan was awarded a scholarship prize valued at two hundred fifty dollars. According to Kaplan, this scholarship was in the nature of a bribe. He had been president of the Blumenthal Society, which was the key student organization, and Adler believed that if Kaplan stayed on, so might the other students. Kaplan refused to remain a senior, for he would be required to attend other classes with younger, less knowledgeable rabbinical students. Only one student accepted Adler's proposal. Elias Solomon, two years older than Kaplan, returned his diploma of 1902 and received it again two years later. Adler, the new chairman of the board of the new Seminary, was furious at Kaplan and the others who had followed his lead. Adler made a special trip from Philadelphia to reprimand Kaplan and his group. "You anarchist!" he shouted at Kaplan. "What right do you have to dictate to us?" Kaplan was merely suggesting a special postgraduate class be set up, but Adler was adamant; he wanted the graduates to stay on as seniors.[31]

Nevertheless, Kaplan did attend the theology course Schechter conducted for the seniors in the Rabbinical School and sat next to Henrietta Szold, who also attended the seminary regularly.[32] The level of the course was much higher than that of Kaplan's undergraduate classes and much more compatible with the studies he was pursuing in the graduate school at Columbia. The material stimulated him and quickly led to new directions in his own thinking. Reticent about expressing his ideas in class, he confined his explorations to the privacy of his diary. Schechter was attempting to show that the thinking of the rabbis constituted a coherent theological system. There were many who disagreed, maintaining that the rabbis had only a deed system, not a thought system. It was natural for Kaplan to begin to think in Schechter's categories. He was frequently impressed by the obvious contrast between the interpretations of the rabbis and the same events as they appeared in the Hebrew scriptures.

Already present in Kaplan's thinking was the sense that traditional views needed to be examined and perhaps in part discarded. He believed "a theology of Reconstruction" (his words in 1904) was necessary and began to think through some preliminary possibilities. He thought, for example, about the attitude toward nature as it appeared in the Bible and as it appeared in the works of the rabbis. For biblical Israel, "Nature is the handiwork of God and has never passed out of his control [Psalm 104]. The fixedness of its laws calls forth admiration." For the rabbis, on the other hand, the view of the world was much more anthropocentric. Since man is higher than the rest of creation, he has greater powers. His "superiority is supposed to manifest itself in the power which the one obeying the precepts of the Torah exercises over external creation." Such Torah power results in magic. It would thus be more in keeping with the scientific view of the modern world if we reverted back to the biblical view. "In order therefore that Judaism survive, nature must be so to say, reinstated. Man must be content to regard himself as unworthy of even the small amount of control he is permitted to exercise over nature, even as the Psalmist said, 'What is Man? that thou art mindful of him.'"[33]

Although Kaplan was still quite traditional, his use of the word *reconstruction* in this passage was significant. It indicated that he did not borrow the term from John Dewey, who published his *Reconstruction in Philosophy* in 1920. Though he was not yet the radical he was to become, Kaplan's thinking involved more questioning than he allowed himself to voice in public. The disparity between his public statements and his private reflections troubled him deeply.

In the fall of 1903, the year of the Kishinev pogrom and two years after Theodore Roosevelt became president, Kaplan assumed his first pulpit. For the high holidays of that year, he preached at Congregation Beth-Israel Bikur Cholim on Lexington Avenue and Seventy-second

Street.[34] This congregation, with its splendid new building, was the home of some of the more prosperous among the traditional Ashkenazi Jews who had already moved uptown. Bernard Drachman, Kaplan's teacher, had briefly served as rabbi when he moved to New York to assume his duties at the seminary in 1887. Although the congregation was traditional, it was split over the matter of mixed seating.[35] Kaplan was to confront a similar problem later on.

Kaplan spoke at a number of congregations in 1903 before he assumed a full-time position at Kehilath Jeshurun that November. In these early 1903 sermons, Kaplan was not caught up in the *halakhic* (Jewish legal) perspective or even in directly exhorting synagogue members to observe the commandments. He spoke about topics such as individuality, holiness, law and liberty, envy, friendship, and atonement, as well as the plight of the Jews in Eastern Europe. In each case, he related the values held by younger Jews to more traditional Jewish concepts. There is no overall philosophy expressed here, nor yet a break in tradition, but rather an articulate example of what good modern Orthodox Jewish preachers were doing at that time.[36] Speaking of individuality, for example, Kaplan interpreted the ancient dictum "Thou shalt not follow the multitude for evil" as meaning, "Be yourself. Pursue what you believe to be the truth even though you get disapproval." To the young people who were eager to break away from their parents' authority, Kaplan said yes, be yourself, but don't be controlled by others who abandon Judaism completely. He spoke of "Individuality, as joy to oneself, a duty to humanity and a duty to God." He upheld the ideal of individuality but used it to exhort his young listeners to turn away from the loose life of their friends. The passage was finely phrased and characteristic of Kaplan. It is also interesting in light of Kaplan's own later struggles with individuality:

> Thou shalt not follow the multitude to do evil! The development of individuality is not only a good in itself but it proves of greater use on occasions that frequently arise in a man's life. I refer to those occasions when duty calls upon us to stand up and say I shall not permit my soul to become the slave of the wills of others. These occasions are of very frequent occurrence in the life of everyone; they are not only to be encountered in mature manhood and womanhood but they present themselves to us while we are still children. . . . There are moments in our life when we have to summon all the courage at our command and face the world and its evils fearlessly. It is then that we have to be aware that numbers never go to make a thing right, that majorities count for

nothing, and that one and with [*sic*] God we are in the majority. Such occasions are the crucibles which refine our character and show whether there is any gold in it or is it a mere heap of dross. These are the moments that give to the world its great men, its heroes. "I would rather suffer," said a great statesman who ventured to differ from his associates, "than that the truth should suffer for want of my speaking."

These sermons demonstrate Kaplan's sensitivity as a preacher, his gift for resonant language, and his ability to speak in a clear and rousing manner. Concerning holiness and the tablets of the covenant, for example, he asserted that God never rebuked Moses for destroying the tablets. Rather, according to the rabbis, the holy letters flew off the tablets when Moses broke them, signifying that nothing is holy in itself but only as "God on the one hand and man on the other hand accepts it as holy. . . . God needs the cooperation of man to render anything holy for us."[37]

At this point, Kaplan still accepted the concept of the chosen people and its ordinary interpretation. In a sermon called "The Mission of the Jew," he did not hesitate to talk of Israel's chosenness: "We understand that it is not in any sense of overweening pride or arrogance that the Jew calls himself priest, chosen of God, but with the full consciousness of the great task before [him] and with the appreciation of the responsibility resting upon him."

Possessing a very strong sense of kinship with his fellow Jews, Kaplan was outraged by the mistreatment of his coreligionists in Russia. During the Easter holidays in 1903, agitation against the Jews in southwestern Russia resulted in three days of bloody rioting in the city of Kishinev. The *American Hebrew* reported the events in detail.[38] Meetings were held all over the United States to solicit money and goods in order to relieve the victims of the pogroms. In addition, these meetings called upon the government of the United States to intervene on behalf of the Russian Jews. Jewish agitation finally resulted in the transmission of a petition to the czar, with the signatures of numerous senators, governors, and other important political figures.

The young rabbi observed these events from a religious point of view; anti-Semitism was a threat not only to the safety of the Jewish people but to the future of their religion as well. Kaplan knew that the Jewish religion also was being threatened in America, where Judaism seemed to be disappearing through the process of acculturation. Every Jew lost through assimilation is a triumph for the anti-Semites. The young rabbi called on his fellow Jews not to give "posthumous victories to the anti-Semites," to borrow the phrase of a later thinker. Kaplan cried out not for vengeance but for steadfastness in the face of the threat: "It is the blood of your brethren crying unto you, the blood of your brethren in Kishineff, the blood of your brethren in Homel, crying to you not for vengeance but crying to you of free America, to you enjoying God-given liberty, to uphold the cause of Judaism for which it was shed."[39]

In the summer of 1903, Zionists met for the Sixth Congress with the massacres of Kishinev fresh in their minds. Kaplan followed the events closely. It was at this congress in Basle that Theodor Herzl offered for consideration an immediate palliative measure for the Jews who wanted to leave Russia. The British government was willing to consider allocating territory for Jewish settlement in Uganda. Herzl considered this only a stopgap solution, not a substitute for a Jewish state in Palestine. The issue split the congress. Herzl was exhausted and disappointed. In his diary, he noted, "Yesterday I gave my report. . . . I presented England and Russia. And it didn't occur to any of them for even a single moment that for these greatest of all accomplishments to date I deserved a word, or even a smile of thanks." The split in the Zionist congress seemed to Herzl to be a mortal blow to the movement.[40]

Kaplan was deeply committed to Jewish nationalism, but, as in the case of Kishinev, he viewed Zionist developments from the religious perspective. Always concerned about strengthening the Jewish people, Kaplan, like other cultural Zionists, believed that Jewish nationalism was the key to preserving Judaism as well as the Jews. National preservation and spiritual preservation went hand in hand. A religious life could be grounded only on the strong bonds of peoplehood. Change was necessary, he believed, but it could come about only if the social bonds among Jews were strengthened. "If we are tired of the old forms and ceremonies (which is no doubt the case with many of them), we have no right to dispense with them as long as our hearts continue beating with love for our brethren, and we are without a home which we can call our own. Reform there must be, but it must be in the direction of nationalism."[41]

Kaplan had not yet organized his thoughts, nor had he devised a conceptual framework. He had many questions but few answers and was tormented by the fact that he had no solutions for the many problems that plagued the Jews. Expecting a great deal of himself, Kaplan was intensely self-critical when he failed to offer concrete proposals to revitalize the Jewish people. Nonetheless, his essential direction was apparent from the beginning — an intense identification with other Jews coupled with the conviction that a radical change was necessary if Judaism was going to survive in America.

◆

In November 1903, Kaplan, still living at home and completely Orthodox in his behavior, assumed his position at Kehilath Jeshurun. It is not surprising that his first full-time pulpit was with an Orthodox congregation. Kehilath Jeshurun, a prominent New York congregation, included many important Orthodox Ashkenazic Jews. These were native-born Americans of Eastern European origin or immigrants who had arrived in the 1880s and 1890s and had prospered. Many were in the clothing business and were active in the Orthodox community in New York City. They had helped to establish Yeshiva Etz Chaim, where Kaplan went to school, and Rabbi Isaac Elchanan Theological Seminary as well.[42] A typical member of the congregation was Harry Fischel. His primary business was real estate, and he had accumulated so much money that between 1903 and 1911, he devoted himself exclusively to communal affairs. He was described as the Russian-born Jacob Schiff. In the 1890s, he helped raise money for the construction of Beth-Israel Hospital.[43] Joseph H. Cohen, another prominent member of the congregation, was the chairman of the board at Beth-Israel Hospital and was to be the moving force behind the Jewish Center on the West Side where Kaplan became rabbi. Abba Baum, the patriarch of the Baum family, also in real estate, primarily on the Lower East Side, had been one of the founders of the congregation. He knew Israel Kaplan well and had been friends with the Kaplan family for many years. He had gone west in the gold rush of 1849 and set up a shop in San Francisco. His daughter Esther Baum Ruskay, an important member of the congregation, was a noted Jewish writer of the time and became a strong Kaplan supporter. She wrote for many of the Anglo-Jewish newspapers in New York and around the country. She was one of the organizers of the National Council of Jewish Women, and her home on Saturday afternoons was a center of the Jewish intelligentsia.[44]

The Kehilath Jeshurun synagogue building on the Upper East Side matched the status of its members. The congregation could boast of having inside toilets for women and a guard (really the janitor) who was dressed up in a gold-braided uniform and greeted the worshipers as they entered the building. Jenna Joselit, the well-known social historian, refers to them as the "reasonable" Americanized Orthodox, who

enjoyed social dancing and mixed swimming but never openly proposed changes in the Jewish law. They were traditional yet acculturated.[45]

It is noteworthy that throughout his life Kaplan served wealthy
Jews. People who could afford the best sought out rabbis who were
intelligent, well-spoken, and articulated a significant program of adjustment to American life. Kaplan was satisfying on all counts. From
his perspective, there was the fear that his congregation might become
just a rich man's club without any spiritual depth. But in 1903, he was
less worried about such things and more concerned with obtaining a
permanent position.

Kehilath Jeshurun had been under the direction of Rabbi Mayer
Joshua Peikes, a traditional Yiddish-speaking rabbi. It met in a "dingy
little building" on East Eighty-second Street. Over the years, many of
the congregants became prosperous, and in 1902 sufficient money had
been raised to construct a building on East Eighty-fifth Street. Some of
the members demanded an English-speaking rabbi who could relate to
the younger, more acculturated congregants. They wanted a fashionable congregation.[46]

Many years later, Kaplan related the details that led to the dismissal
of the old rabbi. Peikes had been pressured to give sermons in English
so that they could be understood by the younger generation. Because
of his limited knowledge of the language, he used notes for these sermons. On one occasion, some of the children stole the notes, and when
he reached for them they were not there. Unable to deliver his sermon,
he was severely embarrassed.[47] Feeling threatened, Peikes sent a letter
to the board in the spring of 1903 stating that once a man is rabbi he
holds the position for life. This letter brought the simmering conflict
to a head, and when the board considered him for a renewal of contract,
the motion was defeated. The board also decided to give Peikes five
hundred dollars as a goodwill gesture.[48]

The trustees then decided to place an advertisement in the papers
and to contact Professor Joseph Asher at the Seminary about securing
a rabbi from England. The ad read as follows: "Wanted by Kehilath
Jeshurun, a rabbi who has *Hatoras Hora'ah* [a kind of traditional ordi-
nation] and capable of delivering lectures in the English language.
Must be able to take charge of a religious school."[49] Asher, in addition
to his duties at the Seminary, also had a congregation at Sixty-fifth
Street and Madison Avenue and may have heard about the sermons
delivered by Kaplan in the neighborhood during the spring of 1903.
After several months spent considering candidates, the congregation
decided to hire Kaplan even without the traditional ordination that had

been specified in the advertisement. He was appointed not as rabbi but as "superintendent of the religious school and also to deliver lectures in the synagogue as often as called upon."[50] Kaplan was to receive sixty dollars a month as a salary. Writing to his Talmud professor at the Seminary, who apparently had recommended him, Kaplan expressed his intention "to do all I can to make myself indispensable to the congregation." He obviously hoped that he would be hired as a rabbi in the not-too-distant future. Apparently, things went well, for in April 1904, the congregation elected Kaplan as minister for two years at a salary of fifteen hundred dollars a year; he was also to be superintendent of the religious school. The designation *minister* was not uncommon at that time. The rabbis in New York City called themselves the New York Board of Jewish Ministers. However, being called a minister was not quite the same as being called a rabbi. Some ten years later, Kaplan wrote in his journal that "knowing, however, that although I had a diploma from the Seminary, the leaders of the congregation were by no means in the wrong in insisting that I have a *smicha* [traditional ordination not granted by the Seminary] from a Rav of the old type whom they could recognize as an authority, I consented to being elected as minister."[51]

It is quite clear that the congregation was divided in a number of significant ways and was in a state of transition. Not everyone was unhappy with Rabbi Peikes. The board vote that dismissed him passed by only a slim majority, nineteen in favor of dismissal and sixteen against. In December 1903, the congregation sent a letter to Peikes asking him not to interfere in synagogue matters. The conflict was between those who wanted a European-type rabbi of the old school who spoke in Yiddish about very traditional matters and those who supported the idea of a young, English-speaking rabbi who would address more contemporary concerns. The attempt to compromise was reflected in the advertisement for a rabbi and in the new by-laws passed by the congregation, both of which stipulated a rabbi traditionally ordained yet able to speak English.

The strains at Kehilath Jeshurun are indicative of the growing pains within the Jewish community at large. Some insisted on preserving the religion they knew from Europe (the resisters, as they have been called), and others preferred to adapt in small ways so that their children would not feel alienated from the synagogue (the accommodators). They wanted to be Orthodox and modern at the same time.[52]

Kaplan thus entered a deeply divided congregation, and his coming created even more conflict and controversy. The conflict Kaplan generated concerned his status as a Seminary graduate. The Orthodox leadership of New York City had attacked the Seminary for years, but now a Seminary graduate was moving into a position in an important New York Orthodox congregation. In the spring of 1904, a few months after Kaplan was hired, the Union of Orthodox Rabbis issued a circular denouncing as blasphemous the use of English in a Jewish pulpit and issued a strong warning to congregations "not to hire graduates of the Seminary who have no right to call themselves rabbis."[53] Kaplan thus came to symbolize the Seminary's threat to the more traditional synagogues in the community. The *American Hebrew* took note of the circular and attempted to explain its origin: "One of the most prominent Orthodox congregations in this city recently appointed a former Seminary student as its religious head and all the fury of these Orthodox rabbis has been directed toward this synagogue and its leaders."

The "righteous" anger of the Orthodox was predictable. The Seminary was rejected by the traditionally Orthodox because of the ways in which it departed from the mode of the European yeshiva. The curriculum included areas of study other than Talmud and Jewish law, and the language of instruction was English rather than Yiddish. The controversy surrounding Kaplan in 1904 focused primarily on this second matter. For some Orthodox Jews, who rejected accommodation, the use of English in the synagogue or in connection with religious matters meant that change and reform were not far behind. In fact most controversies involving Reform in the nineteenth century centered around the use of the vernacular in connnection with religious matters.

In order to understand the Orthodox attack on Kaplan, it is necessary to understand the problems the Orthodox confronted at the beginning of the century. With thousands of immigrants streaming in every year, it was imperative to set up some kind of institutional order to serve their religious needs. In 1898, the Union of Orthodox Jewish Congregations was established in New York City, with Rabbi Henry Pereira Mendes as its first president. The union concerned itself with various issues including matters of *kashrut.* It was a small group at the beginning and did not include many of the congregations on the Lower East Side.[54] In 1902, a group of rabbis banded together to form the *Agudath ha-Rabbanim* or Union of Orthodox Rabbis of the United States. The *Agudath ha-Rabbanim* represented those who would not countenance change or adjustment to their new environment. For some of these traditional rabbis, Mendes's association with the Seminary and the fact that he had a western education branded him as heterodox.

The first problem for the rabbinical union was determining who was a legitimate rabbi. Among the thousands of immigrants, there were learned men who passed themselves off as rabbis without having received the proper ordination. The union also was determined to do everything in its power to weaken the Seminary which graduated "rabbis" but did not confer the traditional ordination (*smicha*). The constitution of the new rabbinical organization stipulated that it could accept as a member only those who had a *smicha* from a well-known European rabbi.[55] Moses Sebulun Margolies, who was chief rabbi in Boston at the time and was to be appointed rabbi at Kehilath Jeshurun, was one of the leaders of this organization. With the issuing of the constitution, the Union of Orthodox Rabbis accepted as members fifty-nine rabbis from different parts of the United States.[56]

The confusion in the Orthodox community is perhaps symbolized most graphically by the death of the chief rabbi, Jacob Joseph, which occurred during the organizational meeting of the rabbinical union. The chief rabbi, who had come to New York with such fanfare in 1888, was unable to bring even a modicum of order to the Orthodox community. Israel Kaplan, Mordecai's father, was thus wise to leave the chief rabbi's entourage when he did. In the mid-1890s, the chief rabbi became bedridden and was barely noticed by New York's Jews. As if to make up for this neglect, his funeral was attended by many thousands of people. A riot occurred at the funeral which was described in detail in the local press and in the *Jewish Encyclopedia*.[57]

One of the first priorities of the Union of Orthodox Rabbis was control of the appointment of Orthodox rabbis to positions in New York City. They thus issued the anti-Kaplan circular of 1904 with its strong condemnation of the Seminary and its graduates. A number of newspapers condemned the circular in very strong terms. The *Yidishe Gazetten*, a paper strongly supportive of moderate Orthodoxy, wrote, "We shudder to think of the depths to which these men would drag Judaism in this country if they had the power — to what extremes their fanaticism would reach." The *American Hebrew* interpreted the circular to mean that a ban or excommunication had been issued against any congregation that took a Seminary graduate. As it turned out later, however, this was not the case. The editorial of the *American Hebrew*, which often spoke for Conservative leaders, went on to say that the ban was a "*hillul Ha Shem* — a profanation of our Holy Faith." It condemned Philadelphia rabbi Bernard Levinthal, the president of the union at the time, saying that the circular was "a disgrace and tends to lower us in the eyes of our fellow citizens of other faiths."[58] Kaplan, quite distressed by the whole matter, brought a copy of the circular to Schechter, who wrote about it to his friend Judge Mayer Sulzberger of Philadelphia: "Mr. Kaplan of the Seminary brought me the enclosed circular. I think you ought to see it. You will also notice Lewinthal [*sic*] of Philadelphia is the 'Hauptmacher' L. impressed me when I saw him as an ambitious Jesuit."[59] The complicated nature of the situation is revealed by the fact that a few years later, Levinthal happily participated in the Seminary graduation when his son Israel Levinthal became a rabbi.

Kaplan was upset by the circular, but his position was not really threatened since he had made a good initial impression at the synagogue and was well liked. His primary duties at this point had to do with the congregational school which he organized and supervised. According to Kaplan, it was the first afternoon school attached to a congregation rather than run as an independent Talmud Torah for poorer children. In November 1904, Kaplan petitioned the board to allow the children to be taught singing and to organize an adult Talmud class which he would teach. Although Kaplan did not teach the young children, he was involved in arranging holiday programs that were presented to the parents. Years later, one of his charges remembered that he would lose his temper frequently and that the students feared him. She had the impression that he hated what he was doing.[60] In later years, Seminary students continued to fear him.

Kaplan also taught a class in *Mishnah* (early rabbinic code) to the older men every morning after services. Although he began to question certain fundamental beliefs at an early age, Kaplan had no trouble teaching and thinking about arcane rabbinic problems. One particular morning, one of the men asked him a question about sacrifices. Musing on the matter later in the day, he noted in his journal that the cessation of sacrifices for two thousand years indicates clearly "there is something inherent in the ceremony which is offensive to the mature spirit of Judaism." Nonetheless, he saw nothing wrong in studying the laws of the sacrifices, because he believed "they are full of the profoundest spiritual suggestions which retain their transparency and truth as long as they are not incorporated within some concrete [form]." Kaplan's ease in relating to rabbinic sources remained with him throughout his life and reflects the time he spent studying Talmud with his father.

As though poised in the eye of the storm, Kaplan seemed calm in the midst of the controversy between the Orthodox and the Seminary. All around him the conflict continued to grow and become more complicated. In June 1904, Rabbi Henry P. Mendes wrote to the Union of Orthodox Rabbis about a number of issues that faced the Orthodox community and required some kind of statement. He asked about the Seminary and the rabbis' attitude toward it. Mendes certainly had in mind the circular that had been issued in the spring. The rabbis' meeting at 156 Henry Street, the home of the Isaac Elchanan Yeshiva, appointed a committee to answer Mendes's letter. While they were considering their response, the rabbis received the news of Theodor Herzl's death on July 3, 1904, at the age of forty-four. Jews all over the world mourned him, and even those who were not strong Zionists were moved to speak out for the Zionist cause as a way of paying tribute to the dead leader. They discussed at length what kind of statement to issue. They finally passed a resolution pledging their support for the Zionist movement, even though many of these same rabbis eventually became strongly anti-Zionist.

The rabbis then appointed a committee to answer the Mendes' question about the Seminary. The committee consisted of Moshe S. Margolies, Joseph Peikes, and the *Slutsker Rav*, a very traditional rabbi who eventually left America because of its impoverished religious state.[61] These men drafted a letter to Mendes which was printed in the *American Hebrew* at the end of the month. It read, "it was never our intention to proclaim a *cherem* [ban], but we do protest against the Seminary calling itself Orthodox since the professors of the Seminary believe in Higher Criticism. Besides the professors in our judgment are not qualified as teachers in the Talmud and the Codes. We protest also against the students who graduate from the Seminary as Rabbis, inasmuch as they are not fit for the position of Rabbi on account of the lack of proper and sufficient learning. We are also convinced that none of the graduates can pass an examination before a competent Jewish authority . . ."[62] It may be that this particular attack on the Seminary is related to an article on "The Law" which appeared in the seventh volume of the *Jewish Encyclopedia* in the spring of 1904. This article, by Seminary scholar Louis Ginzberg, assumed that some of the law codes in the Pentateuch developed over a long period of time and were not all from the Mosaic period. An article in the newspapers by Judah David Eisenstein brought the matter to public attention. Eisenstein was very critical of Ginzberg and pointed out that Schechter was on the board of the encyclopedia and thus bore responsibility.

There is, of course, no doubt that Kaplan could have passed the most rigorous rabbinical examination. He was perfectly at home with all the classical Jewish sources. Rabbinic quotations appear regularly in his notes and journals throughout his life. His lessons in *Mishnah* and Talmud at the congregation certainly convinced many that they had the ideal leader — an English-speaking rabbi with a college education who was easily conversant with classical rabbinic texts. He could relate to those in the congregation who had college educations and understood English well. The rate of acculturation of the children of the congregation is exhibited by the story of one extremely observant member who was leaving his house very early one morning to go to services and met his son coming home from an all-night party.[63] The presence in the congregation of such fathers and sons led in 1904 to a rather bizarre series of events.

During the summer of 1904 Kehilath Jeshurun, with Kaplan as its minister, invited the *Slutsker Rav* to preach for the high holidays. Hiring the *Slutsker Rav* was certainly odd, considering the strong language with which the union and the *Rav* had condemned the congregation and its hiring of Kaplan.

Rabbi Jacob David Willowsky (1845–1913), the *Slutsker Rav*, held a number of important posts in Europe. He had a special interest in the Jerusalem Talmud and was in the process of publishing a new edition, adding his own commentaries to the standard ones. It was to raise money for this project that he first came to America in 1900,[64] touring a number of cities and speaking to Orthodox Jews wherever he could. Kehilath Jeshurun was a logical stopping place; not only was the congregation Orthodox, but many members were wealthy.

Kehilath Jeshurun first turned to the *Slutsker Rav* for advice in 1903. The building they had vacated on East Eighty-second Street was not being used. In October of that year, the trustees of the synagogue were approached by someone who wanted to use it as a stable. The board was troubled and asked the *Rav* whether it was appropriate to sell the building for other than religious purposes.[65]

Perhaps this earlier relationship with the *Rav* explains some of the trustees' again turning to him for help in 1904. The high holidays that year would be the first time the congregation did not have a traditional rabbi who would preach to them with the passion and vigor of the "old-time religion." Without bringing the issue up before the full board, the president and a few board members approached the *Rav* and asked him to preach on the high holidays. As the high holiday season of 1904 approached, the *Slutsker Rav* made it clear to the board that he would not preach if there was any preaching at the synagogue in English. This represented a direct challenge to the congregation, since Kaplan, now leader of the congregation, was hired specifically because of his ability to deliver sermons in English. The significance of the language issue is reflected in a *responsum* (legal opinion) the *Slutsker Rav* wrote later regarding sermons delivered in English on general subjects:

> These sermons contain no true guidance for the Jewish people. They simply make the Jewish people like the rest of the nations. If these practices will not cease, there is no hope for the continuance of the Jewish religion. These sermons will open gates leading our brethren to Reform Judaism. Whoever fears the Lord must protest against

these preachers. If one does not have the power to stop this practice, he must leave the synagogue when such a preacher rises to ascend the pulpit. Due to our sins this practice is now become widespread even in Orthodox synagogues. The masses do not realize the graveness of the danger this presents to Judaism.[66]

The letter perfectly illustrates the mentality of the resister to acculturation.

For Kaplan, the central issue posed by the *Slutsker Rav* concerned the way in which Jews in America ought to confront the future. Would contemporary culture be the context for a new Judaism, or would it be the enemy? Writing to the congregation before the high holidays, he said:

I hereby protest against your resolve not to have me speak on the High Holidays. It is not a question of personal consideration; it is not my honor that I contend. Principle is here involved. Your action in refusing me the pulpit on the most important days of our calendar proves that you still believe that it is impossible to make Judaism compatible with modern culture, that you are concerned that the Ghetto manners and the Ghetto language are the only means whereby Judaism can be saved. If this is the case, I must make known to you that I stand for the very opposite belief. I believe that Judaism need not and must not be afraid to meet and absorb all that is good in modern culture. I believe that the manners and the jargons which are the accretions of the Ghetto must be cast off. I have faith and confidence in Judaism. You have no faith in Judaism's strength nor confidence in me.

This impassioned statement eloquently expresses Kaplan's commitments, his anger, and his pain.[67]

Some seventy years later, Kaplan recounted the incident with amusement, but at the time he was outraged. He learned about the matter too late to alter its outcome and decided to preach in Hebrew but not in Yiddish. Kaplan was not easily intimidated even at this early point in his career:

The *Slutsker Rav* offered to preach on the high holidays. I remember particularly what he said on Yom Kippur. The old *Maggid* [preacher] would have a sing-song voice, and, this congregation being Orthodox, the women were in the galleries. The back galleries were all old women. When the *Maggid* would begin, in his sing-song voice, to say something sad, the women would begin to cry out loud. They were called the weeping choir. So on Yom Kippur, I recall as though it were today, he said, "*Oy meine kinde! Weisst ihr was mir hoben von unser Toyro gemacht? Ihr hoben gemacht von ihr a pamoneche.*" [Oh my children! Do you know what has been done to our Torah? It has been made into a slop pail.] As soon as he said that out loud, the women cried, "*Oyyy.*" Then on *Sukkos* after that, I preached in Hebrew so that he should understand. I would not preach in Yiddish.[68]

The news spread quickly that Kaplan had been forbidden to preach at his own synagogue during the high holidays. The *American Hebrew* expressed a deep sense of outrage. "Such action," declared an editorial, "is a disgrace to the congregation which permitted itself to be dominated by a man whose whole career in America has been that of a mischief-maker. The sooner the *Slutsker Rav* gets out of America the better. . . . Kehilath Jeshurun should make reparation for the disgrace it has brought upon itself and the insult it has permitted to its preacher."[69]

The next week, Esther Ruskay wrote to the *American Hebrew* that the majority of the congregation considered the incident "deplorable and unwelcome." The *Slutsker Rav* was invited by the president of the congregation and one or two trustees. Given this fait accompli, there was no choice but to show common courtesy and "give him [the *Rav*] the respect which he deserved." Kaplan was supported by the entire congregation and comported himself very well, according to Ruskay: "the young minister himself, imbued with the love for learning that the Seminary and the traditions in which he has been reared have instilled into him, was among the first to insist that the president's action be sustained and that the proper need of reverence be accorded the visiting *Rav*."[70]

To understand the incident, it is important to remember how strongly many Jews felt about Yiddish in those days. The uptown establishment considered it the chief obstacle to Americanization. The older Jewish immigrants used Yiddish in their daily lives, but many of their children refused to speak it. Some of the traditional leaders, on the other hand, felt that it was a hedge against complete assimilation which involved not only the use of English but the changing of traditional ways.

One Reform rabbi obviously contemplated the whole situation with great relish because now Conservative Jews were getting a little taste of what Reform rabbis had experienced in the nineteenth century. Writing to the *Reform Advocate*, which was published in Chicago, he described the Conservative Jews supporting the Seminary as "the English-Portuguese-Episcopalian-Jewish Orthodoxy" who are "just as *trefe* [contaminated] as we are." The *Slutsker Rav* is no fool, he wrote, and knows that "preaching in English is the beginning and most effective beginning of Reform."

These issues were hotly debated in the Jewish press that autumn of 1904. The ubiquitous J. D. Eisenstein wrote later in his memoirs that he considered the *Rav* a fine speaker who delivered his talks with great feeling. During the controversy itself, Eisenstein wrote a letter to the *American Hebrew* making the point that many in the congregation didn't understand English anyway. "This congregation is the richest among others consisting of members and seat holders of foreign nativity," he wrote. "Not over 10 percent of them understand the English preacher [Kaplan] although most of them know enough English for business needs. One of the members told me that they consider the English preacher like a fine piano, it being of no consequence, if there is no one in the house who can play it. The younger element is indifferent to both English and Yiddish preaching. The English preacher, the members confessed, was to satisfy the prevailing style of rich congregations." [71]

Eisenstein, however, tended to exaggerate. He was quite Orthodox and critical of the Seminary and its graduates, attacking the institution from its very beginning. There was a sizable group of younger college-educated congregants who would certainly have related more easily to Kaplan than to the *Slutsker Rav*.

Phineas Israeli, Kaplan's Seminary classmate who married his sister, Sophie, wrote a letter responding strongly to Eisenstein's criticism. Israeli believed that Eisenstein had "disparaged" the sermons of the "young rabbi" and characterized Kaplan as "a brilliant example" of the kind of English-speaking rabbis the Seminary was producing. He went on to say that Kaplan was not a mere ornament, for besides preaching, "he personally leads a class of about twenty young men in the study of Jewish Philosophy using a text book — the *Chovoth Halvovoth* of Bachya. . . . He has under him, furthermore a school of more than one hundred children who are learning how to translate Hebrew into English. . . . After these facts will Mr. Eisenstein still prefer the old country itinerant preacher to the modern Orthodox rabbi who devotes himself heart and soul to God? We need a dozen such rabbis." [72]

A woman who signed herself "A Member of the Congregation," wrote that the situation was just the opposite of the one Eisenstein had described, for it was 10 percent who do not understand English and 90 percent who do. (This, too, was perhaps an exaggeration.) Kaplan was a man of "broad liberal culture" with those who are college-bred being "in complete accord with the young minister." Those who do not understand "are the very old men, may Heaven preserve them to the congregation for many years, since in this as in every other congregation, they are the mainstay — the 'old guard,' the precious link that binds the strenuous Judaism of today with the easily satisfied, uncomplaining Judaism of the past. . . . The old men nevertheless seek out the young rabbi as evidenced by their attendance at the early [morning] *Mishnayos* class."[73]

Although Kaplan held up well, the situation was undermining. He had not really settled into his new position and was already being replaced in a sense. The newspaper comments indicate, however, that he was popular with the congregation and was in no danger of losing his job. Well versed in the traditional sources, the young minister had no trouble offering the members of the congregation food for thought: he was, in fact, more sophisticated and somewhat more radical than they realized. Two days before Eisenstein's letter was published in the *American Hebrew*, Kaplan confided to his journal, "If ever with G's help I will carry out the plan I have in mind, viz. first of writing a work which shall be a kind of 'Guide to the Perplexed' and secondly, of purging the 'Shulhan Aruch,' I hope to write a commentary which shall contribute new content to the old forms of prayer."[74] Kaplan was a mere twenty-three years old; he does sound somewhat presumptuous. But he was a man of vision, and the feeling that he had a mission to help save the Jews was evident early on and obsessed and motivated him throughout his life.

3

MIXED EMOTIONS:

Felix Adler and
Moshe Sebulun Margolies

Although Kaplan's life at the congregation was a full one, he still managed to find time to continue his graduate studies at Columbia. In addition to studying, he took up swimming and other sports and built up his naturally fine physique to larger proportions. Although his later life as a rabbi was essentially a sedentary one, he exercised regularly. He enjoyed walking and covered long distances in the city on a daily basis, including the path around the reservoir in Central Park, while discussing the portion of the week as well as general Jewish problems with a comrade. Both colleagues and students were his "reservoir" companions. Judah Magnes, for example, and students such as Max Kadushin, Louis Finkelstein, and Ira Eisenstein, joined him many times.

Like many leaders of his generation, Kaplan believed that fragmentation and divisiveness would be fatal to the Jewish community. In thinking through the problem of unity, he fastened on the central concept of consciousness of kind which he learned from his teacher Franklin Giddings. His reasoning ran as follows: "The fundamental principle of groups of men is consciousness of kind. In the case of other nationalities, the consciousness of kind is based on both the physical and spiritual aspects." Unity within a nation is to be related to a sense of a shared past, he thought. "No experience is ever wiped out but it is

Note: In the literature of that time Margolies' middle name is always spelled with an 's' despite the fact that in Hebrew he is called "Ramaz."

taken up and reconstructed. This is true of racial and national life as well as the individual. The great problem for the Jews, therefore, is how to reconstruct our past experience." Relating effectively to the past ought to be the primary mechanism for promoting unity. He believed that unity would bring strength. "We want to find a common platform whereon Nordau [a key Zionist], Reines [a religious Zionist], the *Slutsker Rav* [an extremely traditional Jew], and Emil Hirsch [a well-known Reform rabbi] can stand," wrote Kaplan in 1906.[1]

Kaplan's reading and thinking moved continually between Jewish and general matters and shifted from the religious to the scientific to the mystical. The following excerpt from his private journal begins with a statement about mysticism; it sums up his state of mind in 1905, when he had completed most of his courses at Columbia. Indeed, this whole discussion might be viewed as a commentary (*Midrash*) on this paragraph which also illustrates the tension in his mind between the scientific or experiential on the one hand and the transcendent on the other.

There is a kind of mysticism which is essential to thought and without which thought is both barren and heartless. That is, the sense of the infinite, which must supplement every concept of the finite. Science does not need it as long as it aims to be particular, but it is sure to grow narrow if it dismisses such mysticism entirely. On the other hand it is of the very essence of literature to embody this sense of the infinite, this longing for the eternal universal Beyond.

To call this Beyond a Person is meaningless, as Arnold has so well proved, . . . *But* if Kant is right then all thought dealing with the infinite must be struck out from religion, or rather to talk less sugarcoatedly one ought to become a positivist with Comte and declare religion as such, untenable? This would necessarily have been the conclusion I would have arrived at, had I not learned that though logic besides being finite, is deceptive and unquestionably in the wrong, as it is in the field of conduct. Thought for instance establishes beyond dispute that our notions of right and wrong have arisen from convenience, custom, etc. The logical conclusion therefore is that when one is a wretch, and a liar and a thief, he is merely at variance with custom and prejudice. In short, as I remember Sidgwick to have well shown in his *Methods*, there is no room in pure logic for the "ought." But the "ought" is there anyhow, and a mighty stubborn and positive thing it is. I shall, therefore, not trust my pure logic to remain insensible to the Beyond, but shall render homage to it and worship it because it is as stubborn and Positive as the ought. Here there is room for a mystical guess which would find the ought in the domain of the Beyond.[2]

In his struggles with the "ought" and with ethical problems in general, Kaplan's teacher Felix Adler was of primary importance. The attraction to Adler was long-lasting but ambivalent. While Kaplan was taking courses with Adler, he was offered a scholarship by the Ethical Culture Society which he refused. Kaplan despised Adler for leaving the Jewish fold in order to found Ethical Culture. He often criticized Adler and was especially distressed when he met members of the university Menorah Societies who were thinking of joining Ethical Culture. Nevertheless, Kaplan himself was attracted to Adler's ethical emphasis and to his universalism. This universalism was Kaplan's great temptation — his demon as it were, which plagued him throughout his life. Everyone has a very private side concealed from others. Kaplan's inner secret concerned his attraction toward the universal and the temptation to move away from the particular, that is, the Jewish people. In moments of despair, when he felt that Judaism had little chance of surviving, he thought about joining Adler's movement. "Time and again it has occurred to me," he confided in his journal in 1916, "that I ought to join the Ethical Culture Movement." His congregation, the Society for the Advancement of Judaism, was patterned after the Society for Ethical Culture. Until the mid-1930s, for example, he called himself the leader as Adler had done, and Ira Eisenstein was called the assistant leader. With the coming of Nazism, Kaplan reverted to the title of rabbi.

Kaplan's ambivalence toward Adler was also widespread within the Jewish community. Commenting on a speech Adler gave at the Free Synagogue on Abraham Geiger, his teacher, the *American Hebrew* praised Adler highly for having "supported with vigor of intellect and lofty sternness every movement for the cleansing of ethical ideals of the American people. . . . He has grasped with rare insight the essence of American principles of life." It also condemned him for running "a Jewish congregation that excluded the Jewish religion."[3]

Adler was born and brought up in New York City and attended Columbia University. His secular education opened his eyes to the world of the intellect and its problems. As for so many others, this experience raised doubts about his religious commitments. Adler's father was a prominent Reform rabbi who expected his son to follow in his path. His Jewish commitments are reflected, for example, in an early essay he published in which he deplored the practice of some Reform Jews who brought trees into their homes at Christmastime. On the other hand, he began to have doubts about some of the fundamentals of Judaism, doubts that were deepened when he went to Germany to continue his Judaic studies. Even the great reformer Abraham Geiger, then advanced in years, could not answer Adler's questions.[4]

Felix Adler (1851–1933), founder of Ethical Culture and Kaplan's professor of philosophy at Columbia. (Courtesy Ethical Culture Archives New York.)

The question that plagued Adler was "Why remain Jewish?" Drawn to prophetic idealism since his Columbia days, Adler was at the same time drifting away from traditional theism. He could not see why ethics had to be rooted in the experience of a particular people — ethics were universal. It was time for Jews to move beyond the narrow confines of their ethnic past. Adler saw Geiger as too timid to take the next step in the process of modernization. The efforts to divest the Jewish religion of its particularity were only partial and must be taken to their logical conclusion, Adler believed.

By the time Mordecai Kaplan arrived in Adler's class in February 1903, the Society for Ethical Culture was well established, and Adler's ideas had already taken a definitive shape. Adler personally expected and received respect. His personality is described vividly by John Herman Randall, who in later years also taught at Columbia; Adler was "Genial, urbane, cosmopolitan . . . he relished and told a good story, and he was an incorrigible punster. First his eyes would twinkle, then a red flush suffused his face, which extended over the top of his hairless head. Adler laughed often, and when he laughed, he laughed with his entire being."[5]

Kaplan had been taking courses in philosophy for the previous three years and also had read extensively in sociology under Giddings's guidance. The doubts he would express in his journal a few years later were certainly already present. Under these circumstances, Adler was extremely important to Kaplan. Although Kaplan never gave up his contempt for Adler as a traitor, the concerns and the formulations of the ethicist were precisely what Kaplan needed to help him deal with his spiritual conflicts.

Adler wanted to capture the essence of religion in order to retain its meaningfulness at a time when science and technology seemed to relegate it to a smaller and smaller place. He sounds very much like the later Kaplan: "There is something in religion besides its doctrines, its symbols and its ceremonies. . . . That which is everlastingly precious in religion is the conviction that life is worthwhile."[6]

Throughout Kaplan's career, he interpreted religion in terms of function. He was drawn to the pragmatism of William James and, later, John Dewey. It is likely, however, that the fundamental thrust of Kaplan's thinking arises from his professor, Felix Adler. Although Adler did not offer a fully elaborated system, he did spell out many of his fundamental assumptions and primary concepts. Again and again, he emphasized the primacy of experience in understanding religion. Many thinkers and students of religion maintained the same point, but Kaplan learned this matter in a contemporary form through Adler: "The religion that shall satisfy must be a religion of progress, of evolution, of development, understood not in a scientific sense but in a moral sense. To the question: How can one get religion? the answer is 'through experience.' We must find in our own inner life the facts which are capable of being interpreted in terms of a religion, the foundations upon which the super-structure of a helpful religion can be built."[7]

Adler also believed that religion must not violate the scientific understanding of the day and must be founded on honesty. He spoke directly to the problem of religious conflict: "Let us found religion upon a basis of perfect intellectual honesty. Religion, if it is to mean anything at all, must stand for the highest truth. How then can the cause of truth be served by the sacrifice more or less disguised of one's intellectual convictions." These were precisely the sentiments that Kaplan needed to hear.[8]

◆

The series of lectures from Adler that Kaplan heard in the spring of 1903 centered on the key problem of justifying the imperative — the "ought" in any ethical system. This primary question, of course, had been asked since the time of Plato, but in the late nineteenth century it took on a different cast. Would the course of action required by self-preservation and the course required by morality be the same? If the answer is yes, then those who survive (we are talking of groups here) would also be the ones that are ethically the most developed.[9] Darwin believed that altruism and survivability went hand in hand. The point is not the virtue of Darwin's position but the fact that at every turn the young Kaplan was confronted by the Darwinian revolution and was presented, in this particular case, with the central issue of justifying ethical imperatives.

The strong ethical and humanistic tendency in Kaplan is in evidence from his early years and may be dependent on Adler's universalism. Kaplan worried about assimilation, but at the same time he was deeply concerned with all humankind. His universalism and his strong Jewish identification remained in a complex symbiosis from his earliest years. The older Judaism, he explained in 1906, centered its attention on the Jewish people: "The new Judaism moves the center from Israel to Humanity. The *Shekina* [presence of God] is in Humanity." If the presence of God is in humanity, then it must mean, according to the young Kaplan, that no one group has a monopoly on the truth. He did not reject the concept of the chosen people until much later; an incipient rejection arose, however, while he was still in his thirties: "It is just as necessary and inevitable that each should represent the spiritual side of life differently from the other as it is necessary and inevitable that each should have features of his own or speak in a way altogether his own. When we recognize the necessity of varied expression, the sameness and the unity of the underlying essence will stand out more prominently."[10]

Theologically speaking, Adler's conception was clearer than Kaplan's later formulations. He stated that when we talk of God, we speak metaphorically because what we say is never literally true, but the metaphor nonetheless stands for something real. The gods, including Jehovah, are creations of the imagination, but the eternal is not. His proof derived from morality, and it was very similar to what is found in Kaplan's later works: "If then, I believe in the ultimate attainment of the moral end, I am forced to assume that there is provision in nature looking to the achievement of that end."[11] Adler's ability to deal with the transcendent certainly made it easier for Kaplan to relate to his philosophy as a whole. Despite his emphasis on the ethical, Adler possessed a genuine sense of the transcendent. "[The] deepest experiences of life have been missed," he tells us, "if we have never been thrilled by the emotions which come from the thought of that vaster life of which ours is a part. It is wonder, evoked by the thought of the vastness, order and beauty of the world that has led men to the idea of God." [12]

In dealing with thoughts that lead a person to the transcendent, Adler discussed not only wonder but also righteousness. It was Matthew Arnold's approach that Adler actually paraphrased, and Kaplan was familiar with Arnold's writings. Speaking of the demand for justice, Adler said, "on the other hand, if the demand for justice is realizable, then in the nature of things there must be provision that it shall be realized; then there must be as it has been expressed, 'a power that makes for righteousness.'"[13] This formulation, which became so important in Kaplan's later thought and which he encountered when he was at Columbia, is taken directly from Matthew Arnold's *Literature and Dogma*. Adler went on to expand the matter, emphasizing God as a power rather than a person.[14]

In 1905, Kaplan wrote in his journal of Arnold and of the Jewish thinker Ahad Ha-Am: "I am more convinced than ever that Achad Ha-Am's conception of nationality plus Arnold's interpretation of Israel's genius for righteousness contains that which could form the positive expression of the Jewish spirit. All it wants is definiteness and detail." [15] Arnold, in *Literature and Dogma*, sets forth his goal of establishing the Bible on some basis other than that of revealed truth. Writing in the late nineteenth century, he assumed that religion was increasingly neglected, because people could not accept the axiom that the Bible derived its authority from the "moral and intelligent governor of the universe." Rather, he said, the authority of the Bible must be based "in something which can be verified instead of something which has to be assumed." [16]

As mentioned previously, Kaplan's first theological doubts came in connection with the miracles in the Bible. When he was a student at the Seminary, he argued with his peers because he could not accept the historicity of events that seemed contrary to the regularities of nature. Eventually, Kaplan was led to doubt not only the miracles but also the Mosaic authorship of the Bible.[17] Arnold was helpful to Kaplan in relating to the Hebrew scriptures as a document that evolved over a long period of time and was the product of many hands. Arnold believed the Hebrews derived their understanding of God from their immediate experience. He perceived them as intoxicated with right conduct and as believing that right conduct brought satisfaction. They were thankful that the world outside themselves, or the world other than their will, was constructed in such a way that righteousness was possible. This world outside the will was referred to by Arnold as "the not ourselves." The Hebrews reified and personified this "not ourselves" which allowed them to be righteous and derive satisfaction from being so. In Arnold's words, "they had dwelt upon the thought of conduct and right and wrong, till the 'not ourselves' which is in us and around us became to them adorable, eminently and altogether as a *power that makes for righteousness;* which makes for it unchangeably and eternally and is therefore called the 'Eternal.'"[18]

The language here is found in Kaplan's *The Meaning of God in Modern Jewish Religion.* Inspired in part by Arnold, he chose to talk about the way God functions in the world and not about his essence. Kaplan, in his lifelong quest for the meaning of God, always focused on what it is that God helps people to do. He repeatedly reformulated his belief in God. "It is because God is to me the warm personal element in life's inner urge to creativity and self-expression that I can conscientiously employ the name YHWH when praying," or, "God is that aspect of reality which elicits from us the best that is in us and enables us to bear the worst that can befall us," or, "God is the assumption that there is enough in the world to meet men's needs but not their greeds for power and pleasure."[19]

All these definitions reveal a shift from the object of the religious experience (the numina) to the religious experience itself. It may be that the shift to an emphasis on the religious experience will yield nothing that contradicts traditional belief or dogma. Yet the germ of the destruction of traditionalism is inherent in this methodological principle, and traditionalists were justified in their later opposition to Kaplan. The emphasis on religious experience assumes that experience is the only area in which we can have real knowledge and certainty. Thus, the experience in a way becomes the essence, while the supernatural or that which is completely outside experience is relegated to the nether reaches of the unknowable.

Kaplan's emphasis on experience is usually attributed to the influence of John Dewey and William James.[20] It may be, however, that Kaplan's pragmatic thrust arises from still earlier influences he encountered while studying at Columbia. His 1902 master's thesis dealt with the philosophy of Henry Sidgwick (1838–1900), who was for many years professor of philosophy at Cambridge University and whose book *The Methods of Ethics* is a significant treatise in the Benthamite tradition of utilitarian ethics. Sidgwick criticized both Bentham and John Stuart Mill but nonetheless remained within the utilitarian school. Kaplan's emphasis on function as well as some of his primary beliefs concerning religion are derived directly from Sidgwick.[21]

Utilitarianism appeared in the nineteenth century with the writings of Jeremy Bentham. Although the doctrine had been enunciated before, Bentham's name is closely associated with the "greatest happiness principle." In evaluating any rule of law or rule of behavior, he believed that the primary consideration was whether the behavior involved promoted the greatest happiness for the greatest number. He identified happiness with pleasure and devised a moral arithmetic for calculating the value of pain or pleasure. The principle of utility, as he called it, consists in evaluating behavior according to the amount of pain or pleasure produced by a certain act. To some degree, Bentham was arguing against the nineteenth-century notion of the self-evident truth. Bentham called this "nonsense on stilts." In his later years, Kaplan was fond of using this phrase but had apparently forgotten its source.

Bentham believed that the moral quality of an act was not self-evident but could be determined only by looking at the results. The utilitarian principle became a significant justification for those who advocated political and social reforms. As a rough rule of thumb, it was valuable to think in terms of the well-being of the individual in a concrete way. Invoking the utilitarian principle to decide specific issues, however, was problematic. Sidgwick is useful, because he closely examined all aspects of utilitarianism, pointing out strong and weak points in the theory and in its application.[22]

Sidgwick attempts at times to relate his philosophy to traditional religious concepts. He finds the fundamental tenet of promoting the general happiness to be in accord with the teachings of Christianity, although he leaves open the precise relationship between God's revealed will and utilitarian principles. He does not believe it possible to prove in any sense that virtue will be rewarded: "A desire that virtue should be rewarded is no proof that it will be, and to say that in some sense it ought to be is simply to restate the problem." Concerning the centrality of prayer, Sidgwick sees its role changing but believes it will remain a "permanent function of humanity." It no longer makes sense to see prayer as propitiating God because humanity has "progressed beyond that stage," Sidgwick believed. It would still be reasonable to consider prayer as a way of transforming the self or increasing self-control. Prayer would thus be a powerful agent in transforming the praying person.[23]

Sidgwick's attitudes toward religion correspond closely with Kaplan's later developments. Particularly with respect to prayer, Sidgwick's perspective resonates strongly with Kaplan's impassioned belief in prayer as symbolic rather than magical or theurgic.[24]

Kaplan's master's thesis is not particularly original or profound. He does not provide a history of the utilitarian movement, nor does he indicate the economic and political uses to which the principle was put. In a rather narrow way, he summarizes the key work of Sidgwick and offers some criticism and suggestions. At certain points in the thesis, Kaplan can hardly be disentangled from Sidgwick, so dependent is he on Sidgwick's thought.

The whole first section of Kaplan's thesis dealt with the origin of ethical ideas. As in Giddings, some attempt is made to trace the "higher" ideas such as ethical beliefs back to qualities that one could also find in the animal world. Darwin initiated this conceptual direction, but Kaplan, influenced by Sidgwick, regarded the entire project as irrelevant to the ethical enterprise. "The question of origin," wrote Kaplan, "is altogether irrelevant, for in ethics as well as in mathematics, the validity of its ideas are not established by virtue of any particular genesis."[25] Ethical value is determined not by origin but by the consequence of an action; one needs to look not behind the act but in front of it and ask what followed. A few years later, in Kaplan's first publication, he considered the origin of the Torah and its rules and asserted clearly and strongly that origin was not the key to justification. He used the word *function*, more properly a sociological term; but in talking of the function of an institution or a ritual, he certainly was talking of nothing more than the consequences of behaving in a certain way.[26]

Kaplan was in excellent command of the issues, writing with force and clarity. He exhibited analytical and critical faculties that were not always evident in the sermons from this same period. Maintaining a sophisticated analytical level, whether he was criticizing Sidgwick or presenting his ideas, Kaplan ended his thesis by characterizing the significance of Sidgwick. He dealt with the two major ethical theories that flowed from different views on the nature of man. One view saw man's essence in his feeling, the other in his reason. The former found expression in Bentham and Mill; the latter approach is the rational approach to ethics which finds its most outstanding exponent in Kant. Sidgwick united both points of view, and Kaplan tried to show that Sidgwick criticized the hedonic philosophy and ended up with a form of rational hedonism.[27]

Kaplan was not only influenced by philosophy and the social sciences but also by the novels he read. Some seventy years later, he vividly remembered *The Way of All Flesh* by Samuel Butler. This novel "spoke" to him in a fundamental way and became an event in his life, not just a passing pleasure. Butler's popular narrative centers on the life of a young clergyman and his conflicts, mostly religious, with his clergyman father and with society at large. As one critic put it: "Since it first appeared Butler's novel has seemed to thousands of people peculiarly exciting and liberating. 'Coming at such-and-such a point in my life,' they are likely to say, 'it altered my whole outlook. It helped me to stand up against the tyranny of my family . . . or of my school . . . or of the Church. . . . It made me begin to think for myself.'" The book constituted an attack on the religious hypocrisy and obscurantism of its time, commenting intelligently on all the major contemporary religious issues including biblical criticism and Darwinism. At a strategic point in Kaplan's life, the novel goaded him into thinking more freely and productively. It reflected his state of mind and helped to propel him forward.[28]

With the help of his mentor, Franklin Giddings, Kaplan's thinking became sociological. Sociologists inevitably distance themselves from institutions, traditions, and ideas and analyze their function. They are almost inevitably led to relativize. The influence of sociology was complemented by Kaplan's study of philosophy, experienced primarily through Felix Adler. Adler valued religion while seeking to demythologize it. His emphasis on the experiential aspects of religion made an indelible impression on Kaplan, as did some of the novels he read. The young scholar and rabbi was attracted to the field of ethics and wrote his master's thesis under Adler's direction. Kaplan's reading in utilitarian philosophy was in accord with his sociological studies; in both cases, value is assessed by results or consequences, not by appeal to self-evident truths or revealed law.

◆

The salary increases Kaplan received at Kehilath Jeshurun indicate definite satisfaction with his work. Although he preached frequently, his growing philosophical sophistication never entered into his remarks from the pulpit. He tried to keep the various parts of his life separate, but the effort was complicated and painful. Even so, there were members of the congregation who were unhappy because the young Kaplan lacked traditional ordination. In September 1905, a committee of the board was appointed to confer with him about engaging Moshe S. Margolies as "an associate." As Kaplan remembered it, the *Slutsker Rav* played a key role in bringing Margolies (*Ramaz*) to Kehilath Jeshurun. On October 31, 1905, it was recorded that Kaplan had no objection to engaging Margolies, and so he was hired as rabbi. Kaplan would

*Mordecai Kaplan as Minister of Kehilath Jershu-
run. (Courtesy Library of JTS.)*

continue to serve as minister and superintendent of the religious
school. However, Kaplan did not like Margolies and was angry with the
new arrangements. He had just managed to establish himself, and Margolies's appointment represented an obvious demotion. Margolies, because of his background and reputation, would be *the* rabbi and Kaplan
his assistant, even though the term was never used. Margolies's appointment was a victory for the resisters within the congregation. At
the same time, his willingness to work alongside a Seminary graduate
such as Kaplan showed considerable flexibility on Margolies's part.[29]

Morris S. Margolies was born in 1851 in Kroza, Russia, and had a
traditional yeshiva education, receiving *smicha* from Rabbi Lippa Halpern, a great rabbi of the day. He served as rabbi of Slobodka before
coming to the United States, where he served as chief rabbi of Boston.
Margolies was one of the founders of the Union of Orthodox Rabbis
and was also a strong supporter of Rabbi Isaac Elchanan Theological
Seminary. In late 1905, the yeshiva was experiencing problems with its
students, who went out on strike because they wanted to learn English
as well as Talmud. Margolies entered the fray as a mediator and helped

to resolve the conflict. He was "known to be a man of great tact, patience, and gentleness and was held in high esteem for his cool and even temper." These qualities helped the two rabbis of Kehilath Jeshurun to get along.[30]

Although unhappy about the situation, Kaplan had no trouble working with Margolies. "We did not come into conflict at any time," Kaplan said some years later, "because once they decided to take Margolies, I accepted him." In the morning, Kaplan continued to teach his class in *Mishnah*, and Margolies taught a class in Talmud. When Kaplan would finish one of the six divisions of the *Mishnah*, he would invite Margolies over for the final celebratory ending (*Hadran*).

Kaplan's conflicts were not between himself and Margolies but rather within himself. He was studying sociology and philosophy at Columbia, and these studies naturally led him to doubt many traditional beliefs. He was aware of the developing science of biblical criticism which maintained that the Torah was the product of many hands over a long period of time. Such assumptions undermined traditional beliefs about the origins of the Torah, and Kaplan felt constrained, perhaps largely because of Ehrlich's influence, to accept the new criticism. (Ehrlich continued to visit his home during this period.) The question was how to maintain the authority of the Torah under such conditions. His sociological training led the still uncertain young Kaplan to consider function rather than origins. "If it can be shown," he wrote in 1908, "how much purer and more spiritual and moral the myth of the Torah is than the contemporaneous myths of the surrounding nations, then we are duty bound to cherish the Torah." The Torah was no longer the center of Jewish life as it once had been. For assorted reasons, Jews were looking elsewhere for truth and inspiration. Kaplan felt this personally as a crisis of major proportions within his own life as well as in the life of the Jewish community. Undoubtedly he was talking about himself when he said, "We are sick of the timidity about radical beliefs and the self-complacency about the lack of positive doctrine. We want both to know and to understand what we believe." Tormented by his lack of courage to speak out, he did not yet have a very precise idea where he was going in terms of his religious ideology.[31]

At times, Kaplan was quite traditional in his thinking, fearing that if traditional views were discarded, Judaism would be in mortal danger. The organic image of Judaism as a living entity, which was to become so important in his later thinking, appeared at this early point but in a traditional context. "Perhaps it may be said," he wrote, "that the relationship between Judaism and divine authority is not the same as between edifice and foundation but more organic and therefore like that which obtains between stem and root, and whenever you kill the root the stem must die with it."[32]

His thought was not yet radical; later, Kaplan talked almost exclusively about the function of religious belief. Here we find rather more willingness to discuss the immanence of God in the world in a traditional way. The sense of God's presence and the concept of function existed side by side. In the more mature Kaplan, we rarely read about God's presence as traditionally understood. In the early writings, he sometimes sounded quite contemporary in his spirituality. "Prayer is communion," he wrote in 1907. "To commune with God is to put oneself in touch with the source of cosmic energy." He pointed out that not only prayer but the other commandments as well help to bring together the divine within man and the divine outside man. He also understood the divine in a functional sense when he emphasized that "everything is the result of divine inspiration which is enunciated by one man and is then adopted by great masses and bodies of human beings."[33]

Although Kaplan's humanism was an essential part of his thinking and of his personality, he was highly critical of Reform Judaism because, despite its universalism, it was not grounded in an emotional attachment to the people of Israel: "Reform Judaism has shaken off Jewish nationalism and has dwindled down to a sick colorless half-hearted cosmopolitanism." Throughout his life, he advocated an ethical concern that reached far beyond the confines of the Jewish people. Yet he believed the Jews could never survive if they denied their own needs as a people. He embraced both the universal and the particular without any sense of conflict.

Because the Jews are a people with a rich and varied past, a Judaism built on a nationalist basis would be the most solid. The young Kaplan did not fully define his nationalism, but he seemed to mean at the very least that Judaism should have at its core the sense of a common past. Focusing on this sense of a shared historical experience would allow the Jews to be traditional or Reform and yet continue to identify with one another.

We first see Kaplan's nationalism in a reaction to a lecture given in December 1906 by Professor Israel Friedlaender. He respected the Seminary professor but was dissatisfied with his remarks on this particular occasion. Friedlaender had spent his lecture analyzing the nature of culture, whereas Kaplan thought he should have concentrated on the nature of Jewishness in defining the topic "Jewish culture." Hearing Friedlaender stimulated him to attempt his own definition of Jewishness: "whether we are orthodox, atheists, anarchists, or socialists," he thought, "we issue from a common past. . . . It is thus with all those who go by the name Jew; they go by that name as long as they are conscious of their ancestors having lived the same sort of life, believed in the same things, and given their lives for the same objects as did the ancestors of all the other people who call themselves Jews." After analyzing the matter of Jewishness, Kaplan then turned to the question of culture. Culture must be conceived not only "as product but also as process. . . . It should be the cultivation of all those powers possessed by the Jewish people in a spirit which would tend to reinforce the consciousness of kind which otherwise might die out." [34]

Kaplan's own sense of Jewish identification was intense. His private musings continually reveal his feelings that Israel's fate is his fate. When the Jews were attacked, he felt attacked. One day, he read an article charging the Jews with a high crime rate, attributing it to the lack of religious commitment. He was furious, and took the insult personally. "The unlimited audacity of those greasy Christians," he exploded. "They are liars and hypocrites and should not talk about criminality when Christianity is responsible for the blackest crimes that have been committed under the sun." [35]

Strange as it may seem, he did admire some who attacked the Jews. Christian missionaries who sought to convert the Jews to a belief in Jesus and to a more ethical life were very much in evidence in the Jewish neighborhoods, and Kaplan valued their energy and passion. He wished that he had the courage to go out and convert people to his point of view. "O," he muses, "if only I were strong enough to break with the empty formulas of custom which asks me to observe moderation and restraint." The prophets responded to their inner voices, but "I sit at home or in the University gnawing away at cold and senseless debates about flimsy nothings." Considering all of Kaplan's later controversies, these self-doubts may seem somewhat incongruous. The very assertive Kaplan, however, coexisted with a more timid person who was ambivalent about going out into the world and attempting to reconstruct it. The ambivalence emerged throughout his life and can be attributed to a propensity for the realm of words rather than things. Kaplan enjoyed being controversial but was not always ready to implement his programs. He liked a good fight, but his ambivalence, which is not wholly conscious, shows us that he had not yet found himself. He yearned to be a prophet with a great mission, but the prophets had courage and he did not.

His deep-seated conflict appeared in many guises. He had been reading Nietzsche and copied some favorite quotations from *Thus Spake Zarathustra*. "Of all the writings I love only that which is written with blood," Kaplan quoted Nietzsche, obviously stirred by the sense here that passion was primary in any authentic advocacy. He certainly felt less than completely honest in his position as an Orthodox rabbi in a traditional congregation. Having quoted Nietzsche's stirring words, he became defensive. As if to defend his own passion, he continued: "I do not copy these things because they merely sound pretty and paradoxical, but they are the formulas of my life and thought." (So at least he wanted to believe.) The passionate romantic element was a very important part of his self-image, but he did not always live up to his own expectations.[36]

After Kaplan left Kehilath Jeshurun and freed himself from the constraints of a traditional congregation, he did indeed speak out boldly on a great number of topics. Evidently he enjoyed a good scrap and later on took pride in being considered the enfant terrible of the Conservative movement. Nonetheless, his inner tension between action and inaction persisted.

We see that Kaplan's inner life during these years reflected a growing skepticism and impatience with traditional Orthodoxy. "The Talmud is tolerable," he wrote in 1905, "considering the age they lived in and at times there really sparkles a gem of thought or morality but the *Poskim* [codifiers of Jewish law in the Middle Ages] . . . their modes of thought, their narrowness, their absolute slavery to the past . . . are below criticism, that I have to spend time upon these ridiculous laws, makes me chafe at my fate." He also felt, as did so many of the younger members of his congregation, that many rituals were no longer meaningful: "there is no doubt as to the deeply religious character which rites and ceremonies had for our fathers. But on the other hand, there is equally no doubt as to the failure on the part of these same rites and ceremonies to call forth any authentic religious response in us." At one point, almost casually, he reflected, "Taking up the *Shulhan Arukh*, let us see how much thereof we can retain."[37]

He even grew impatient with the daily rounds of prayers and rituals: "are not these [the entries in the journals] more truly prayer and confession than the infinite repetition of the daily prayers in our ritual, from which I find it necessary to desist occasionally in order to be able to recite it all without getting nausea?" His religious conflicts would give him no respite. "Oh God, what anguish of soul! How doubt tortures me," he wrote in his diary in 1905. His spiritual uncertainties and the feelings of disgust made life very difficult for the young orthodox rabbi. Yet living at home, he did obtain some relief from his parents. He apparently shared his thoughts with them. His father expressed confidence in him and in his eventual return to the traditional fold.

This support certainly helped Kaplan to think freely, as he deeply valued his relationship with his father. Once, when he was in a depressed mood over his conflicts, his father noticed and asked whether they might study together. After two hours or so of Talmud (*Baba Metzia*), Kaplan went back to his room and exclaimed, "O the joy of activity. How sweet the hope of attainment."[38]

It gradually became clear to him, however, that his doubts certainly would stand in the way of advancement within the rabbinate. He was troubled not only by the questions but also by the fact that he did not really have a message. On the one hand, he had a strong sense of himself and his abilities, while his uncertainty made it difficult for him to preach to others. "I little thought that at this time of my life, I would find myself so aimless. In the way of personal ambition . . . stand my altered religious beliefs. On the other hand, it has not pleased God to endow me with convictions and ideals sufficiently strong to crystallize themselves into a spiritual mission. I find a perfect photograph of my mental life in the book of Koheleth [Ecclesiastes], in its skepticism, in its fear of God, in its worldliness and in its threadbare spirituality." He felt cast adrift from his moorings as a traditional Jew. His religious life was difficult because he could not give himself wholeheartedly to the daily round of prayers and rituals.[39]

Eventually, he concluded that he had to submit his resignation at Kehilath Jeshurun. He went to Cyrus Adler and related his problems. "What do you do for recreation?" Adler asked. "I walk around the reservoir [in Central Park]," answered the young rabbi. "Well," Adler said, "when I was young, I had my doubts, too. Go and take another walk around the reservoir." Kaplan had in fact gone to Adler to ask him for a recommendation. He was considering applying for a position at the New York Life Insurance Company and he wanted a recommendation from Adler. He also may have considered going to law school at the time.[40]

Kaplan's parents were very disturbed over his plan to leave Kehilath Jeshurun. In November 1906, he sent a letter to the trustees advising them he was ready to resign. He did not mention his religious doubts but rather referred to congregational matters with which he was unhappy: the lack of a school committee with which to work, the lack of decorum at services, and the fact that there were many members who did not send their children to the religious school. A committee was formed and ultimately acceded to Kaplan's specific requests. They also agreed to give him a leave to study for his doctorate. Obviously, they believed that he was working too hard and needed time off for his own scholarship.[41]

His diary reveals his inward state. "Why do I stay where I am, you will ask. Well I did send in my resignation and it nearly broke my parents' hearts. Nor would I have yielded even then, had I known that I have sufficient intellectual power and force of character to make my ideas known. The tragedy of my life no one knows or wants to know. The lie which I live is so clear and palpable to me and yet I cannot tear myself loose from it. My sermons are mental tortures to me, for I have to wriggle so as not to offend. Enough." Other aspects of his life exacerbated his depression. He wrote, "of the vast lump of pleasure which exists in this world is there not just one little crumb for me. . . . I have no message to bring which would make others love me and think me in a way indispensable. My life lacks music." He was lonely. "I shall for once conquer my senseless prudishness for which I have to thank M [mother?] and say that the void in my life is due to the absence of love."[42]

Soon after these diary entries, Kaplan met and married the woman who was to be his helpmeet and the mother of his children, Lena Rubin. The Rubin family was prominent at Kehilath Jeshurun and in the community. Lena's father had died while the Rubin children were still young, before they came to America. Altogether there were seven brothers and two sisters, Lena being the second youngest. The oldest brother, Jacob, came to America in 1890 to prepare the way, and the rest of the family arrived soon afterward. The brothers prospered in the clothing trade and opened their own shop. One of them, I. C. Rubin, became a famous gynecologist. He was the inventor of the Rubin test for determining the potency of the fallopian tubes.

Mrs. Fruma Rubin was reputed to be a very strong woman. After her sons moved out, they all came to visit regularly and felt that in some significant sense "she still ruled the roost," as one granddaughter put it. She had her own apartment on East Eighty-first Street and would brook no interference in her life from her very successful sons. She was an intelligent woman who learned English quickly and was able to read Yiddish literature with ease. Although arrogant and somewhat difficult, she always sided with her daughters-in-law and was very devoted to her family. She may not have agreed with Kaplan's ideas, but she always supported him, and there was never a split in the family because of his philosophy.

Lena was the baby of the family, and everyone doted on her. She was a very attractive young woman, who dressed most fashionably and was introduced to all the eligible young men in the community. According to family legend, the sons of many wealthy Jewish families avidly pursued her. Her beaux would take her ice skating in winter and

*Lena Rubin in 1908, at the time of her engagement
to Mordecai Kaplan. (Courtesy Hadassah K.
Musher.)*

horseback riding in spring and summer. From time to time, she worked
at the family business keeping the accounts.

There are a number of different family stories about how Lena and
Mordecai met. In one version, a meeting was arranged. In another,
Kaplan visited the Rubin household because one of Lena's nieces had
been acting up in the Hebrew school. Supposedly they met as she was
coming out of the house with one of her suitors.

Kaplan was a shy man despite his professional experience with
social situations. He did not mix easily in informal settings and seems
to have had virtually no private social life before he met Lena. His parents did not pressure him to get married — or, if they did, their efforts
made no impression on him, and he left no record of it anywhere. He
apparently had no active sex life before he got married and came to a
knowledge of female anatomy and the facts of reproduction quite late.
When he was at the Seminary and the class studied Talmudic material
dealing with menstruation, he was confused by the discussion.

The courtship was short. Although the Rubin brothers were happy
with the match, their children were not. Some were in the Hebrew
school at Kehilath Jeshurun where Kaplan was the principal, and they
were terrified of him. The Rubins were not learned people, but they

95

were active in the congregation and liked the fiery young rabbi. Lena and Mordecai were married on June 2, 1908.[43]

Kaplan requested a leave to go abroad. The leave actually had two purposes. One was for a honeymoon, the other a visit to Rabbi Isaac Jacob Reines for *smicha*. Reines, who had been the rabbi in Kaplan's hometown, was quite close to Kaplan's father, and was well known throughout the Jewish world.

Kaplan was clearly unhappy with his status at Kehilath Jeshurun. The coming of Margolies, a man much older and better known than Kaplan, was disconcerting for the young rabbi — a rabbi in everything but name. An indication of this occurs in the congregational minutes for 1907, where the recording secretary wrote "Rabbi Kaplan" and then crossed it out and wrote "minister" instead. Traditional ordination in America would have been awkward for him because Margolies was one of the few people who could give it.[44]

Smicha was a general problem which also concerned Rabbi Margolies. The Rabbi Isaac Elchanan Theological Seminary had no organized system for conferring *smicha*. Although the yeshiva was founded in 1897, it was not until 1906 that a *smicha* board was established. It was composed of three scholars, among whom was Rabbi Margolies. When a student felt ready, he would go to each of the rabbis on the board separately to be examined. Each rabbi would then write on his own letterhead in a prescribed formulation that the student was worthy of being a rabbi and therefore should receive *smicha*. Primarily because of his many years of study with his father and with private teachers, and also because of his attendance at the Seminary, Kaplan possesssed the knowledge required for a *smicha*. However, it would have been an embarrassment for him to go to Margolies for certification as a rabbi. What was needed was another recognized authority, respected by all; Reines was exactly the right person.

Reines was happy to reestablish contact with the Kaplans, because he respected Israel Kaplan and retained fond memories of their time together in Sventzian. Apparently, there had been some disagreement between them and they had lost contact. When Kaplan visited Reines, the rabbi examined him and found him worthy of being a rabbi according to traditional standards. Upon Mordecai Kaplan's return to New York, the congregation welcomed him and officially recognized his new status as rabbi.[45]

Approximately one year after the congregation declared him rabbi, he tendered his resignation in order to take up a position at the Jewish Theological Seminary. The board of Kehilath Jeshurun expressed its regret that he was leaving and made him an honorary member of the

Menu from the wedding of Mordecai Kaplan and
Lena Rubin, 1908. (Courtesy of Hadassah K.
Musher.)

congregation. They were sorry to see him go and presented him with a
silver loving cup.[46]

For his part, Kaplan was happy to leave. Although he enjoyed being a congregational rabbi, his intellectual movement away from

97

Orthodoxy made his position untenable. He felt like a hypocrite; he was living a lie. Behaving outwardly as a traditional Jew, he had come to doubt many of the fundamentals of Orthodoxy. A position at the Seminary would free him from congregational restraints, allow him to develop his thinking openly and to speak his mind at last.

4

THE PUBLIC ARENA:
Schechter and Benderly

Kaplan's arrival at the Jewish Theological Seminary in 1909 was a turning point in his life. No longer primarily a pulpit rabbi, he became absorbed in the education of rabbis and teachers and in the elaboration of his own philosophy. His new position stimulated the development of his thinking in a number of basic areas. His public speaking increased, and he thereby moved out of relative obscurity to become a significant figure on the Jewish scene in New York City and on the East Coast generally. While at Kehilath Jeshurun, Kaplan had lamented that he had no distinctive message; during his first years at the Seminary, a clear direction and philosophy emerged. His philosophy arose as a result of his new institutional context and his participation in the work of the *Kehillah* (organized Jewish community) of New York. He was also strongly influenced by Solomon Schechter.

The Seminary to which Kaplan returned in 1909 was a different place from the school he knew as a student. The Old Seminary building on Lexington Avenue had been a converted brownstone; the new location on 123rd Street was specially constructed as a school and was much more spacious. Jacob Schiff bought the land and donated the building without much consultation. It soon became apparent that the Seminary was not well situated. The Jewish neighborhoods were on the Lower East Side or Yorkville (East Nineties), and Jewish Harlem was not immediately adjacent to the new building. The Teachers' Institute under Kaplan's direction eventually (1916) secured space downtown near East Tenth Street, much closer to the centers of Jewish population.

No students lived in the building on 123rd Street as they had at the first seminary. The new Seminary, although it did have two undergraduate divisions, a preparatory course and a junior course, was also a graduate institution. Although Columbia was nearby, the Seminary was now surrounded by the countrified atmosphere of Morningside Heights, and the immediate area was still rather sparsely settled.

Solomon Schechter dominated the new institution through his philosophy and by his mere presence. Schechter came to New York with high hopes and a great vision. The Seminary would be "a theological center which should be all things to all men, reconciling all parties, appealing to all sections of the community," he said in 1902. It would stress the search for truth about all things Jewish and would uphold the Torah as the center of Jewish loyalty. Although the teaching at the Seminary would be "largely confined to the exposition and elucidation of historical Judaism," it would be deemed a complete failure if it did not produce "such extremes as on the one hand a raving mystic, who would denounce me [Schechter] as a sober philistine, on the other side, an advanced critic, who would rail at me as a narrow-minded fanatic, while a third devotee of strict Orthodoxy would raise protest against any critical views I may entertain."[1]

Schechter fascinated Kaplan personally and interested him philosophically. Schechter was a person of great enthusiasm, attributed by some to his Hasidic background, while others compared him to Ram Dass, the Indian god who had a fire in his belly. Despite his "god-like capacity for wrath" he usually could be appeased with a joke. As one rabbinical student put it, "I soon learned to provide myself with a goodly number of jokes and humorous stories before going with him, for there was no way of telling when he will indulge in one of his fiery outbursts. . . . Most people would wait for the storm to abate and then laugh it off and Schechter would laugh the loudest — the laugh of a healthy child." Schechter never took himself too seriously, and his "ordinary conversation sparkled with brilliant epigram and genial good humor." By contrast, Kaplan frequently looked serious; Schechter noticed Kaplan's countenance and described him as a *"brogezer misnagid"* (an angry anti-Hasidic type).[2] Kaplan admired Schechter on many levels but also saw in him "a good deal of the European ghetto trait of spying and gossiping. . . . The saying went that before a member of the faculty formulated an idea in his own mind, Schechter was already aware of it."[3]

Schechter brought new blood to the Seminary but retained some of the faculty Kaplan had known as a student. Bernard Drachman, who had been one of Kaplan's principal teachers and was the dean before Schechter's arrival, was demoted to the rank of instructor. Kaplan scorned Drachman, and Schechter in some ways seemed to agree. Joshua Jaffe, who had lived at the Old Seminary, continued to teach Talmud, but Henry P. Mendes, who had worked so hard to maintain the Seminary in difficult times, held no position in the new organization. Schechter had little use for Mendes, whom he considered to be just another meddling rabbi and not really a well-known scholar. Both Mendes and Drachman became strong supporters of Yeshiva University and were quite bitter about their experiences with Schechter.[4]

Schechter hired a group of brilliant young scholars who would become the core faculty of the rabbinical school for the next forty years. These were the men Kaplan lived with as a member of the Seminary faculty. All of them had their doctorates and came from Germany. Kaplan never received his Ph.D., and the feeling that he was not respected by this core group caused him much pain. Schechter first appointed Louis Ginzberg, who had been working for the *Jewish Encyclopedia*. Ginzberg had only recently come from Germany, where he studied for his doctorate at Berlin, Strasbourg, and Heidelberg, and he possessed a traditional as well as a western education. His doctorate dealt with rabbinic legendary material found in the works of the Church Fathers.[5]

Kaplan taught homiletics and was in charge of the student sermons given in the Seminary synagogue. One Sabbath in the spring of 1915, as they were coming out of the synagogue, Ginzberg asked, "When will the students be done with their preaching?" "Why do you favor the sermons at all if they are such a nuisance?" Kaplan shot back. "After all, scholarship does little more than study sermons that were given two thousand years ago." "Well," Ginzberg retorted, ". . . a laundry bill of today you throw away, while one of Ashurbanipal's time constitutes an important discovery." Professors at the Seminary valued scholarship much more than they valued the congregational rabbinate. Kaplan, on the other hand, dismissed scholarship unrelated to the problems of Jewish life and preferred to teach material relevant to the pulpit and to religious life in America.[6]

In the summer of 1903, Schechter went to Europe and returned with two new faculty members, Israel Friedlaender and Alexander Marx. Marx was to teach history and become head of the library. Friedlaender, a young man born in Poland and with a good Hebrew background, studied Arabic and Syriac philology at the University of

Strasbourg: "slight of build, of medium stature and regal bearing, meticulously groomed, Friedlaender was a fine figure of a man. A short dark beard framed a straight-featured bespectacled face that was almost handsome. To young men from old-fashioned homes, he was the epitome of courtliness and grace." Schechter hired Friedlaender to teach Bible. Schechter decided, however, that there were to be no courses in the Pentateuch because of the difficulties of dealing with biblical criticism. According to Kaplan, Schechter chose to ignore the issue by assuming that all entering students knew the Pentateuch well. The truth was that they did not, and for years Kaplan's class was the only one at the Seminary studying the text of the Torah. Friedlaender taught courses in the prophets and the wisdom literature, but his focus was not narrowly academic. Writing to Schechter of his plans, he said, "I do not intend to treat the Bible as a document of the past of mere antiquarian interest. Instead, in the spirit of Historical Judaism, I will demonstrate how it will form the basis of the Judaism of the present and the future."[7] Kaplan admired Friedlaender; their approaches to Judaism turned out to be quite similar.

Kaplan's coming to the Seminary grew out of problems the Seminary was having in connection with its teacher program. The first teacher's course began in January 1904 and consisted of four class hours a week for three years, after which a diploma was issued. Students fifteen years or older were eligible to attend. Ninety-three people registered for the first term. In the second term, the number rose to one hundred thirty-five. But the registration did not hold; with each successive term, the numbers decreased. Some years later, Kaplan maintained that the location of the Seminary on 123rd Street made it too difficult for young people to attend. A downtown branch was briefly considered, but this idea was never implemented. By 1906, Friedlaender, Schechter, Drachman, and Israel Davidson, the new registrar and a Ph.D. from Columbia, were teaching courses in Bible, Hebrew, prayer book, Jewish history, and the *Ethics of the Fathers*.

Registration did not improve. In May 1907, Schechter wrote to Adler, "with regard to the Teacher's Course question, I wish only to say that everything at present is against it. The place is not suitable, as the Seminary is too far away from the center of town." Schechter reported the need for additional staff: "I think there is also a great deal of truth in what Dr. Friedlaender says, that such an institution cannot be treated as a mere appendix to another institution whose teachers are already fully occupied."[8] At the end of the 1907–8 academic year, Schechter informed the board that he planned to discontinue the courses for teachers.

In November 1908, Schechter appointed a committee chaired by Louis Marshall and including Cyrus Adler to formulate a proposal on the training of teachers. It was clear that a new institution of some kind had to be created. As in so many other situations, Jacob Schiff came to the rescue. He offered to establish a fund of one hundred thousand dollars — the "Jewish Teachers College Fund." Schiff allocated half the income from this fund for training teachers "east of the Alleghenies" and the other half "west of the Alleghenies"; that is, the income would be divided between the Seminary and Hebrew Union College. Adolf Lewisohn, another strong supporter of the Seminary, offered twenty-five hundred dollars a year for five years. The board of the Seminary stipulated that a model school should be established in the Lower East Side.[9]

The first order of business was the selection of someone to organize the new department. By the beginning of May 1909, nothing had been done and Adler was getting nervous. "If the thing is not done within the next few weeks," he wrote to Marshall, "we will lose a year and we will be in an awkward position, too, if the School in Cincinnati was started and ours was without funds." The committee's first choice to head the school was a 1907 graduate of the Seminary, Jacob Kohn, who declined the position.[10]

According to Kaplan, it was Henrietta Szold who first brought him to Schechter's attention as a possibility for the position of principal of the new school. Szold and her mother had just moved across the street from the new Seminary and gradually became an important part of the Seminary family. Szold was much more involved with the core group of professors than Kaplan was. In the early years, Friedlaender and Marx took English lessons from her. In 1903–4, most of the teaching at the Seminary was done in German because of the language problems of the new professors. Translating a considerable amount of material from Ginzberg's monumental six-volume *Legends of the Jews* while at the same time serving as editor of the Jewish Publication Society and editing the *American Jewish Yearbook*, Szold became Ginzberg's close friend.[11] Szold attended a service at Kehilath Jeshurun in the spring of 1909, where she heard from the women in the congregation how well the school functioned. She also listened to Kaplan preach. Afterward, she recommended him to Schechter, who, at the time, was looking for someone to head the new Teachers' Institute. Kaplan was active in the alumni organization of the Seminary and addressed the group in June 1909. Schechter heard the speech and was very impressed.[12]

Kaplan's speech concentrated on Jewish nationalism as the core of a religious commitment. He began by pointing to the new circumstances created by Jewish emancipation and the fact that neither the Reform Jews nor the Orthodox advanced a version of Judaism adequate to the new situation. When he talked of Jewish nationalism, he did not have in mind a narrow version of the Zionist enterprise. Nationalism as a movement "degenerates into a mere matter of charters and transportation," he asserted. Only Jewish nationalism considered as a religious creed could save the Jewish people. Such a creed "would read something like the following: 1. that the Jew cannot find the fulfillment of his spiritual nature except through the entire people past and present; 2. that the Jewish people cannot fulfill its spiritual nature except through the physical appurtenances of what is commonly called national life, and to show how it is impossible to have Judaism without these assumptions." People ordinarily identify Judaism with a set of beliefs, and Kaplan, although realizing the importance of belief, desired to move away from the emphasis on dogma. "Doctrine is the response of a collective consciousness of a given age to its experiences," he explained, and these experiences had changed drastically in recent times. Doctrine, therefore, must follow the shift in authority. It is only by faith in the community of Israel that Jews can unite and that Judaism can survive.[13]

After the speech, Schechter invited Kaplan back to his office and discussed with him the position as head of the new teachers' department. Kaplan expressed interest but gave no definite answer and promised to get back to Schechter in a few days. "He is a strong man," wrote Schechter to Marshall, "his English accent is pure, and he is very greatly interested in pedagogics." Schiff approved of the choice and agreed with a contract that involved five hundred dollars more than they had offered Jacob Kohn.

Kaplan believed that Adler took offense at his appointment because it was made by Schechter without consultation. Adler still may have harbored resentment toward him because of his refusal to agree with Adler's 1902 scheme of deferring graduation to 1904. Kaplan imagined that Adler had written something quite negative about him to Schechter. For his part, Schechter felt that Kaplan was "inspiring and stimulating."[14] Later in June, Schechter invited Kaplan to his home in the country. He seemed satisfied with his choice: "I think we have found the right man," he wrote to Adler. "This is also the opinion of Mr. Marshall who knows him and from whom I heard yesterday." Schechter also mentioned that Kaplan would take a summer course at Columbia in "pedagogics."[15]

Kaplan's duties as principal commenced in the fall of 1909. At first, the new institution was called, perhaps with Columbia in mind, the

To the Tannersville Station. Solomon Schechter
meets Mordecai Kaplan, 1909. (Courtesy RCC.)

Teachers College of the Jewish Theological Seminary. Schechter may
have hoped to develop an American institution that was much more
than a rabbinical school. When the Teachers College opened, an optimistic Schechter wrote to Marshall, "The Seminary with the help of
God is destined to become the Jewish University of America."[16]

The beginning, however, was certainly modest. Classes met in
the Uptown Talmud Torah on East 111th Street and later in the
Downtown Talmud Torah on East Houston Street.[17] Eventually, the
Teachers' Institute moved to larger quarters of its own at the Hebrew
Technical Institute at 34 Stuyvesant Street. Kaplan was not yet the
maverick he was to become, but it is perhaps symbolic that the location
of the Teachers' Institute was on an unusual street: "Stuyvesant Street
continues to run due east and west in stubborn opposition to the surrounding Manhattan grid, which follows the axis of the island instead
of the exact points of the compass."[18] Stuyvesant Street is between
Ninth and Tenth streets in the East Village not far from the Lower East
Side. Thus, the problem of access to the downtown Jewish population
center was solved.[19]

During that first year, 1909–10, just as Kaplan was beginning his
new position, he had to take on added responsibilities at the Seminary

as professor of homiletics. Professor Joseph Mayer Asher, who taught homiletics to the rabbinical students, died. Asher was an English Jew, the son of a rabbi who went to Eastern Europe to study with Rabbi Isaac Elchanan Spektor in Kovno and met Schechter when he later studied at Cambridge. Asher served as a tutor to the Schechter children; in 1900, he came to America as rabbi of Congregation Bnai Jeshurun, then located on Madison and Sixty-fifth Street, a few blocks from the Old Seminary. In 1903, Schechter appointed him professor of homiletics. Asher helped Kaplan secure his first pulpit at Kehilath Jeshurun. Kaplan delivered the eulogy at Asher's funeral because Schechter was a *Kohane*, or priest, and was, according to Jewish law, not allowed to come to the cemetery. Asher was thirty-seven years old when he died.[20]

The Seminary stimulated Kaplan to speak his mind more freely and to develop his ideas systematically. Soon after he arrived, he became involved in an exciting intellectual adventure known as the *Achavah* Club. Judah Magnes, the head of the New York *Kehillah*, intended to assemble the most interesting minds of the day to address the problems facing the Jewish community. The group met every two weeks at a different home. Among the members were the core faculty of the seminary (Ginzberg, Marx, Davidson, Kaplan, and Friedlaender) as well a diverse group of Jewish leaders including Louis Lipsky (Zionist leader), Chaim Zhitlovsky (Yiddishist and socialist), Max Radin (professor of law), Samson Benderly (Jewish educator), and Gedaliah Bublick (journalist and religious Zionist).

Kaplan attended the meetings regularly during the two and a half years of the club's existence. The group discussed a wide spectrum of problems: "Assimilation in New York and How to Combat It" (Bublick), "The German and Russian Jews" (Friedlaender), and "Race and Religion in the Light of Jewish History" (Ginzberg). The minutes reveal that the young Kaplan did not present a lecture or participate often; he was somewhat intimidated by the group, most of whom were older and more experienced than he. When Benderly gave a lecture on Jewish education, however, Kaplan spoke up. Benderly outlined the novel situation for Jewish education in America where the home and the synagogue had lost much of their power in educating the young. The school thus had become the primary source of Jewish values. Zhitlovsky, who was in the chair, added that formal Jewish education should be primarily nationalist in character, with religious education being left to the individual home. Kaplan disagreed, asserting that education needed to be simultaneously nationalist and religious: "The aim of education was self-preservation, i.e., the preservation of the social soul of the respective social group. This self-consciousness was in itself religion. As for Judaism, the aim of Jewish education ought to be preservation of Jewish nationalism as religion."[21]

Judah Magnes lectured to the club on "Some Suggestions for a Religious Organization in New York City" which anticipated to an amazing degree the Reconstructionist approach. He expressed his concern that so many Jews in New York City were unaffiliated or "unchurched," as he put it. A new way must be found that would be neither Orthodox nor Reform: "It would appeal to those who believe in a Jewish people which embraces all shades of belief and opinion and expresses itself in all the functions and activities connected with a people, who adhere at the same time to the conception of history and believe in the mutability of Judaism."[22]

Kaplan's "religious nationalism" expressed at the *Achavah* Club is based on the belief that Jewish nationalism was the greatest hope for the spiritual salvation of the Jewish people. Certainly, Magnes assumed this, as did Friedlaender, Schechter, Szold, and others who were influenced by the writings of Ahad Ha-Am. Kaplan considered himself a disciple of Ahad Ha-Am, the primary advocate of cultural Zionism, but at the same time he significantly departed from his mentor. Writing to his brother-in-law Phineas Israeli on the eve of his coming to the Seminary, Kaplan explained: "You identify me too much with Ahad Ha-Am. I grant you that I drew my first inspiration from him, but I went much further than he did. His nationality is a barren unproductive idea. I have converted it into a fruitful idea by giving it a religious significance. Thus with me the nationality of Israel is the best proof of the divine government in human history." Although Ahad Ha-Am advocated a spiritual revival of the Jewish people, he had little use for traditional religious beliefs or practices. For Kaplan, Magnes, and Schechter, Jewish nationalism was not only a bulwark against assimilation but a way of putting a new foundation under the crumbling edifice of Judaism — the religion.[23]

Kaplan's relationship with Schechter began very positively but later deteriorated as Schechter became better acquainted with Kaplan's thinking. Although Kaplan was certainly quite occupied during that first year of 1909–10, the two men saw each other frequently. Kaplan sought out Schechter as a mentor and friend, while Schechter took a fatherly interest in his new protégé. Schechter spent his 1910–11 sabbatical abroad in England and Europe with a side trip to South Africa to visit his daughter Ruth. Israel Friedlaender directed the Seminary in Schechter's absence, and although Kaplan found he could work with Friedlaender, he longed for Schechter's caretaking presence. In the spring of 1911, Kaplan wrote to Schechter, "I need not tell you how much I miss your counsel and guidance, and I dare say there are but few who await your coming as eagerly as I do. You will have to help me both in my work as a student and in my work as a teacher. Problems are constantly presenting themselves to me before which I stand helpless, and I have no one to turn to. I have no doubt that I could have gained a great deal from some of the men on our faculty, but the trouble with me is that I am too retiring a nature to thrust myself forward to their attention, and that I have to be encouraged to present my difficulties." Kaplan mentioned that he saw Friedlaender frequently, but every time he talked with him at length he was "conscience-stricken" that he was taking away time from Friedlaender's work. "Sometimes," Kaplan confided, "I forget myself [with Friedlaender] and talk as much as I feel urged to." Friedlaender respected Kaplan and always consulted him whenever a student was recommended for a pulpit.[24]

Schechter came to hold Kaplan in high regard, although he did not always give Kaplan the attention he craved. Kaplan had begun work on a critical edition of a classical Hebrew text dealing with the Song of Songs (*Shir Ha-Shirim Rabbah*), and Schechter encouraged him to devote himself to this. One afternoon in June 1915, Kaplan spent more than two hours with Schechter. Kaplan was pleased with the attention: "He was quite genial and frank with me. For once he seemed to display some interest in me personally. He told me that I have a great future before me. He said . . . I should finish the edition of *Shir Ha-Shirim Rabbah*." Kaplan worked on this scholarly project for many years, intending perhaps to use it as a doctoral dissertation. In 1908, he had copied a manuscript in Frankfurt which he used in connection with other more well-known manuscripts of this Midrash to establish a critical edition, and he hoped such a text would be published by the Seminary.[25]

Schechter was also responsible for assigning to Kaplan the translation and critical editing of the eighteenth-century ethical work *The Path of the Upright* by Moses H. Luzzatto. Kaplan received the Schechter letter informing him of the project on November 19, 1915, the day Schechter died.[26] A few months before he died, Schechter had told Kaplan, "[You] ought to get into the ring." Kaplan believed that Schechter had him in mind as a successor.[27]

Kaplan, encouraged by Schechter, directed his attention toward developing the Teachers' Institute curriculum. In his own courses at the Teachers' Institute and also in homiletics class, Kaplan began his teaching career by using the Torah as a text. "Besides administering the Teachers' Institute, I was to give instruction in religion. . . . In the past, the belief that every word in the Pentateuch was divinely dictated was sufficient to make religion an exciting affair for the Jew. With that belief gone, I felt that we had to discover the deep underlying spiritual motives which actuated the final redaction of the Pentateuch. If we could only retrieve these motives, Jews would once again find the Torah inspiring." The primary problem was authority. Biblical criticism undermined the Torah as a divinely revealed work and as the preeminently authoritative text it had been in the past. He wrestled with the question and by June 1912 had evolved the beginning of an answer. Speaking to the Seminary alumni at Tannersville, New York, he confronted the basic issue head on: "[Does] it necessarily follow that if we accept the method of criticism, we must surrender the possibility of its [the Torah] being authoritative and eternal? That this is certainly not the case becomes clear when we take note of what is involved in the terms *authoritative* and *eternal*." Kaplan went on to explain that the Torah's authority depends on "not whether it is a direct creation of God, but whether we are willing to accept as authoritative that which Israel has hitherto accepted as such." The Torah is eternal also if Jews continue to make it the center of their lives.[28]

Two years later, Kaplan published this paper with some revisions in the student annual of the Seminary. To his pleasure, it sparked "some discussion among the graduates and [seems] to have aroused a few of them from their apparent indifference to the fundamental questions of Torah, revelation, etc." Schechter told Kaplan that he was "walking on eggs." Schechter warned him that he must not commit himself to any views about the Bible, views he might have to retract lest his career be jeopardized. Even some of Kaplan's close friends had reservations about the article in the annual. Julius Greenstone, Kaplan's roommate at the Old Seminary, wrote him in July 1914:

> That the Torah is supreme in Jewish life is agreed, but that the basis of this supremacy is the fact that Israel has made it supreme is open to contention. The secularization of Judaism, which has become almost a dogma in some Zionistic quarters, is opposed to all tradition and to the very essence of our fundamental ideals. Without the religious sanction, without the belief in revelation as the compelling motive for leading a Jewish life, the nature of Judaism and of Jews will become so completely changed as to be unrecognizable.[29]

Kaplan explained his ideas more completely in a series of articles he published in the first issue of the *Menorah Journal* in 1915. The *Menorah Journal* reflected the many Menorah Societies established by the Jewish students at colleges and was destined to have a major influence on the intellectual life of American Jews. It also occupied a significant place in Kaplan's life. Henry Hurwitz, who created and edited this journal, constantly prodded him to publish in it. Kaplan was eager to contribute, as he was driven to clarify and develop his ideas. For him, the survival of the Jews was at stake. Until his last days, he was constantly revising his basic formulations.

His article was entitled "What Judaism Is Not" and was followed the next month by another entitled "What Is Judaism?" Here he emphasized that religion could be understood only when the social sciences and particularly sociology were used as the method of investigation. He proceeded to elaborate his understanding of Judaism and of religion in general. Schechter was disturbed by the first article, which appeared in October 1915, and said to Kaplan, "I'm going to answer you." A few weeks later, he died.[30]

Although Kaplan was grateful to Schechter for helping him professionally, he did resent Schechter's critical attitude toward his methods and was pained by Schechter's lack of approval. In 1933, Alvin Johnson, the editor of the *Encyclopedia of Social Sciences*, requested a biographical piece of four-hundred words on Schechter. Kaplan refused.

> I regret I do not see my way clear to writing the article on Schechter because I do not hold the majority opinion about him. I do not question his eminence as a savant and as an outstanding personality. He was a Jewish Samuel Johnson but I cannot act as his Boswell. While I consider his contribution to Jewish scholarship as worthy of the Historical School to which he belonged, I regard his contribution to the problem of Jewish adjustment as more confusing than helpful. He belonged to that school of thought which views life as something self-evident and to be accepted as a God-willed destiny and as bound to become soulless and meaningless as soon as it is treated as a problem. The social sciences were to him the work of the devil, and those who invented the Jewish problem, the devil's disciples. Since he probably classed me as one of those disciples, although we were always on the friendliest of terms, I feel someone else ought to do his biography.

Kaplan never sent this letter. The day after he wrote it, he recorded the facts in his journal: "I wrote the letter to Alvin Johnson and Lena typed it. She objected to my sending it. I yielded to her objection and instead wrote the usual excuse of not having time." The years, however, dulled Kaplan's pain; he dedicated his final book, *The Religion of Ethical Nationhood*, to Solomon Schechter, "who granted me the opportunity to transmit [the spiritual reality of the Jewish people] to my students."[31]

A little more than a year after Schechter died, Israel Kaplan passed away. Kaplan grieved deeply over his loss. He had been very attached to his father and appreciated the intellectual freedom his father had allowed him. Israel Kaplan believed that no matter how far his son strayed from the tradition, he would always return. Kaplan's father had been the first and most important teacher, and the two men studied Talmud together until Israel Kaplan's last years. A few months after his father died, Mordecai Kaplan organized a group of students to study Talmud with him in his home. He missed the sessions with his father. Some believe that a man does not really depart from the ways of his father until the father's passing. Such was not completely the case with Mordecai Kaplan, although it is nonetheless true that the full dimensions of Kaplan's radicalism became public only after his father died.[32]

◆

The Teachers' Institute monopolized Kaplan's attention throughout this period. It grew steadily but was not without its problems both as an institution and as part of his life. The school moved a number of times to larger and more appropriate quarters, remaining downtown in the East Village until 1929, when it moved into the new Seminary building on 122nd Street and Broadway. There were also changes made in the curriculum, with the shifts from a three-year to a four-year course, from an English-speaking institution to a totally Hebrew institution, and from an afternoon and evening school to a school that required morning attendance for almost half the time needed for the degree. All these innovations were carried out under Kaplan's direction during the first decade of his administration.

In 1919, Kaplan dropped all elementary courses at the Teachers' Institute while opening a series of extension courses. These were taught entirely in English, the function being to train Sunday school teachers, club leaders, and the laity generally. In 1921, after Friedlaender's murder in the Ukraine Kaplan renamed the extension courses "The Israel Friedlaender Classes" and appointed Israel Chipkin, one of Benderly's proteges, as director.[33] Chipkin worked closely with Kaplan for a long time. The Friedlaender classes grew quickly in an era when Jewish studies were not taught on the college level. During the 1920s, Kaplan opened branches in Borough Park, Brownsville, Bensonhurst, the Bronx, and Newark. In 1928, there were 212 students registered in all the divisions of the Friedlaender classes including those held at Stuyvesant Street.[34]

Kaplan, his father, Judith, Lena (pregnant with Naomi), and Hadassah, August 1914. (Courtesy Dr. Naomi Kaplan Wenner.)

Another major accomplishment for Kaplan was the founding of the Seminary College. The original suggestion for a college of Jewish studies that would supplement the Teachers' Institute seems to have come from Leo Honor, a Benderly follower, in the mid-1920s. The Teachers' Institute was overflowing. Many applications sought admission, but not all were interested in taking up Hebrew teaching as a profession. The Friedlaender classes were too elementary for these people whereas in the Seminary College all instruction would be offered in Hebrew. Kaplan repeatedly presented the proposal to Adler, but the Seminary was having economic problems sustaining the departments it already had. These difficulties reached the point where Kaplan had to ask the students to pay for the cost of printing up their diplomas. There were some who felt that the Teachers' Institute was too much of a burden for the Seminary and that it might be run more effectively by the Jewish Education Association. Despite all these problems, Kaplan convinced Adler of the importance of the college, and in 1931 the new institution was established.[35]

Kaplan also created a joint program with Columbia University under which Teachers' Institute students received about sixty credits toward a diploma from Teachers College. Dean William F. Russell of Teacher College opposed the arrangement because he thought the courses were too sectarian. But after the intervention of Samson Benderly, Kaplan's friend, who explained Kaplan's philosophy of Judaism and his civilizational approach, Russell gave in.[36]

To what degree did Kaplan actually influence major developments and the day-to-day life at the Teachers' Institute, as Benderly maintained? The answer is that his influence, while considerable, is not always easy to specify. A principal (Kaplan's title until 1930) molds his school as much by what he is as a person as by what he says. Kaplan's actions reflect a deeply committed Jew, open to change and devoted above all else to the survival of his people. He took seriously any strategy or ideology that could help revive Jewish life and Jewish culture. The curriculum offered a very broad definition of the Jewish heritage. (There were classes in Jewish music and drama in Hebrew.) It was a curriculum built on a dedication to the Jewish people rather than any narrow or sectarian view of Judaism. The faculty never saw themselves as apostles of Conservative Judaism but rather as agents of the Jewish cultural renaissance. The primary manifestation of this "nationalist" focus was the emphasis on Hebrew. Kaplan and his faculty viewed the Hebrew language and Hebrew literature as the primary products of Jewish creativity. Neither biblical nor rabbinic civilization was given exclusive attention; they took their places alongside the Hebrew poets of the Golden Age of Spain and the writers of the twentieth-century Hebrew renaissance. Students lived the philosophy of Judaism as an evolving religious civilization, whether or not they used this term.[37]

The Teachers' Institute began as an English-speaking institution, but by 1920 it had become thoroughly hebraized. The use of Hebrew, however, was not without its problems. At no time did Kaplan ever speak against the use of Hebrew either as the language of instruction, as the language in which the classical sources ought to be studied, or as the standard to be used in judging whether a given work ought to be included in the curriculum. But he was personally self-conscious about speaking Hebrew extemporaneously before his peers and his faculty. It is perfectly clear that he was at ease reading classical and modern Hebrew sources and that he wrote well in Hebrew, but speaking was problematic. His diary recorded his distress that year after year he opened the Teachers' Institute in the fall with a speech in English because he did not want to put forth the effort to prepare a talk in Hebrew.

In 1925, he finally did prepare his opening remarks in Hebrew, and this, together with the fact that his daughter Judith was playing the piano, gave him much satisfaction. His speech was well received.

Teaching in Hebrew was likewise troublesome for him. He was in the habit of reading in the Hebrew periodical literature before he went to class so his mind would be in a Hebraic mode. On one occasion he could not prepare himself in this way and had trouble expressing his thoughts. And yet "he did not have the courage to do what in his heart he believed to be right, i.e., speak English." Although pressure to teach in Hebrew was strong, he could not refuse when some students complained that they were not getting the point; Kaplan immediately switched to English, "to my relief and to the relief of my students." Samson Benderly, who is credited with originating the method of "Hebrew in Hebrew," had his own doubts about the use of Hebrew in classes; he saw it as a "fog that rests on all that we do."

In the course of time, even such a devoted Hebraist as Hillel Bavli, a member of the faculty from 1918, had second thoughts about insisting on Hebrew. "Perhaps we are too demanding," Bavli wrote in 1959, "in asking that all subjects be given in Hebrew thereby restricting the freedom of thought and the freedom of expression of the students." In one of his angrier moments, Kaplan vowed that someday he would create "a scandal among the Teachers' Institute staff by declaring war against this miserable slavishness to mere language."[38] He never did anything about it.

But Hebrew was not the sole problem. Of far greater significance in terms of Kaplan's primary commitment was the issue of religion and the degree to which his understanding of religion was communicated at the school. Evidence indicates that his ideology was reflected in only a limited way and primarily through his own classes. The sequence of courses in religion and ethics taught by Kaplan was required of each student. The courses were arranged so that each year the students would be exposed to the most important religious and ethical questions. He began by dealing with the biblical period and ended by considering contemporary attitudes toward religion. In actuality, he was dealing with the contemporary right from the beginning. He was not the only faculty member who taught religion, and the fact that at times others taught it was not accidental.

Samuel Dinin, longtime registrar at the Teachers' Institute and a very strong supporter of Kaplan, remembered Kaplan's conflicts with the more traditional students who came from Orthodox homes on the Lower East Side or in Brooklyn. Once, when students were reduced to tears, Kaplan called Dinin in for help. Paul Chertoff took over some of the religion classes, easing matters for those students who felt threatened. Kaplan worried that the different methods of teaching the *Chumash* (Pentateuch) would be confusing to students. In moments of depression, he considered withdrawing from teaching *Chumash* altogether because the traditional mode was really more in line with what the Talmud Torahs wanted from their teachers.[39]

Another limitation on Kaplan's philosophic influence was the faculty. Were they in any sense followers of Kaplan? The answer is yes and no. For example, Kaplan's devoted disciple Max Kadushin taught for a few years in the 1920s after he graduated from the seminary in 1920. Dinin taught courses in education. Israel Chipkin, who ran the Friedlaender classes, was very close to Kaplan; at his death, Kaplan delivered the eulogy, speaking of him as a brother. "We were bound to each other by bonds of mutual love and influence," Kaplan said in 1955. Leo Honor, who had been one of Benderly's followers, was at the Teachers' Institute from 1918 until 1928 and was also close to Kaplan but cannot really be considered a disciple. Milton Steinberg, who graduated from the rabbinical school in 1928, taught philosophy full-time as a senior rabbinical student and afterward taught part-time through the 1930s and 1940s. Nevertheless, the core faculty who remained over the long haul were not really Kaplan followers. This core faculty included Moshe Levine (1912), Zvi Scharfstein (1915), Hillel Bavli (1918), Paul Chertoff (1924), Joshua Ovsay (1921), and Abraham Halkin (1929). They all may be described as devoted Hebraists who were also ardent supporters of the Zionist ideal.[40]

Kaplan had no hesitation about working the faculty hard. Between the Teachers' Institute, the Seminary College, and the Friedlaender classes, a full-time faculty member usually taught more than twenty hours a week. Although there were disagreements from time to time, the faculty respected Kaplan, who treated them well and did not rule with a heavy hand. Cuts in salary during the depression were met with protest, but everyone understood that these budget decisions were not Kaplan's. For his part, Kaplan was rarely satisfied with the way the institution functioned. Sometimes he blamed himself; he did not put in enough time, he had little patience with details. At other times he felt that the faculty was the fundamental weakness of the institution. They were secularists and had little real understanding of religion or spirituality. In his address to the National Conference for Jewish Education, Kaplan proposed that the teaching of religion be restored to Jewish schools. "The secularization process has gone too far," he told his audience. "The teaching of history and language and literature has been encouraged and promoted at the expense of religious training." Religion could not be well taught by "doubtful [doubting] instructors and skeptical Hebraists but by men and women who have achieved for themselves a full and unquestioned integration of the Jewish religion."

The curriculum at the Teachers' Institute had to be revised to include more rabbinic and medieval material, and less from modern Hebrew writers. He maintained that much of modern Hebrew literature was "bare of permanent values." [41]

Kaplan had a keen sensitivity to opponents and guessed accurately the nature of their dissatisfaction. He often felt opposition from all sides. The Orthodox criticized him for turning out graduates who were heretics, while the faculty of the Teachers' Institute resented any religious emphasis in the curriculum and wanted the institution to be totally devoted to Jewish nationalism. Hebraists outside the Seminary thought the graduates knew too little Hebrew, while Adler and the trustees thought there was too much emphasis on Hebrew and Hebrew literature, preferring to offer public school teachers a few lessons in the Jewish religion. [42]

◆

In addition to the rabbinical school and the Teachers' Institute, Kaplan's communal activity after 1909 centered on the organized Jewish community of New York. The *Kehillah* was a kind of Jewish self-government which had existed in the preemancipation period. During the first decades of the twentieth century, the Jews of New York City attempted to create a *Kehillah* that would be appropriate to America — a great social experiment which Kaplan admired and supported. It fomented an uneasy alliance between the uptown German wealthy Jews and the downtown Russian poorer Jews, presenting the astonishing phenomenon of the Jewish community, religious and nonreligious alike, working together under the leadership of a non-Orthodox rabbi, Judah Magnes. For a brief moment, the community came together despite different values and varied priorities. It was, in a word, ecumenical. This Jewish ecumenism, this taste of unity, was enormously appealing to Kaplan. Although the experiment failed, it succeeded in suggesting a model of Jewish community. Throughout his life, Kaplan talked about the concept of organic community, and what he meant was a strengthened *Kehillah*. Many criticized the *Kehillah* because they thought it was too powerful. Kaplan thought it was not powerful enough.

Kaplan and Judah Magnes were natural allies. Born in San Francisco, educated at Hebrew Union College and at Heidelberg, Magnes believed strongly in pluralism, democracy, and Zionism. Kaplan met the young Reform rabbi when the latter came to New York in 1904 to assume a pulpit in Brooklyn. Magnes advanced quickly to become associate rabbi at Temple Emanu-El in Manhattan, where the Schiffs, the Guggenheims, the Warburgs, and the Marshalls were all members. He moved further into the German-Jewish aristocracy when he married the sister of Louis Marshall's wife.[43]

The two young rabbis were close.

> He [Magnes] also moved in the circles in which I found myself, namely, the Seminary circle, with Dr. Schechter at the head. And so, Dr. Magnes and I became quite intimate, particularly when, as a result of his dissatisfaction with the Temple Emanu-El position which he occupied, he became Rabbi of a Conservative congregation, in other words, when he found the Reform movement unfriendly to his nationalist conception of Judaism, to his Zionist efforts and to his interest in Jewish life as a whole. It was at that time that I cooperated with him in his efforts to formulate in general his ideas about Judaism through the preaching of sermons that he delivered in the new synagogue, B'nai Yeshurun.

Magnes, for his part, considered Kaplan a respected friend.[44] There were times when Kaplan was critical. He was uneasy about the close connection of the Seminary, the *Kehillah*, and Magnes to the wealthy uptown Jews. Kaplan thought that Magnes was snubbed by the Zionists because of his connections with Schiff, Warburg, and Marshall.

The origin of the *Kehillah* may be traced to a specific set of events. In September 1908, an article was published by New York's police commissioner, wherein he stated that "with a million Hebrews, mostly Russian, in the city perhaps half of the criminals are of that race." The Jewish community was up in arms over this anti-Semitic slur and reacted strongly. This situation made it very clear to a number of Jewish leaders that the community suffered because it could not react in unity easily. Meetings were held in the wake of the commissioner's statement which brought together Jews of very varied backgrounds and commitments. Within a short time, the commissioner retracted his statement, but, more importantly, the process toward a unified community structure was initiated.[45]

In February 1909, a Constituent Assembly was held which declared that "a Jewish Community of New York be formed." There were more than three hundred delegates to this meeting at the United Hebrew Charities Building on Second Avenue, each of whom represented an organization in the city. Among the three hundred was Mordecai Kaplan, who represented his congregation Kehilath Jeshurun. There were also representatives of "74 synagogues, 18 charitable societies, 42 tual benefit societies, 40 lodges, 12 educational institutions, 9 Zionist societies, 9 federations and 9 religious societies." [46] In the course of that spring, an executive committee was set up which elected Judah Magnes chairman. The executive committee of twenty-five in turn appointed committees in several areas such as religious organization, Jewish education, social and philanthropic work, and propaganda. Kaplan was appointed to the education committee, headed by Israel Friedlaender and including Rabbi Moses S. Margolies (still serving Kehilath Jeshurun), Maurice Harris (a Reform rabbi), Henrietta Szold, and Dr. Bernard Cronson (a local public school principal).

Both Kaplan and Friedlaender felt caught in the middle between Schechter and Samson Benderly, who was head of the Board of Education. Schechter never became active in the *Kehillah* and indeed turned quite antagonistic toward it. He, like the other Jewish leaders, was mobilized by the events of 1908 and offered his name as one of the forty-two nominees for the *Kehillah* executive committee. Out of these forty-two, twenty five were to be selected. Schechter did not even make the first round; he was insulted and severely disappointed. The Board of Education set up by the *Kehillah* during Schechter's sabbatical in 1910 seized the initiative from the Seminary in organizing a new Jewish educational system in New York City. [47]

The first item on the agenda of the new *Kehillah* education committee was to gather information regarding Jewish education in New York City. Cronson conducted a survey which Kaplan presented to the second *Kehillah* convention in February 1910. The convention was held in the large hall of the Charities Building. Five hundred to six hundred people attended, representing a myriad of organizations. The *American Hebrew* realistically noted that a few delegates were present who didn't know what the *Kehillah* was. But many felt they were embarking on a great adventure. Magnes opened the session with a statement of the goal: "how to form a cohesive, conscious body out of the million Jews in the city, without coercion from without, and with a large number of Jewish institutions already in existence." [48]

After Magnes's general remarks on the committees and their functions, Kaplan, the acting chairman of the education committee, rose to report on the survey. His report described Jewish education in New York. It began by dividing Jewish schools into five categories, describing the schools in each category along with a sense of the problems and the strengths of each type of school. The report advocated that the *Kehillah* should centralize these educational institutions so that adequate facilities could be built and maintained. Most of the teachers were not American-born, and their knowledge of English was meager.

Henrietta Szold (1860–1945), founder of Hadassah, who recommended Kaplan to Schechter. Kaplan and Szold worked together for the Kehillah. Photo ca. 1910. (Courtesy Library of JTS.)

"It is inevitable," Kaplan told his audience, "that the type of teacher who will succeed, will be the one who had received both secular and Jewish training in this country and who will not look upon his work merely as a temporary means of support. The *Kehillah* should encourage students who are preparing themselves to teach in the city schools to attend the Teachers Institute so they might also become teachers in Jewish schools."[49]

After Kaplan finished speaking, an announcement was made that a "friend of the *Kehillah*" had donated ten thousand dollars a year for the next five years in support of the educational arm of the *Kehillah*. The next morning, Magnes announced that the fifty thousand dollars would be used for the Bureau of Jewish Education. Arthur Goren, noted historian of this period, emphasized the significance of this report: "Overnight the [education] study provided benchmarks in an unsurveyed field. Heretofore, problems of religious education belonged to the province of small isolated groups, motivated by personal philanthropy or private gain. The *Kehillah*, at its 1910 convention, transferred such discussion into the public realm."[50] The Kaplan report, in other words, began the process whereby Jewish education was to be considered a community responsibility.

Kaplan's enormous influence on Jewish education was partially a result of his collaboration with Samson Benderly and the New York *Kehillah*. The Bureau of Jewish Education was to be headed by Benderly and officially opened its doors in the fall of 1910. Benderly became an important colleague and one of Kaplan's most intimate friends.

An unusual man with a unique background, Benderly came not from Eastern Europe or Germany or England, where so many American Jewish leaders had their roots, but from Safed. There, in the place where Isaac Luria taught the *Kabbalah* and Joseph Karo compiled the *Shulhan Arukh*, Benderly was born on March 31, 1876. He studied in Beirut and received his bachelor's degree from the American College in 1896. After beginning his medical studies in Beirut, he immigrated to the United States, where he finished his training at the College of Physicians and Surgeons in Baltimore. Eventually, he became active in the Jewish community as an educator, headed a small school called the Hebrew Free School for Poor and Orphaned Children, and at the same time served as a resident physician at a local hospital.[51]

Benderly was boldly experimental with his school. He introduced the *Ivrit Be-Ivrit* method (teaching Hebrew in Hebrew), established clubs outside the classroom, worked out programs related to the holidays which included music and dance, established play areas for recreation, and physical exercises conducted in Hebrew. All of these educational activities are familiar and widely practiced today, but in 1905 they were a rarity.[52]

The cooperation between Benderly and Kaplan is easy to understand. As Kaplan put it many years later, "He needed trained people and the Teachers' Institute was looking for students to train." Along with Benderly, Magnes appointed an advisory group to the Bureau who were known as trustees. The trustees were Israel Friedlaender, Louis Marshall, Henrietta Szold, and Kaplan. Kaplan knew Benderly before he came to New York, having visited Baltimore shortly after assuming directorship of the Teachers' Institute. The two men had much in common. In 1949, Kaplan wrote of his colleague and friend, "Having fully absorbed and digested the teachings of Ahad Ha-Am and Herbert Spencer, he had become obsessed with the passionate purpose of utilizing education to transform the Jews into a prophetic people."[53]

Kaplan felt the impact of Benderly's work quickly. In his 1914 Seminary commencement address, he noted that "the standard both of admission and of graduation is far higher than what it was when the Institute was first organized. The curriculum has correspondingly been made more inclusive and intensive." Some years later, Kaplan commented that the Hebrew high school that was established by the bureau extended the preparation of entrants to the Teachers' Institute by three to four years. "For the first time it was possible for the Teachers' Institute to draw upon a student body who had received a uniform Jewish training that paralleled their secular high school training."[54]

Benderly and Kaplan together played a major role in creating the profession of Jewish education in the United States. Their cooperation was effortless, despite their significant differences. Part of Benderly's strategy was to bring new, fresh talent into Jewish education. The group of young men Benderly gathered around him were known as the "Benderly boys." Originally, he thought he would seduce young men from the Rabbi Isaac Elchanan Yeshiva into Jewish education by giving them money to attend a local college. With the secular education at college and later in graduate school, plus additional Jewish education, he would be able to turn out first-class Jewish educators. Alexander Dushkin, one of the first Benderly boys, a leader in Jewish education in the United States and later in Israel, describes the plan: "For us he outlined his three-fold training on the job: (a) To employ us immediately as teachers in the model schools which he planned to establish, and to give us pedagogic supervision and guidance while in service; (b) to enable us to pursue studies in education toward M.A. and Ph.D. degrees at Teachers College, Columbia University; and (c) to arrange special courses in Judaic Studies at the Teachers' Institute of the Jewish Theological Seminary." Benderly's huge success is reflected in the collective biography of this group, which would actually be a history of Jewish education in the United States for the next forty years.[55]

Kaplan records in his journal that initially he had little faith in the scheme. Nonetheless, when he encountered young men he thought might be capable, he recommended them to Benderly. In this way, he brought a number of young people into the group, including Alexander Dushkin and Isaac Berkson. The group would meet with Benderly in the morning before the college day began for a combination of "ceaseless chatter, delightful epigrams, and stories and practical guidance." The relationship of the group to Benderly had in it something of the master-disciple relationship. "There was the quality of the Hasidic *rebbe* in Benderly, and he molded us into a comraderie [*sic*] of believers," wrote Dushkin in his memoirs. "We considered ourselves a band of pioneers who were 'hastening the footsteps of the Messiah.' Benderly was not a religiously observant Jew in the traditional sense . . . yet he was imbued with the deeply emotional mystical background of Safed. I remember his singing Hasidic chants with tears streaming down his face."[56]

In addition to their "seminars" with Benderly, a special class was organized by Kaplan. He started to teach "the boys" informally during the spring of 1912. During that summer, Friedlaender taught them

Bible and history while Kaplan dealt with principles of education. In the next few years, Kaplan continued to teach the group, devoting himself to the study of the Bible according to his interpretation as well as the study of Talmud. He derived great satisfaction from teaching the "Benderly boys" and felt that in many ways they were more zealous than the students he had at the rabbinical school. Benderly's philosophy of education appealed to Kaplan, for he maintained that Jewish education should be a coordinated community enterprise, not a disorganized morass of private and philanthropic activities. Accepting the fact that American Jewish children would attend public school, Benderly worked around that reality by building supplementary Jewish institutions. He was a follower of Ahad Ha-Am and saw the aim of Jewish education as "the preservation of the Jews as a distinct people, existing and developing in the spirit of the Jewish religion." Nevertheless, Benderly did have several blind spots: "He failed to see the synagogue as the inevitable unit of American Jewish life, and as growing in educational importance on all age levels. He was opposed to Jewish day schools which aim to teach both Judaic and general studies." It is thus understandable that "the Conservative rabbis accused him of being a 'secularist' and the Reform Jews opposed him as a nationalist." [57]

There were the normal student-teacher problems, such as the one in May 1915 when the Benderly group complained about Friedlaender's teaching of history. Kaplan and Friedlaender handled this awkward situation well. Friedlaender was approached by Benderly, and Kaplan called a meeting at his house with Friedlaender, Benderly, and the group of students. Kaplan recorded the incident in his journal:

> Although I anticipated unpleasant developments at the conference because some of the men mistake rudeness for outspokenness, it concluded with a definite understanding of where the fault lay, and every one of us felt better for having participated in it. Friedlaender did a great deal to smooth the way by frankly stating his weaknesses. He put the matter quite plainly by saying that in the instruction of history he was no specialist and that he therefore could not go at a rapid pace because it involved more preparation than he could give the subject. It developed that the real lack was that of a definite schedule and objective to the work. I promised to work out one. [58]

Kaplan worked closely with Benderly. Physically, their centers of activity were not far from each other. The bureau was located at the Hebrew Charities Building on Second Avenue and Twenty-first Street, while the Teachers' Institute was off Second Avenue near Ninth Street.

Philosophically, Kaplan and Benderly shared an abiding dedication to the Jewish people but differed on the matter of religion and its function. Benderly's neutrality toward religion disturbed Kaplan, who believed that his attitude was a reflection of Ahad Ha-Am. "I must say," wrote Kaplan in 1914, "that Dr. B. is perhaps the only man who is working out Achad Ha-Amism in *Golus* [exile] in a systematic and organized way. I had always missed something in Achad Ha-Am's conceptions of Judaism, but certainly its realization in practice I have always found jarring to me. It is wanting in appreciation of the indefinable religious longings and aspirations. . . . It is this spirit that has taken possession of the men [under Benderly] and I have found them strange, unresponsive to the deeper appeals of Judaism."

Kaplan also regretted Benderly's encouragement of his "boys" to go for doctorates in education rather than into the Seminary to study for the rabbinate:

> [He] urges them to work for the Doctor's Degree in Columbia expecting that when one of them will swoop down on an out-of-town Jewish community as Dr. So and So, the Jewish populace will be so overwhelmed that he will have no difficulty in carrying out his educational plans. This sounds well in theory but I do not think feasible in practice. This tendency in the Bureau which I do not find to my liking is probably the main reason for the bitter antagonism which exists between Dr. Schechter and Dr. Benderly. What to me is only jarring is to Dr. S. hateful and offensive. . . . If I had anyone else more like-minded to turn to and cooperate with I would never have much to do with Dr. B.[59]

Benderly obviously wanted to control, or even take over, the Teachers' Institute. In a report issued by the bureau in May 1911, he asserted, "It is our opinion that the Teachers' Institute must stand out as an institution by itself. That is to say, detached from the Seminary." The Seminary was too far uptown, he claimed, and also lacked room for a teachers' school of the scope that Benderly required. In Benderly's plan for Jewish education in New York, it was obvious that the institution that trained the teachers would play a central role. This report reveals Benderly's strong opinions about both curriculum and faculty. He believed, for example, that a full humanities component should be part of the offering. Courses in English language and literature, general history, and civics should be given along with courses in classical Jewish texts, Hebrew, and Jewish history. The kind of institution Benderly had in mind was a very different organization from the one Schechter set up and Kaplan led.

Benderly was in constant consultation with Kaplan, but it is not known which elements in the Benderly plan met with Kaplan's approval. In February 1911, Benderly wrote Magnes of his dissatisfaction: "After many visits to the Institute and many talks with Dr. Kaplan, its principal, I have come to the conclusion, with which Dr. Kaplan is in accord, that the Teachers' Institute as at present constituted cannot solve the problem of Jewish teachers." The Teachers' Institute must graduate a hundred teachers a year, Benderly believed, and should have a budget of fifty thousand dollars each year.[60] If Schechter was disturbed by Benderly, he had good reason.

Kaplan seemed to vacillate between the positions Schechter and Benderly represented. On the one hand, he agreed with Benderly's reforms even though he disliked his secular emphasis. But on the other hand, he was loyal to Schechter and was not ready to hand the Teachers' Institute over to Benderly for expansion. As time passed, things became more difficult for Schechter and the Seminary. By 1915, Schechter's health failing, he may have been thinking about retirement. The Jewish community's resources were concentrated in the *Kehillah* and in war relief; money was thus harder to obtain, and the Seminary lacked sufficient scholarship funds. Kaplan, who fancied himself something of a novelist, gives us a graphic description of a Seminary faculty meeting and of Schechter in May 1915:

> [Something] seemed to be disturbing Dr. Schechter and he called for the list [of those who had applied for scholarships] . . . one could see that a storm was brewing. One name was mentioned, then another without aim or purpose. Schechter was at a loss what to do. He was reluctant to refuse scholarships to men who had received them before. When questions of that kind were discussed, Professor Ginzberg usually leans back as far as he can in his chair, in serene indifference to the situation, and puffs away at his cigar. This, of course, only adds fuel to the fire. Finally, Schechter burst out. He fairly screamed at the top of his voice; he banged at the table, he jumped up and ran about the room hurling invectives. He aimed particularly at Friedlaender. "Do you think I am jealous of Magnes the '*Manheeg Ha-Dor*' [the leader of our *generation*], or of Benderly when I say that since they have come the Seminary has gone down? There used to be a group of about twenty people to whom I could come for money whenever I needed it. That has now become impossible, because the 'Burau' [so he pronounced it] has to have three hundred thousand dollars a year. I need scholarships and there is nobody to help me to get them. See what they are doing at Cincinnati. They give each man twice the amount we give. If we can't offer scholarships, we can't have any students.

There used to be times when I could approach a member of the board for money to buy some rare manuscript. That is gone now, because the 'Burau' wants to swallow up everything. Unfortunately, the last days of my life have become bound up with the Seminary and I hoped to see it before I die established on a firm footing. Instead of that it is going down and down." . . . Later on he calmed down somewhat and said, "I am really sorry that I have had to speak out this way, but it hurts me and I can't help myself." [61]

Kaplan considered both Schechter and Benderly narrow in their outlooks. Schechter exaggerated the threat from Benderly's secularism, and Benderly failed to appreciate the potential of the synagogue as the focal point in the life of the Jews in America. Both Kaplan and Benderly diverged from the uptown philanthropists who saw Jewish education only as a means of Americanizing the immigrants. The philanthropists perhaps feared the Benderly, Kaplan, and Friedlaender trio because, in the words of a leading scholar of that period, they might "use Jewish education to convert immigrant children segregated by circumstances into separatists by choice, to philanthropists — their funds were, perhaps stamping out one evil — the obscurantism of the *heder* master — by abetting another evil — the rampant ethnicism of Zionist leaders." [62] As a matter of fact, Kaplan's philosophy of community and his efforts to implement his ideas were much more complex than the concept of simple ethnic separatism would indicate.

Kaplan articulated his philosophy of Jewish education in an article he published in 1916. He began by asserting that democracy does not call for the amalgamation of all groups into the general culture. While rejecting the "melting pot" as a form of "social tyranny" he also rejected self-segregation as a "menace to peace and progress." He opted for a middle road that he called partial segregation and that he might call healthy democratic group life. The aims and functions of groups, especially religious ones, are analogous to those of families: "The main claim that a religious community can put forth is that it is serving the same kind of purpose in the body politic as the family group though on a larger scale." Such groups foster self-fulfillment of the individual, teach decent values, and help to maintain needed social control. In a democracy, the individual has a right to pursue his or her own happiness, and this logically entails the right to form groups that might pursue a common goal. Group life thus becomes essential to any democratic society.

The right of any group to a separate existence would be meaningless if that group were not given the right to perpetuate itself. This perpetuation takes place through education. A group such as the Jews should use its educational agencies and institutions to foster Jewish consciousness. By Jewish consciousness, Kaplan meant "becoming so integrated with the House of Israel that he conceives for it a loyalty which gives meaning to his life and value to his personality." Such loyalty should not be construed as in any way being in conflict with the loyalty of the Jew toward the society at large in which he lives. Jewish consciousness will not endure, Kaplan insisted "unless by means of it, our children will make better citizens of the state, unless it will fit them spiritually for the larger world in which they must live [and] unless it will give them worth and character." The goal of Jewish education is thus particularistic and universal at the same time. It should foster "adjustment to environment and not to abstract principles." It should create "in the child a sense of warm intimacy with the Jewish people . . . and a sense of exaltation in those experiences of his people which have constituted for the human race the very footprints of God."[63] Although many of the *Kehillah*'s supporters were still concerned about the Americanization of the immigrants, to Kaplan and some of his colleagues (Samson Benderly, for example), it was already apparent that the problem was not Americanization but survival and distinctiveness. Americanization was succeeding all too well; Kaplan was concerned even at this early period with the survival of a community that was becoming too thoroughly Americanized.

The Teachers' Institute and the Board of Jewish Education constitute a series of beginnings and a series of conflicts. In his involvement with the Teachers' Institute and with Benderly and the bureau, Kaplan helped to create the profession of Jewish education. The conflicts that emerged around him centered on the matter of what kind of functionary and what kind of institution would most effectively serve the Jewish community. Schechter and people at the Seminary believed it would be the rabbi and the teacher as located within the synagogue. Benderly and others looked to a community educational system with a support apparatus of Jewish welfare agencies as the bulwark of Jewish survival. In one vision, the rabbi was primary; in the other, it was the social worker.[64] As we shall see below, Kaplan eventually came to believe that there might be one institution, a Jewish center, that would perform both the religious functions and the social functions and thus be the means of creating a genuine Jewish community in America.

5

INTO THE COMMUNITY:

The 92nd Street Y and Collective Consciousness

The life of Mordecai Kaplan and the history of the Conservative movement merge into a seamless web at many points. Ever the ideologist, constantly searching for new and better ways to formulate his ideas, Kaplan recognized the need for clarified thought and believed deeply that only on the basis of such thought would the Jewish people be able to remake themselves. Yet the institution that had become his home lacked coherence and direction. Conservative Jews, then as now, had a difficult time defining themselves. Many believed that the Seminary and its various institutions did not constitute a separate denomination with its own ideology. Kaplan, more than anyone else at the Seminary, became obsessed with defining the nature and the purpose of the Conservative movement, alienating many in the Seminary family because of his search.

While Kaplan and Judah Magnes, among others, believed in formulating a distinct ideology for Conservative Judaism, Adler and Schechter opposed the idea. Schechter by his mere presence imbued the Seminary with direction and clarity. Yet even before Schechter's death confusion existed. Did the Seminary and its community constitute a denomination, a distinct ideology? Moshe Davis, in his seminal work on the early history of the Conservative movement, answered in the affirmative by his attempt to link the Conservative movement of our day with the Historical School of Jewish scholarship in the nineteenth century. This mode of thought arose among a group of Jewish scholars in Germany who initiated the scientific study of Judaism through research into classical Jewish texts. The *Wissenschaft des Judentums*, or science of Judaism, emphasized the importance of studying the Jewish religion from a historical and scientific point of view. Davis attempted to establish a link between the *Wissenschaft* movement and the Conservative movement as embodied in the early Seminary. Of course, there is such a link, but mere dedication to a method of studying the Jewish past constitutes neither a full-blown ideology nor a denomination.[1]

Toward the end of his life, Schechter focused his effort on the United Synagogue; Kaplan's attention was naturally drawn to this new institution. The United Synagogue became the primary organization of the synagogues that were affiliated with the Seminary. This institution came into being in 1913 as an attempt to organize the synagogues in America that were not part of the Union of American Hebrew Congregations. The goal was to include synagogues that were clearly Orthodox and those that had initiated reforms. Kaplan served as one of the vice presidents but did not play a key role in creating the organization. The movement that culminated in the United Synagogue began during the first decade of the century as a push for a Conservative union. This concept meant different things to different people. Some saw it as a merger of academic institutions (Jewish Theological Seminary, Gratz College, Dropsie College), but that idea was abandoned at an early stage. Others saw the new initiative as a means of gaining support for the Seminary, of helping congregations in isolated communities, and perhaps as the beginning of a new denomination. Cyrus Adler opposed any policy that might prove divisive. He felt strongly, for example, that the word *conservative* should be removed from the title of the organization. The change was debated at successive meetings of the Seminary alumni in 1911 and 1912, and eventually Adler got his way. The official title would be *"Agudath Jeshurun — A Union for Promoting Traditional Judaism in America."*

Schechter was of two minds. In some small way, he hoped that all American Jews might be members of the union so that his idea of catholic Israel, or *K'lal Yisrael*, might find some concrete expression. On the other hand, it was evident that establishing a new union (alongside the Union of American Hebrew Congregations and the Union of Orthodox Jewish Congregations), no matter what it was called, was an important step toward a new denomination and an acceptance of the fact that "catholic Israel" would exclude many Orthodox as well as most of the Reformers. Adler warned Schechter, "I for one do not want to be drawn into any separatist movement by these young men and you, I think, do not want to be drawn into one either. It would, in my opinion, be a fatal mistake at the outset." Adler believed that the new union "may even detract somewhat from the Seminary as the authoritative center of Conservative Judaism in this country." [2]

In 1913, at an important meeting of the United Synagogue, when the new organization was still in the process of setting up its constitution and bylaws, Judah Magnes and Mordecai Kaplan proposed that the organization declare itself the center of a new movement. The motion was vociferously defeated by the meeting. The leaders of the United Synagogue were not yet prepared to accept an increasingly plain reality: the Seminary and its affiliates did constitute a new movement. Just a few years later, Kaplan and his followers, through a new organization they founded called the Society for Jewish Renascence, were ready to support a more radical new denomination than might have been acceptable in 1913. Throughout the 1920s, Kaplan and those close to him continued to push for a clearer and more extreme definition of the Conservative movement.

The young men who supported a new denomination were Rabbi Herman H. Rubenovitz, a Seminary graduate (ordained 1908) who had a congregation in the Boston area and eventually became a very strong Kaplan supporter, and Rabbi Jacob Kohn (ordained 1907) of Congregation Ansche Chesed in New York. Kohn, although critical of Kaplan, was also attracted to his ideas. Although Kaplan felt keenly the need for the clarification of a Conservative ideology, he was also as convinced as Adler that fragmentation could only weaken the Jewish community in America. Kaplan's ambivalence on the question of denominationalism was to become a major problem in the development of the Reconstructionist movement.

◆

Like all members of the Seminary faculty, Kaplan participated in the United Synagogue from the beginning. He served as one of the vice presidents and was a member of the executive council as well as the committee on propaganda and the committee on education. Rubenovitz, who had worked hard to bring the organization into being, was also on the executive council and the committee on propaganda. Jacob Kohn was recording secretary.

According to Kaplan, the name United Synagogue was suggested by Rabbi Joseph Hertz, a Seminary graduate who was to become chief rabbi of the British Empire and was in New York in 1913 for the opening meetings. Kaplan tells an entertaining story about himself and

*Menorah Society at City College, ca. 1912. Kaplan
is seated second from right; Judah Magnes is seated
to Kaplan's left. (Courtesy RRC.)*

Hertz in 1913. Hertz had come down to the New Jersey shore to visit
Kaplan, who was vacationing with his family. Kaplan was a healthy, ro-
bust person and invited Hertz into the water, desiring to venture out
where it was deep. "No! No!" replied Hertz. "I have to be careful now
that I'm chief rabbi."[3]

Kaplan was a natural supporter of the United Synagogue. When
the Jewish Center of New York City, a new kind of synagogue that
Kaplan helped establish, opened in 1918 with Kaplan as rabbi, there
was no doubt that it would join the new organization. The center identified itself as Orthodox though it did have a compromise on seating,
the policy being to have women's sections on the right and left and the
men in the middle with only a token divider between them. Denominational lines were not yet clearly drawn. Kaplan encountered no difficulty in bringing the center into the United Synagogue despite the fact
that the lay leaders considered themselves Orthodox. The United Synagogue included a number of synagogues with separate seating but
without a traditional barrier (*mechitza*), and Adler stipulated that
separate seating was not opposed to the kind of Judaism the Seminary
represented.[4]

Just what kind of Judaism the Seminary and its new organization
did represent was harder to explain. In terms of general policy, there
were those who only worried about having the largest number of congregations (Adler) and those who believed an effort should be made to
have the congregations be more uniform (Kaplan). Schechter was com-

mitted to *K'lal Yisrael,* catholic Israel, and wanted everyone included. He attempted to reassure the Orthodox, telling them at the first convention that "his sympathies and convictions lie largely with the Orthodox" and that he wanted all to understand that "cooperation [in the United Synagogue] should not be construed as the organization's approval of all those innovations which some of its constituent bodies may have introduced." He was convinced that the policies of the United Synagogue ought to minimize the differences between the congregations, not emphasize them. Although Schechter reassured the Orthodox in public, in private he resented them, especially the more sectarian Orthodox. "We cannot well work together either with the *Hayot Ha-Kodesh* [Holy Beings (Beasts)] of the *Agudat Ha-Rabbanim* or the Oyster Saints of the West," he wrote to Magnes in disgust.[5]

Kaplan's hopes for the United Synagogue as a radically innovative force quickly faded. The organization could demand only a bare minimum from its members because meetings were held only twice a year, and the key issues seemed to be recruitment of more members, rather than matters of substance. He served on his committees and attended the annual conventions but the United Synagogue was a disappointment to him as well as to his younger colleagues and former students who had worked so hard to bring the organization into being. He would have to look elsewhere for an institution that would become the embodiment of his ideas.

◆

Kaplan was always a busy man. Today we would call him a workaholic. With the Teachers' Institute, his classes at the rabbinical school, his public speaking, and his work with the New York *Kehillah,* he was fully occupied. After his departure from the pulpit at Kehilath Jeshurun, he was without a regular congregation. The rabbi within needed expression; he served on an ad hoc basis at a number of congregations in the city. Together with Magnes, he also was drawn into religious work at the YMHA at Ninety-second Street and the founding of the Young Israel movement. All these community endeavors helped him to sharpen his sense of what kind of institution would be appropriate for a revitalized Jewish community in America.

The Young Men's Hebrew Association in New York City had been established in 1874. It had moved several times before the beautiful four-story building was erected at Lexington Avenue and Ninety-second Street in 1900. The building had a large gymnasium, reading rooms, bowling alleys in the basement, and a billiard room, and in 1911 a pool was added in the building next door. The activities of the "Y" included sports, a literary society, a chess and checker club, a camera club, and dances. The young people danced to the latest rhythms, and sometimes things got a little "out of hand." As the bulletin noted in 1913, "If however . . . they came for the purpose of doing Half-Time and Turkey Trotting, then for their own benefit, dancing had best be stopped for good." The Y also ran its own high school and provided a full range of academic and commercial subjects.[6]

The Y's Committee on Religious Work organized services every Friday night and on holidays. Judah Magnes chaired the committee for two years; then, in 1913, Kaplan succeeded him and held the post for a number of years. In 1912, he conducted services eleven times, Magnes three times, and Israel Friedlaender once. The attendance averaged about one hundred fifty people. Kaplan was constantly instituting new schemes to bring in more people or to keep those he had. In 1915, he reported to the board of directors that he had organized a Sabbath circle of young men who met after the services and discussed the sermon over refreshments. At one point, he instituted services on Sabbath afternoon. Many young people attended a matinee on Saturday afternoon; Kaplan felt religious services could offer an alternative. Even observant young men sometimes went to a show and kept within the bounds of the Jewish law by buying their tickets beforehand.[7]

At times Kaplan became impatient with his youthful congregants. At one Purim celebration, the boys were in high spirits and started to tell dirty jokes. Not one for tolerance in such matters, Kaplan reported this incident to the board of directors as proof that the Y needed not only social activities but a religious orientation that might influence moral character. After the weekly services were over, everyone rushed into the social room for the refreshments and wine. Kaplan was appalled. He sensed that the understanding of the group was limited; they found it difficult to follow an idea unless it was a simple one.[8]

Although on a day-to-day basis Kaplan was often distressed, his activities at the Y stimulated him to think about the larger context of Jewish communal needs. The Y, he felt, should not only function as a temporary means of keeping young men from "worse places" (e.g., gambling), but it should also be a positive force in their lives. The Y should "seek to stimulate in them a positive enthusiasm for Judaism." Instituting services, he maintained, was not the solution. The method must be more indirect. Kaplan viewed religion as the effect of personal growth and moral behavior, not the cause. "A group of those already interested in religion should be formed and activities of a cultural sort arranged by this group. Then perhaps services would come as a natural development later." A suggestion to this effect was eventually published in the Y bulletin: "Our Friday night services fall flat, the reason is that they are artificially imposed on our men. The service is the same and doesn't come from them. In our Friday evening work we must fashion our own form of service, we must express our own individuality, we must actually worship and not have our leaders praise God for us."[9]

The YMHA did have nonliturgical programs with substantial Jewish content. There were lectures in which Kaplan and other well-known figures participated. In the spring of 1913 we find Solomon Schechter speaking on "The Synagogue," Henrietta Szold on "Women in Israel," and Louis Marshall on "Aspects of the Jewish Spirit."[10]

The YMHA afforded Kaplan a much-needed forum for self-expression. From the pulpit of Kehilath Jeshurun, he dared not voice his doubts or his heterodox views. His life at this time was consequently more fully integrated, for he could publish his views in liberal journals and preach these same ideas from the pulpit at the YMHA.

In 1915, he used the high holidays to talk about the most pressing problems of Jewish life — the lack of a clear direction and the need for community. He began by pointing out that when one entered the "Days of Repentance" in earlier times, the meaning was clear: "in the past . . . there were certain standards of uprightness, self-restraint, holiness which everybody was expected to live up to, and to fall below which constituted one a sinner. Therefore, when the season of repentance would come around the conscience of the individual would be aroused when he would consider how much there had been in his life which ran counter to the ideals or standards of the community. But when the Jews took up the wandering staff and went to find a new home in this great land of freedom and opportunity, the old standards had, of necessity, to be shaken." The only change, Kaplan believed, was that "while formerly [the immigrant] was one of a community he is now an individual." Being an individual, of course, allows one "room for development of his own individuality, but the fact is that the little decency and humanity that still abides in the person, he could have gotten in no other way than through the life of the community."

Community life sometimes may be repressive to individuality and to freedom but not necessarily so. The Jews in America needed to create genuine community. If America were to consist merely of individuals without subcultures, the public welfare would not be well served. A subcommunity serves to help build character and inculcate moral standards and loyalty. "The Jew to be a true American must be a better Jew. This means that he must belong to a Jewish community where the ideals, by means of which he is to help mold American life, are to be developed. To be a Jew means to participate in some form of Jewish community life where the standards of right and wrong are to be clearly formulated and accepted."[11]

It would be natural, Kaplan maintained, to consider the congregation the center of such a community effort. To be sure, the people who meet in congregations have an advantage, yet they do not possess a real community: "They neglect the most potent forces and seize upon only the one of custom and tradition. People that belong to congregations usually meet only in prayer; they do not have the social life developed." To this large Y group, therefore, he did not recommend the immediate formation of a congregation. They should first become a community, and religious expression would come later: "I have learned from experience that it would be futile to expect you to organize along congregational lines, and to make worship the main purpose of your association. You are not ready for that as yet. You have to know each other better; and it is the problem of how you are to know one another better that you ought first to undertake to meet. You ought to constitute yourselves a neighborhood association, with the only aim of broadening your lives through mutual acquaintances. You ought to take your pleasures together."[12] Religion, Kaplan believed, comes as a result of group life but does not create it. A group that worshiped together but did nothing else in common would not endure.

In that year, 1915, Kaplan not only spoke at the Y on Rosh Hashanah but had already preached on the previous Passover. Naturally, he spoke about freedom and attempted to emphasize "the present truths of Passover." "Passover tells us," Kaplan said, "that God is the power that makes for freedom." The God of freedom, he explained to the audience at the YMHA, "is a God each one can experience because each one has an immediate awareness of his inward striving to liberate himself from the besetting forces of earth and temptation. Men are not born free and equal but are born to become free and equal. It is the goal of all social endeavor to bring about equality in the inequality into which men are born. It is the goal of spiritual endeavor to make men free."[13]

Kaplan joined the YMHA in 1913 and remained a board member until 1919. His attendance at meetings indicates that his interest in the organizational process was superficial. He attended regularly for only a short time. He was discouraged by the secular character of the YMHA and the lack of respect for Jewish law that was frequently in evidence. In September 1915, the board meeting was held at the Manhattan Club on Twenty-sixth Street and Madison where the luncheon consisted of

*Reading room of the 92nd Street Y, where Kaplan
directed religious activities, ca. 1910. (Courtesy
92nd Street Y Archives.)*

oysters on the half-shell and chicken. Needless to say, Kaplan was much offended.[14]

The board's fund-raising function never excited Kaplan's interest, even though at the Teachers' Institute, he raised money over a long period of time. In the case of the YMHA, he did not feel he had the necessary contacts and considered withdrawing from the board because of the pressures put on him. "I realize only too well," he wrote to Felix Warburg in 1915, "the truth of your contention that each director of the YMHA ought to make himself responsible for an increase in the revenues of the association."[15]

On one occasion, Kaplan was invited with other board members to the home of Herbert Straus to entertain a group of wealthy people organized to help the YMHA. Each guest praised the work of the YMHA. When Kaplan's turn came, he had had trouble thinking of something to praise. He was critical of the "self-complacency and hollowness" of the donors who felt they were in a position to teach morals to the youth. In his more cynical moments, he thought of the Y as "a toy to those rich men to amuse themselves with in their off-hours" and an institution that "had no definite policy worth upholding; and that it moved along aimlessly."[16]

In the ordinary course of events, Kaplan worked well with the powerful people he knew, but at times a strong egalitarian streak surfaced.
In an angry moment, it occurred to him that "the moneyed powers have
no interest in Judaism except as a means of maintaining things in their
status quo, and they are using us as tools. The Seminary and the Bureau
of Education and the *Kehillah* are nothing but social pacifiers." Kaplan
was not completely at ease when he was invited into the home of a
member of the Jewish aristocracy. One evening in April 1915, for example, he attended a dinner at Felix Warburg's house in honor of
Magnes. Warburg, the son-in-law and partner of Jacob Schiff, strongly
supported Magnes. Through the medium of an organization called the
Society for the Advancement of Judaism (no connection to Kaplan's
congregation by the same name), Warburg raised money to support
Magnes. At this time, Magnes was without a congregation, and according to Kaplan approximately seventy-five hundred dollars a year was
collected by the society.

When Felix Warburg introduced Kaplan, he praised his work at
the YMHA and emphasized Kaplan's great skill and patience in building a sense of community out of elements that were so diverse: "He
spoke of what I did to improve the moral tone of young men at the
YMHA while I know that it amounts practically to nil. This is an illus-
tration of how people get credit for what they never do." Whether Kaplan helped to raise the moral standards of young people at the YMHA
is a moot question, but his work was obviously significant at the very
least because it served as a stimulus to his own thinking.[17]

Kaplan had definite ideas about what policies the Y ought to follow.
Jewish spirit and Jewish consciousness ought to be more in evidence.
At the large annual public meeting in 1914, he spoke along with borough president-elect Marcus M. Marks (whom Kaplan hailed as one of
the few Jews to earn distinction outside the Jewish community). Speaking with vigor and eloquence, Kaplan hammered away at his basic message. "The Jew in the past," he told the large crowd, "was threatened
by corrosion and disintegration." The Y contributed toward Jewish survival, Kaplan told his audience, but "that was not enough. Let us be
Jewish rather than Hebrew, and make religion and not race the basic
principle of our efforts even as the Young Men's Christian Association
does." As head of a committee to study conditions at the Y, he did not
hesitate to mention that at the YMCA they consistently stressed the
importance of Jesus. There was no reason, he believed, why there could
not be a corresponding religious emphasis at the YMHA.[18]

In 1916, Felix Warburg resigned the presidency of the YMHA, and
it passed to Judge Irving Lehman, the brother of Herbert Lehman.

Lehman was an eminent jurist who became a member of the state supreme court and later served on the federal circuit court. On taking
office, he met with some of the directors. Kaplan disagreed with Lehman over the ultimate goal of the Y. He believed "every activity in the
YMHA ought to be dominated by the Jewish spirit." Lehman countered that "Judaism was only one of the means of character development." Kaplan emphasized that "Jewish social consciousness is the aim
and individual character development is the means." [19]

The leaders of the YMHA had their own visions about how to serve
the Jewish community and help it survive. They wanted to prevent
young people from becoming "victims" of the vices of the street. In
1908, the police commissioner of New York City asserted that a large
percentage of criminals came from Jewish families, and Jews were legit-
imately concerned. The Jews who lived in the neighborhood of the
YMHA had less to fear, for the area was more solidly middle-class and
was much less crowded than the teeming tenements on the Lower East
Side. Kaplan worried about the morals of Jewish youth, but his concerns for the future of Jews were broader by far. He looked toward a
communal life which would be an integrated whole — organic, to use a
later term. He did not find this at the Y, nor did he find it possible to
influence conditions significantly in such a setting. He would have to
look elsewhere.

During this period, Kaplan not only devoted himself to the Y but
also became involved with other institutions that he hoped would provide for the spiritual needs of American Jews. By associating with
"Young Israel," he hoped to serve the alienated young people of the
second generation in a more directly religious way.

Young Israel is a system of synagogues associated with Orthodox
Judaism. The genesis of the organization, however, clearly involved
Seminary men like Kaplan. The actual specifics of its origins are un-
clear, but sometime in 1912, a group of young men approached Judah
Magnes, the head of the *Kahillah*, and asked him to help them form an
organization of programs geared especially to unaffiliated young
people. The name "Young Israel" may have come from Magnes. [20]

From the beginning, the avowed purpose of the group was nondenominational: "to arouse the Jewish consciousness of young people
without regard ... to reform or orthodoxy." The *American Hebrew*
stressed: "It is not zionistic or socialistic. It intends to awaken Jewish
young men and women to their responsibilities as Jews in whatever
form these responsibilities be conceived." [21] In arranging for Friday-
evening lectures in the downtown synagogues, the young organizers
decided that they would always be delivered in English. The lecturers

included Magnes, Friedlaender, Joseph Hertz, Abraham Newman, and Kaplan. In 1915, a synagogue was formed, called the Model Synagogue. There were sermons given in English, congregational singing, Friday-evening lectures, and classes for adults.[22] The atmosphere was warm and inviting. Gradually, other branches were formed, and in the early 1920s, these banded together into a council.

Kaplan asserted that he was a founder of Young Israel, but, bowing to pressure, he was forced to resign after members of the organization learned of his heterodox views. Reconstructionist literature also reflects this version of Young Israel's history. The hard evidence indicates that the organization was indeed guided by Conservative leaders such as Friedlaender and Kaplan at its inception. The extent of Kaplan's involvement, however, is difficult to gauge. The organization, small at the outset, probably occupied a very minor part of his schedule; it is not mentioned in his journal. Later on, Kaplan was fond of startling people by relating his association with Young Israel and perhaps exaggerating somewhat. Jeffrey Gurock, a noted scholar on this period, points to the earlier Jewish Endeavor Society, established by seminary students around the turn of the century, which involved Kaplan and was a precursor in many ways of Young Israel. The nondenominational character of the early Young Israel, which later disappeared, and the emphasis on Jewish consciousness, however, both reflect Kaplan's influence.[23]

◆

The Jewish community during these years was in considerable ferment. Kaplan, though aware of developments affecting the Jews, remained in significant ways an observer, not a participant. The most important development was the war in Europe which began in the summer of 1914. Jewish men fought in the armies of all the belligerent nations, and many were decorated for heroism. Jewish communities, especially those in Eastern Europe, suffered dislocation, loss of property, or loss of life if they happened to lie in the path of the advancing armies. The chaos generated by the Russian Revolution made the Jews fair game for the pent-up hatred of many Slavs and Russians. In the Ukraine alone, there were hundreds of pogroms as the war came to a close and immediately afterward. The small Yishuv in Palestine also suffered considerably, cut off from the offices of the Zionist organization in Europe as well as from markets for their citrus and wine products.

Before America's entry into the war, the American Jewish community was split over the conflict. Jews from Germany and Austria supported the countries of their birth, as did other German-Americans. Eastern European Jews were divided, but eventually most came to support the Allied cause. At the Seminary, for example, there were arguments between the pro-German faction of Marx and Friedlaender on the one hand and Schechter and Adler on the other, who were both strongly pro-English from the beginning. Judah Magnes felt that because Jews were fighting on both sides, Jewish leaders ought to be neutral. After America entered the war in 1917, Magnes called for a quick end to hostilities and supported a radical pacifist position. This stand led to his becoming increasingly unpopular in the Jewish community.

The fate of the Jews of Europe would be determined by the treaties at the war's end, but many within the American Jewish community believed it was necessary to organize sooner. The American Jewish Committee, which had been established to guard Jewish rights after the Russian pogroms of 1903 and 1905, had represented the cause of the Russian Jews to the American government many times in the years preceding the war. Those who controlled the committee, the *Yehudim* — the wealthy German Jewish aristocracy — naturally thought they would represent the cause of the rights of the Jews at the international peace conferences. At the same time, Schiff, Adler, and Marshall were aware that the committee did not represent all sectors of the American Jewish community. They proposed a conference that would be organized by the committee to which other constituencies would be invited. The American Zionist movement, on the other hand, led by Louis Brandeis, Stephen Wise, Louis Lipsky, and Jacob De Hass, supported the calling of a large representative body, a congress, that would represent the cause of the Jews. The wealthy leaders of the American Jewish Committee opposed the calling of a congress. As Schiff put it, "With the actual holding of the proposed congress, the coming of political anti-Semitism into this land will be only a question of time. There is no room in the United States for any other congress upon national lines except the American Congress."[24]

The year 1916 witnessed a number of large rallies organized by the supporters of the congress movement. In July, the American Jewish Committee held a meeting at the Hotel Astor in New York, still hoping to stem the tide of a congress movement which by this time had gained strong support from many leaders of the Eastern European Jewish masses. Kaplan attended this meeting as a representative of the United Synagogue. Although he was not involved in the congress fight, he had a firm grasp of the issues and a distinct interpretation of what was happening:

> Those who favor the congress are, for the most part, drawn from the Zionist ranks. What they want, therefore, is to establish here a semi-autonomous Jewish group life. They are using the congress idea simply as a means of getting the Jews together for that purpose. They want to utilize the predicament of the Jews in Europe as a means of organizing the Jews in America. The conference people, on the other hand, who are of the better placed class, dread nothing more than the furtherance of Jewish group life. Their interest in the Jews of Europe is based on philanthropic principles and they fight bitterly any attempt to convert philanthropic Judaism into national Judaism. This is why the debate during the greater part of the afternoon was waged about the question whether the congress should be called for the sole purpose of obtaining rights for the Jews everywhere or whether the congress should become a permanent organization.

Kaplan also saw the conflict as a political struggle which he found personally repellent:

> Joined of course, to this question of principle is the matter of personal ambition and love of power. Marshall, Adler and Magnes are jealous of the popularity of Brandeis and Stephen Wise. The latter again wish to wrest the power from the moneyed interests. With all that the higher interests of the Jewish people would not be compromised by these squabbles — every people has similar ones — if we had some terra firma to stand on. The very need our Jews have of some outward calamity to bring them together and the total apathy toward any internal improvement is indication of the final dissolution. The very freedom which will be won for the Jews will help to put an end to Judaism.[25]

The congress finally met in December of 1918 and once again in Philadelphia in 1920. Cyrus Adler continued to oppose the movement. A congress gives "the Jews the appearance of being a separate nationality within the United States," he wrote to Judge Mack in July 1918. However, neither the fears of the aristocrats nor the hopes of the Eastern European masses were realized. Kaplan for his part stayed aloof. Bernard Richards of the congress tried to involve him. At one point, Kaplan wrote back describing himself as "an interested observer rather than a participant. There is so little being done in the way of constructive Jewish thinking and teaching that few of us who feel qualified for that kind of work ought practically to keep out of everything else."[26]

A significant phenomenon appears here. Kaplan, although associated with many organizations, was active in few of them. He was not in any meaningful sense an organization man. His urgent endeavors were directed toward the institutions he headed — the Teachers' Institute, the Jewish Center, and the Society for the Advancement of Judaism. What Kaplan really wanted at this time was to devote himself to his scholarship and his writing. In 1916, Dr. Harry Friedenwald, a Jewish leader and Zionist from Baltimore, wrote Kaplan a congratulatory note, to which he replied: "If I had the opportunity, I should have devoted myself entirely to that kind of work [the series of articles in the *Menorah Journal*] because I believe that nothing is so essential to Jewish life at the present time as the reinterpretation of the values of Judaism in terms of modern thought."[27]

◆

Before Kaplan came to the Seminary, he lamented the fact that he had no message to offer. The stimulation of his communal activity led him to formulate the fundamentals of his ideology. The primary concepts of functionalism and collective consciousness which he articulated at this time became and would remain the cornerstones of his approach to Jewish life.

The context of Kaplan's thought was framed by the special needs of second-generation Jews, particularly in New York City. His appeal as well as his significance result from the fact that he spoke to the problems of the children of the immigrants, who spoke the English language and were beginning to "feel at home in America."[28] The pressures on them to be part of the culture in which they lived were very intense. They sought education in order to succeed and enrolled heavily in the city's high schools and colleges. Families moved from the Lower East Side up to the Bronx or out to Brooklyn but continued to live in Jewish neighborhoods, and their children attended schools with other Jewish children. The schools were a great socializing force and helped the immigrant children to forge a strong secular Jewish identity.

The road before the second generation was arduous. They struggled with the depression and also with the anti-Semitism often present in their lives, albeit without the virulence of the European strain. There were quotas in colleges and professional schools, and in many areas of employment it was difficult for Jews to rise above the

*Kaplan cutting wood, ca. 1913. (Courtesy Hadassah
K. Musher.)*

lowest levels. To assimilate outright was not easy, either. Only a few
took this road. Most Jews lived poised between two cultures or two
civilizations, often feeling somewhat alienated from both. This sense of
alienation became the subject for endless movies, novels, and short
stories. It also became the primary concern of Jewish leaders and
rabbis.[29]

Kaplan was without exaggeration the primary ideologue for the
second generation. He was a spokesman for the minority of the minority, the "thinking people," who yearned to be Jewish and American
at the same time. He knew their language and understood their problems. Kaplan's ability to speak to Jews of the second generation flowed
from personal experience. He came into his adulthood during the period of the great migrations. By the time the majority of second-
generation Jews reached their adulthood (in the 1920s), he had already
worked out his philosophy and presented his views in many different
forums. He understood the second generation because he belonged to

it. He had matured in America and could provide answers to problems that the generation of the 1920s was only beginning to face.

As a rabbi, Kaplan was continually confronted by the reality that Jews did not find their religion compelling. Their values, their hopes, and even their sense of identity emerged on the whole from the domain of the secular. The children of immigrants found Judaism obscure and oppressive. For them, it was not part of the new and modern life in America. In short, America was an open society, and Jews, like other ethnic and religious groups, fully embraced the values of pluralism and toleration. But this very openness also constituted a threat to Jewish identity. The individual Jew, in search of life's meaning, was free to go in almost any direction. Such freedom often led to fragmentation and weakness which endangered the Jewish community itself. Some Jews questioned the need for a Jewish community altogether in a society where the opportunities seemed unlimited. So many of the functions of the traditional Jewish community had been appropriated by one level or another of government that it was difficult to see what significant functions remained.

Kaplan was very much a product of his time and place, and this long-recognized fact is both his strength and his weakness. He shared the view of the world common to young educated American Jews. He was optimistic about the future and believed strongly in America. He lived and thought in the American idiom — the idiom of the pragmatic and the functional. His philosophy was attractive because it so well suited the American landscape of change, growth, and opportunity. He embraced the ethics of progress and was concerned with what would actually work. Kaplan essentially asked himself two basic questions: How could he help the Jewish people to survive when the community and the religion seemed to be in a state of rapid disintegration? And how could Jewish thinking and Jewish attitudes be changed so that Judaism would again serve the Jewish people in helping them to live more complete lives as individuals and as members of the community? He sought a realistic, vital religion and a God related to his experience as a person living in the twentieth century. Although in many ways a radical, Kaplan, like Janus, always looked in two directions.

He embraced the social sciences, particularly sociology, rather early in his career. When he examined behavior, he did so not as a psychologist might, from the point of view of motivation, but rather in terms of function. Sociologists who deal with this concept often distinguish between manifest function, or that which is seen as the goal of an action by the actor, and latent function, or the unforeseen or unintended result of a particular action. Both uses are found in Kaplan's writings. His early reading of nineteenth-century utilitarians and his master's thesis on Henry Sidgwick also may have influenced him to think principally in terms of the consequences of a particular belief or mode of behavior. Kaplan's concept of functionalism appears in a journal entry of 1917: "the question 'What is Judaism?' therefore resolves itself into the question 'How do these beliefs and practices function? . . . for the function of a thing practically constitutes its essence." [30]

His concept of function had direct application to ritual. Concerning ceremony in general, he noted that in the ancient world ritual, and especially worship, was a form of recreation. Prayer and sacrifices were often accompanied by music and sometimes by dance. In the modern world, recreation and worship are completely separate. Judaism, then, must restore this sense of the joyful to prayers and rituals so that they can function again the way they once did. [31]

The most important application of the concept of function was to religion itself. Throughout his career, Kaplan offered many formulations to his basic definition of the function of religion. "What we want," he wrote in 1915, "is a religion that will help us to gain our bearings in the world, that will keep down the beast in us and spur us on to worthy endeavors in the field of thought and action." [32] Kaplan always believed strongly that if religion was to retain its function, it needed to be flexible and progressive. Most Americans tended to identify the Western monotheistic religions with reaction and rigidity; such have frequently been the characteristics of organized religion. A distinction exists, however, between religion as an individual experience and religion as it becomes structured and organized through communal institutions. Kaplan never doubted the primacy of the individual experience in religion, even though he continually emphasized that unless the religious experience became part of a group context, it would not survive. Regarding religion as experiential emphasizes that it is constantly growing and changing. Any formulation or creed is only a temporary version of some deeply held insight or profound and ineffable experience. Therefore, further experience and insight inevitably lead a person to reformulate his or her beliefs.

Kaplan's commitment to flexibility is well known. The challenge of ceaselessly revising creeds the better to reflect experience is extremely demanding. It would be much easier to hold on to what one believed. In a profound sense, however, the experience of the transcendent is always an approximation. There is no way to capture once and for all the numinous aspects of experience. A fixed creed or dogma, therefore, would inevitably become idolatrous, mistaking that which ought to be considered transitory and limited for that which is permanent and infinite. Kaplan tied this point to the Second Commandment regarding the making of graven images in a sermon he delivered at the Jewish Center on March 29, 1919: "It is not merely the letter of the Second Commandment that is essential to progress in religion. Its spirit is especially necessary today. The spirit of that commandment is that no idea, creed, dogma, political belief or institution must assume finality. Every one of our ideas must be held in a state of flux subject to reconstruction upon our acquiring more knowledge of things affected by them."[33]

A commitment to the experiential was also a commitment to the pragmatic. Pragmatism carried with it the connotation of a non-dogmatic philosophy, fact-oriented and scientific in its approach to problems. Kaplan displayed all of these qualities but not in a rigorous philosophical sense. He continually looked to the consequences and the way in which ideas function, but at the same time he entertained notions (such as the concept of the collective mind) of a highly abstract and almost metaphysical nature.

The pragmatic tradition is intimately linked with the works of John Dewey. It frequently has been maintained that Kaplan in his functionalism was decisively influenced by Dewey. However, in all of Kaplan's early writings, we find few references to the philosopher of pragmatism. The bulk of Dewey's popular work came out in book form after Kaplan's thinking had already been molded by the sociological tradition. There is no doubt that philosophers of the pragmatic persuasion share much in common with the sociological thinkers; it is easy to see how pragmatism might have influenced Kaplan. The primary source of that influence was not Dewey, but William James. When a group of seminary rabbinical students in 1915 asked Kaplan to teach them about religion, Kaplan chose works by James as the basis for discussion. They convened at Kaplan's house every Saturday night to deal with the nature of religious experience.[34]

Pragmatism is a particularly American philosophy and was just coming into its own when Kaplan came into intellectual maturity. William James's *Pragmatism*, published in 1907, developed from a series of lectures he delivered in Boston at the Lowell Institute and in New York City at Columbia University. Although he preferred to call himself a functionalist rather than a pragmatist, Kaplan operated clearly within the pragmatic frame of mind as defined by James. "The Pragmatic method," wrote James, "is to try to interpret each notion by tracing its respective practical consequences. What difference would it practically make to anyone if this notion rather than that notion were true?" Even the most rigorous pragmatic thinker will not seek to verify each and every statement he or she accepts as true. The pragmatist does believe passionately, however, that all true statements must, at least in principle, be capable of verification through experience. In this sense, we may classify Kaplan as pragmatic.

Kaplan's clearest statement on pragmatism is found in an unpublished manuscript entitled "The Meaning of Religion" which he wrote in 1929. The passage is worth quoting in full:

> We do not have to accept Pragmatism as a philosophy of life or as a means of getting at the ultimate and metaphysical nature of reality to accept it as a method of knowledge or as the logic of scientific procedure. We make no philosophic or metaphysical commitments when we identify the nature of a thing (for purposes of manipulating it or setting it right when there is something wrong with it) with the manner in which it functions, with the difference it makes in other things. Applying this pragmatic method of getting at the nature of religion we learn as much as there is to be learned about religion for purposes of adjustment and manipulation by having a correct and clear idea of the way in which religion has functioned in the numerous guises which it has assumed in the different civilizations and eras of human development.[35]

A fundamental tool of Kaplan's thinking emerges here. His first question about a religious or Jewish matter was: What function did it fulfill when it originated? Then he would ask: How did this function change throughout Jewish history? Next: Does this matter now fulfill the same function that it did in the past? And finally: If it doesn't, what will take its place and now serve the same goal? These questions were applied by Kaplan to the belief in a supernatural deity, to prayer, to the concept of the Chosen People, to the concept of the world to come, and to many individual *Mitzvot*.

After the passage just quoted, Kaplan continued to elaborate the principal functions of religion:

> (1) As a supposed means of effecting desirable changes in the environment which could not be effected by empirical and humanly controlled factors.

> (2) As a means of salvation emphasizing the values of life which have the quality of holiness. (Kaplan later reinterpreted the concept of salvation to mean life abundant.)

> (3) As a means of faith making man feel at home in the world by inculcating in him a sense of confidence in the inherent tending of the uni-

verse to make for man's security and happiness, providing he conform to its nature and controlling agencies.

In Kaplan's earliest published writings, his pragmatic emphasis came through as a hard-hitting attack against abstract theology in favor of the experiential. "A condition indispensable to a religion being an active force in human life is that it speaks to men in terms of their own experience. . . . [The] language of theology might have a certain quaintness and charm to the ears of those to whom religion is a kind of dreamy romanticism. But to those who want to find in Judaism a way of life and a higher ambition, it must address itself in the language of concrete and verifiable experience." In his journal in 1914, he noted that the reconstruction of Judaism could only take place, "on the basis of natural human experience within the reach of every one of us." Such an emphasis on experience would lead, of course, to considerable diversity of belief and practice in the religious sphere; Kaplan was always willing to accept this diversity as a sign of health. At one point, he explained to his congregants at the Society for the Advancement of Judaism, "A religion of experience would allow each person to work out for himself the method whereby he can best express himself religiously." [36]

The doctrine enunciated here seems to advocate a kind of anarchy where every man or woman is his or her own religious guide, and where there is virtually no uniformity. Kaplan, of course, never endorsed such an idea, but on the other hand he believed that modern religion could never achieve uniformity of belief within the ranks. The best traditional faiths could hope for, and the most they should work for, was a unity of commitment along with a diversity of religious belief.

The rationalist (i.e., the opposite of the pragmatist), according to James, is a person who believes the truth is absolute. The pragmatist believes it is not. "We have to live today by what truth we can get today and be ready tomorrow to call it falsehood," James said. [37] Kaplan believed this very strongly, and consequently it was not difficult for him to embrace the whole notion of religion as constantly evolving. In his 1915–1917 *Menorah Journal* articles, Kaplan attacked the idea that there was a specifiable set of doctrines incumbent on all Jews. The doctrines were ever-changing. Not beliefs but the underlying life force — the life of the Jewish people — bound the generations to each other. One must see Judaism "not in any one doctrine or sum of doctrines but in the innermost life force which has vitalized the Jewish people and has made of it the most self-conscious social group of any upon the face of the earth." Kaplan's basic thrust here suggests Bergson and his *elan vital*, but there is no direct evidence that he was influenced directly by the philosopher of creative evolution.

Kaplan spoke a great deal about "energy" in talking of the group or the nation or God. Energy is the basic commodity of the modern era, and thus it appears to be emotionally, intellectually, and spiritually compelling:

> The main cause for misapprehending the true character of Judaism is the proneness to regard it merely as a form of truth, or at best, as the effect of a truth upon thought and conduct, and to overlook entirely the fact that it is a living reality. . . . We must break completely with the habit of identifying the whole of the Jewish religion with merely certain beliefs and duties, while ignoring completely the living energy which has operated to produce them. They are only the static residue of something that is essentially dynamic.[38]

The novelty of Kaplan's formulation can be fully appreciated only if set beside the common approaches of this period. Both Reform and Conservative Jews were eager to show that Judaism embodied a set of beliefs that constituted a rational picture of the universe and not merely a set of rituals and customs. Judaism entailed a whole theology which was embedded in rabbinical dicta. (Hence the title and the purpose of Solomon Schechter's great work, *Some Aspects of Rabbinic Theology*.) Reform and Conservative leaders argued over the relative importance of this or that belief, but no one except Kaplan questioned the notion that Judaism consisted of a series of rational beliefs about the world and the commandments that flowed from them. Kaplan completely redefined Judaism; in doing so, he moved the discussion to a higher level. The question was not which belief to retain and which to discard in order to strengthen Judaism but how to nurture the life energy of the Jewish people — the life energy that constituted its essence. Moreover, the Jewish consciousness, which the vital energy sustained, could be fostered in myriad ways. "It may be the Synagogue, the Hebrew Language, the Zionist movement, Jewish education or even student societies," Kaplan wrote to his friend Henry Hurwitz in 1916.

In attacking dogmatism, Kaplan again placed himself within the pragmatic tradition and exhibited the sociological bent of his thinking: the pragmatic person must always be ready to discard a cherished belief if he or she finds evidence that will invalidate it. William James offered a guiding principle in the search for truth with which Kaplan would certainly concur: "If there be any life that it is really better we should lead, and if there be any idea which, if believed in, would help us to lead that life, then it would really be better for us to believe in that idea, unless, indeed, belief in it incidentally clashed with other greater vital benefits."[39]

The study of sociology predisposes sociologists to view truth in relative terms. Exploring different classes and different cultures, comparing and contrasting their values, describing the social conditions under which certain ideas take hold, it is inevitable that "truth" becomes viewed as a tentative phenomenon. Kaplan's continued exposure to sociology during his education led him to doubt the possibility of discovering eternal truths. He stated the idea eloquently in a lecture at Columbia Teachers College in 1917: "The conception of religion as the highest manifestation of group life, instead of as a revelation of absolute and eternal truth valid for the whole human race, hangs together with our modern notion of truth. Considering the power of an idea to function as the truth of that idea, the various beliefs entertained by different religious groups may be said to be true for each respective group, insofar as they function beneficially for that group." Nevertheless, Kaplan never advocated a relativity of truth with regard to ethical standards. At an early point, he even went so far as to maintain that "the moral order of the universe, of which man alone happens to be the exponent, is as much an actual reality as the natural order."[40]

Here is a key element in Kaplan's view of religion. Although the religious impulse is almost always institutionalized, many might agree with Alfred North Whitehead when he defined religion as what man does with his solitariness. Religion seems to be on first consideration the particular and very individualistic way in which people confront ultimate questions. But Kaplan believed the individual to be a social achievement. What a person may become is predetermined by society according to the range of accepted roles available. Each person builds up a set of values out of the commitments of those who nurture and educate him or her. Society is primary in creating individuals, not vice versa.[41]

The beliefs and values which the members of any group hold in common constitute their collective consciousness. The concept of collective consciousness was basic to Kaplan's thinking. The collective consciousness worked through men and women, and in them, to establish the range of possibilities that existed in any situation where people must make a choice. The collective consciousness had a force and power all its own. Ordinary social conventions, for example, represent a primary expression of the collective consciousness, sometimes referred to as the collective mind. Kaplan at times maintained that the collective mind was as real as the individual mind: "Social science is gradually accustoming us to regard human society not merely as an aggregate of individuals but as a psychical entity, as a mind not less but more real than the mind of the individuals who constitute it."[42]

The concept of the collective mind is more intelligible if it is perceived as analogous to the individual mind. Although philosophers have debated the existence of other minds, the ordinary person feels no reason to doubt their reality. Only the functioning of the mind, however, can be observed — never the mind itself (we can observe the brain, but the brain and the mind are not identical). The individual mind is real even if unobservable. In the same way, the collective mind is not a metaphysical entity; it is created by the collective functioning of many individual minds and like these is real though unobservable.

◆

Kaplan believed that the individual mind had certain qualities that can also be ascribed to the collective mind. The collective mind, for example, has memory, as is illustrated so well in the case of the Jewish people. The individual mind also may be described as having imagination and powers of adjustment. Kaplan saw these abilities as exhibited by the Jewish people throughout history. According to Emile Durkheim, an important authority for Kaplan, the collective consciousness functions differently, depending on the fundamental organization of the society in question. In societies we would call primitive, the collective consciousness includes almost the totality of the consciousness of individuals; social imperatives govern the whole of life, and it is rare that individuals really distinguish themselves from one another. In more highly developed societies, where there is a greater division of labor and more significant differentiation among individuals, the collective consciousness embraces less of the consciousness of individuals. In a more advanced society, there are more circumstances in which an individual can choose to modify social imperatives. According to Durkheim — and Kaplan — one of the key concerns of modern life becomes the problem of coherence and unity. As society becomes more complex and differentiated, the individual becomes freer, and community consensus is weakened. Since values are to a degree collective rather than individual, group functioning is the key to the moral life. Language presents a similar pattern. Although speech is individual, language significantly structures the way we look at the world. So, although behavior is an individual matter, it is significantly structured by the fact that people are social animals and that our values emerge from and are acted out in social situations.

Religion, Kaplan believed, deals with values and thus is fundamentally related to the collective consciousness. Religion concerns itself with morality and with the perfection (i.e., salvation) of the individual. Inescapably, the group will exert major influence in determining the nature of religious beliefs and habits. Many, including William James, locate the essence of religion within the mind of the individual, but for Kaplan, even in the case of unusual or charismatic individuals, the social element is paramount: "Even where the experiences seem most personal and entirely isolated from the environment as is the case with visions, trances and hallucinations, a closer examination will inevitably reveal the operation of social forces generated by the religious life of the group to which the highly sensitized individual belongs." [43]

The relationship between the collective consciousness and religion is also reciprocal, each influencing and molding the other. Not all shared beliefs and values concern matters of importance in the religious sphere. Religion reflects primarily the commitments that are of a spiritual and moral nature. Kaplan defined religion, then, as that part of the collective consciousness which deals with fundamental and ultimate concerns about the nature of man, his goal as an individual, and his obligations to his fellow man: "Religion is the unity of aim which a social group develops whereby each individual in it shall attain the highest degree of perfection." [44]

This definition may apply to religion in both its organized and its unorganized states. A distinction between the real religion of an individual and his professed religion must be borne in mind. The distinction is an ancient one even if not made explicit in this particular form. The real group values that guide our decisions (quest for money, power, status, pleasure) constitute our real religion. It is out of this set of values that our god is created. At the same time, we may profess group values of altruism, self-sacrifice, honesty, and spirituality, which are part of the organized religion with which we are associated but which do not really guide us in our actions or our thinking. Religion assumes its highest form when the values of individual perfection *and* social cooperation become part of real, as well as professed, religion.

Kaplan believed that an organized religion confronts a crisis when the religion no longer reflects the collective consciousness of the group. To put it in terms of the distinction just made, the real religion of the group is too much out of line with the professed religion. It also may be that the group has ceased to function as a group and thus the collective consciousness has faded. The fate of any religion is thus tied inextricably to the quality of the group life of its members.

There are many ways in which Kaplan's analysis of the collective consciousness applies to Judaism and to the Jewish people. It is clear, for example, that Judaism should not be considered a fixed set of beliefs about God, the afterlife, and so on. Any set of beliefs is the expression of the collective mind at a particular point and is liable to change as circumstances change. If Judaism consists of a set of values, as Reform Jews used to maintain, then it is extremely vulnerable, because these values may be found easily somewhere else: "If monotheism is the truth, and it is the truth, it is not confined to Judaism."[45] But since Judaism is the life energy of the Jewish people and gives rise to these values, it becomes incumbent on interested Jews to do all they can to enhance and nurture this life force. The life force is its own justification, and the values it expresses will be judged by the degree that they contribute to the enhancement of the lives of Jews as individuals and as a group.

The key to the Jewish problem, then, becomes the preservation and enhancement of *group life*. Kaplan, writing in the first decades of the twentieth century, saw both Orthodox and Reform Jews being vanquished in the struggle to preserve Jewish life. The Orthodox cut themselves off from the mainstream of modern thought and from American life. The natural process of integration meant that Jewish consciousness was becoming more and more Americanized, and therefore the Orthodox consensus was more and more out of line with what people actually felt and believed. The answers offered by Orthodox Judaism may have met the needs of a past era, but could not meet their current needs. The Reform Jews, on the other hand, sought to integrate to the point where they were losing their individuality as Jews. The content of their beliefs did not differentiate them from non-Jews, and they were not committed to the Jewish people other than as a congregation of believers.

Preserving the Jewish people required strengthening the collective consciousness of Jews as Jews. When this happens, the community gains power at the expense of the individual. Kaplan was ready to accept such limitations as the price of survival. He believed that democracy and freedom had to be limited if there was to be any kind of real community among Jews.

Community was fundamental for Kaplan, not freedom. He was widely criticized for not understanding the spiritual side of religion, for overemphasizing its communal aspect, for equating religion with the life of the group. In response, Kaplan would argue that he did not reduce religion to group life but that his critics tended to reduce communal life to religion. Religion is important, spirituality is important, but religion comes only as a consequence of community.

> To expect worship to constitute the principal motive of social togetherness in the same way as professional or business interests, golf or gambling, is to put a strain upon average human nature. To make religion in its commonly accepted sense, the aim of social cooperation is like organizing eating clubs, for the purposes of having their members say Grace together. The one unmistakable principle which emerges from the scientific study of religious phenomena is that in order to have religion in common, people must have other interests in common besides religion.[46]

It was one thing to talk about the psychosocial energy and the collective consciousness of the Jewish people and quite another to find the appropriate institutional expression for that energy. Both the 92nd Street Y and Young Israel had severe limitations. Some other kind of institutional context was needed which would be more appropriate for the religious setting of modern life.

6

THE QUEST FOR COMMUNITY:
The Jewish Center

T he Jewish center movement and the name of Mordecai Kaplan are inextricably connected. Supporters and critics alike credit Kaplan with the concept of the movement and the establishment of the first concrete example, the Jewish Center in Manhattan. Kaplan preached regularly at the center. With eloquence and power, he put forth the idea of a new institution to embody Judaism as a living civilization. It was in connection with the center that he first began to refer to Judaism as a civilization and to analyze the implications of the concept. Considering Judaism as a civilization rather than as a religion was a natural outgrowth of his reading and thinking in the social sciences. However, Kaplan was not only a sociological thinker, he was also a rabbi. The spiritual side of Kaplan is revealed in the sermons he was giving at this time. He preached every Sabbath at the center and was able to develop his style, his delivery, and, most importantly, the spiritual content of his thought.[1] Kaplan's tenure at the center was very short. The building was dedicated in April 1918 and actually not completed until July 1920; within a year and a half, Kaplan and a large group of supporters had left the center to establish the Society for the Advancement of Judaism (SAJ). Kaplan hardly had time to begin.

The origin of the center movement is complex. Kaplan does indeed formulate the idea of a new kind of Jewish institution to meet the needs of a new generation, but he is not alone in this endeavor. The concept behind the center was being considered on many fronts. It was an idea whose time had come.

The term *center* can mean a variety of things. In 1923, a prominent social worker proposed that the word be used "to include every type of organization which attempts to provide leisure activities for the entire Jewish community or for a part thereof."[2] Such a generic definition would include the settlement houses intended for the immigrant generation as well as YM/YWHAs and community centers that were not primarily philanthropic in nature. The Jewish community centers established in the 1920s and 1930s were essentially secular institutions, while synagogue centers — "the pool with a *shul* and a school" — were, of course, religious. Kaplan's name is connected with both the secular and religious centers.

Given Kaplan's ideology, the concept of the synagogue center is logically implied by his understanding of the relationship between religion and community. Kaplan believed that historic religions grew or declined depending on the vitality of their group life. The spiritual search of the individual constitutes the core of the quest for meaning, but unless the individual finds himself or herself in some living group his or her spiritual creativity will wither and die. There is no way religious life can be detached from group life. Even the solitary monk lives in a community and lives out the ideals of his community's tradition.

Kaplan was troubled by the "thinness" of contemporary religious life. Traditionally, Jewish life had been bound up with the life of the community as a whole. Religion and the rest of life were coextensive. Since the emancipation, religious life had become for many Jews a sometime thing. Kaplan believed that the only way Judaism would survive was if the Jews lived a life beyond merely praying together. Community precedes religion and gives rise to it. A thriving community inevitably will crave religious expression to give form and context to its joys and its pains.

Judaism is thus a total civilization and not a set of beliefs, a notion Kaplan had been thinking about for a long time. It seemed that now (1915–1918) everything was falling into place. He believed that just as the synagogue helped to rescue the Jews after the destruction of the Temple in Jerusalem, so the synagogue center would help rescue them now. The center would help restore Jewish life because it would embrace all facets of life: "The Jewish Center in insisting that Judaism must be lived as a civilization, will endeavor to have us work, play, love and worship as Jews." Kaplan's congregants, for example, would learn to bring their Judaism into the workplace. Rather than voicing pious platitudes about economic justice, they would engage in ethical living. Kaplan wanted to emphasize "the need for Jews who exercise power in the dominion of industry and traffic to come together in the name of their faith . . . to see what they can do to ameliorate the evils and to improve the relations between employer and employee."

In dedicating the center building in March 1918, he had put forth a new ideal. His ideology was the map with which the congregants would orient themselves and clarify their goals. It is important to understand the ideal and the degree to which it became a reality in the new Jewish Center.

The Jewish Center grew out of an obvious and definite need. A number of prominent Jews had moved from the Upper East Side, an area of a large Jewish population and many synagogues, to the Upper West Side. The West Side had virtually no prominent houses of worship. Many of the new West Siders were wealthy Eastern European Jews who had been successful in the clothing business. As Kaplan said many years later, they wanted a synagogue that would make Judaism fashionable. The world would know that one could be rich and be an observant Jew and also live on the West Side of Manhattan. Some of the West Siders turned to Kaplan because he was well known in the New York area and respected for his work with the *Kehillah* and the Teachers' Institute and his fine speaking ability. He was young, dynamic, and college-educated, and he spoke English without an accent.

Kaplan was without a congregation at this point, working hard at the Teachers' Institute, lecturing widely, and publishing his thoughts on the nature of Judaism in the *Menorah Journal*. When the West Side group came to him and asked for his help in forming a synagogue, he began to consider concretely the implications of what he had been thinking. The synagogue had to become something new in order to meet new needs: "it would not only provide a place to worship for the elders and a school for the children but also an opportunity to all affiliated with it to develop their social life Jewishly."[3]

Although the idea for an expanded synagogue was not well established, it was also not incompatible with a traditional understanding of Judaism. The West Side group had no trouble accepting Kaplan's plans for the structure and program of the synagogue. His concept of a synagogue center was new but not radical. However, his general conception of Judaism represented a clear departure from tradition. He rejected the cardinal concept of traditional Judaism that the Torah (Pentateuch) was given to Moses at Mount Sinai and publicly accepted biblical criticism.

The West Side group was clearly Orthodox. Its head was Joseph H. Cohen, a wealthy clothing manufacturer who was quite active in Jewish affairs. A member of Kehilath Jeshurun when Kaplan was rabbi there, Cohen had taken a fatherly interest in Kaplan. He was active in the Jewish community and especially interested in Beth Israel Hospital, which was the sole hospital in Manhattan that was conducted in accordance with Jewish Orthodox principles. In talking with the West Side group, Kaplan wanted them to understand his general position on Judaism. He made a special point of reading Cohen his notes on Genesis which he used for teaching at the Teachers' Institute. These notes indicated his acceptance of Darwin, evolution, and biblical criticism. Cohen seemed unconcerned with matters of belief. He was a practical man, and he wanted Kaplan's commitment on certain religious forms he considered crucial. Kaplan was less concerned about "particulars" (seating, order of the service) and so was willing to give in on all the details. He did, however, insist on support for the revival of Hebrew and for the rebuilding of Zion. Kaplan also agreed to be "tactful and circumspect" about his religious views.[4]

As is often the case, we have two parties talking past each other and neither really hearing the other. Kaplan was satisfied because he had warned the group about his radicalism. The *Baale Batim* (community movers and shakers) cared little for ideology as long as they got their way on practical matters. They certainly thought they could control Kaplan if he stepped out of line. They didn't take his growing radicalism seriously, and he didn't regard their Orthodox commitments as a problem. Kaplan perceived signs of flexibility and a willingness to try new ideas. There was some basis for this perception, however slight. Cohen, for example, expressed interest in "the good points of Christian Science" and also suggested to Kaplan that the center might hold services in the vernacular during the week. Nonetheless, Cohen and his followers were Orthodox. At this time, Kaplan wrote in his journal that though he was radical in his thought, he was completely Orthodox in his own religious behavior. The statement was true then but not later. Kaplan in his later years allowed a number of historians to read the first volume of the journal and to quote from it. They inaccurately assumed this particular statement to be a description of Kaplan's behavior throughout his life. It is evident from the later diaries that his religious observance changed significantly as time passed.[5]

Kaplan was exhilarated by the meetings with Joe Cohen and the West Side group. He was in his early thirties, possessed of a strong sense of his own mission and the contributions he contemplated. Although the Teachers' Institute kept him busy, it was a limited operation.

A new kind of synagogue meant "a method in religion," Kaplan told the group one Sabbath afternoon, and not just another *shul*. After one of the meetings, he confided to his journal, "I find myself at the beginning of a new spiritual enterprise which holds out great promise." Kaplan experienced such feelings at frequent intervals. Throughout his life, he was spawning new ideas and convening groups together to discuss them. He was very excited by the whole process, feeling he was always on the verge of some great breakthrough. Perhaps the process was as important as the product.

The discussions that began in earnest in the spring of 1915 continued through the summer and fall. Cohen wanted Kaplan to assume the position of rabbi as soon as the building was completed. The two men met frequently for lunch at the Waldorf to discuss their plans for the center. Kaplan noted that the waiters all knew Cohen and made obvious efforts to meet his religious needs so he would not be embarrassed in washing his hands or saying the *Motzi*.

The people who supported Cohen in establishing the center were Jewish laymen who had served with him at Beth Israel Hospital. They were second-generation Jews, energetic self-starters, and already well-known in their particular fields. Otto Rosalsky, for example, born and educated in New York City, was appointed to the Court of General Sessions as a judge in 1905. His father was one of the best-known butchers on Allen Street and very knowledgeable in Jewish matters. Rosalsky served on the bench for thirty-one years, with very few reversals. Kaplan described him as long-winded, with a propensity, when talking in private to individuals, toward summarizing speeches he had given. The judge and Julius Schwartz were the only members of the center board who were not manufacturers. Schwartz, also born in New York City, was a staff member of the *New York Tribune* and later organized the Jewish Biographical Bureau which published early editions of *Who's Who in American Jewry*.[6]

The other members of the board were all businessmen; their average age was forty. Almost without exception, they owned their own companies, predominantly in the clothing industry. Israel Unterberg, for example, who came to America alone at the age of ten, established a shirt company at twenty-one. He, too, was active in many Jewish organizations, serving as a board director of Montefiore Hospital. Unterberg, a strong Kaplan supporter and one of the founders of the Society for the Advancement of Judaism, later donated a large sum of money to the Teachers' Institute. His daughter married I. C. Rubin, Lena Kaplan's brother.

Joseph H. Cohen, founder of the Jewish Center,
20th Anniversary Celebration — The Jewish
Center, *1937. (Courtesy Rabbi J. J. Schachter, The
Jewish Center.)*

The center board members were also powerful lobbyists for religious causes other than the center. Most of them were active with
Rabbi Isaac Elchanan Theology Seminary (RIETS), raising money and
serving in various capacities. The Lamport family, which had four
members on the center board, was especially important to Dr. Bernard
Revel, the head of RIETS, because they labored diligently for the institution. Nathan Lamport, the paterfamilias, had given more than two
hundred thousand dollars to RIETS during his lifetime. Samuel C.
Lamport, who took over the family business, became one of the largest
exporters of cotton goods in the United States. He was widely known
for his philanthropy and patriotism; he bought more than one million
dollars' worth of liberty bonds during World War I. His brother Arthur
entered investment banking and formed his own firm. The Lamports
were "star workers" for the center and made their presence felt in all
branches of the synagogue.[7]

*Israel Unterberg (1863–1935), businessman, strong
Kaplan supporter at the Jewish Center and SAJ.
Later donated funds for new TI building. (Courtesy
RRC.)*

The center was constructed in a relatively short period of time. By
the summer of 1917, the building began to go up. Wartime did not
seem to retard the process of planning and construction. The Jewish
community, and that included the center leaders and members, was involved in raising money for relief of Jewish communities in Europe, but
the center supporters seemed to have enough money for all their needs.
The men building the center spared no expense in erecting a fine building. They started out with a four-story structure, but by the time it was
completed in 1920, the building reached nine stories.

Kaplan conferred frequently with Cohen and the group to resolve
problems. One particular question was the issue of seating, mixed or
family seating being a hotly debated issue at this time. Reform Jews had
introduced mixed seating in the middle of the nineteenth century, but
it did not present a problem until the early twentieth century. The
movement for the emancipation of women was gaining ground, and the
question of seating became the emblematic issue that differentiated
more liberal (i.e., Conservative) synagogues from the more strictly Or-

thodox. Kaplan, a strong supporter of the emancipation of women in general and of women's right to vote in particular, wanted mixed seating. The board on the whole wanted separate seating. They arrived at a compromise: separate seating with the women sitting on the two sides of a large center section but with no curtains or dividers between the two groups which thus remained in full view of each other. Cohen consulted Rabbi M. S. Margolies on the matter, "not so much for the purpose of knowing the actual law, but how to be sufficiently within the letter of the law and yet please the members." Part of the compromise package also included a stipulation that in all synagogue matters women were to have a vote equal to the men.[8]

Wherever possible, the backers of the center arranged a ceremony to celebrate a stage in the completion of the project. This procedure gave them important publicity and perhaps helped them gain members. It also reflected their belief, certainly influenced by Kaplan's rhetoric, that they were engaged in a venture of heroic proportions. At the groundbreaking ceremony, which took place on May 22, 1917, Kaplan declared that this was not just a foundation that was being dug but a "well" which would become "a fountain of new and inexhaustible energy for living the Jewish life." He raised the event to a higher plane when he said that those building the center were "the tools of a will not their own and higher than their own to perpetuate the life of the Jewish people."[9] Students of Kaplan may want to speculate about whose will Kaplan was speaking of here. Although he leaned toward a naturalistic theology even at this early period, Kaplan continued to use expressions like "God's will." Whether he had in mind God or the Jewish people, he seems to be expressing a significant sense of the transcendent. We also see a case of Kaplan's inflated rhetoric. He viewed this situation *sub specie aeternitatis* rather than as one more synagogue in New York City. Kaplan's propensity to inflate the importance of his activities was a strength and a weakness.

At the ceremony marking the laying of the cornerstone, during the summer of 1917, he again emphasized that what was needed was not just another synagogue or rich man's club with a chapel to outdo the gentiles. He harped on the theme that community needs superseded religious needs: "we have established a Jewish Center that shall enable us to live together as Jews, because living together as Jews is an indispensable condition to Jewish religion."[10]

After all the work he put into the planning of the center between 1915 and 1918, it is hard to fathom why Kaplan hesitated to serve as rabbi. The reasons for his hesitation are revealing. Objectively, he was very busy. The Teachers' Institute was growing quickly and taking more and more of this time. He spoke frequently not only in New York but also in the Midwest, and to Menorah Societies up and down the East Coast. He spent time on his writing and scholarship. He was preoccupied with his family, which already consisted of four young girls.

But there were other reasons for his ambivalence. Kaplan loved the Jewish people in general, but in the particular he found them irritating. Deep down, he had contempt for the center members and the class they represented. His constant repetition of the conviction that the center was not to be a rich man's club represented his private fears that this was precisely what it would become. He was always ready to judge the center leaders harshly. In talking about the size of the building, for example, he said that it would only serve to make the center leaders smug and complacent. He had no illusions about the spiritual depth of the people he was dealing with and referred to them more than once as a "group of typically successful bourgeois type."

The other major factor in his hesitation to become rabbi of the center involved his sense of himself as a writer and scholar. In 1915 and 1916, he had published his series of articles in the *Menorah Journal*, enjoying not only the creative process but also the recognition he received. On the other hand, he was only beginning to exercise his creative powers and had doubts about his ability. The choice in taking the center position seemed to be between an uncertain future as a writer-scholar and the immediate respect and influence that the position at the center might bring: "I have not much confidence in my literary ability and I am afraid that if I let go of this opportunity of becoming a public factor, I might be a disappointed man in later years." Kaplan did not envision that he would become important both as a writer and as a public figure in the course of his very long life.

So deep was his ambivalence that he considered leaving professional Jewish life completely. While at Kehilath Jeshurun (1903–1909), he had seriously contemplated going to law school or selling insurance. In 1917, he investigated the possibility of entering business. Bernard Revel's brother-in-law had numerous investments, and Kaplan turned to him for advice. Kaplan was told that the best thing for him to do was to get some capital together and set up his own company — possibly in oil — and invest in a place like Oklahoma. Kaplan turned to his brother-in-law, Jacob Rubin, who advised him against this venture when Rubin found out that Revel's brother-in-law had a rather unsavory reputation.[11]

The center board reluctantly started looking for another rabbi. They did not conduct a real search and interviewed only one candidate, Kaplan's colleague and distant cousin, Hillel Kauvar. He came from

Denver, preached at the synagogue, and was interviewed by the board. Kauvar enjoyed a long and distinguished career in Denver, but he was no match for Kaplan, and the center rejected him.[12]

On Sunday evening, April 21, 1918, Judge Rosalsky and Abe Rothstein tried to persuade Kaplan again to accept the position of rabbi. This time he accepted and was voted in by the congregation the following week. All that remained was salary. Kaplan, the ideologue, showed himself the true idealist when he adamantly refused to accept any salary at all. The center board was understandably perplexed about the refusal of the seventy-five hundred dollars they offered him — certainly a considerable sum for those times.

In refusing the salary, Kaplan had a number of considerations in mind. First and foremost, he wanted maximum freedom to express himself. Every congregational rabbi is caught between his function as a leader of the congregation and the fact that the congregation also pays his salary. It is not easy to bite the hand that feeds you. Moreover, Kaplan held the moneyed classes in genuine contempt. He did not want to belong to them. Once his income rose, he would be tied into a higher standard of living which would enslave him. He had, of course, many expenses, and with four young children the decision was not an easy one. His wife, Lena, was genuinely supportive of his idealistic stance, a proof of her strength of character, since she was the one who ran the household and balanced the budget. He recorded his struggle in his journal: "I would become the slave of a higher standard of living or at best save up another fifty thousand dollars in the course of the next ten years. Besides, I am convinced that unless those who are at the helm of Jewish life display something of the spirit of sacrifice that now permeates the nations of the world, the Jewish people have no chance for survival. . . . I pray to God that I be strong enough to resist all temptation to accept a salary from the Center." Kaplan and the board agreed that his salary should be given to the Teachers' Institute, where it would be used for scholarships.[13]

The center bulletin joyously declared that Kaplan had accepted the call to be the rabbi. It characterized him as "the thinker and spiritual elder who called the Center idea into being and who helped to bring it to its present stage of development." Kaplan was represented as combining "in himself so completely the authority of the old and the new learning, as well as the social vision and individual power as thinker and leader." During the summer of 1918, Kaplan and his family moved from 120 East Ninety-third Street to One West Eighty-ninth Street.[14]

In the midst of the negotiations, the building, or at least its first four floors, was completed, and it was time for another ceremony.

The Jewish Center, West Eighty-sixth Street,
N.Y.C. 20th Anniversary Celebration – The
Jewish Center, *1937. (Courtesy Rabbi J. J.*
Schachter, The Jewish Center.)

The Center was called "the Shul, with a pool and a
school"; Jewish Center pool, 20th Anniversary Al-
bum, *1937. (Courtesy Rabbi J. J. Schachter, The*
Jewish Center.)

Judge Rosalsky presided, with Rabbi M. S. Margolies offering the opening prayer. In addition to Kaplan, Louis Marshall spoke, as did Mathilde Schechter, who represented the women of the center. The occasion brought together diverse parties within the Jewish community, for Kaplan himself had not yet alienated the Orthodox and was well known in both Reform and Zionist circles. He clearly envisioned the center as an exemplary institution when he told the group, "[We] must create for ourselves the kind of recreational, cultural and religious opportunities which we shall then have the right to provide for others." [15]

The most accurate way to describe life at the center is to understand it as a "modern Orthodox" or Conservative synagogue. The reality fell far short of the vision, but nonetheless Kaplan did institute a wide range of activities, an innovative educational program, and a meaningful service in the synagogue despite the fact that it was not experimental in character, and did not introduce changes in ritual. The community never achieved the cohesiveness of which he had dreamed. In comparison with what had existed in traditional synagogues before this period, however, the center marked a very significant step toward a bold and innovative American institution.[16]

In educational activities, the center offered apparently two tracks, an afternoon Hebrew school and a day school. The afternoon school, which started in 1918 with some forty children, Kaplan described as being "very small and very expensive." Kaplan's eldest daughter, Judith, attended this school, and Max Kadushin, later to become a noted scholar of rabbinics, was her teacher. Kadushin's teaching may have been a major cause of the split that led to Kaplan's leaving the center.[17]

The day school was extremely innovative for its time and was one of the projects Kaplan barely had time to begin. He started with a kindergarten in 1918, and by the time he left the center in 1922, the school had three or possibly four grades. Naomi, Kaplan's third eldest daughter, attended the day school from its inception. It was much more experimental than the other schools she attended. The pupils learned carpentry, tie-dying, and candle making and studied arithmetic by using paper money. She remembers that there was much "Isadora Duncan"-type dancing at the school and a musical program as well. Kaplan himself invited people in from Columbia, where John Dewey was holding forth about experimental education. Patti Hill of Teachers' College — the woman who composed the song "Happy Birthday" — also visited. It is curious that the day school was never instituted at the SAJ.[18]

In adult education, Kaplan gave weekly lectures on the Bible and later formed a *Hevra Shas* which met for five hours a week to study

Talmud. In the Bible class, he used the same material he had prepared for his students at the Teachers' Institute. He felt relaxed with these classes and expressed himself freely on the origins of the Jewish people and the development of the biblical text. "Now and then there would come to the class someone who was in search of heresy and he would not have to wait long before he got what he had come for. Such a man would then complain to Fischman or Cohen, but the latter would always find some way of drawing his fangs." [19]

In addition to education, the center provided activities in music and the dramatic arts. Kaplan engaged Amelia Morganroth, a local drama coach, to supervise the plays and the drama groups. She apparently was well liked by the young people, but nonetheless the youngsters were often more interested in doing vaudeville than plays on biblical themes. Seminary children such as Eli Ginzberg participated in the center plays, as did Shaw Benderly, the son of Samson. Kaplan had little patience with the adolescents, describing the girls as "foolish gigglers" and the boys as "rich boobs."

Morganroth functioned in several capacities at the center. As a teacher of elocution, she criticized Kaplan's Sabbath sermons, analyzing the modulation of his voice, his use of gestures, and his general delivery. It is no accident that he spoke so well. She reacted to everything from his pronunciation ("would you" came out "woodje," "could you" was "coodje," she told him) to the quality of his voice ("there really was a smile in your voice") to a general evaluation of the content ("the subject was a monstrous one and most clearly put before your listeners"). She sometimes quoted back to him particularly good lines she liked — "Man must primarily live right and then God will take on form — according to his way of living and thinking." [20]

Music also played a prominent role at the Kaplan synagogue. In the era of the great cantors, the center was not to be outdone. Cantor Pinhas Jassinowsky, with his beautiful high tenor voice, sang each Sabbath and on holidays. Congregational singing was coming into vogue in the more traditional congregations, and so, in order to help things along, the center hired a man who sat in the back of the congregation and sang along with the congregants. During the week, there was a choral society and other opportunities for center members to learn the hymns for Sabbath services. The school put a strong emphasis on Zionist songs, and on the occasion of the British Mandate (April 1920), Judith Kaplan remembers being on a float constructed by the Jewish Center: "Several thousand men and women formed a parade when the first reports concerning Palestine came . . . and marched through East Broadway and other streets. They sang 'The Star-Spangled Banner,'

'*Hatikvah*' and 'God Save the King' and were greeted with cheers by spectators."[21]

With all its extra activities, the center was nonetheless still a synagogue. Although it could be described as fairly Americanized, this synagogue reflected little of the innovative ritual or changes in liturgy that would characterize Kaplan's work at the Society for the Advancement of Judaism. There were no late Friday-evening services. Kaplan felt that Friday evening should be a family time; he never held late services. The preaching at the center was in English, with a very limited number of English readings during the services. Honors were not auctioned from the pulpit. In 1919, he experimented with a forum method from the pulpit, but it did not succeed.

Kaplan's greatest strength and his unique contribution to the synagogue was as a preacher, having a strong voice and the ability to turn a fine phrase. Having taught homiletics at the Seminary since 1910, he understood the structure of the sermon and what distinguished a great sermon from a mediocre one. Most often, his theme derived directly from the Torah portion of the week. He would begin with the text, but by the time he finished, he was far afield into important ethical and religious issues. His sermons also reveal his thinking on a wide variety of subjects and have a special tone not present in his articles and books.

As a form of thought and expression, the sermon has been held in rather low esteem. The essay informs or analyzes, whereas the sermon exhorts, although some degree of analysis may be included. In a sense, it is much easier to exhort than to analyze. Exhorting also may reflect a limited understanding of the way things actually are. The analytical aspects of Kaplan's sermons may have been too sophisticated for many in his congregation. They were, after all, ordinary people, businessmen and their wives and children who came to hear him week after week. His principal weakness as a leader was his inordinate faith in preaching. There was perhaps excessive analysis in his sermons and too much exhortation in his essays. His true feelings were only thinly disguised when, in a sermon in May 1918, he denied the overriding significance of preaching. "Bear in mind," he told his congregation, "that preaching is not a means to the solution of all difficulties in Jewish life." (Who besides Kaplan ever thought it was?) He went on, "If it can diagnose the evils and at least create a demand for the proper remedy, it is discharging its function." Underlying Kaplan's assertion here was the question of change and how to achieve it. He naively believed that people needed only to be told "the right way," and then they would automatically change their habits and their behavior.

Kaplan did exert a strong influence on those who heard him. He was a passionate, rousing speaker, and his congregants could not help but be moved when he spoke. He made them feel part of a great adventure. The center journal reflects the members' feelings that theirs was a very special institution and that "they were the vanguard of a new direction in Jewish life."

Kaplan's sermons dealt with topics ranging from theology (God as healer) to religious practice (the nature of public worship) to economic issues (the five-day work week) to the pressing matters of war and peace. The "war to end all wars," the Great War, was constantly on everyone's mind, and Kaplan talked about it frequently. He was a strong and unwavering supporter of Woodrow Wilson. Wilson's idealism elicited a deep response from him as it did from many other Jewish leaders. When America entered the war in 1917, he spoke at the 92nd Street Y and encouraged young men to go willingly to the army when they were drafted.

He framed the conflict in metaphors of Genesis, telling his congregation that the war had been a clash of nations seeking power but was transformed when Wilson proclaimed the League of Nations and the rule of international justice as the only worthy outcome of the conflict. Comparing Wilson to Abraham through the concept of the test or trial, he asserted that, "Ideals are distorted as soon as we attempt to put them into practice." If we continue to believe in them despite the distortion, we might be said to have withstood the trial. President Wilson was undergoing such a test just as Abraham had done. At another point, Kaplan used the image of Jacob wrestling with the angel to comment on Wilson and the League of Nations. As the war ended, he tried to draw some lessons from the conflict. He emphasized that "the forces of bestiality were always there ready to break up the coherence of civilization." Unfortunately, "to restore the world to sanity, it is necessary to become mad and irrational." Soldiers are brutalized by war, and there is inevitably a loss of freedom at home. Most importantly, the insanity must not be prolonged.[22]

Kaplan's support for the war and for Wilson flowed from a strong sense of patriotism. His feelings of loyalty and gratitude were the consequences of the immigrant experience. But Americanism to him did not imply any diminution of Judaism. Instead, like Horace Kallen, he insisted that "Americanism is falsely regarded as demanding the surrender of all group traditions, values and loyalties. It is thought that being a good Jew prevents one from being a full-time American. The discussion of this question is relevant to the celebration of Hanukah because we commemorate on this festival Judaism's triumph over the melting pot idea."[23] Parallel to his strong patriotism was his commitment to democracy and the ideals of pluralism: "Democracy's conception of preeminence is the full development of one's distinctive and individual traits and capacities. It is distinctiveness that makes for distinction."

In some of his sermons, Kaplan even managed to present his Zionism as compatible with American loyalty. It took a bit of twisting and turning, but the chain of argument does reveal the strength of his loyalty to America. If we see Wilson as the emancipator of the nations, Kaplan argued, we must still understand that full emancipation did not come to the Jews until the Balfour Declaration. Kaplan suggested that the anniversary of the Balfour Declaration should be called *Yom Ha-Geulah* — the day of redemption. "The Jews were slaves before, because a slave is one who accepts from another the purposes which control his conduct," and until the Jews have their own land, they will not be in a position to control their destiny. Thus, the slogan "making the world safe for democracy" really means making the world safe for nationalism, and the job "of the Jews is to make nationalism safe for the world. . . . Nationalism misapplied is dynamite but nationalism together with the goal of righteousness and social justice makes Zionism and American loyalty not incompatible."[24]

Kaplan presented to his congregation a very broad definition of Zionism. He put forth the notion he later called peoplehood when he asserted that, more than anything else, Zionism reflected the identification of Jews with one anther. To the Jew gifted with sympathy and imagination, Kaplan suggested, "nothing Jewish is alien or indifferent." He believed that the Zionist movement alone could restore unity to the Jews, ensuring their survival. Zionism was a mode of developing "new standards of fraternity and solidarity" among the Jews. Such solidarity would not be narrow or chauvinistic, however. He strongly rejected the kind of group pride that sees little value in others. Such chauvinism, backed up by force, was called imperialism. When not coupled with violence, it results in "proud self-isolation." Jewish loyalty, however, called for a wider perspective, because "of the fealty to the God of Israel who is [also] the God of Humanity."[25]

It might seem that Kaplan was softening his Zionism to make it more palatable for his congregation. Surely the recently successful clothing manufacturers who made up the bulk of Kaplan's flock had little interest in emigration for themselves. They could nonetheless be easily drawn to philanthropic Zionism, to the idea that "we need a homeland for those who suffer but not for ourselves." Kaplan was not a hard-line political Zionist who despaired of the Diaspora. In a rather remarkable journal entry from this period, we see again the strength of his Americanism. Even in the privacy of his diary, he had to turn his Zionist understanding and longing into an aspect of his devotion to the United States. In December 1918, he briefly contemplated emigrating to Palestine and consulted with Jacob De Haas, a key figure in the Zionist movement. Feeling guilty about his actions, he wrote the following in his journal: "Does this mean ingratitude to America? To love America is simply to love myself, for it is only in this blessed country that I could have achieved what I value most in myself. . . . If I will go to Palestine it would be not only for the purpose of helping to interpret my people to itself, but also of interpreting America to her own people. Very few of her own people understand her."[26]

The setting for the newly developing sense of Jewish solidarity as fostered by Zionism was the synagogue, or more precisely the synagogue center. Kaplan saw Jewish solidarity (Zionism) as the goal and the synagogue center as the means. Kaplan's Zionism at this time was perfectly compatible with the needs of his congregation to feel fully loyal. It was a Zionism that envisioned a Jewish community in Palestine that would complement and enhance the Jewish life of communities around the world. He never thought the Jewish future would be ensured by emigration alone.

The reinterpretation of Judaism was a frequent theme of his sermons, but his understanding of the main theological issues differed from the theology he later espoused. At this early point in his life, he retained a strong sense of the spiritual as it is traditionally understood. The synagogue setting perhaps encouraged him to be somewhat less rationalistic when he spoke about theological matters. Considering his later attacks on supernaturalism, his calls at this time for an effort to make God more real are striking: "We have to cultivate a sense of the reality of things spiritual," he told his congregation. "God should be so real to us that in place of fear and distrust which overcloud our lives, we should be possessed of such peace, poise, and power as to render us free and joyful and give us a sense of dominion." The only way to experience the reality of God was "by having our inner life permeated by 'Kedushah' and 'Bitachon,' inward holiness and faith." His optimism was present here as in everything he touched. In one rousing sermon about Sinai and the drama of revelation, he contrasted the power made manifest at the mountain with the still small voice Elijah heard in the wilderness. The Jewish spirit moves between these extremes. "The significant fact about the Jewish Spirit," he said, "is that no matter how near extinction it may appear, it is not only imperishable but resurgent. . . . [The] voice that spoke at Horeb may no longer thunder forth its divine message but it can never be completely silent."[27]

In his later writing, Kaplan talked frequently about God as the power that makes for salvation. This formulation has been attacked and criticized as being metaphysically muddled and unsatisfying. At this early point, however, his theology was less naturalistic, and was expressed in traditional terms. At times, he even sounds mystical:

> It is only that kind of community (i.e., a true and close one) that develops associations, traditions, and memories that go to make up its soul. To mingle one's personality with that soul becomes a natural longing. In such a community one experiences that mystic divine grace which like radiant sunshine illumines our lives when joyous and like balm heals them when wounded or sore-stricken. Then all questions about saying this or that become trivial, for the real purpose is attained in having each one feel with the Psalmist: One thing have I asked of the Lord, that will I seek after, that I may dwell in the house of the Lord all the days of my life, to behold the graciousness of God.

With such formulations, Kaplan easily might have remained within the Orthodox community had he not subsequently attacked it. His theology here is not alienating but has a unifying and synthesizing effect. In the sermon just quoted, he reaffirmed, "there is no justification at the present time for any part of Israel inaugurating changes without the authority of Catholic Israel."[28]

It is in connection with his stand on women and Judaism that we observe Kaplan and the dynamics of the congregation in all their complexity. The center seemed reasonably progressive in regard to women's issues. Statements in the center journal strongly supported women's rights but presented them in a somewhat defensive manner. For example: "We are the last to subscribe to the German idea of *Kuche*, *Kinder* and *Kirche*. Women must play a significant role in the great social changes that are taking place." Wherever possible, women were included in important ceremonies. As part of the dedication of the center, a *Sefer Torah* (Torah scroll) was finished with each person writing in a letter. The center journal noted proudly that "all the women as well as the men participated in the ceremony."[29]

But the synagogue was Orthodox. Seating was separate though equal, and there was never any question of altering the synagogue ritual to include women. The major question of the day was women's right to vote. Kaplan advocated the emancipation of women. In his preaching, he went beyond mere support of the vote, which he took for granted, but he did not argue for changing any rituals to include women. In the fall of 1918, he took the occasion of the *Sidra* (Torah portion) "*Haye*

Sarah" to deal with the issue of women's rights. Preparing the way for the sermon, the center journal published the following question during that week: "Shall the Emancipation of women be merely a duplication of men?" On Sabbath morning, Kaplan pulled no punches when he said, "Judaism of the *Galuth* [Diaspora] has said nothing and done nothing to lay claim to any share in the Emancipation of women." The major religions, moreover, always lagged behind when it came to movements for social justice. He asserted that "the movement to emancipate women was nothing more than the logical extension of democracy."

If Judaism in general offered no help on the issue of women's emancipation, Kaplan suggested looking to the Bible for guidance. He pointed out that there are many strong holy women in the Bible, including Deborah, Miriam, and, of course, Rebecca, who was the focus of the week's portion. If Genesis presented the matriarchs, however, it also presented the curses of Eden. The curse on Eve reads, "Toward your husband shall be your lust, yet he will rule over you" (Genesis 3:16). It is clear, Kaplan maintained, that women are destined to be redeemed from this curse at the end of time just as men will be redeemed from their curse. We know this because Genesis also tells us that God said, "Let us make humankind, in our image, according to our likeness! Let *them* have dominion over the fish of the sea." The key word here is *Veyirdu;* "they," both male and female, shall rule the earth together. The ideal is that men and women were meant to be equal, and the world as we know it violates that ideal.

Kaplan looked closely at Rebecca and used her as a model. Man's essential sinfulness stems from his lust for power; the same is true for women. Women in the past have sought to gain power through their charms. Women have both gained and lost because of this — in Kaplan's words, "What if not her desires to entrance man with her charms has caused man to look upon her as his doll and plaything to minister to his wants?" Thus, the enslavement of women has resulted from their femininity, "the power of the eternally feminine," as Kaplan called it. Now women must be emancipated, not essentially for more power but for greater service. Just as Rebecca went the extra mile in her service to Abraham's servant, so must all women follow her example. It is almost as if Kaplan were talking about women in the same terms as Jews in general have always talked about themselves — as the Chosen People. The Jews are the only ones whom God has known, says the prophet, and therefore they have a higher standard to follow. If women were really free, Kaplan says, they would revolutionize the political sphere by lifting it to a higher level. The chosenness of women, Kaplan believed, made them more humane: "Women will purify politics, make industry more humane and make justice to the consumer instead of profits to the producer the standard of the market." Emancipation is not aimed at power, "neither her own particular power, nor that masculine power which has contributed so much to the destruction of the world." As Hannah so eloquently put it in her hymn of thanksgiving to God, "for not by strength shall man prevail."[30]

Kaplan was often at his best when he attempted to recast traditional concepts. At one point, he reiterated the idea that reverence for the individual was more basic than the concept of "Love thy neighbor." Being created in God's image was the biblical way of talking about the absolute value of human life: "the reason it is wrong to take human life is that the human being wears the image of God, therefore, when a human being is slain, something more than that which is merely human is destroyed, the very image of God is shattered." The proper attitude toward fellow human beings is respect, the same awe and respect "we associate with the idea of God." Human life is revered because "it is a spark of that life that animates the universe," Kaplan told his congregation. He explained that acting out of reverence was a higher principle than acting out of love: "It is only after mankind will have acquired the principle of reverence for man that it will be possible to love man as he should be loved, not merely 'as thyself' but as the reflection of the Divine. 'Beloved is man,' said R. Akiba, 'for he was made in the image of God.'"[31]

In his sermons and publications, Kaplan continued developing his thinking concerning the spiritual. It was clear to him that the concept of the spiritual fundamentally concerns unity and oneness. He believed that when human beings realize their kinship with one another, they are lifted to a higher level, the level of the transcendent. Any activity that helped people to be one with the world was considered to be a spiritual activity. Thus, the center of the Jewish liturgy calls upon Jews not only to affirm that God is one but also to affirm the consequences that flow from this affirmation. If God is one and is the center of the universe, then the universe also embodies an essential unity. To the unschooled eye, the world may seem variegated and diverse. To experience the world as one — as a unity — Kaplan believed, is the primary challenge of the religious life.

The reality of this unity is related to the sense of God's presence in the world. The presence of God, or the *Shekhinah*, is how Jews designate God's presence as it touches humankind. The *Shekhinah* relates to those moments when a person is lifted above the profane and the fragmentariness of the everyday. The primary question is whether the transcendent state is merely a subjective condition, an inner "high," or whether it reflects the existence of a unitary force or a form of energy or power that exists apart from ourselves and our transcendent moments.

Most students of Kaplan's theology understand him to be advocating what has come to be called a predicate theology. In the words of one contemporary advocate of this approach, a predicate theology involves the "belief in the reality of the predicates and atheism is their denial. The critical question for predicate theology is not 'Do you believe that God is merciful, caring, peacemaking?' but 'Do you believe that doing mercy, caring and making peace are godly?'" The issue is not whether God possesses a particular attribute or quality but whether the quality is worthy of the highest respect and constant cultivation.

Kaplan in his later work undoubtedly advocated a predicate theology. He talked more about creativity than about the creator, more about divinelike qualities than about the divine essence itself. This kind of thinking also appears in his writings in the early twenties. "If instead of affirming that God is love, spirit, courage, devotion etc. there were a new religion to proclaim that Love is God, that spirit, courage, devotion, etc. are all aspects of the love that is God, we might have a religion that is in accord with reality as man knows it to be. Only when the term *God* will come to have an adjectival force instead of being a substantive will it exercise a wholesome effect upon human life."[32] In the present era, many people do not take God or the concept of God seriously because they do not *believe* in God, do not believe in God viewed as subject. Kaplan believed that when people learn to focus on the predicates and to use the concept of the divine to support ultimate concerns, then God or the divine would again assume spiritual importance in their lives. In other words, when American Jews revised their view of God, God would become functional once more.

Kaplan spoke endlessly about the idea of God and how it functions in human life. In this area he had no peer. The reality of God and His qualities, however, was another matter. The sociologist of religious belief was always present, but there was also another Kaplan. This other Kaplan, especially in the early period, talked of the presence of God and seemed to intend more than just the qualities in question. He seemed at times to be endorsing the existence of a numinal presence in the world. In the 1920s, Kaplan's predicate theology and this more numinal theology coexisted.

For example, he was quite at home with traditional religious language. "God in his essence is transcendent," he wrote in his journal. "As such He represents the mystery which we cannot help sensing behind the phenomena of the cosmos."[33] The category of mystery was no problem for him, and he was fully aware that it is an essential aspect of the religious consciousness. He explained that religion in its traditional formulation encompassed all fields of knowledge and thus overextended itself. The modern scientific spirit was pervasive and religion seemed increasingly limited. Yet he hoped that modern men and women would regain the sense of the mystery and see it as obviously compatible with the rational and the scientific: "Religion will be restored to its rights. It will once again react naturally to the supernatural and will find truer and more apt analogies to answer to the deepening sense of mystery."

That Kaplan appreciated the mystical should come as no surprise. A rationalist who craved a religion that was understandable, he was at the same time keenly aware of the mystical tradition and felt there were aspects of it that he could embrace. Needless to say, he could not relate to any mysticism that involved superstition or magic. Nonetheless, there was a kind of religion, which he called saintly mysticism, "which is the state of mind attained through a sense of divine presence and which gives rise to various emotional experiences from serenity to ecstasy and to actions testifying to such experiences. The psalmists, the saints and the ascetics manifest this type of mysticism. It is this type which we should mean and aim for in public worship and private devotions."[34]

Kaplan also took a traditional stand on the matter of immanence and transcendence. Traditionally, God as transcendent is unknowable, but God as immanent is knowable. Kaplan believed that "through his attributes [God] is immanent. The ethical implications of religion are derived from God as immanent." At times, he viewed the matter historically, emphasizing that although both conceptions (transcendence and immanence) are present in all periods of Jewish history, one sometimes dominates the other. In the present era, the doctrine of God's immanence predominates. Kaplan believed that there was development in our knowledge of God as there is development in our knowledge of the world, and "with the progress of time, God comes to be better known and better understood."[35]

The rabbinic use of the concept of the *Shekhinah* (divine presence) was important to Kaplan. "The term *Shekhinah*," he once wrote, "implies that God is not aloof from human life with all its defeats and triumphs but that he is in the very midst of it." He believed that the rabbis saw God not only as immanent insofar as Israel was concerned but as present for all mankind as well: "they say that when a man suffers for his sin, the *Shekhinah* cries out, 'Oh my head, oh my arms.' The *Shekhinah* thus moves from Israel to all humanity."[36]

Kaplan's ease in the use of traditional language was particularly evident in his sermons. Sometimes he was the modern thinker, attempting to reinterpret some classical notion; but frequently in the same sermon he switched to a traditional point of view. In one particular sermon, for example, he reinterpreted the concept of the *Shekhinah* and then reverted to completely traditional language. He ended with a conventional reference to God as having gone into the Diaspora with the Jewish people and voiced his hope for God's return: "Thus may the *Shekhinah* which has ever been with us in the *Galut* return with us to the land where it first revealed itself."

Kaplan moved easily back and forth between traditional and contemporary formulations and felt no conflict between them. Regarding God as subject, he seemed unable to convince himself that man was the highest form of consciousness in the universe—an implication that would clearly follow from a strictly adjectival or predicate theology. Thus, he wrote a few years before the appearance of *Judaism as a Civilization*, "It cannot be that the universe as a whole is a blind mechanism whereas the infinitesimal being—man—has mind. We might as well believe that any cell of the body has more psychic energy than the entire body."[37]

His predicate theology and a numinous theology co-exist sometimes in the same written piece. In one diary entry, Kaplan talked about different aspects of the human mind and their connection to the religious experience: "God equals that aspect of mind which gives one the power to live." In such a functional definition, certainly a useful one, God has become transmuted into an aspect of the way the mind works. A few sentences later, however, comes a much more numinous sense of the divine. Relating to God as divine energy, Kaplan mused, "implications of modern conception of God, analogy of lightning and electricity. God manifest everywhere and at all times . . . God is manifest in different degrees, in different objects, persons and collectivities."[38]

Kaplan's later formulation, "the power that makes for salvation," seemed to be more of a theological axiom needed for his system than any kind of compelling reality. "Power *that*" instead of mere "power" is unnecessary reification. It would be preferable to use the concept of energy or life energy, as Kaplan does in the following statement where he suggests a fine sense of the numinous: "[Man's ability to triumph over evil] is spiritual and serves as a means of insight into the nature of the universal life compared with which our life is but an insignificant and passing moment." There seems to exist a large reservoir of life-giving energy that we can tap into if we could just lift ourselves high enough. In the same passage, he went on to say, "calling upon Him to help us is a means of calling into actuality whatever portion of that power is dormant within us."[39]

In *Judaism as a Civilization*, a whole chapter was devoted to what he called his functional method of interpretation. He gave many examples, among which is a very brief discussion of God's attribute of helper and protector: "God as helper and protector may be identified with the powers of nature which maintain life, and with the intelligence that transforms the environment by subjugating and controlling the natural forces for the common good of humanity." Here Kaplan seemed to be wholly the naturalist whose God has been completely absorbed into the forces of nature and into man's constructive energies. But a few years before he wrote his magnum opus, he worked on a full-length manuscript entitled "The Meaning of Religion" which is in a sense an extended treatise on the functional mode of interpretation. In this earlier manuscript, when he talked at length about God the helper, a very different sense emerged.[40]

In "The Meaning of Religion," he focused on the benevolent and life-giving energy that allowed human beings to exist in the first place and in addition lifted them to higher levels: "God is experienced as helper every time our thought of him furnishes us an escape from the sense of frustration and supplies us with a feeling of permanence in the midst of the universal flux." Part of viewing the world in a spiritual way leads us to focus on how people help one another in mutual nourishment and sustenance. Such cooperation is also a manifestation of God as helper, for "Cooperation is from the standpoint of the universe the functioning in the human soul of God's love or helpfulness." Kaplan was close to a predicate theology here but moved beyond its boundaries with the phrase "from the standpoint of the universe." Cooperation, then, is more than a human activity viewed from a human vantage point, for "benevolent energies are not confined to man" but are everywhere around us. One could argue that Kaplan was simply calling cooperation divine, but the following words are quite unambiguous: "to be at home in the world one must have a sense of security and permanence that only God as the absolute can give." Clearly a sense of security does not flow from predicates and adjectives.[41]

Unfortunately, Kaplan never spelled out what he meant by the absolute. If he failed to offer his readers a complete metaphysics, then so did Maimonides, who refused to talk about God's essence except in terms of what He was not. The *Kabbalah* is similarly blameworthy, seeing God in his aspect of *Ein Sof* (the infinite) as beyond our ken.

Contemporary students of Kaplan have tended to identify him with recent process theologians such as Charles Hartshorne and Alfred North Whitehead.[42] According to these thinkers, God ought to be understood not as a person or as an entity but as a process or processes within the universe. Kaplan began to talk in process terms quite early in his career. In a fragment from the 1920s, contemplating the Tabernacle, the *Shekhinah*, and holiness in general, he mused on "the recognition of the ultimate unresolvable element. [Mystic.] The will to divine presence and manifestation — God as process and not as static structure, as character of the universe in operation and not as entity."[43]

Ironically, Kaplan's profound spirituality was rarely appreciated. Indeed, he was even accused of contributing toward the secularization of the Jewish community. This accusation obviously distressed him, for in the introduction to *Judaism in Transition*, published in 1936, he called attention to it and tried to refute it. "The main misunderstanding," he said, "is that it [his book and the concept of Judaism as a civilization] reduces Judaism to a secular culture." Of course, the charge of secularization is an old one insofar as liberal Jewish thinkers are concerned. In the nineteenth century, it was consistently leveled against the early reformers. Yet the reformers helped to retain those Jews who were on the fringe and who would otherwise have assimilated. The same was true of Kaplan. He always appealed more to those disaffected but searching for some way to relate to their Jewishness. He had only one purpose. "Our object will be attained," he once wrote, "if these studies will set the reader on the road to seeking God. To very few it is given actually to find God. All that we need do, all that can be expected from us is that we should continually be in search of God, and not allow a day to pass without pondering on the mystery of life and the duty of man — 'Seek me and live.'"[44]

7

A NEW DENOMINATION:

The Society for Jewish Renascence

There was no Rabbinical Assembly when Mordecai Kaplan entered the Jewish Theological Seminary faculty; the alumni of the Rabbinical School convened both formally and informally.[1] In those early years, the Seminary Alumni Association functioned as a kind of proto-Rabbinical Assembly. Kaplan, ever active, was always ready to meet with his rabbinical colleagues and former students to discuss his ideas for solving the problems of American Jewry. It was at the Seminary Alumni Association that he delivered his 1909 speech "Nationalism as a Religious Creed," which so impressed Schechter.

Many of the younger graduates were excited by him. He offered them an ideological alternative to Reform Judaism. Rabbi Herman H. Rubenovitz wrote to his friend Charles Hoffman of Newark: "The only vital force able to fight a barren inane universalism is Jewish nationalism. There can be no doubt that Jewish nationalism as . . . the latest manifestation of the Jewish vital force or life power, will exert a powerful influence over the course of Jewish thought and in this way determine the form of Jewish dogma. To this extent I am in agreement with Dr. Kaplan."[2] In 1912, at Tannersville, Kaplan addressed the alumni concerning "Tradition and the Bible" and was daring enough to accept the conclusions of biblical criticism while attempting to rethink the basis of the authority of the Torah. Kaplan served on the executive committee of the Alumni Association and in August 1914 was instrumental in assembling a group in Long Branch, New Jersey, for three days of meetings.

He organized this conference with his younger colleague and friend Rubenovitz. About fifteen attended, including Rabbi Charles I. Hoffman, the president of the alumni; C. H. Kauvar; Julius Greenstone; and Jacob Kohn. Kaplan felt that these men were ready "to take up the theoretical [religious] problems at once," whereas the other rabbis were not. In the 1920s, the more radical wing of the Seminary alumni would rally directly around Kaplan, but even in this early period his leadership was vital.

Several younger rabbis spoke first, exploring a fundamental question that faced all those who were willing to reform or discard Jewish laws: What principle should be used for preserving some commandments while dismissing others? Kaplan emphasized reason and experience while at the same time attempting to shift the focus of the discussion. He asserted that the essence of Judaism did not reside in one belief or another, or even in the performance of all the commandments, but in the psychosocial energy of the Jewish people:

> The dynamic force in Judaism is none other than the socio-psychic vitality of the Jewish people. The problem, therefore, cannot be reduced to a question of preserving certain abstract concepts whether they belong to the past or the present. Our only concern is that the Jewish people be worthy of being Israel. . . . The Reconstruction of Judaism on the basis of natural human experience within reach of every one of us is not carried out to its legitimate length because we have so little confidence in human reason and experience. The fear is analogous to that entertained by those who have ever opposed the democratic form of government.[3]

As yet undetermined was whether the Seminary leaders had the courage to initiate the reconstruction of Judaism that Kaplan envisioned. One reason of the Seminary's attitude toward change related to the matter of Jewish law, its status, and the possibilities for reform. Not long after the formation of the United Synagogue in 1913, a committee headed by Louis Ginzberg recommended that a standing committee on Jewish law be included within its framework. The debate at the United Synagogue Convention in 1918 is instructive because clearly most of those assembled wanted only an advisory committee rather than a stronger "authoritative council" which would initiate substantive change. Ginzberg believed that the United Synagogue (and perhaps the American Jewish community as well) was too diverse for substantive changes in the *Halakhah*. The committee was set up to be reactive. It would not initiate change but would only respond to questions from

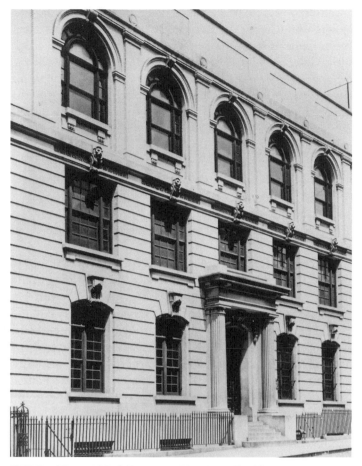

JTS Building, 123rd Street, 1903–1929. Building constructed by Jacob Schiff. (Courtesy Library of JTS.)

rabbis in the field. Kaplan, on the other hand, voiced his conviction that steps should be taken toward the establishment of a genuine rabbinical court at the Seminary.[4]

The restiveness among some of the younger rabbis was very deep and palpable. Kohn and Rubenovitz came to Kaplan in December 1918 to discuss establishing a new party within the American Jewish community — a third party, as they called it. Neither the United Synagogue nor the Seminary seemed to offer a definite ideology. These young rabbis were not thinking in terms of a departure from Conservative Judaism but rather of providing the Conservative movement with shape and direction. They seemed to vacillate between hoping the United Synagogue could serve as the vehicle for the third party and fearing that the organization would remain a mixed group with a primarily Orthodox character. Until late into the 1920s, the popular image of the United Synagogue remained essentially Orthodox. In 1929, for example, a former congregant of Rubenovitz who was then on the board of another synagogue asked him for help in formulating a definition of Conservative Judaism for a new charter: "although I understand and appreciate the fact that the United Synagogue of America has aligned itself with Orthodox Judaism, I cannot, as a layman, fail to take notice of the fact that many of its members are Conservative congregations." Shouldn't it be the task of the United Synagogue, the writer asked, to formulate a definition of Conservative Judaism? If not, then the Conservative synagogues needed to get together and establish an organization of their own.[5]

Kaplan's reaction to the proposal for a new party is startling. He was very excited about the idea but paradoxically was unwilling to do anything to initiate it. "Nothing could be more in accord with my wishes than to organize those who take their Judaism seriously enough to demand of it that it satisfy their spiritual yearnings." Yet at the same time he was honest enough with himself to write, "I must admit that I am too dogmatic in my way and unless I could carry out my wishes to the full, I would not be satisfied. . . . If I am to launch out on a spiritual adventure, I do not want to be hampered by a sense of yielding and compromise."[6] He desired above all to remain in his own world — the "universe of words," where he could devote himself undisturbed to formulating his goals.

Jacob Kohn admired his colleague but was aware of his weaknesses: "It is not yet certain to my mind, that Kaplan with his peculiar mixture of theoretical radicalism and practical inertia, will actually help to initiate our movement." Kohn pinpointed one of Kaplan's fundamental problems, especially in regard to the Seminary. Kaplan never hesitated to strike a radical stance, but was reluctant to take any action that would have led to a separate denomination and to abandonment of the Seminary.

But Kaplan was always exciting. Barely a month after his remark doubting Kaplan's helpfulness, Kohn heard him speak at the Menorah convention and was overwhelmed by the lecture: "I was not quite prepared, however, for the really sweeping statement he made. He embodied our whole program in the paper he read and anyone who heard him could be left in no doubt as to his intention of leading a new alignment with a theoretic and a practical program that would differentiate it both from Orthodoxy and from Reform." The students at the Seminary and the alumni were all talking about the speech; one can sense the excitement and electricity from Kohn's letter.[7]

The following months, April and May 1919, were filled with activity that bore fruit. On June 9, 1919, the six (Kaplan, Israel Friedlaender, Julius Greenstone, Jacob Kohn, Max Margolis and Rubenovitz) called for a meeting to be held at the Seminary, to consider the fundamental issues facing the Jewish people. They would "state frankly what we believe in and what we believe as authoritative in Jewish practice." They believed that "no good can come to Judaism either from a petrified traditionalism or from individualistic liberalism." Although the invitation letter never mentioned the establishment of a new denomination, this was clearly implied.

Louis Ginzberg received the letter, as did the other members of the Seminary faculty, the alumni, and the students in the Rabbinical School. Henrietta Szold also received an invitation and attended the initial meeting. Ginzberg was not only a member of the faculty but also head of the institution, operating in Adler's place while he, the acting president, was at the Paris Peace Treaty Conferences. A few days after receipt of the letter, Ginzberg wrote to Kaplan telling him that the meeting could not be held at the Seminary because that would amount to an endorsement of the proceedings. Kaplan and his group decided to hold the meetings at the 92nd Street Y.[8]

The day before Ginzberg received the June 9 letter, both he and Kaplan addressed the graduates of the Seminary at the commencement exercises. As if to presage the many debates to come before the Rabbinical Assembly in the late 1920s and afterward, Kaplan and Ginzberg seemed to be talking as much to each other as to the graduates. "Hold fast to your faith," Ginzberg told the graduates, and don't be "tossed by every wind of religious thought." Answering the letter of June 9 before he even received it, Ginzberg addressed himself directly to the topic of denominationalism: "Your faith in Israel must be strong enough to raise you above the narrow confines of partisanship . . . you are graduates of the Jewish Theological Seminary without any tag attached to it."

Kaplan, on the other hand, urged the young rabbis to teach Judaism in a vital fashion, and he called for a new formulation of that Judaism. He declared, "the theology of Schechter . . . is already in need of further development and application. I trust therefore that you will not shirk the duty of contributing toward a clearer point of view in Judaism than has yet been formulated."[9]

Most of the details of the meeting at the 92nd Street Y are lost, but a few very important remnants have been preserved. Kaplan's speech at the Y was eventually published in the *Menorah Journal*. In addition, there exists a description of Friedlaender's reactions, written many years later but going to the heart of the issue. One participant reports, "[We] all waited to hear what Dr. F. would say. Dr. F. pointed out that never before in our history, had any group come together to make changes in Jewish life and observance. You cannot, he said, say to the Jewish people, in the name of a small group of experts, this you should do and this you should not do basing your decision on what you as experts believe times demand." [10]

The whole incident is very revealing. The six who signed the letter were at the center of Seminary life, not some fringe group of the radical left. Kohn and Rubenovitz were both key figures in the founding of the United Synagogue, and Julius Greenstone also was active though he lived in Philadelphia. The lines were obviously drawn between those who wanted to move in the direction of a third party and those who did not. On the one side stood the signers of the letter and their supporters; on the other were Ginzberg, Adler, and Marx, all of whom were concerned to avoid schism at all costs. They did not perceive themselves as members of a distinct denomination and thought such self-perception divisive. Most of those attending the conference stood somewhere in the middle, believing in the need for change yet opposed to starting a new party. Kaplan ultimately sided with his colleagues on the faculty against his own position on the matter of schism. Above all else, he wanted to help unify, not divide, the Jewish community. Consequently, from 1919 on, he was continually putting brakes on his followers when they argued for independence. He also knew that once he moved out of the realm of mere talk, he would lose control of events and would be forced to compromise. As long as his primary activity was the formulation of an ideology, there was no need for him to compromise. He was willing to speak out but reluctant to enter the sphere of action.

Almost a year passed before the group reconvened, this time at the Jewish Center on West Eighty-sixth Street. They had appointed a subcommittee to draw up a series of propositions that would be the basis of a program to keep Judaism in America in harmony with the tradition but at the same time would reflect the needs of modern life. At the second series of meetings, they decided to constitute themselves into an organization called the Society for Jewish Renascence (SJR), with Kaplan as its president. The main figures were all active in Seminary affairs, although only Kaplan was a member of the faculty. Jacob Kohn, Eugene Kohn, Max Kadushin, Solomon Goldman, Paul Chertoff, and a young recent Seminary graduate named Louis Finkelstein attended regularly. Max Margolis, a Bible scholar who taught at Dropsie College in Philadelphia, was the most important outside figure. [11]

Deliberations began with tentative formulations of the shared beliefs that bound them together and which would stand as the foundation of their advocacy. Some felt they should not formulate a binding creed (Finkelstein) while others felt that the elements of such a creed should be held to a bare minimum, such as belief in God as the "Conservor of Values" (J. Kohn). Kaplan maintained that those who could not assent to a majority theological formulation ought to be asked to withdraw. Paul Chertoff, a recent Seminary graduate, helped put matters in focus. After much wrangling about a possible theological statement, he made an obvious point: what the group primarily desired was to "show that Judaism has meaning." It was not really necessary to spell out particulars about God or revelation. These might be better left to the individual. Kaplan strongly disagreed, believing that a strong theological statement was necessary. "We want the idea of God to function," he told his friends and former students, and this couldn't be done with some kind of empty theological statement. For Kaplan, the God idea was essential: "we cannot as Jews work together without the God idea." Theological disagreement on fine points, however, had always existed among Jews and had not prevented them from working together. Kaplan was wrong and somewhat overbearing here, but he was telling about himself, expressing his passion for clarity and precision in theological matters. For him, the formulation was always the key. The belief that Kaplan gave up God easily and early is erroneous. The truth is that he continued throughout his life to formulate, refine, and wrestle with his belief in God.

There were, obviously, theological differences within the group, and it was decided, as Chertoff suggested, to avoid any theological statement. The principles approved by the conference certainly represent the commonly held beliefs of most people associated with the Seminary and with the United Synagogue at the time:

1. We believe in the continuance of the Jewish people as a distinct group with a religious culture of its own in the lands of the Diaspora.

2. We reaffirm the abiding need for humanity of faith in God because we hold that whatever else the belief in God means, it denotes the belief in the dignity and sacredness of human life, in the reality and worth of human progress and in the ultimate establishment of freedom, justice and truth.

The third principle had two formulations; the difference between the two is important. The first formulation was brought by the committee and emphasized the preeminence of scripture. The second and final resolution was adopted by the conference as the platform of the SJR. It also mentioned scripture but pointed rather to the total spiritual experience of the Jewish people as the key source of values. The first formulation was more traditional than the second despite the fact that Kaplan and his young radical supporters (Rubenovitz and Kadushin) were all on the committee.

> 3. A [from the Committee] — We accept the spiritual experiences of the Jewish people recorded in scriptures as the principle Revelation of the Divine. [Kaplan was on this committee.]

> B [as passed by the conference] — We accept the spiritual experiences of the Jewish people from the earliest days to the present as the Revelation of the Divine recognizing the basic character of the experiences recorded in scripture.[12]

Kaplan's remarks in these discussions again and again hammer at the principle that the essence of belief in God is not thought but experience. At one point, he emphasized the important distinction between the holy text and the experiences it records. "My idea is that we should not deal at this point at all with the literary expression of Revelation but simply with the fact that we understand that God reveals himself in actual events, in experiences, spiritual experiences or inner experiences."

Throughout these discussions, Finkelstein talked little and listened much. What he did say was not very impressive. He later regretted his involvement with SJR. "It was only out of respect for you" he wrote Kaplan, "and because of our relations that I joined the Renascence. You will remember how I tried to avoid joining it or coming to its first meeting. I never forgave myself for that act, which once done had to be followed by more compromises with myself. I do not intend to commit such an error again."

The SJR group sometimes expressed a strong universalism as when they adopted a resolution stating that they viewed the Divine revealed in the experiences of all humankind. At the same time, the group was quite clearly Zionist. In talking about divine revelation and the experiences of the Jews, Kaplan, although avoiding the Chosen People concept, asserted his belief that the Jews were unique: "We believe such revelation to have taken place in the experiences of Israel throughout its history to a degree unparalleled by any other people. If I had not believed this, I would have devoted myself to the American people."

Although most of the participants were graduates of the Seminary or otherwise connected to it, they did not regard the Seminary as the primary agency for a third movement. Everyone seemed to agree that the Seminary by its charter did not represent a particular philosophy. The commitment of the Seminary was to be noncommitted. According to Max Margolis, "there is nothing in the original constitution that says it is Orthodox or anything. You will be met by the answer that the Seminary is noncommittal and will remain noncommittal." Kaplan understood the inertia of the Seminary; to a degree, he suffered from it himself. At the same time, he and others at the meeting hoped for change and believed, however unrealistically, that the faculty might accede to their proposals. Margolis thought the Seminary should declare itself a third party, but such a declaration did not appear feasible to most in the group. The problem these young men faced, including Kaplan, was that the Seminary, however inadequate as the center of a third denomination, was still a going concern. They did not want to destroy the "parent" that had given birth to them as rabbis.

Herman Rubenovitz, speaking in favor of forming a separate denomination, made the obvious point that "what we are doing the minute we organize is organizing a third party." But Kaplan took strong exception to "going denominational." "I do not think we ought to in any way create what appears as a divisive influence," he told the group. In September 1920, he wrote to Elias Solomon, the president of the United Synagogue, about the new organization, going out of his way to emphasize that it was no threat to the Seminary. A few months later, at a meeting of the executive committee of the SJR, Kaplan made a rather amazing statement which rendered the organization completely and absolutely innocuous. He told his executive committee, "I believe you are all cognizant of the fact that we are primarily an organization to further Jewish study and to popularize Jewish study and to make Jewish study an essential aspect of Jewish life. Personally, I consider it our main function." The committee then discussed the suggestion that the rabbis of the group could organize Bible study groups in the spirit of the SJR. But, as Paul Chertoff pointed out, there was nothing particularly new in a rabbi organizing a study group. This kind of proposal accounts for the fact that the SJR, which had started out with great hopes, ended up doing virtually nothing — and Kaplan was largely responsible.[13]

Many were critical of the new organization, of Kaplan, and of the direction in which the Conservative rabbis were going. The first criticism arose from within the organization itself. Jacob Kohn resented the characterless aspect of the Seminary and its lack of direction but was not ready to endorse Kaplan; moreover, Kaplan really didn't seem to be moving anywhere. "Kaplan, as I always thought he would, has proven himself a broken reed. For purposes of harmonious action, I was willing to accept what was preeminently his formulation of our position. I neither share his ponderous immobility in the sphere of Jewish life nor his revolutionary audacity in the sphere of Jewish thought. I do not believe that pragmatism introduces a new era in religious thinking. The Renascence Society as a harmless study group has my approval but cannot command my enthusiasm." [14]

Some of Kaplan's colleagues objected to the nationalist thrust of the society's platform. Kaplan's old friend and faithful critic Julius Greenstone wrote him, "I am unable to agree to the philosophy underlying the platform which places Israel before God, making the idea of God dependent on the conception of him by the people." Some liberal critics seemed to resent Kaplan's easy equation of Zionism with Judaism. Non-Zionists who were also not Reform Jews might have been interested in joining Kaplan. Louis Finkelstein in an interview hinted that contending factions within the society and internal conflict led to the organization's demise.[15] But whatever caused the failure of the Society for Jewish Renascence, Mordecai Kaplan himself was a major part of the trouble.

Nonetheless, Kaplan's preeminence as an ideologue is forcefully illustrated throughout these proceedings. His thoughts clearly dominated the society. The paper he delivered in June 1919 at the opening of the proceedings eventually became a brilliant article in the 1920 summer issue of the *Menorah Journal*. The article was a clarion call to the broad mass of American Jews to embrace a program that would suit their new situation in twentieth-century America. This article, viewed by some as the beginning of Reconstructionism, nevertheless must be understood within the context of its time as an attempt to bring clarity and organization to the Conservative movement. It was primarily a call for the Conservative movement to organize itself.

Kaplan's argument was unambiguous: neither Orthodoxy nor Reform was adequate to ensuring the continued existence of the Jewish people. Orthodoxy would fail because it could not keep pace with the times and stifled creative change: "It precludes all conscious development in thought and practice, and deprives Judaism of the power to survive in an environment that permits of free contact with non-Jewish civilizations." One might think that Reform allowed for creative interaction and evolution in a modern critical vein. But Reform was likewise inadequate, Kaplan asserted. It is "merely a negation of Judaism" and has "as little in common with historic Judaism as has Christianity or Ethical Culture." Reform had shifted Judaism's emphasis to the individual Jew and completely neglected the communal aspects of the Jewish past and the Jewish future.[16]

The solution begins, according to Kaplan, with the Zionist perspective. Ahad Ha-Am had shown the way in which a revitalized Jewry would be the concomitant of any political salvation in Palestine. Reestablishment of the Jewish people would be meaningless unless it was accompanied by the resurrection of the spiritual life of the Jewish people, and this could not wait for developments in the *Yishuv* (the settlement in Palestine). Restoration required a fundamental change in the way Jews related to their religious life. In Kaplan's stirring words:

> We are faced with a problem no less than that of transforming the very mind and heart of the Jewish people. Unless its mythological ideas about God give way to the conception of divinity immanent in the workings of the human spirit, unless its static view of authority gives way to the dynamic without succumbing to individual lawlessness, and unless it is capable of developing a sense of history without, at the same time, being a slave to the past, the Jewish people has nothing further to contribute to civilization.[17]

Transforming Judaism entailed an alteration in the concept of religion in general. Usually we conceive of religion as a body of ideas about the world, the afterlife, or the meaning of existence. Kaplan proposed a shift from the ideational to the social realities. The "social viewpoint" required a shift in the "center of spiritual interest from the realm of abstract dogmas and traditional codes of law to the pulsating life of Israel. We will then realize that our problem is not how to maintain beliefs or uphold laws, but how to enable the Jewish people to function as a highly developed social organism and to fulfill the spiritual powers that are latent in it."[18] Whatever will not advance the revitalization of the Jewish people must be changed. Or, conversely: whatever contributes to Jewish renascence, whether it be the Hebrew language, upbuilding the *Yishuv*, or efforts at Jewish defense on the political scene, must be viewed positively as a part of the total life or civilization of the Jewish people.

Kaplan envisioned a three-point program. First, it was necessary to reinterpret the Jewish tradition in modern terms. Second, Jewish solidarity must be fostered through building the community in Palestine and establishing stronger communities (*kehillahs*) in the Diaspora. Third, a new code of Jewish practice must be formulated.

Kaplan's ambivalence about denominationalism was nowhere clearer than in this essay. On the one hand, he would have the reader believe that individuals had only to think in a new way in order to organize in a new way: "The achievement of our purpose will be facilitated if our initial activities identify us in people's minds as a new school of thought in Judaism, rather than as a new brand of Judaism." And he concluded that "to carry out the aims of such a program, we have to call into existence a type of organization that is new in Jewish life. We should not constitute ourselves a third party in Judaism. There is already enough fragmentation and division among us without creating a new sect in Jewry." On the other hand, in discussing the conduct of the individual Jew, he unfolded a set of proposals that were clearly denominational. He spoke about laws of personal conduct that any Jew of any persuasion would certainly accept, but then he continued to call for changes in the ceremonial observances. With regard to the prayers, for example, he stated that "not only are its contents and length entirely out of keeping with the requirements of present day life, but there are parts in it which have been made entirely obsolete by changes in social conditions and in the intellectual point of view." Without explicitly advocating the elimination of the second day of festivals, for instance, he mentioned such an alteration as a serious consideration which, however, ought to be put off until a coherent justification could be worked out. He also considered the idea of moving the Sabbath to Sunday, but he never stated this in print. In December 1919, he discussed the matter with a visitor and recorded the meeting in his journal: "I suggested that if Judaism is to survive in the Diaspora it must abandon its uncompromising attitude toward the Sabbath and by an act of will adopt Sunday as the Seventh Day." [19]

To the many young men and women of college age who read the *Menorah Journal* and were unable to reconcile their secular American education with their traditional background, Kaplan's analysis came as an inspiration. His approach showed the children of the immigrants that Judaism could stand up under the most rigorous scientific scrutiny and emerge stronger and more appealing because of this new analysis.

It is not surprising that the Orthodox reacted quickly to the article and condemned Kaplan in very strong terms. At a meeting of the *Agudath Ha-Rabbonim*, the Orthodox Rabbinical Union, some sixty rabbis listened to speeches that denounced the "half-Orthodox" and the SJR platform as poisonous to innocent Jews who were not fully aware of Kaplan's goals. [20] Kaplan had made it clear that he did not depart from Orthodox practice. The rabbis saw him as a wolf in sheep's clothing who, because of his position, was much more dangerous than any Reform or secular Jew. As Bernard Drachman, the past president of the Union of Orthodox Jewish Congregations and Kaplan's former teacher at the Old Seminary, put it, "These views would have been bad enough coming from the lips of an avowed representative of radical Reform but emanating as they do from one who holds a high position on the faculty of a Theological Seminary which declares that it stands on the platform of Orthodox Judaism and who is spiritual guide of an Orthodox congregation [the Jewish Center], they are amazing and disconcerting in the highest degree."[21]

Kaplan was also charged with reducing religion to nationalism. Leo Jung, a leader of neo-Orthodoxy and after 1922 rabbi of the Jewish Center, believed that Kaplanism reduced the Jews to the level of the "Eskimos, Poles and Magyars." The Jews would become one nation among many, albeit with wonderful capacities. Jung believed that nationalism plus Reform was the essence of Kaplanism and the most dangerous threat to Orthodoxy. He did not deny that Orthodoxy was in trouble and indeed felt the Orthodox were indebted to Kaplan, who by his threat helped to whip the remnant of Israel back into shape. "The only answer to Kaplanism," Jung asserted, "is the immediate convention of a living Orthodox body to work out a systematic educational scheme for the reassertion of Orthodoxy, absolutely faithful in principle, absolutely fresh in method."[22]

Some emphasized the naturalistic tendency of Kaplan's thought as the most serious element in his heterodoxy. Drachman maintained that according to Kaplanism there could be no such thing as divine revelation in any real sense and that to Kaplan Judaism would become a purely "worldly, national and social system."[23] Needless to say, these Orthodox leaders presented Kaplan's ideas with considerable distortion. Kaplan, without trying to answer specific allegations, wrote in the *Morgen Journal* (in Hebrew, though it was a Yiddish newspaper) that he had no intention of undermining the beliefs of young Orthodox Jews but was only interested in those who were indifferent to Judaism because of their secular education. Rather defensively, he asserted: "The Torah and the Jewish religion are dear to me and my associates no less than they are to the assembled rabbis who condemn me before bringing me to judgment."[24]

◆

It is difficult to understand how Kaplan thought he could condemn Orthodoxy as vehemently as he did in his *Menorah* article without creating havoc at the Jewish Center. The article turned out to be the last and most serious in a succession of problems that ultimately led to his exodus from the center.

His troubles commenced with remarks regarding ethics in the workplace which he continually made from the pulpit. Genuine concern for the worker is not enough by itself, he said, for it might still lead the misguided to benevolent despotism over those whom they control. A real relationship of respect, however, involved "giving the employee a share in the management, since it is only through having a share in the management that he can exercise his right to be responsible. This may be considered poor economics, but it surely is good religion, and religion is not satisfied with prayers. It also means business."[25]

Kaplan was not afraid to condemn economic injustice even though it seemed to put him at odds with the many center members who were successful businessmen. His sentiments on economic questions were made abundantly clear in a Passover sermon he delivered in 1919. He saw the two social systems (capitalism and socialism) in moral conflict — one based on competition and one based on cooperation. Those who believe in the virtues of competition do so, he said, not because they think it will call forth the best in people but because they profit from the process. He spoke of the "moral bankruptcy of the competitive system" and advocated the minimum wage, health insurance, and the five-day week. With such sermons, and considering the times, it should not be surprising that some of his congregants began calling Kaplan a Bolshevik. He was never one to shrink from a fight and went so far as to use the term *Bolshevik* in reference to the prophets. On one occasion, he talked from the pulpit of Amos as "the wide-eyed preacher" and "this radical Bolshevist." He did not hesitate to attack the evils of wealth and told his followers that "power and luxury are the very antithesis of the spiritual."[26]

Kaplan's identification with the working classes was very strong. At times he attempted to be even-handed and critical of the Bolsheviks, for this was the time of the "Red scare," and many were afraid the revolution would come to America; he was not emotionally detached from the issue. In a sermon entitled "Democracy vs. Bolshevism," he condemned the Bolsheviks for seeking to abolish the distinctions between man and beast. But a few years later (1924), looking over the text of this sermon, he penciled in the following remark in the margin: "As I read these lines, I feel ashamed to think that I allowed myself to be bamboozled by the journalists, preachers and other white collar slaves who were engaged in fighting their masters' battle against Bolshevism." While Kaplan was proudly calling the prophets Bolsheviks, others such as Rabbi Herbert Goldstein were preaching on "the crime of radicalism."[27]

One very practical issue of the day involved the five-day workweek. Many unions went on strike demanding that the workweek be reduced and standardized at forty-four hours. Kaplan and observant Jews supported the five-day week. Sunday blue laws were still in force, and Jewish Sabbath observers were severely penalized in the workplace. Kaplan, in a rare activist mood, arranged for a meeting of leading Jewish manufacturers in order to discuss the issue. Jacob Schiff was scheduled to speak but never came. Magnes and Kaplan addressed the group, and Kaplan was surprised that there was relatively little opposition at the meeting to the idea of a five-day workweek.[28]

Kaplan's whole attitude toward wealth was anomalous, because the concept and the facilities of the center assumed support by wealthy people. In his journal, he continually ridiculed his congregants for their vanity and materialism, yet he was unquestionably proud of the ten-story building completed in the summer of 1920. The poor masses of Jews on the Lower East Side had neither the time nor the resources to develop their "Judaism as a living civilization." Kaplan needed his wealthy congregants, but he never ceased to regard them with contempt: "The men are busy making money and the women spending it, and they have no taste for the intangible realities which the Center is to further." In 1941, he noted that Professor Louis Ginzberg of the Seminary faculty attacked him for producing a Judaism only for manufacturers. He did not mind being called names, but he pondered whether such diatribes would allow people to dismiss his views without really thinking about them. He thought about a statement by George Bernard Shaw, who said that "under the present system clergymen are nothing but chaplains of pirate ships," to which Kaplan replied, "Precisely so; and what ships have a greater need for chaplains."[29]

Judging from Kaplan's journals, there evidently were some quite vulgar people in the congregation. One board member who always seemed to find fault with the building was scheduled to celebrate his son's bar mitzvah. He had planned to conduct it out of town, but William Fischman, a key member of the board and later president, induced him to hold the ceremony at the center. Sabbath morning came, and he didn't show up until the honors of the Torah reading were half finished. On another occasion, the high holidays came early in September, and Kaplan and the board were afraid that many members would remain at the shore and not return. A meeting was called at Far Rockaway to make plans for getting members to come back to the city in time for Rosh Hashanah.[30]

Kaplan's persistent harping on economics took its toll with the congregation, and when the opportunity came his opponents grabbed it. Undoubtedly his general views on religion formed what might be called the necessary condition for his leaving the center, but the alienation caused by his strong stand on economic questions was certainly the sufficient condition. Joseph Cohen, like an angry father, remarked in the spring of 1921, when things were coming to a head: "You wrung our hearts every time you spoke on the industrial question. If you had taken my advice to gather around you a sort of cabinet you would have refrained from saying and doing many of the things that should not have been done."

Kaplan's exodus from the center was partly a consequence of his growing career. No longer was it possible for him to be identified with traditional Judaism. His views had been evolving over the previous decade, but it was not until 1920 and his *Menorah* article that he finally took a clear and irrevocable stand against traditional Judaism. After his father's death, Kaplan found it easier to publish his criticisms of Orthodox Judaism. It is true that he had been open and aboveboard with the center leaders and that at their retreat in Tannersville during the summer of 1917 he had explained his philosophy fully. They had also heard him preach every Sabbath in the synagogue for a number of years. However, the sermons were by no means theologically radical, and in any case he had never attacked Orthodoxy from the pulpit. His article in the *Menorah Journal* provoked immediate reactions from the Orthodox community. Even his mother got into the act, telling him: "change — give up some of your ideas. You don't have too many followers, better try to work with Cohen again because the Center will suffer without you as well as without him. I hope my dear you will do the best as it is possible and God shall bless you that you shall live a long and happy life and then you will make happy all of us."[31]

Kaplan attempted to explain himself to his congregation. There was a strong show of support at one pivotal meeting. Judge Rosalsky, certainly the most respected member of the board, praised him highly, and as if to address his attackers, he said, "As much as you may strike him and the more that you stab him behind his back, the nearer will we be drawn to him." Sam Lamport, another strong Kaplan supporter, referred to him as "one of the finest and most erudite men in the American Rabbinate." The group, however, wanted to hear Kaplan himself, because the press was ascribing radical ideas to him and they sought reassurance. Kaplan attempted to be as conciliatory as possible while remaining honest: "I want to make clear to you that historical traditional Judaism is what I stand for and what I work for." He said that he was using the new weapons of psychology and social science to support old verities. Then he got down to some basic issues. Some people believed that he advocated doing away with the second days of holidays. He explained his position that the second day was not really necessary, but as long as the law (*Halakha*) was there, it must be obeyed. People had the right to express their dissatisfaction, however. He emphasized that his remarks were directed primarily at those who were having difficulties in their observances. To the person who observed two days and had no difficulty in doing so, he recommended no change. In essence, he said the same thing about the Sabbath. People should observe as much of the Sabbath as they can; one hundred percent if possible, but if not, then seventy-five percent. In other words, keep as much as you can. "If you must violate some of the Sabbath laws," he told the group, "don't feel that you have to overthrow the whole institution." Without disguising his beliefs, he hoped to heal the wounds he might have caused: "we all stand for a Hebrew Judaism, for a Torah Judaism and for a Zionist Judaism . . . we stand on tradition and history."[32]

Many meetings took place during the spring of 1921, both public and private. Kaplan was of two minds about the situation. On the one hand, he wanted to stay at almost any cost, because he genuinely believed that if he left, the center would not survive. He was willing to agree to almost any compromise no matter how unworkable it might seem on the surface. For example, at a number of meetings in May, an agreement was hammered out whereby the congregation and especially the school would be run according to strictly Orthodox principles but Kaplan would be free to say whatever he wanted from the pulpit. The issue of the school arose in connection with one of the pupils in Max Kadushin's class who had been instructed not to reveal to her family what she had been studying about the Bible and Mosaic authorship. Kaplan agreed that a committee would bet set up to supervise the school and ensure its Orthodoxy. In a moment of profound naïveté, he thought: "I hope that I am not compromising with myself nor with the principle of intellectual honesty by consenting to the appointment of a committee that would most likely render the instruction Orthodox. The people know my views and if they are liberal enough to tolerate me, why should I not be liberal enough to tolerate them."

At times, however, he admitted to himself that such solutions were clearly untenable and that the only path open to him was to leave the center. His friends and colleagues were supportive of his leaving. Herman Rubenovitz wrote him that "The Renaissance [Society for Jewish Renascence] movement demands that you free yourself from the trammels, which association with intolerant and bigoted men must of necessity impose upon you." Rubenovitz suggested that he and others would raise money so that a synagogue could be founded that would embody the principles Kaplan stood for. In late April 1921, Kaplan asked for a year's leave of absence so he could devote himself to his writing and scholarship.[33]

Joe Cohen, the central figure on the board, wanted the center to be Orthodox. It had become increasingly clear that Kaplan was not dependable in this regard. The board, however, was split. Many still supported their rabbi. On May 12, the board convened to consider Kaplan's request for a leave. A long harangue opened the meeting, with Cohen accusing Kaplan of trying to foist a new Judaism on the center. He referred to Kaplan's article in the *Menorah Journal* and to the Society for Jewish Renascence, both of which he said indicated that Kaplan had broken with Orthodox Judaism. Kaplan replied that he was ready to compromise and was willing to have the center run according to the *Shulhan Arukh*, but he would still be free to state and to teach his views, even if they proved to be unorthodox. A committee would be appointed by the board to supervise the school. Thus, Kaplan might preach heterodoxy from the pulpit, while at the same time the children would learn Orthodoxy in the school. After two hours of debate, Abe Rothstein stepped in and stressed that Kaplan had agreed to board supervision of the school; he proposed that Kaplan be reelected rabbi. There was some wrangling about the motion, with Unterberg and Rosalsky supporting it, and it carried. Kaplan's salary was to be twelve thousand dollars.[34]

The issues seemed settled; of course, they were not. In his heart, Kaplan knew that the compromise was unworkable, and he continued to think about leaving the center. The summer and the holidays came and went, and the maneuvering continued on both sides. By the end of the year, Kaplan had his fill and finally decided to resign. In his letter to Fischman, the president of the board, he stated that the board knew his approach to Judaism from the start, and Cohen especially "knew me as well as I know myself." He said he did not want to take any money: "I wanted my contribution to the Center to be a whole offering to God." He found himself "hampered at every turn by the Board of Trustees" and thus felt compelled to resign.[35]

Although some were happy to see Kaplan leave, his exodus together with about half the families at the center put the very existence of the institution in jeopardy. A few months after Kaplan left, Israel Unterberg, who had left with him, wrote to Ike Phillips, a member of the board, for a donation to some Jewish cause. Phillips, still smarting from the split, wrote a very angry response, revealing how the "other side" felt: "A number of gentlemen who are supposed to advance Judaism simply laid down on their contracts, laid down on their words, refused to pay dues and in so many words told the handful of men who were already overburdened with responsibilities to go to hell." It took many years before the center was again on solid financial ground. In 1931, the center reincorporated itself with a new charter stipulating that it would always be Orthodox unless ninety-five percent of the membership agreed that it be changed.[36]

The split at the center had reverberations outside the synagogue itself. It certainly meant a weakening of the liberal forces within the Orthodox community. There were many traditional Jews who in 1920 did not perceive the Seminary as representing a new denomination. For those who had supported the Seminary and perceived themselves as Orthodox, the whole situation was very uncomfortable. Apparently, a group of center members, sometime after Kaplan left, came to the Seminary and asked Cyrus Adler to fire Kaplan. They threatened to withdraw their financial support if Adler did not comply.[37]

The center experience is vital in understanding Kaplan the man as well as Kaplan the ideologue of American Jewry. The experience marked a turning point in his life, his final divorce from the traditional Jewish community. Perhaps he struggled to stay so long because on some level he knew that the break would be irreparable. There was no turning back. With the publication of his article in the *Menorah Journal* and his dismissal of Orthodoxy as a viable alternative in America, he had, as he put it, "crossed the Rubicon" of his career. He had incessantly lambasted his congregation on the economic injustices to which they were a party. His overt rejection of Orthodoxy in his 1920 article was the last straw. The *Menorah Journal* article, though published in 1920, was first offered in 1918 as a speech and was written the year before, a short time after Israel Kaplan's death.

That Kaplan lived on the level of his ideology and was rather inept politically was a strength and a weakness. We see this problem with the Society for Jewish Renascence as well as with the center. Because he was ambivalent about a new party, he ended up destroying the Renascence movement. He dominated the movement from beginning to end. The many meetings resulted only in the formulation of a set of principles, but these principles were provocative and helped to clarify the possible fundamental commitments of non-Orthodox Jewry.

The center started off with a great vision of genuine community. That vision still stands as a goal to be achieved. It broke new ground in showing what a synagogue could be in America. Yet it fell far short of what Kaplan himself could have accomplished there. It became the model for a host of centers built in the 1920s and 1930s which only began to promote an understanding of Kaplan's profound insight that people who only pray together do not really stay together on any significant level. Kaplan wanted a community, and he got a synagogue.

◆

Kaplan's experience at the center is significant in other respects. He is ordinarily credited by both his critics and his supporters with giving birth to the center concept. There were actually two kinds of centers, one with a synagogue at the hub and one that was secular and resembled, more than any other kind of institution, a Y. Most scholars consider him the ideological father of both types of institutions. Such an important contention warrants close examination.

In the case of the secular community centers, even strong supporters of Kaplan find it difficult to marshall hard facts about his contribution. In a tribute to Kaplan in the early 1950s, Louis Kraft, a longtime disciple, began an essay on Kaplan and the center movement by saying, almost apologetically, "that Dr. Kaplan at no time had an official role as a member of any of the governing bodies of [the Jewish Welfare] Board," the umbrella organization for Jewish community centers all over the United States. Kraft briefly discussed Kaplan's concept of the synagogue center and then went on at length to show that Kaplan supported the secular community center.[38] There is no doubt that Kaplan believed in the pluralism inherent in the community center and in the commitment to Jewish culture that these institutions represent. But particular ideological underpinnings are not essential to such developments. The Y movement long predates Kaplan and probably would have developed extensively after World War I in any event.

The Americanization of the synagogue was proceeding apace without special influence from any one individual. The immigrant synagogues proved insufficient to meet the needs of the younger generation. On the Lower East Side, the Young Israel offered lectures in English geared to attract the young and the unaffiliated. Uptown on the East Side, such synagogues as Kehilath Jeshurun went out of their way to lure an English-speaking rabbi. In Harlem, a large number of young rabbis were experimenting with late Friday-evening services, English sermons, and a greater decorum not usually associated with the Orthodox *shtibl.* Rabbi Henry Morais, the son of Sabato Morais, and others conducted thoroughly respectable services; the urge for respectability was perhaps the Jews' strongest social need at this point.[39]

The synagogue center was a logical extension of developments already present within the Jewish community. The orientation of the younger generation of New York rabbis led to an expanded synagogue that would include significant new activities in addition to the traditional educational and religious programs. Kaplan did not create the synagogue center trend but rather rode the crest of an already existing development. There were other institutions being created that were more appropriate to American Jewish life than the old-style European synagogues. If Kaplan had never lived, the synagogue center and the other institutions like it would have developed anyway.

One of the most interesting projects meant to serve the needs of the second generation was the Central Jewish Institute (CJI). This experiment combined a whole range of social and recreational activities with a school at the hub. The philosophy underlying the CJI is similar to the ideal put forth by Kaplan at the center, but the CJI was more the creation of Samson Benderly, the director of the Bureau of Jewish Education, Rabbi Herbert Goldstein, and Isaac Berkson than of Mordecai Kaplan. Yet Kaplan is usually credited with establishing the institution.

The CJI grew out of the establishment of the Talmud Torah, a kind of Hebrew school, at Kehilath Jeshurun. Although Kaplan was no longer rabbi at the congregation, the board continued to rely on him for advice concerning the enlargement of their Hebrew school. Many years of planning and fund-raising resulted in the construction of a new building next door to the congregation. Because of his long association with Kehilath Jeshurun and his splendid speaking ability, it was natural that Kaplan be invited to be the featured speaker at the cornerstone-laying ceremony in May 1915. Some three thousand invitations had been sent out, and a large crowd gathered at the site on East Eighty-fifth Street on a Sunday afternoon. M. S. Margolies, the rabbi at Kehilath Jeshurun, delivered the opening prayer but decided at the last minute to make a speech. The other speakers included Samuel Hyman and Marcus Marks, the president of the borough of Manhattan. Kaplan's speech was short but powerful. He addressed himself directly to the central problem of the modern period when freedom and opportunity had given Jews a completely new kind of life. He pointed out, however, that "business is so pressing, time is so scarce, pleasure is so abundant, that there seems to be no room left for Judaism." The only answer, he told his audience, is "to increase the spiritual power of the Jew that he shall not feel the burden that God has placed upon him." That power, he went on, can be increased only by increasing Jewish knowledge. "However, the Jew must not only have the power to think clearly, independently and spiritually, but he must also will nobly." Kaplan did not hesitate to emphasize also the special place the Jews held in the total scheme and that the idea of assimilation must be rejected.[40]

The building to house the Talmud Torah was completed in the course of the next year, and planning for the school proceeded apace. In the spring of 1916, Friedlaender, Benderly, and Kaplan were called in to make recommendations regarding a director for the institution. Kaplan was convinced that they had already settled on Goldstein, one of Kaplan's former students who had become rabbi at Kehilath Jeshurun, and that the consultation was just a formality. One important issue was raised at this time, however, that reflected Kaplan's goals and the direction of his Yorkville friends. The name of the school was changed from the Yorkville Talmud Torah to the Central Jewish Institute, indicating that it would be the meetingplace for all kinds of Jewish organizations in the city. Kaplan, however, believed in a close-knit community; he felt strongly that the institute should serve only the immediate neighborhood and not the Jewish community in general.

The formal dedication took place on May 21, 1916, with much solemnity and with Jacob Schiff at the center of the ceremonies. Herbert Goldstein, the new director, also emphasized the ideals of traditional Judaism and patriotism. Kaplan spoke at the dedication of the auditorium which had been endowed by his brother-in-law, Jacob Rubin. He again "warned against the possibility of this institution undertaking too much and reaching out over the city instead of confining itself to constructive intensive work within a certain area."[41]

The CJI was an original American creation. It offered classes for all ages, in addition to choral music, an orchestra, a gymnasium, folk dancing, an employment bureau, and public lectures on a wide range of topics. Kaplan's participation in the running of the CJI was peripheral. Though he was on the board during this period, he referred to himself as a "stationary director" who did relatively little. He spoke at the CJI from time to time, using the opportunity to formulate the principles that gave shape and purpose to the institution. This was his contribution. But the institution certainly would have grown and prospered without him.[42]

In the area of synagogue innovation, the Institutional Synagogue of Herbert Goldstein was almost an exact parallel to the Jewish Center which Kaplan helped to create. Kaplan, however, had nothing to do with the Institutional Synagogue, which began before the Jewish Center was established. The name derives from a Protestant experiment in the late nineteenth century called the Institutional Church. The YM/YWCA movement was so successful that a number of ministers, particularly in the New York area, conceived the idea that their churches could be expanded easily by opening their doors during the week for community leisure and recreational activities. Goldstein adopted this idea and advocated it publicly in connection with the synagogue as early as 1916: "My plea for the future is the Institutional Synagogue which would embrace the Synagogue, the Talmud Torah and the YMHA movements. . . . If we desire to perpetuate the real Judaism of the past, we must so shape Jewish spiritual activity that it will all find expression in one institution . . . instead of a man belonging to three separate institutions, he could pay a little higher membership in the Institutional Synagogue which would include all the advantages of the three separate institutions." [43]

In April 1917, for reasons never divulged, Goldstein resigned from Kehilath Jeshurun and the CJI for a rather uncertain future. He quickly became involved in two ventures, both Jewish adaptations of Christian modalities. The first was the revival. Goldstein was quite a forceful preacher and organized large rallies in the Harlem area. Meetings were held on Sundays, when even those who worked on the Sabbath could attend, and the Mt. Morris Theater was usually packed, sometimes with more than a thousand people. Goldstein also invited prominent public figures such as Nicholas Murray Butler to attend and to speak. [44]

Goldstein's second venture was the Institutional Synagogue. The synagogue was to be Orthodox but at the same time "high-class, clean and American. . . . There will be decorum at all times as well as a dignified reverential spiritual Orthodox service." The 1917 constitution of the Institutional Synagogue commits the corporation to a wide range of activities and concerns. "The objects and purposes of the corporation shall be to promote the religious, civic, moral, social and physical welfare of the Jewish youth and to maintain a school for the same purpose." Goldstein began his experiment in a brownstone on 116th Street, where he held regular services plus programs late on Friday evenings. These programs could best be described as an *Oneg Shabbat* with a speaker and refreshments. Goldstein attempted to combine a Y and a synagogue by the presence of a gymnasium consisting at first of little more than a bare room with a basketball hoop. There were also clubs, music groups, and eventually a pool. In the early 1920s, a Benny Leonard Club was devoted to the Jewish boxer who once appeared at the synagogue. [45]

This expanded synagogue center paralleled Kaplan's efforts but was not derived from him. It is easy to see that the synagogue center was a logical outgrowth of the YM/YWHA, the Central Jewish Institute, and the Institutional Church. Yet Herbert Goldstein is all but forgotten and Mordecai Kaplan lives on in the minds of many as the center movement's founder. The reason is that Kaplan, more than anyone else, gave eloquent expression to the center concept and placed it on the agenda of ultimate concerns. Kaplan himself inadvertently supported this hypothesis on the origins of the synagogue center: "Let us not characterize the Jewish Center as a Club, or as a synagogue with social attractions or as a Jewish analogue of an Institutional Church."[46]

8

THE WORLD AS CLASSROOM:
The Jewish Theological Seminary

Throughout the meetings of the Society for Jewish Renascence, Mordecai Kaplan's relationship with the Seminary surfaced as an obstacle. Both his supporters and those who did not think he should be president of the SJR felt that his Seminary connection was a key problem. His final election was a recognition that for better or worse, the society and all its activities were tied to his name. Kaplan's 1920 article in the *Menorah Journal* had been severely critical of historical Judaism; no doubt, his colleagues at the Seminary were distressed. Kaplan was unhappy at the Seminary and the desire to leave became the leitmotif of his inner life for many years. Even when he finally retired from the Rabbinical School in 1963, the chancellor, Louis Finkelstein, did everything in his power to persuade him to remain. On the one occasion when he finally mobilized himself to leave, his departure lasted only a few months. This ambivalence toward the Seminary both illustrates his profound inertia in the key area of his life and highlights his ideological radicalism.

The Seminary graduation exercises of 1916 proved to be the inception of unending discord between Kaplan and Cyrus Adler. Schechter had died the previous November, and Adler as the acting president certainly was anxious to succeed. Seven graduates from the Rabbinical School and twenty-two from the Teachers' Institute attended the ceremonies at the Aeolian Hall on Forty-second Street. A promising young rabbinical student named Louis Finkelstein received a prize for his

Gates to the Seminary at the time of their dedication, 1934. (Courtesy Library of JTS.)

essay "The Life of Rabbi Bezalel Ashkenazi and the Contents of His Library Traced from His Responsa and His Novellae." All the speakers paid tribute to Schechter, and Adler stressed Schechter's "distinct genius for constructive leadership." Kaplan called for a rededication to Jewish education and took the opportunity to comment on an important current matter — Jewish patriotism: "We are told it is more important to be a good American than to be a good Jew or that we should be Americans in public and Jews in private. . . . It is carrying coals to Newcastle to preach to Jews about loyalty to America. We only make ourselves ridiculous by this tawdry music hall patriotism." America was, of course, not yet officially at war, but patriotism was very much on everyone's mind. Anti-Semites were quick to use the large German-

Jewish community in America to impugn Jewish loyalty. Jews became sensitive on the loyalty issue, and many saw Zionism as an inappropriate policy at this juncture.

Kaplan was apparently responding to remarks by Jacob Schiff. When Schiff read the news report in the *New York Times*, he was furious and wrote to Adler: "I never called into question the patriotism of Jews in general, but have only pointed out that rabid Jewish nationalism and loyalty to America are in my opinion not compatible." Adler tried to soothe him: "I consider Dr. Kaplan's address very much out of place." Adler explained that Kaplan spoke each year because there were Teachers' Institute graduates and then went on to play down the significance of Kaplan's remarks: "Indeed it is probably a mistake to take either college presidents or college professors out of their academic seclusion and put them in the forefront of communal and political life. The temptation to play to the galleries is a very strong one." [1]

It was Adler's dedication to traditional Judaism and his deep desire not to have the Seminary affiliate with or become a separate denomination that constantly brought him into conflict with Kaplan. At a rather early point, he explained to the faculty that he wanted a particular kind of person at the Seminary: "those who naturally accept tradition and who entertain doubts only when there is strong proof against what tradition affirms." On the central matter of Jewish law, Adler's stand was equivocal. He wanted to embrace all points of view without threatening the fundamental traditionalism of the Seminary. This point is illustrated in an address he delivered before the Rabbinical Assembly Convention at Long Branch, New Jersey, in 1923, entitled "The View of the Seminary on the Authority of Jewish Law." Adler told the rabbis: "We welcome legalists, rationalists, mystics, always provided that they recognize the validity of the Jewish tradition and the Jewish law and are willing to live under it even though their explanation thereof may be different." Adler's response on the matter of mixed seating also revealed his vacillation. Rabbi Solomon Goldman wrote to Adler apparently because there was a split in his congregation; Goldman wanted to initiate mixed seating. Adler urged him to wait: "It is not our purpose to depart from the mainstream of rabbinic Judaism. . . . I recognize that we cannot control either the Rabbis or the Congregation, but I have always hoped that the result of the Seminary's teaching would be the maintenance of traditional worship." [2]

Adler was not a theorist or philosopher but rather an administrator, a practical man opposing any kind of particular theology for the Seminary. By calling the movement "traditional" and by resisting any prescriptive platform, he allowed Orthodox and traditional Jews to continue to identify with the movement. Many didn't want to think they were changing; others could see themselves as traditional while covertly introducing changes such as the English sermon and late Friday-evening services.[3] When Adler used the term *Conservative Judaism,* he had in mind a movement that *conserved* traditional Judaism rather than a new movement with a new ideology called "Conservative."

Adler wanted no part of any new faction or party. In 1919, he wrote that "the word 'Jew' and 'Judaism' should not be supplied with any adjectives by us. . . . I remember saying this a good many years ago, and was held up to scorn by a Yiddish paper for being a Jew without a party. I accept that designation as a title of honor." Asked to state the position of the Seminary with respect to Orthodox, Conservative, and Reform, Adler began by saying without any hesitation "that the Seminary was not the creation of any particular party in Judaism." In his hatred of factionalism, he went so far as to maintain that *Orthodox* and *Conservative* mean almost the same thing: "When the Seminary was founded, therefore, it was the institution of the Orthodox, or Historical or Conservative School and there was no question as to the propriety of the union of such forces for the maintenance of the Jewish tradition." Adler's traditionalism was much closer to the Sephardic style than to Bernard Revel and Eastern European Orthodoxy. Although Adler himself was thoroughly traditional, he could nonetheless praise the work of I. M. Wise because Wise did not seek to be divisive. Wise "did not have a partisan or factional tendency . . . his original thinking was union not factionalism."[4]

On a number of significant occasions, Kaplan and Adler clashed. In January 1921, Kaplan delivered a paper to the United Synagogue which he had also delivered to his congregation at the center and to a group in Buffalo. "The Function and Organization of the Synagogue" is a tour de force that deplored current synagogue operations and attacked the synagogue as spiritually impotent. Once the core of the vital concerns of the Jewish community, synagogues since the Emancipation had become more and more devoted to worship, which in many cases became their sole raison d'être. To regain its position, Kaplan believed, the synagogue must again relate to all the primary needs of Jewish people. Worship, of course, had its place: "mending the broken will, strengthening the despondent heart, recreating the weary soul by offering an escape from the noise and dust of everyday life." But despite its lofty goals, worship became one form of entertainment competing with others. The rabbi was judged by his charms and was subjected to a completely distorted set of standards: "The synagogue instead of developing rabbis who are true teachers and scholars, makes them spineless, spiritless footmen, with disgust in their hearts, milk on their lips and cobwebs on their brains." The synagogue should not be primarily a house of worship but rather a social center for the Jewish community. There should be a wide variety of activities at the synagogue; the social life of the Jewish community should converge there. The real concerns of the Jews about their livelihood and their personal lives should be mirrored in synagogue life. The synagogue, Kaplan believed, could be saved from irrelevance only by being transformed back into a communal institution with the emphasis on learning and study. It must again be a "*Bait Midrash*. Judaism is a civilization and the synagogue is the only institution the Jews have in the Diaspora for transmitting that social inheritance or civilization."[5]

Kaplan had sent Adler a draft of the paper, and Adler replied, strongly condemning the tone and content of Kaplan's remarks. Adler believed that the passage just cited "whittled down Judaism to what you call social inheritance." Adler was further annoyed by a rather casual remark Kaplan made about an important issue. Kaplan maintained: "What we so often fail to realize is that one is a Jew neither by race nor by choice. Being born to Jewish parents is getting to be less and less of a reason for remaining a Jew. Being a Jew is not a matter of blood. Judaism is not a biological fact; it is a spiritual fact." Adler countered: "I take issue with you and I am inclined to think that the whole of Jewish tradition and law would take issue with you on the question as to whether a person is a Jew by birth or not."

Kaplan's speech was an attack. He had harsh words not only for the rabbis but for the *baale batim* (important laypeople) as well: "attendance at synagogue, and participation in activities, are usually in inverse proportion to the amount of money that one possesses, and that one contributes to the synagogue." Adler thought such passages in "bad taste" and the paper on the whole "offensive and destructive." He concluded that "if our men are to be able to be sent out with a lack of belief in the past and antagonism to the only surroundings in which they can be useful, then indeed I see little hope for the future."

Adler believed deeply that one brings about a renaissance "not by attacking others" but by "positive work." Kaplan was always ready for the fray and never would shrink from controversy. He was fully ready to own his heterodox opinions and enjoyed startling people. Adler was a more cautious figure. He disliked Zionists because they made so much noise, thereby giving grounds for attacks by anti-Semites. In short, Kaplan was a scrapper, Adler was not.[6]

Writing to Kaplan in 1923, Adler told him that his 1920 *Menorah Journal* article caused him "a great deal of trouble" because of the strong reaction it had elicited. S. A. Israel had attempted to dislodge Kaplan from the Seminary because of his "poisonous doctrines." Israel and Adler corresponded in 1921 and 1922 about Kaplan, and a year or so later, much to Adler's regret, Israel published the private correspondence in an Orthodox weekly, *Idishe Licht*. Israel maintained that the "Seminary should not tolerate the teachings of a man who robs Judaism of all its sacred laws and precepts." Adler responded weakly that Kaplan taught homiletics, and "if he were professor of theology, the matter might be quite serious." This response did not satisfy Israel, and he pressed Adler for an interview. The meeting took place in April or May 1922. It is not known what transpired at this meeting, but it seems that Adler talked to Israel about getting rid of Kaplan. The subsequent correspondence included the following communication from Adler: "Concerning the matter about which we spoke I have nothing definite to say to you as yet." Israel answered: "Should you, however, be satisfied with permitting Kaplanism to continue in the Seminary and the Teachers' Institute I will have to force the issue." It is not clear how Israel could force the issue of Kaplan's dismissal. Perhaps he intended to persuade a group of Seminary supporters who disliked Kaplan to withdraw their support from the Seminary. The editor of *Idishe Licht* also advocated that Kaplan "be forced to sever his relations with the Seminary and other religious institutions and thus put an end to his pernicious activities." This exchange of letters prompted Kaplan to open negotiations with Stephen Wise about accepting a position at the Jewish Institute of Religion.[7]

Kaplan's feeling of unease at the Seminary had just cause and stemmed from situations both ideological and personal. Between 1910 and 1934, Kaplan's moods of depression were usually associated with the Seminary. In recording his impressions of one uneventful faculty meeting, Kaplan went away thinking "I wonder if I shall ever feel at home in the Seminary." He often felt slighted and unrecognized. Once, at a Seminary dinner in 1924, all the faculty members were brought up for public commendation except Kaplan. Afterward he pondered, "there never takes place an affair in the Seminary without something to give me a sense of inferiority." Kaplan had not yet produced any major work, but he came in daily contact with scholars of great repute. He was constantly reminded of his own meager output: "I shall soon be forty-six and not a single book to my credit. What a shame! Still I must not give up." Even some of his students seemed to outstrip him when it came to publication.[8]

For a time, he was self-conscious about speaking Hebrew before his colleagues or in public forums. The opening exercises of the

Teachers' Institute were particularly painful, because the circumstances demanded an address from Kaplan in Hebrew, but he usually spoke in English: "Here is another failure I have to register against myself. Due to the lack of energy necessary to train myself to speak and write Hebrew with ease, I am afraid to venture on those occasions to give an address in Hebrew." On one occasion, when he was at Professor Marx's house for a *minyan* (in this case a prayer service), he mispronounced a word in the passage he was reading from a classical Jewish text. The incident troubled him for a week.[9]

Kaplan underestimated his abilities and judged himself harshly. "I live inwardly as though I had but a short time to live and wanted to accomplish something substantial before it is too late. I suppose most people who combine mediocrity with inordinate ambition are always in a hurry." This ambition drove him constantly forward and resulted in a prodigious literary output. At the same time, he believed that it hampered him in his capacity as head of the Teachers' Institute. he felt that he did not devote enough time to the institute because financial constraints required him to seek other employment (mostly speaking at universities and synagogues around the country) and because he had to do "literary work." In March 1926, after meeting Bialik, who had come to the Seminary to present a lecture, Kaplan thought to himself, "Mine is the hell of being a mediocrity and knowing it."[10]

The colleague with whom Kaplan most frequently clashed during this period was Louis Ginzberg. More than anyone else, Ginzberg exemplified the Seminary's values. Traditional in his religious practice and utterly devoted to the scholarly understanding of the rabbinic tradition, he was admired, indeed revered, both at home and abroad. In the seminary community, including the Conservative rabbis, there was never any doubt that Ginzberg's word was final insofar as Jewish law was concerned. His stature is reflected in a report of the Law Committee offered to the United Synagogue in 1920 by Rabbi Louis Epstein. Epstein first lamented the fact that some rabbis and laymen had taken it upon themselves to introduce innovations in their congregations without consulting the committee. Then, referring to Ginzberg, he remarked, "it is all the more unbecoming of Rabbis to act on matters that involve the integrity of Jewish ceremonial life without consulting their master, our chairman at whose feet they sat."[11]

Throughout the Adler era, Ginzberg (*Der Kleine*) and Marx (*Der Grosse*) were at the very center of Seminary life. Adler was head of Dropsie as well as the Seminary and was frequently absent. Kaplan was "definitely outside the inner circle," according to Ginzberg's son Eli, who attributes this to Kaplan's concerns with the Jewish Center and to

Louis Ginzberg (1873–1953), Talmud scholar, colleague of Kaplan at JTS and primary adversary in 1920s and 1930s. (Courtesy Library of JTS.)

Alexander Marx (1878–1953), historian and colleague of Kaplan at JTS.

commitments at the Teachers' Institute that was located downtown for many years.[12] But there were other reasons, too.

Ginzberg was preeminent in the field of Talmudic law, and it was here that he and Kaplan battled throughout the 1920s and 1930s. Ginzberg's philosophy of law was on the whole traditional. Although it may have been merely a flash of rhetoric, in one speech he went so far as to say that no authoritative codes existed outside the Bible and that no changes could even be thought of without convening by some future authoritative body. In speaking to the United Synagogue Convention in 1921 (where Kaplan read his paper on the synagogue), Ginzberg "made clear the position of the [law] committee whose function was to interpret the law not to modify it or change it."[13]

The Kaplan-Ginzberg debates at Rabbinical Assembly conventions were a major attraction during the late 1920s and early 1930s. The conventions usually were held in June or July at some location on the Jersey shore. One particularly illuminating series of sessions occurred in Asbury Park in July 1927. Some seventy graduates of the Seminary attended, many reading papers on a wide variety of topics. Ginzberg gave a paper on the nature of Jewish law which bothered Kaplan on a number of levels. He was personally annoyed with Ginzberg because of his imperious manner and the "oracular" nature of his pronouncements. Kaplan felt that Ginzberg perceived him as a threat to his prestige with students and graduates. "He sees in me a menace," Kaplan confided to his diary. "Whenever voices are raised in defense of any policy that takes life into account he begins to boil with rage. He treats such voices as defiance and rebellion. He grows hysterical, he screams at the top of his voice, he foams at the mouth and shakes his fist as he cries . . . you are destroying Judaism." During one session, Kaplan was so distressed that he left the room and decided to have a cup of tea. Feeling guilty, he returned and found a heated discussion under way. He listened for a time, and then he and Ginzberg raised their hands simultaneously, Kaplan noting jealously that Ginzberg got the floor first.

When the law was being discussed, Ginzberg maintained that whatever changes were introduced by rabbis in the past were of an "unconscious nature." They always believed that the changes suggested were implicit in the written law. Those who advocated a deliberate break with the past "are undermining the very existence of Judaism." Then, turning to the rabbis seated in front of him, he thundered, "to you I say hands off the law."

Kaplan stood up after the harangue and answered Ginzberg, feeling that the assembled rabbis supported his response. He introduced a distinction between different routes toward change. One way was to approach the law with contempt for the ancients, thinking that they were completely wrong. "The other type of change is the kind of deliberate change which proceeds from the assumption that the situation with which we happen to be dealing presents new and unprecedented aspects which could not even have been contemplated by the ancients." To change by considering new situations did not really constitute a break. Kaplan was happy with his rejoinder; he felt he had "demolished Ginzberg, this time."[14]

Although change in the law could not be decided at public forums such as the Rabbinical Assembly convention, this discussion led to the Law Committee being transferred in 1927 from the United Synagogue to the Rabbinical Assembly. The public exchanges between the two are significant in that Ginzberg's public position may have been hardened considerably by Kaplan's.

There were other matters of contention between these two defenders of the Jewish cause. In March 1923, Kaplan published a booklet marking the first anniversary of the Society for the Advancement of Judaism. He showed it to a number of his colleagues on the faculty. Ginzberg was hostile. He was irritated by Kaplan's characterization of Judaism as a civilization rather than a religion or a theology. On this basis alone, he was ready to condemn the booklet. He suggested to Kaplan that copies be circulated to all members of the faculty and that a meeting be called to discuss "the attitude of the Seminary toward free expression of opinion on matters affecting traditional belief." The meeting never took place.

Ginzberg and Kaplan also differed on the extent to which they desired to approach religion from a rational point of view. Speaking at the installation of Louis Finkelstein as rabbi at Kehilath Israel in New York, Ginzberg said, "A religion which neither irritates the reason nor interferes with comfort, a religion not from love and fear but from good sense, will in the long run satisfy neither the heart nor the head of man."[15] Kaplan was clearly trying to introduce "good sense" into the understanding of religion in general and Judaism in particular. Ginzberg was a rationalist as well but was somewhat more restrictive in the way he defined "good sense."

Kaplan and Ginzberg also disagreed about the nature and purpose of Seminary education. Ginzberg highly valued traditional scholarship and never lost an opportunity to tell students and graduates that scholarship was the only thing that counted. "Your sermons will be forgotten," he told them at one convention. Kaplan, on the other hand, was convinced that traditional scholarship was frequently used as a means of escaping from life and its problems.[16] "If not for my encouraging the majority of them [the students and graduates] to insurgency against the policy of evasion," Kaplan wrote in 1926, "he would have had his way with them in intimidating them into a slavish fear of rabbinic law, and here comes along Kaplan who hasn't even any pretensions to Jewish scholarship and tries to overthrow his authority and influence. Yet I can't see how I can act otherwise. My heart bleeds as I think of the tremendous opportunity that Ginzberg has had to put new life into Judaism, an opportunity that he has abandoned."[17]

Ginzberg was not the only traditionalist unhappy with Kaplan, especially after the publication of his article in the *Menorah Journal* in 1920. He was branded as heterodox and seen as a distinct threat to the Orthodox community. In 1921, when Kaplan was scheduled to give a paper before the United Synagogue, one writer maintained that "A professor confessedly unable to accept the foundation of all Orthodox Jewish teaching should no longer attempt to teach and preach that in which he does not believe."[18] A delegation of Orthodox supporters of the Seminary came to Adler sometime in 1920 or 1921 and threatened to withdraw financial support from the institution if Kaplan was not fired.

Kaplan's association with the Seminary was exploited by those who wanted to prevent the merger of the Seminary and Rabbi Isaac Elchanan Yeshiva. This merger, from today's standpoint almost bizarre in its remoteness, was in the 1920s considered a desirable goal by a segment of the leadership of each institution. Kaplan proved to be a primary stumbling block. The story is both interesting and significant.

Rabbi Isaac Elchanan Theological Seminary (RIETS) and the Jewish Theological Seminary have had roughly parallel careers. The yeshiva was organized in 1898, the Seminary in 1902. Bernard Revel, the yeshiva leader who turned RIETS into Yeshiva University, came into office the same year that Cyrus Adler assumed power at the seminary. Both men died in 1940. In the mid-1920s, both institutions embarked on major fund-raising drives. Revel launched a collegiate division within the yeshiva and sought a new physical complex to house the growing educational institution whose quarters on the Lower East Side on Montgomery Street near East Broadway were too small. In 1924, the yeshiva purchased land in Washington Heights for the construction of a new school. The Seminary was also feeling the need to expand. The Teachers' Institute had always been downtown, far away from the Seminary's main building on 123rd Street. Kaplan had convinced Israel Unterberg, a member of the SAJ, to donate two hundred thousand dollars toward the construction of a new building for the institute. At about the same time (1926), Louis Brush, a New York lawyer, died, leaving almost one and a half million dollars to the Seminary. Some of this money was to be used for a new dormitory for rabbinical students. The new buildings at the yeshiva and at the Seminary not only would require a very large initial investment but also would entail a large annual outlay for maintenance. To some, it seemed that the American Jewish community might benefit if the campaigns were consolidated and there was only one traditional Seminary instead of two.[19]

Just how the merger first became a public issue is hard to establish. Kaplan believed that the initial impetus came from Judge Rosalsky, a member of the Jewish Center and a strong supporter of the yeshiva. It also may have begun with Nathan Lamport, a member of the Jewish Center, who donated a total of two hundred thousand dollars toward the Washington Heights complex and was also interested in seeing the two institutions consolidated. From the Seminary side, the strongest encouragement came from Louis Marshall with the concurrance of Adler. Marshall had written to Rosalsky and S. C. Lamport (Nathan's son) in December 1925 and received a positive response about the possibility of merger. The point has been made many times that laymen never see the theological niceties observed by rabbis and scholars. Marshall, a Reform Jew, saw no reason why there shouldn't be one strong traditional Seminary instead of two weak ones. He believed that a merger might help put an end to the yeshiva's plans to establish a college. Marshall denounced the college plan publicly as an attempt to establish a "Ghetto Institution." While he supported religious institutions, he nevertheless believed that secular higher education was an important element in the acculturation of Jews in America. To have a "secular" college in a yeshiva setting would constitute a large step backward.[20]

Numerous people, according to Marshall, perceived Kaplan as an obstacle to the merger. Joseph H. Cohen, his old adversary from the center, and even S. C. Lamport, ostensibly a friend, thought strong opposition from the yeshiva rabbinical leadership might be forthcoming. "[S. C.] Lamport, although a very warm friend and admirer of Kaplan, expressed the opinion, that if [Kaplan's] presence at the Seminary were to operate as an insuperable objection some way would have to be found to deal with that problem which would permit consolidation."[21]

Rabbi Bernard Levinthal, an Orthodox leader very active in yeshiva affairs, visited Adler in February 1926. Levinthal had ties to the Seminary; his son Israel Levinthal had graduated in 1910. He believed that some kind of consolidation might be possible if the units within the new institution remained relatively autonomous. He was critical of the Seminary curriculum and told Adler that he believed a college education was superfluous as a requirement for a rabbinic career. Adler said he would bring the whole matter to the Seminary faculty.[22]

The merger proposal was laid before the Seminary faculty in the spring of 1926. According to Kaplan's report of the meeting, Marx and Finkelstein approved the merger proposal and Ginzberg opposed. Kaplan believed that Ginzberg distrusted the yeshiva rabbis, and Ginzberg maintained that as yet no concrete plan had been put forth for the structure of the new institution. Kaplan opposed the whole idea. When he first heard about it in 1925, he thought, "Ye gads, that's all I need."[23]

The yeshiva leadership held its own conferences in 1926, and sometime early in 1927 the two groups met. Representing the Seminary were Adler, Marshall, and Ginzberg; the yeshiva was represented by three rabbinical leaders and two laymen. (The rabbis were probably Bernard Revel, M. S. Margolies, and Bernard Levinthal.) The conference put an end to all talk of merger, for the rabbinical leadership of the yeshiva remained unalterably opposed.

In 1928, Revel, the *Rosh Yeshiva*, wrote a paper called "The Seminary and Yeshiva" in which he outlined his objections to the merger. The two institutions differed in curricular structure, in the religious standards expected of students and associated congregations, and in their ultimate goals. The Seminary was a training school for rabbis, whereas the yeshiva was dedicated to the study of Torah as a mode of revitalizing American Jewry. Revel also maintained that the two institutions could never come together as long as the Seminary tolerated a man like Mordecai Kaplan. Revel wrote that Kaplan was the "most influential member of the Seminary faculty" and that he publicly "denies Divine Revelation and the Covenant at Mt. Sinai. The Seminary authorities are aware of his publicly taken attitude; the implication drawn from their silence is that such an attitude may consistently be presented and followed in an Orthodox Rabbinical Seminary."[24]

The merger proposal confirms several important points. Kaplan's presence at the Seminary was a key factor in the way the institution was perceived by other segments of the American Jewish community. The denominational status of the Seminary was not clear. Consolidation with the yeshiva certainly would have meant significant concessions on many fronts. Adler seemed to have no trouble, and Marshall didn't care. The documents also reveal that there were those at the Seminary, perhaps even including Marshall, who would have liked to have dismissed Kaplan.

◆

Teaching was Mordecai Kaplan's metier. He was always teaching, no matter where he was or to whom he was speaking. Behind his teaching was much time and effort devoted to the clarification of his thought on fundamental issues. His ideology influenced his teaching, and his teaching served as a significant metaphor that influenced his ideology. He had the teacher's naive faith in the transforming power of the word. In his heart, he believed that if he could only get people to listen, he could dramatically transform their thoughts and behavior.

On the matter of scholarship, Kaplan was ambivalent. He was beyond doubt knowledgeable in many areas, yet he never considered himself a scholar in the professional sense. On the one hand, he held in contempt the scholars around him whose arcane interests bore no relationship to contemporary issues. On the other hand, he was always the careful and informed thinker who observed the canons of critical inquiry, who very much desired the approval of his scholarly colleagues, and who was obviously himself engaged in scholarly pursuits.

His deepest concern as a scholar was to demonstrate the relationship between the social sciences and religion in general and Judaism in particular. Generally speaking, his career as a scholar falls within the broad movement known as *Wissenschaft des Judentums* — the science of Judaism. In the early nineteenth century, the methods of critical contemporary inquiry came into use in interpreting the Jewish past. The most outstanding exponent of the early *Wissenschaft* was Leopold Zunz, who devoted his long life (1794–1886) to the study of traditional Jewish literature, tracing its development over time and also its relationship to its historical context. Judaism as a historically evolving phenomenon was at the center of the *Wissenschaft* movement. Through the careful use of the oldest rabbinic documents, these nineteenth-century scholars established the outlines and the foundation for the historical study of the Jewish experience and of Jewish literature. In almost every case, this scholarship was seen by its creators as significantly related to the present interests of the Jews. As Kaplan himself wrote of the *Wissenschaft*, "It was expected that such knowledge would open the eyes of non-Jews to the fact that the Jews, throughout their historical career, had been the creators of significant cultural values and that they did not have to justify their continued existence as a People on the ground of their belonging to a supernatural order of reality."[25]

Kaplan accepted the general approach of the *Wissenschaft* movement even though he did depart from his fellow scholars in a number of significant ways. Many Jewish scholars associated with the *Wissenschaft* considered the Bible off limits to the application of critical methods; Kaplan did not. Kaplan accepted the conclusions of the critics and said so publicly. However, he did not want to identify the essence of the Torah with its origin; only the significance of the Torah mattered. He believed that the Torah must regain its preeminent place among the Jews, but this goal, he was convinced, would not be achieved by seeking to reestablish Mosaic authorship.[26] The central goal of Kaplan's ideology was to establish the supremacy of the Torah on a naturalistic basis.

The *Wissenschaft* movement found its primary expression in the field of history with Heinrich Graetz, the most important scholar-historian of the late nineteenth century. Jewish scholars of that era painstakingly examined Hebrew manuscripts in the principle libraries of Europe and attempted to establish authoritative critical editions of the classical texts of the Jewish tradition. Once a correct text was established, it could serve to show the development of Jewish thought in a particular area. For Graetz, the history of the Jews meant a chronicle of Jewish spirituality and Jewish suffering.

Kaplan must be credited with expanding the notion of *Wissenschaft* to include the newer social sciences of his day in addition to history and textual criticism. At the turn of the century, sociology, anthropology, and social psychology were just beginning to gain acceptance among the educated elite and to find their way into the halls of academe. Kaplan's training under Franklin Giddings and his continued reading after he left graduate school led to the heavily sociological character of his thinking. He was a sociologist writing intuitively, as so many did in that generation; yet he was also a rabbi, and it was natural for him to use the social sciences in the service of religion. Indeed, one of the fundamental aspects of Kaplan's legacy was his conviction that the social sciences were essential for the survival of the Jewish people. Religion had ceased to function in the modern world; only a deep understanding of the origins of religion and of the present religious situation could help to restore it. "Only in the light of what these newer sciences of human life have taught us," Kaplan wrote, "can we comprehend what is amiss with this spiritual condition today and lay plans for making religion function again."[27] In a sense, Kaplan was simply continuing the *Wissenschaft* conviction that scholarship ought never to be detached from the greater social utility it might serve. There were, however, many who feared the application of the social sciences to the Jewish religion, believing that spirituality would become irrelevant and piety disappear. Kaplan rejected such fears. He was convinced that the salvation of the religious impulse depended on the use of critical faculties.

Kaplan's application of sociology to religion began with the assumption that religion was primarily a social phenomenon. He was fully aware that there was always an individual component to religion, but he was convinced that the group side had been neglected. Studies of religion such as William James's *Varieties of Religious Experience* gave primacy to the exalted individuals identified with the origins of the great religions. While never denying the significance of the charismatic believer, Kaplan was persuaded that the experience of such individuals had meaning only in a social context: "Religion is primarily a social phenomenon, to grasp its reality, to observe its workings, and to further its growth we must study its functioning in some social group." The group was the vehicle by which religion survived from one generation to the next: "The individual and his development or perfection may constitute the sole aim of religion, but the fact and substance of religion cannot exist completely and exhaustively in an individual." Kaplan has been much misunderstood on this point. More than one critic has mistakenly described Kaplan as reducing religion to the values of the group.[28]

Kaplan did not compartmentalize his life. Engrossed as he was in reading and thinking about social science, he naturally incorporated this material into his teaching of rabbinical students at the Seminary. Many liked his general approach and wanted more exposure to the scientific study of religion. Several students went to Cyrus Adler requesting a course on religion from the standpoint of the social sciences. Adler leaned back, put his feet up on his desk, and said, "You mean the thing they call social psychology . . . I don't believe in the whole business. There is no such thing as a psychology of the Jewish people. Anyone that would undertake to teach such a subject is a charlatan."[29]

Other faculty members agreed. Although Ginzberg never made any direct statements on the matter, his attitude was clear. He believed that the most important study for rabbis was textual. While he himself related the *Halakhah* to political and social realities, he was nonetheless opposed to the newer social sciences making inroads into the curriculum. "Dr. Ginzberg had a great contempt for the social sciences and for psychology," Louis Finkelstein later said. Ginzberg in the 1920s was an outspoken critic of biblical criticism and was against certain aspects of the scientific study of religion. He may even have had Kaplan in mind when he wrote in an article on "Judaism and Modern Thought": "Do not be deceived by those who maintain that sensible experience and the verification of the phenomenon of sensible experience will yield the living philosophy of the future."[30]

In a sense, Kaplan was making precisely this point, that the ideology that would help sustain the Jewish people would be an empirically based system of thought flowing out of a scientific understanding of the Jews and Judaism. This issue is important. Is it true that the social sciences and psychology when applied to religion empty the numinous of all significant content? Is it the case that the more it is analyzed, the less potent the mystery becomes? Or might it be that as understanding increases, so does appreciation? Is it possible that wonder and *Wissenschaft* can coincide? Kaplan addressed this point many times throughout his life. "The Scientific Basis for Adjustment of Judaism to Modern Life," a 1918 essay, is one particularly cogent formulation. "Religion," he said, "cannot be considered apart from the rest of life. The tools of science, or of social science that help us to understand human beings in general will help us to understand the religious facet of our nature and the institutional forms of religion. We need to understand that religion must be studied just as we would study a rock or a flower, but our studying it does not mean that it is less a divine creation. Religion though subject to natural law is nonetheless divine." After all, we analyze the beauty of a poem or the lyrical quality of a piece of music. When we come back to the experience, we are richer and more appreciative because of our understanding. "Explaining religion does not mean explaining it away. That the interaction of the individual with society should give rise to a belief in an invisible order is itself a divine mystery." Kaplan was convinced that once it was understood how religion works, it could be developed and restored to its previous strength. Just as God does not disappear as creator because there are laws in physics, so God does not disappear as an object of belief because the origins and growth of these beliefs can be explained scientifically.

The restoration of religion will not be easy or automatic, but there is no doubt that the social sciences help the individual in understanding the numinous dimension of experience and its integration into people's lives. If we understand the way the religious impulse functions, and if we can penetrate the essence of that functioning, we will at least understand the goal toward which we should be working: "The creeds, rituals, and ceremonies of the established religions are not vital . . . because they are detached from the basic interests of life. Instead of being rooted in the things which make up the work and play of modern man, they are based upon the work and play of ancient man. . . . Living religion is not universal abstract truth but local and concrete experience. Idealism and spirituality that are not derived from the immediate actualities of life and do not refer directly to them make for the so frequently deplored divorce between religion and life."[31]

It has often been maintained that there is in Kaplan's work a slavish inclination toward modernism and particularly toward contemporary knowledge. Today many are painfully aware that all problems cannot be solved through science and technology, that indeed a great many new problems have been created by "advances" in understanding and manipulation of the environment. Kaplan lived in the era of great optimism regarding science and technology. He shared that optimistic attitude. But when he spoke of the benefits of living in the modern age and of the usefulness of contemporary knowledge, he often had in mind the scientific study of the human condition. Focusing the light of systematic critical inquiry on the origins and the workings of religion — finding out how things "really were" — was tremendously exciting. There is, of course, a naïveté in such attitudes, but an understanding of human nature and the striving for the transcendent have been significantly advanced through scientific studies.

One little-known example of Kaplan's scholarly application of the social sciences to Judaism was his analysis of rabbinic Judaism. Our view of Kaplan is distorted by the fact that his writing dealt exclusively with the adjustment of Judaism to the conditions of modern life. On a day-to-day basis, however, he was teaching rabbinic material at the Seminary and studied Talmud regularly. There exists solid evidence that Kaplan "learned" often until he was forty years old. After his father died in 1916, he continued to form special study groups devoted to Talmud learning. Max Kadushin reports that the same group that discussed contemporary sociology with Kaplan also studied *Bava Batra* (a Talmudic tractate) — a very clear example of living in two civilizations.[32]

During the 1920s, Kaplan attempted to apply his ideas on social psychology to the rabbis. He wrote a book-length manuscript outlining the contours of the collective consciousness of traditional rabbinic Jews. His purpose, as he indicates in the introduction, was to consider the rabbis objectively, not distorting their views to make them harmonize with what moderns believe. "The eagerness to find traditional beliefs acceptable," Kaplan stated, "leads the harmonizer to turn his blind spot upon those beliefs which might prove difficult to reconcile with current thinking."[33]

Kaplan was frequently accused of distorting traditional texts in order to bolster his own ideology. Here, however, he chided the harmonizers who did not look objectively at the texts. His whole approach was roughly similar to the work of the German Protestant theologian Rudolf Bultmann (1884–1976). Bultmann was associated with a method of interpretation known as demythology. In this approach (which has been subjected to much criticism recently), a writer might attempt to separate the essence of the message (the *Kerygma*, as it is called in Christianity) from the "mythological" context in which it first appeared. Only by removing the myth would it be possible, according to Bultmann, for the message to sustain itself in the modern world. At other times, however, Bultmann (and also Kaplan) looked carefully at the concept in its original setting, trying to see the concept on its own terms without any attempt whatsoever to reinterpret the idea. Bultmann did this in his magisterial work, *The Theology of the New Testament*, and Kaplan did the same in his work on rabbinic ideology. One can sometimes take an idea as a metaphor or reduce it to its core, while at other times one might objectively observe it in its original context. If distance is maintained and current interests do not intrude, the concept may suddenly look very different.

Kaplan's work with rabbinic ideology flowed directly out of his general analysis. In the introduction to his volume on the rabbis, he sought first to justify his approach and to explain his method. "Human societies," he stated, "have always been held together not only by common interests but also by common ideas and ideals." These ideals Kaplan called "folk ideology." Folk ideology helped to meld the people "into an organic unity" which would aid them in attaining a "sense of historic continuity with their ancestors." He set out to describe this ideology in its most developed form, in its classical rabbinic incarnation.

He divided rabbinic ideology into three different areas: group consciousness, or ideas about the origin, nature, and destiny of the group; law consciousness, or ideas about the duties, obligations, and standards intended to control social life; and God-consciousness, or ideas about God and his relationship to the group. Throughout his introduction to this work, Kaplan emphasized that one must accommodate to rabbinic ideology whether one accepts it or not: "So long as a person is identified as a Jew, he must reckon with the complex of traditions which has been known to differentiate him from the non-Jew. For better or for worse, he is committed to his folk ideology. He must make peace with it, otherwise it will give him no peace."

Attempting to look dispassionately and objectively at the rabbinic concept of God, Kaplan found, for example, that the rabbis believed God to be a being who occupies space. He was not immaterial. Kaplan emphasized that it never occurred to the rabbis that God might be inherently invisible. At times, the rabbis say that his presence fills the "heaven and earth" as in the scriptures, but at other times, they "seriously discuss the amount of space occupied by the Divine substance."[34] They never freed themselves from the notion that God resides essentially in heaven. They also believed that God can easily change himself, so at times the divine substance is unlimited and at other times it is confined to a narrow area.

In the section on Israel, Kaplan contrasted the rabbinic idealization of the Jewish people with the more realistic, full-blooded portrait in the scriptures. In the *Tanakh* (Bible), we see all the warts, even though Israel is still the center of God's promise. But for the rabbis who suffer the yoke of oppression, there is a new, transcendent concept of Israel: "God has fostered the people Israel with the intention of ultimately making it the heir of all human kingdoms and through Israel to exercise His sovereignty over mankind." Israel thus idealized is the rival and successor to Rome. The rabbis portray Israel as a nation, a political entity that will be restored to its land, *and* as the Ecclesia of God.

Their status on the one hand as a nation, a political entity, and on the other as an Ecclesia, a people of God destined for salvation, seem to be incompatible. The contradiction is resolved by the difference between the Days of the Messiah and the World to Come (*Olam Ha-Ba*) which follows the Days of the Messiah. The Days of the Messiah look to the restoration of Israel as a nation, and the World to Come looks toward the salvation of Israel as the Ecclesia of God, of all those loyal to God. Kaplan stated explicitly that he thought Maimonides was wrong in identifying *Olam Ha-Ba* with the immortality of the soul immediately after death. The World to Come appears *after* the Days of the Messiah and is the time of resurrection and miracles. The wolf will become a house pet, and manna will again appear as it did in the desert.

This brief summary of the rabbinic mind gives a glimpse of Kaplan as a historian of ideas and, more particularly, as a student of rabbinic Judaism. While working on this manuscript in 1926, Kaplan consulted his colleague Louis Ginzberg. With his wife, Lena, he visited the Ginzberg household and reported the incident in his diary, indicating his respect for Ginzberg as well as the tension he felt in approaching him. The evening began with much small talk which made Kaplan impatient. He was also somewhat oversensitive: "He hardly looked at me and had not a word to say to me. He sat sideways from where I sat so that he shouldn't feel the necessity of addressing me." After about a half-hour of palaver, as Kaplan called it, he asked Ginzberg whether they might talk alone. Ginzberg led him into the study, where Kaplan opened the discussion by asking him some questions on one of his notes in *The Legends of the Jews*. He then told him about his work on the ideology of the rabbis and read him some passages from his manuscript. Kaplan was quite happy, because "he seemed to be well impressed [and] on one point in particular I found that I had more exact knowledge than he did."[35]

Kaplan believed that scholarship should be useful. Since all Jews had to come to terms with the tradition, his work on rabbinic ideology seemed to him eminently significant. One had to know the rabbinic mind before dismissing it. He was contemptuous of a scholarship that had no direct relevance to contemporary concerns. His feeling was that rabbis should be trained directly in the knowledge and skills they would need to function in the American pulpit. Others assumed that as long as the rabbi had the relevant knowledge of classical texts, he would be able to function effectively. Professor Ginzberg, as one might expect, believed that scholarship was the way. "We ought to train scholars as scholars, not merely train rabbis," he wrote. "I am not opposed to train-ing rabbis, but I want our rabbis to be scholars also — greater scholars than they are now."[36] Ginzberg's priorities were always clear. Scholar-ship was the most valuable commitment a rabbi could make.

There existed at the Seminary an "anti-rabbinical" attitude — or, to be more precise, a contempt for the active pulpit rabbinate. Rabbinical students devoted to scholarship always felt more valued than those whose interests lay in congregational work. This attitude toward the active congregational rabbinate originated with Schechter himself, and was very distressing to Kaplan. Writing a few years after her husband's death, Mathilde Schechter noted in her memoirs that Schechter "did not care for the pulpit and often related smilingly how once in his life he had been about to preach on the High Holidays in place of a sick friend. He prepared his sermons but his friend got well and so he never preached the only ones he was ever called upon to deliver." In his younger days, Schechter wrote to a friend that he thanked God he was free of the "onus" of being a rabbi: "As you know I always abhorred that profession." Kaplan felt that Schechter actively and openly denigrated the congregational rabbinate while he was president of the Seminary: "It was he that used to wither the souls of the students with his ill-timed jests about rabbis and their calling. It was he that made it fashionable for all scholars and near scholars in and about the Seminary to turn up their noses at the term *rabbi*."[37] As Neil Gilman, a Seminary professor, so aptly explained, the faculty was clearly devoted to teaching classical texts, and the religious message, if any, "was left to the student to ferret out on his own." Questions of a fundamentally religious nature were simply not dealt with directly. The text was the focus, not the religious experiences that lay behind it.

Kaplan, on the other hand, dealt directly with the ultimate questions in all the courses he taught. He sought to influence his stu-dents' thinking, not just their reading of a text. In the early 1940s, for example, he made it a practice to submit a series of questions to his rabbinical students at the beginning of the course in order to ascertain their fundamental religious beliefs and whether or not they related to particular biblical stories as factual, wholly mythical, or primarily re-ligious metaphors. He was always willing to give his students extra help with their preaching. On one occasion in 1929, a group of students had arranged to meet informally to practice speaking extemporaneously. They invited Kaplan to attend, and he was delighted with the whole project. The next day, he saw Professor Davidson in the hall and excitedly reported his experience. Davidson made a joke of it. Offended, Kaplan noted angrily in his diary the "practice in vogue among the members of the faculty to speak contemptuously of rabbis and preaching, a practice that was inaugurated by Schechter."

The explanation for this bizarre state of affairs may be found in the nature of the modern rabbinate itself. The traditional rabbi was an expert to be consulted on matters of Jewish law (*Halakhah*). He preached little and did not serve his followers as a "pastor." The obligation to visit the sick (*Bikur Holim*) and to comfort those who had lost a loved one (*Menahem Aveylim*) was incumbent on all Jews. The rabbi had no special obligations in this area. Nor was he seen as a religious philosopher who interpreted the eternal verities in terms of the needs of the moment. His function related primarily to the law and its interpretation. It may be that Schechter and Ginzberg were relating to the older model of the rabbi. Contemporary rabbis in America, on the other hand, are rarely called upon to give legal opinions. Indeed, rabbis outside the community of sectarian Orthodox are almost never asked questions regarding Jewish law. The rabbi's functions have increasingly related to the role of pastor and sometimes interpreter and spiritual guide to a congregation. How important is the rabbi's scholarship in this new context? What skills does the rabbi need when the function is that of a pastor and not that of an expert on Jewish law?

For Kaplan himself the priorities were self-evident. He had no patience for the arcane concern with "stupid Geniza fragments" or "dry as dust scholarship." Individuals who spent their time in these areas ought to turn their attention to contemporary concerns. "I hold Jewish science in proper respect," he once confided to his journal, "but I would not permit any but those who are crippled and maimed to pursue it and I would compel men like Ginzberg, Davidson and Friedlaender, who are men of brains to help build up a living Judaism with content to it."[38]

The rabbi's primary means of constructing a living Judaism was preaching. Kaplan taught homiletics from the time he first came to the Seminary. He was himself a great preacher, never actually questioning the centrality of preaching in the life of a rabbi and convinced of the efficacy of sermons. This point is illustrated by his preparation of a particular Hanukkah sermon involving the theme of the Maccabees and moral courage. In reading how he worked out his thoughts in his journal, one can sense his conviction that if he formulated the concept

Reading room at the Seminary. (Courtesy Library of JTS.)

of moral courage adequately he would thereby inspire his listeners to be more courageous. "What could be simpler than an appeal to people to exercise their moral courage?" he asked himself. It was almost as if the appeal were equivalent to the result.

His devotion to preaching may also be illustrated by the fact that on a number of occasions he contemplated sacrificing all his other activities, including the SAJ, and devoting himself fully to the teaching of homiletics. Eventually, he went to Adler with the proposal. Adler said he would pursue the matter with the board, suggesting that Kaplan might have a total salary of twelve thousand dollars if he were to teach homiletics full-time. However, the reality was that students did not always take the subject seriously. On one occasion, Kaplan asked a number of students to hand in extra sermon outlines before graduation. The students were so burdened with work that they were late in submitting their sermon outlines, and Kaplan received them the very same day as the last faculty meeting of the year when decisions were made about graduation. He was unhappy, to say the least. Very hard on his students, Kaplan often criticized their sermons severely. Occasionally, he became genuinely excited. Henry Rosenthal, a student in the late 1920s who eventually taught philosophy, impressed Kaplan with his student sermon. "He certainly possesses an inner beauty of soul which spurns the ugly and the spurious in art, morality and religion . . . he is fully alive to the vulgarities of Jewish life and its sterility and nevertheless deeply in love with it."[39]

The other course Kaplan taught every year was *Midrash*. Since the *Midrash* is really a collection of homilies, many of which may have been delivered originally in the synagogue, it was a natural resource for future sermons. Kaplan loved the *Midrash* because it stood at the center of the traditional attempt to make the text of the Hebrew scriptures relevant. The central question for any student of *Midrash*, but especially for the future rabbi, is whether these past attempts at relevance could be made to live again. For Kaplan, the *Midrash* was a storehouse of useful interpretations of the holy text. It was the most important text a rabbi could study.

Here lay Kaplan's greatest talents. One of his most famous students, Robert Gordis, characterized him as "Master of *Midrash*." Louis Finkelstein, the future head of the Seminary who studied with him during World War I, remarked, "His *Midrash* classes were extraordinarily illuminating. No one ever missed a class unless he was sick." Kaplan did not need to call the roll, because everyone was always there.

Gordis reports that he pleaded with Kaplan to write an introduction to the methodology of *Midrash*, but he never did. Indeed, in all of Kaplan's writings there is very little material that deals directly with the text of the *Midrash*. Kaplan may cite *Midrashic* sources that support a particular idea he is discussing, but his focus is almost never the rabbinic text per se. Kaplan was absorbed in the exposition of his own ideology and never found the time or the interest for writing on the *Midrash* directly.[40]

We are fortunate, however, in having some fragmentary material that sheds light on Kaplan's *Midrash* teaching.[41] He had great sensitivity to the text and a real talent for grasping the issue the rabbis were discussing and explaining it in contemporary terms. The rabbis sometimes speak in metaphors, and the meanings must often be elicited. They say that the Tree of Life (Genesis 2:9) was so large that it took five hundred years to travel from one end of it to the other. Kaplan's explanation is that to the rabbis the universe was five hundred years long. "The tree of life or salvation was offered to the entire world, not for Israel alone. It coincides with rabbinic universalism that all mankind is eligible for salvation or eternal life."[42]

The *Midrash* itself constantly reads meanings into the text: only by such a reading can the text be kept alive. The Jewish tradition — any tradition — only lives if we make it our own, relating it to our world and our experience. This is precisely what Kaplan did when he commented on the *Midrash*. In Genesis 2:8, for example, is the word *MiKedem*, which means "east," that Eden was in the east. The rabbis, however, point out that the word can also mean "early." They assert that the garden was actually created on the third day while Adam was created on the sixth day. Man's reward was there before he did anything to deserve it. The *Midrash* is explicit when Adam says, "the Holy one Blessed be He, prepared a reward for me before I even started to act." Kaplan then commented on the notion of reward as it may be understood here: "Reward for righteous living is a difficult notion to apply today. We must phrase the concept in its modern equivalent — self-realization. We see that self-fulfillment was inherent in the moral order outlined by the rabbis . . . the interpretation of *MiKedem* shows us that the world is so conditioned that self-fulfillment is inherent in the universe for one who lives the moral life." The rabbis are saying that reward is built in — that the world is a rewarding place. The interpretation is pure Kaplan, and yet it does fit the *Midrash*.

Elsewhere, Kaplan demonstrated his skill in applying the *Midrash* as rabbi and preacher. The *Midrash* on Genesis presents several rabbis speculating about what kind of tree the Tree of Knowledge actually was. Their conclusion is that "The Holy One Blessed Be He did not reveal [the name] of that tree." We don't know what kind it was lest every glance at such a tree prove a constant reminder of man's weakness. At stake are man's honor and self-respect, his *kavod*, as the *Midrash* puts it. Kaplan then dealt with self-respect and the dignity of the individual. "The honor of the human being must not be impugned. Adam or humanity in general must not be degraded. The belief in God comes through the belief in man. We cannot remove the idea of man's dignity and still have religion (because man is created in the image of God). All those who speak of the humanist movement in religion as irreligious do not appreciate the problem." Kaplan was perfectly traditional here in talking about the dignity of the individual, but suddenly he took a significant leap which radicalized the whole statement, suggesting to the reader the essential way in which humanism and religion fit together.

These examples aid us in understanding Kaplan's methods of teaching *Midrash*. Year after year, rabbinical students passed through his *Midrash* class and were profoundly appreciative of his talent in explaining the *Midrash* and in helping them to appropriate it in a way that would be useful for their own preaching. "Kaplan provoked and inspired students to think about things that they had taken for granted before. He was brilliant in the way he handled the text." [43] Many rejected his philosophy, but all valued his teaching.

Kaplan's classes were not exempt from ordinary problems. As strict with his students as he was with himself, he was much in favor of tightening the standards, "in order to cut down on the number of nincompoops the Seminary graduates annually." Though an excellent teacher, Kaplan did have temperamental days. He portrayed himself as often rushing to class because he so looked forward to the teaching. On one particular day, he was late and took a taxi from his home to the Seminary at 123rd Street. When he entered the building, he found the students loitering in the hallway, not making a move to enter the classroom even though the bell had already rung for the session to commence. He was livid and reprimanded them severely.

Kaplan's dilemma in teaching *Midrash* at the seminary is very graphically illustrated by his fear of "being found out." A student in one *Midrash* class once asked him to mimeograph his lectures so that the students could read them before class. He declined; he worried about other faculty members discovering exactly what he was teaching. "If some of the material I give in class were to fall into the hands of any of my colleagues, they would raise the roof off the Seminary." [44]

Kaplan's need to teach seems to have known no bounds. He was always organizing private groups that would meet regularly at his house to read some of the latest sociological literature or to discuss the problems of Judaism in the modern world. The groups were informal, given without charge, but always taken seriously by Kaplan. They included rabbinical students who wanted more study or who came from Orthodox backgrounds and were having problems adjusting to the Seminary. In one instance, the rabbinical students found that a club they had formed in homiletics to practice their preaching was not working out, so they came on Monday nights to Kaplan for extra help. Most frequently, they would read some relevant theoretical work such as Josiah Royce on loyalty, William James on pragmatism, William McDougal on social psychology, or William Bagehot's *Physics and Politics*. The groups sometimes consisted of community leaders who were friends or former students of Kaplan's. The 1923 membership included Alexander Dushkin, Leo Honor, and Henry Hurwitz, the editor of the *Menorah Journal*, among others. [45]

Kaplan organized these groups as much for himself as for those involved. He needed to think through and clarify his ideas and the teaching context provided an excellent opportunity. His classes at the Teachers' Institute and at the Rabbinical School were exciting whether or not the students agreed with his approach and his philosophy. Students admired him and some embraced his philosophy. Yet disciple-ship is not easy to unravel, nor was being a disciple an unmixed bless-ing. Nietzsche, who had many admirers but few disciples, understood the process very well when he said, "one repays a teacher badly if one always remains nothing but a pupil."[46]

Kaplan remained at the Seminary for such a long time that a list of his students would include all the leaders of Conservative Judaism in the twentieth century and a significant group that graduated from Teachers' Institute but were never formally linked with the Conser-vative movement. Among the most important of Kaplan's students, but never fully a disciple, was Louis Finkelstein, perhaps the best known of the Conservative leadership. Born in 1895 in Cincinnati, he attended City College and entered the Jewish Theological Seminary in 1911 in what was then called the junior class. In the fall of 1915, he enrolled in Kaplan's course in homiletics and remembered Schechter sitting in on the student sermons and making his comments first before Kaplan commented. Finkelstein's traditionalist tendencies were apparent from the beginning of his association with Kaplan. He early asserted his be-lief that "the existence of Judaism was endangered if the traditional conception of revelation and miracle be denied." Finkelstein was not, however, unequivocally dedicated to the rabbinate and once told Kap-lan that "if he had his choice he would have taken up law rather than the rabbinate." Attracted to Kaplan's ideas, Finkelstein in 1917 joined one of the groups that met at Kaplan's house. Ten years after grad-uation, Finkelstein responded to a paper Kaplan had delivered at the 1929 Rabbinical Assembly convention. "After all, we are all proud to have had you as teacher and master and want you to keep acting as our guide. Sometimes we forget what we owe you, but that is only for the moment, in our hearts we always feel it. What you have done for me personally, you know better than anyone else. I shall never forget the pains you took with me in the first years after my graduation when I used to come to your house regularly. But in talking to the other men of my debt to you I find that all of them feel in a greater or less degree similarly indebted."[47]

The ups and downs in the early Kaplan-Finkelstein relationship uniquely illustrate the complexities of protracted personal dealings with Kaplan. After his graduation in 1919, Finkelstein took a pulpit in the Bronx. At Kaplan's urging, he attended the meetings of the Society for Jewish Renascence but was never comfortable there. More to his liking, perhaps, were his regular walks with Kaplan when they discussed the Torah portion of the week. Throughout his life, Kaplan walked vigorously on a daily basis. Living on the Upper West Side, it was convenient for him to walk around the reservoir in Central Park. Finkelstein, Max Kadushin, Samuel Dinin, Ira Eisenstein, and at an earlier period perhaps even Judah Magnes walked around the reservoir and discussed Torah with Kaplan. Finkelstein was a good listener and used the material from their discussions as a basis for his Sabbath sermons. This relationship went on for more than a year, with the result that Finkelstein gained what he thought was an undeserved reputation as a forceful preacher. In April 1921, he wrote to Kaplan, "it will mean a heavy burden on me to live up to the reputation I established with your help. I begin to doubt whether it was right to deceive my people as I did."

Many years later, Finkelstein remembered these conversations with Kaplan, from which he obviously had gained much more than had Kaplan. More importantly, he felt that the Kaplan he took walks with was not truly radical, and the "identical sermons" they both delivered could very easily have been given by any rabbi in the Conservative movement. When asked in an interview why he stopped meeting with Kaplan and whether or not he felt that Kaplan was overbearing, he responded that he had no such feelings. He had left the sessions because others wanted to join and he had no interest in being part of a group. But in a very revealing diary entry from the early 1920s, Kaplan noted: "He [Finkelstein] came to see me today. I proved to him that he was entirely unjustified in assuming that I wanted to do his thinking for him or that I expected him to undertake work uncongenial to him. We parted friends and decided to work jointly on the subject dealt with in the sermon 'God the Liberator.'"

The very letter Finkelstein wrote to Kaplan when he ceased to meet with him proves that while Finkelstein did not want to offend his teacher, he yet felt stifled by the association. "My deep respect for you," Finkelstein wrote Kaplan, "prevents me from saying frankly to you what I feel and so I must resort to writing this letter. For I do not think that I ought to continue to work under you. The work has been of unquestionable advantage to me. It is a pleasure to come in contact with a vigorous mind, and it is stimulating to get new ideas. Yet I feel that if I were to continue to work as we have for the past year, my own growth would be hampered. For it is evident that our minds do not work in the same way. . . . I have plans, I even have ambitions just as you have. Being younger they are less developed and less clear, but I do not want them to be stunted."[48]

As the years passed and Finkelstein's power and influence at the Seminary grew to significant proportions, the strain between the two men also increased. Always ill at ease at the Seminary, Kaplan began to

Kaplan and Dr. Louis Finkelstein, ca. late 1930s.
(Courtesy Library of JTS.)

feel in the early 1930s that Finkelstein was working to have him re-moved. At one point, Kaplan wrote in his diary that he had "Finkitus." But at other times, he wondered "who is to blame for this strained re-lationship between Finkelstein and me, he or I?" Many years later, Fin-kelstein freely admitted that he did everything in his power to limit the spread of Reconstructionism. Even before he became president in 1940, Finkelstein had considerable power, because Adler was always coming and going and after 1934 left much of the day-to-day running of the institution up to his assistant. Finkelstein's primary goal seems to have been to prevent schism. His famous speech in 1927, "The Ties That Unite Us," was clearly a message to the Conservative rabbinate that divisiveness only weakens the movement and the Jewish people.

Nevertheless, Finkelstein was Conservative with respect to *Hal-akhah.* Kaplan's deep conviction that the commandments ought to be understood as folkways rather than laws surely alienated him. Of the changes in Kaplan's *Haggadah* (1941), Finkelstein said "we were out-raged by the *Haggadah.* There was a general feeling that the *Haggadah* was the first step in a real breach. I opposed it." However, Finkelstein never went so far as to sign the letter in *Hadoar* which strongly con-demned Kaplan on the occasion of his prayerbook (1945). Professor

Neil Gilman once asked Finkelstein directly, "Why didn't you fire Kaplan?" Finkelstein responded, "Because he was my teacher." When Gilman pressed him on the issue, Finkelstein added, "I wanted to make the Seminary a first class academic institution and you can't have that if you fire people you don't agree with." In spite of these tensions, Finkelstein and Kaplan strove to be cordial. In 1935, finishing up his biography of Rabbi Akiba, Finkelstein wrote Kaplan, "when it is finally finished, I am sure you will find many traces of your influence and exegesis in it."[49]

Eventually, the Seminary lost money because of the opposition to Kaplan and was deliberately ignored by more traditional Jews. In 1952, Finkelstein was in Jerusalem and met with the chief rabbi, who told him, "Your Seminary would be a very good seminary and I would be entirely on your side if you didn't have Dr. Kaplan." Chief Rabbi Herzog was very happy to meet with a few members of the Seminary faculty on his New York visit, but because of Kaplan he refused to step inside the Seminary building. At one point, Finkelstein said to Herzog, "It can't be as bad as you think if [Saul] Lieberman sits on the faculty." In the 1950s, relations improved considerably, and when Kaplan was ready to retire, though he was in his early eighties, Finkelstein implored him to remain as a teaching member of the faculty.[50]

Finkelstein was never clearly a Kaplan disciple, and the strain in their relationship is understandable. With some of Kaplan's more devoted followers, relationships were more complex. One of Kaplan's most faithful students in the early years was Max Kadushin. Born in 1895, Kadushin came to the United States when he was two years old and grew up in Seattle. He studied at New York University and entered the Seminary on the preparation level while he was in college. While at the Seminary, he became devoted to Kaplan, teaching classes at the Jewish Center while Kaplan was rabbi there. Kadushin's biographer maintains that Kaplan was a father figure to the very bright rabbinical student. His classmates at the Seminary sarcastically referred to him as "his master's voice" because of Kadushin's devotion to Kaplan. In the early 1920s, Kadushin wrote a number of essays that exactly mirrored Kaplan's concept of Judaism and his proposals for a center that would reflect the enlarged Judaism his teacher was advocating.

In the late 1920s, Kadushin was among the most politically radical of Kaplan's circle. In one of Kaplan's fits of depression, he considered leaving the SAJ and suggested that Kadushin be asked to replace him. Nothing ever came of the idea, but Kaplan's confidence in his former student was obvious.[51]

After leaving New York, Kadushin drifted away from Kaplan. Obtuse at times about human relations, Kaplan was conscious of the fact that his young devotees seemed to be less ardent after they left the Seminary. He once approached Finkelstein on the matter. Finkelstein responded supportively, explaining that Kaplan attracted strong men of independent minds who would naturally strike out on their own. Kadushin felt his divergence from Kaplan was gradual and in part a function of his maturing interests which diverged from those of his teacher. There may have been other reasons. Apparently, Kadushin's wife, Evelyn (née Garfiel), herself an ardent follower of Kaplan and one of the early female Ph.D.'s, once went to Kaplan and told him of her unhappiness with the fact that Kaplan was dominating her husband.[52]

Kadushin was interested in rabbinic Judaism, and produced some very original works in this area, specifically on the problem of the coherence of rabbinic thought. He wanted to know in what sense rabbinic thought constituted an organically unified system. Kadushin certainly was influenced by Kaplan's concept of Judaism as a civilization, but the coherence of rabbinic thought was not something Kaplan questioned or even examined. Kadushin developed his own focus, even becoming critical of his teacher. Kaplan, in dismissing the concept of the Chosen People, had maintained that it was a central organizing notion in rabbinic thought. Kadushin believed that to be central or foundational, a rabbinic concept must exist primarily in a noun form. The concept of "chosenness" does not really have a Hebrew noun word that denotes it but is usually referred to by using the verb form. Additionally, Kadushin believed that salvation, a central idea to Kaplan, though it is found in the Bible, is essentially a Christian concept, or, to put it more precisely, Kadushin simply could never get the Christian associations of "salvation" out of his mind. Kadushin believed that salvation in rabbinic thought should be rendered by the words *Olam Ha Bah* (the World to Come). Although the idea of *Olam Ha Bah* may have been important to the rabbis, it was not foundational according to Kadushin; he would not use it as a key concept from which most other rabbinic concepts could be derived.[53]

At the end of his life, Kadushin, looking back, regretted that he had not kept in closer touch with his teacher, although at the same time he admitted that as he grew older he became less enamored of change and referred to himself as an "unreconstructed traditionalist." Kadushin never denied Kaplan's greatness: "Kaplan is bigger than Reconstructionism," he said in 1974, "and nobody was more concerned about Judaism than Kaplan. This is an emotional contribution of no mean order."

It is not possible to speak individually of all the students who passed through Kaplan's classes and were significantly influenced by him.

Simon Greenberg (born in 1901), is one of the many students who deeply appreciated Kaplan but who never became a disciple. Greenberg was a student in the Stone Avenue Talmud Torah in Brownsville, Brooklyn, where Louis Finkelstein was his teacher. Joseph Bragin, Kaplan's emissary, visited the Talmud Torah and literally begged the students to come to the Teachers' Institute. It meant traveling a long way, because in those days the subway did not go under the East River. Passengers had to leave the train and then reenter the subway on the other side. Greenberg entered the Teachers' Institute in 1917 and studied religion with Kaplan. He remembered the first day of class, when Kaplan drew a diagram on the board of how the universe would look if one took the first chapter of Genesis literally. "Nothing Kaplan said ever shocked me," Greenberg maintained many years later, "because no one ever hammered into my head that God dictated the Five Books to Moses." In the Rabbinical School, Kaplan had his circle of devotees, but Greenberg was never among them. Nonetheless, Kaplan inspired him. "He is significant," Greenberg later said, "because he made me think through my objections to him — that kind of person has a very great impact." Rabbi Robert Gordis, the outstanding Bible scholar at the Seminary, felt the same way. "The necessity for countering the Reconstructionist critique of Judaism led me to evolve what theories I have had concerning Conservative Judaism."

A rather interesting case of discipleship was Milton Steinberg. Born in Rochester in 1903, Steinberg attended City College, where he studied with the great philosopher Morris Raphael Cohen and went on to become an outstanding rabbi with a lifelong devotion to academic and Jewish philosophy. While in high school, he befriended the Eisenstein brothers, Myron and Ira, and exerted a very strong influence on the younger Eisenstein. At the Seminary, Steinberg quickly became a Kaplan admirer and studied privately with him for two hours every Wednesday, "the most exciting hours of the week," Steinberg's biographer and colleague, Simon Noveck, says. When he was an upperclassman, Steinberg became president of the student body and headed the delegation to Adler that asked for a total revamping of the Seminary curriculum. There were too many class hours, and "except for Morris Levine and Mordecai Kaplan, the students regarded most of the members of the faculty as pedants who did not encourage originality of thinking."

Steinberg's admiration was clearly evidenced by a letter he wrote to Adler on the occasion of Kaplan's resignation, in which he eloquently expressed his feelings about Kaplan as a teacher and a model. Kaplan, in turn, was fully aware of Steinberg's potential. Steinberg would sit in the back of the class, and then all of a sudden a voice would say, "But Professor . . ." and Kaplan would stop what he was saying. "Yes, Steinberg," he would answer, and then listened intently. In Steinberg's senior year, Kaplan asked him to teach at the institute. It was rumored that all the girls were in love with the handsome young rabbinical student. Upon his graduation, Kaplan offered him a position as assistant rabbi of the SAJ, but Steinberg refused, perhaps feeling it was necessary to leave New York and prove himself on his own. Ira Eisenstein, who was to become the preeminent Kaplan disciple, later admitted, "if [Steinberg] had accepted the position at the SAJ my whole life would have been different. I was a definite second choice."[54] Eisenstein once quipped in talking about the Reconstructionist *Haggadah* that people often referred to the "Trinity of the Movement, namely the Father [Kaplan], the Son-in-law [Eisenstein] and the holy-ghost writer [Eugene Kohn]."

Born in Harlem in 1906, educated in New York City, Eisenstein attended Columbia College. He was significantly influenced by his Orthodox grandfather, J. D. Eisenstein, a well-known scholar and writer on the New York Jewish scene who published many works including a number of Hebrew anthologies. (Ira was very much impressed when he learned that his grandfather had translated the Declaration of Independence into Hebrew and Yiddish.) Eisenstein attended synagogue regularly as a child, and when he was a teenager his father, who enjoyed hearing different preachers, took him to the SAJ. "This stern and forbidding man with a black goatee," Eisenstein later wrote of his first encounter with Kaplan, "was giving a learned talk on the mythical and pagan origins of some of the laws in the Bible. I think the subject was the red heifer, but it does not matter. Here was another arrogant disbeliever. How in the world could he say those things about one of the most important institutions in biblical days. All the way home I excoriated Kaplan."

Although Eisenstein endured a period of doubt and soul searching, he finally decided to become a rabbi and attended the Seminary at night while studying at Columbia. When he finished Columbia and finally entered the Rabbinical School, he studied with Kaplan. Many years later, it was the terrifying aspect of Kaplan that was fresh in Eisenstein's mind: "with him you didn't fool around. When he marched into the building on Wednesdays . . . the students began to shake and shiver in advance. His reputation was terrifying. He would bellow and roar if he thought you were talking without thinking the matter through. He would call off the class if students became lax about promptness. He would tear a sermon apart mercilessly if it did not meet his standards of organization and clarity. Most of all, he demanded intellectual honesty of us as he demanded it of himself. He would settle for nothing less."[55]

Eisenstein frequented the SAJ in order to hear Kaplan preach. Eventually, he was invited to the Kaplan household, where he conversed freely with his teacher. Eisenstein also became part of a study group, even though he thought that Kaplan was not at all selective: "Kaplan needed a group with which to meet. Some groups were of a high quality as with Kadushin or Mortimer Cohen or Solomon Grayzel but he didn't always discriminate."

"You never knew when the volcano was going to erupt," Eisenstein said later. Kaplan was impatient with students who didn't know the right answer or with any remark he considered to be "primitive" and unreasonable. It was his "monumental explosive anger that students worried about. When it happened the whole earth shook." Eisenstein felt that this anger discouraged long-term disciples. Students appreciated Kaplan's honesty, his questioning, and his attempts to deal with fundamental issues, but their fear drove them away. For some reason, Eisenstein himself never experienced this fear. "What they never understood was how I had the nerve to go into the lion's cage. I was never afraid of it and Kaplan appreciated that."

Students left Kaplan "because they did not want to be vulnerable — or be the recipient of his temper." Then, too, there was his demand for loyalty: "If you didn't agree with him one hundred percent he thought you misunderstood what he was talking about. He lost dozens and dozens of disciples because of this." Eisenstein, the quintessential disciple, paid the greatest tribute to Kaplan not in his autobiography but in an early letter to a man organizing a dinner in Kaplan's honor:

> It has become one of my major joys to indulge in enthusiastic praise of Dr. Kaplan, and one of my most cherished ambitions to convert the rest of civilized Jewry to my enthusiasm. . . . Jewish life has produced in him a new kind of saint. One who does not flee from life but who grapples with it. We should take heart to behold a man, sincere, uncompromising, bold, of brilliant mind and unbroken faith, who finds in Judaism something to declare to the world . . . such a man makes our calling a dignified and significant one. He gives meaning and promise to the course we embrace, and when we do him honor, we do at the same time reaffirm our belief in the possibilities of Jewish life.[56]

◆

Teaching was central to Kaplan's life and thought; other activities were more or less surrogate. As a teacher, Kaplan was a master, but unfortunately he related to every other activity as if it were also an opportunity to teach. His pedagogic obsession constituted his essential greatness and his major flaw. Interpreting the term *Torah* to refer not only to the product but also to the process, we might understand Kaplan as one who was wholly and completely devoted to the Torah and to the study of Torah — Talmud Torah. Unfortunately, there was a sense in which he never managed to make the transition from study to deed.

It is not just that he was teaching regardless of the activity at hand but that the naïveté of the teaching function penetrated to other areas where it was entirely inappropriate. The stock-in-trade of the teacher is the spoken word, and the teacher's goal is to enlighten. The teacher's efforts rest on the assumption that people behave in a way that reflects their beliefs; if one can change their beliefs, one can change their behavior. The new behavior would emerge directly from the change in belief. No institution need mediate. It is quite surprising that a man whose understanding of social forces was so clear and penetrating could not see the more complex truth: human behavior changes in response to a wide variety of forces, most of which are unconscious in the mind of the individual. People are swept along by many internal and external pressures, most of which are outside their awareness.

Kaplan was trapped within the confines of the teaching function. In the early 1940s, the newly established Reconstructionist Foundation gathered to formulate a strategy to spread the word. The members met frequently, devising ways to strengthen the movement. Kaplan still insisted that the Reconstructionist movement was not a new denomination but a school of thought. On this particular occasion, as on many others, there were some members who were not content with this policy. One such person advocated that the Reconstructionists begin to think about capturing the boards of trustees of carefully chosen congregations; after the board, the congregation; and after the congregation, a number of congregations in the region. Kaplan cried out — and one can hear him banging his fist on the table and shouting — "No, what we have to do is to change human nature!" It is certainly the teacher in Kaplan that led him to make such statements, statements that reveal a complete lack of political and organizational sensitivity.

Kaplan's world was essentially a world of words, not things. This *res et verba* distinction goes back to ancient times. For some people — and Kaplan is one of them — words fill up the world and become the overarching concern. He was forever engaged in formulating and reformulating, in trying to get the thought exactly right; the formulation was so critical because ultimately it would carry the day. The words themselves become constitutive, become the totality. Once he had succeeded in stating the formulation, his task was completed.

This explains why Kaplan never could teach enough. On one level, his workaholic passions can be seen as a devotion to the Jewish people, which they certainly were. But on another level, there was a compulsive quality in his need for teaching and ceaseless articulation. He constantly brought students home; he was forever forming groups, not only of students but of his colleagues as well. He was in the grip of his unending lectures, given in synagogues up and down the East Coast and across the length and breadth of the land. Considering all the people he taught and all the lectures he gave, it is amazing that the Reconstructionist movement remained small. But Kaplan wasn't trying to build an organization and a movement at all; he was trying to convince, to arouse, and to force people to question their assumptions and beliefs, so that they would comprehend and share his vision. He was a prophet, not a political strategist or an organization man.

The world of words is in a sense an easy place to live in. If one doesn't like the formulation one gave yesterday, one can always give a new one today. Actions ("things"), on the other hand, commit in a way words never do. It is far easier to achieve clarity when one is concerned solely with verbal formulations.

Kaplan the diary keeper is another dimension of his involvement in words, not things. Throughout his life, Kaplan wrote regularly in his journal. Keeping a journal is a way of naming things and bringing order into the universe of the everyday — a mapping of experience. Kaplan created the map but did not always take the journey. The journal also represents a form of speech. Speech is objectified thought directed at the "other"; the diary qualifies as speech, since there is always an implied readership. So he was teaching and formulating not only when he was with students or colleagues or congregants. He was also formulating and teaching when he was alone. The diary, he felt, confirmed his existence. For Kaplan, to exist was to formulate ideas, and so the continuous need for self-confirmation led him to keep the diary as a constant companion and a ready outlet. The diary also helped to satisfy his yearning for immortality. Writing about his diary keeping and observing himself as from a distance, he said, "After every such writing spell he would experience a sense of calm as though he had succeeded in accomplishing something that had permanence to it, something that rescued his life from the vortex of time."

That Kaplan was caught in the web of his own words was clear to the master himself. He understood that he never built the necessary organizational structures because he didn't want to. He realized, in moments of insight, that he was a man of words and not an organizer or a man of action in any significant sense. In the late 1920s, he tried to

Faculty of the Rabbinical School of JTS, mid-1940s. From left: *Max Arzt, Alexander Sperber, Robert Gordis, H. L. Ginsberg, Mordecai Kaplan, Louis Ginzberg, Louis Finkelstein, Alexander Marx, Saul Lieberman, Boaz Cohen, Hillel Bavli, Simon Greenberg, Moshe Davis. (Courtesy Library of JTS.)*

write the diary in the third person, but after a few weeks dropped the idea. The entries for this limited period are interesting, especially where he described himself. In one passage, he wrote, "He had a weakness for formulas. Never having had the fortune of experiencing the thrill of firsthand contact with things, he lived in a universe of words." To have lived in a universe of words means that he followed in a long line of rabbis and religious teachers who saw their primary spiritual activity as learning and formulating. Their whole life and Kaplan's whole life were an exercise in Talmud Torah.[57]

9

Torah and Salvation:
Interpreting the Bible

The *Menorah* articles Kaplan wrote from 1915 to 1920 constitute the outline of an ideology of Jewish life. All the basic concepts of his system are there: Jewish peoplehood, Judaism as a civilization, and some tentative formulations of the meaning of God in human experience. A comprehensive theory dealing with the Torah is lacking. Kaplan is associated with an ideology of Jewish life, but rarely is he perceived as an interpreter of the Torah. To be sure, he frequently based his arguments on Torah texts, and we do find explications of his concept of Torah,[1] but nowhere does there exist a systematic discussion of his biblical theology or of his work on the more well-known biblical narratives or of the major critical problems that confront the student of the Bible.

The many rabbis who have studied with Kaplan are, however, well aware of his views on every aspect of Bible study, for it was in his classes at the Jewish Theological Seminary, particularly in his courses on homiletics, that Kaplan examined the Torah with his students.[2] He insisted that before his students could preach, they had to have something to say; this meant studying the Bible and the philosophy of religion. In 1915–16, Kaplan taught a course entitled "Interpretation of the Bible" at Teachers' College of Columbia University. The course was repeated again with a slightly different emphasis in 1918.[3] Year after year, Kaplan preached weekly, first at the Jewish Center and later at the Society for the Advancement of Judaism.

Eugene Kohn, a student at the Seminary when Kaplan began teaching homiletics, is the author of the sole monograph on Kaplan's method of biblical interpretation.[4] In "Mordecai Kaplan as Exegete," Kohn rightly tied Kaplan's understanding of the Bible to the problems of the preacher. More than anything else, Kaplan wanted to make the text relevant. The need for a further elaboration on his method was recognized by Kohn: "We have not yet, for example, produced a single Bible commentary that is based on the reinterpretive approach [i.e., Kaplan's method]."[5] The commentary Kohn wanted was indeed begun by Kaplan himself, unbeknownst apparently even to those closest to him. Thus, we will examine the specifics of Kaplan's method, without having to speculate.

Before we can fully understand Kaplan's contribution to the study of the Bible and the conflicts he encountered, we must note the state of biblical scholarship in the early years of the twentieth century and the atmosphere in which Kaplan worked.

At the beginning of the century, Jewish scholars found it difficult to avoid the challenges put forth by Christian biblical critics. Julius Well-hausen, the most prominent Protestant Bible scholar, postulated a slow evolutionary development of Israelite religion from a primitive ani-mism in the patriarchal period to the ethical monotheism of the literary prophets. The document known as the Pentateuch was thus the prod-uct of many hands and received its final shape in the time of Ezra (fifth century B.C.E.). Jews reacted to this theory in different ways. Traditional Jews totally ignored the German-Protestant critics and never took the whole enterprise of biblical criticism seriously. On the other end of the spectrum, secular Jewish nationalists believed that the Bible was the record of Israel's spiritual groping and revealed the soul of Israel rather than the word of God in any direct sense. Ahad Ha-Am did not hesitate to call for a more scientific investigation and reinterpretation of the scriptures. Leaders of Reform Judaism followed in Abraham Geiger's steps and accepted the critical view.[6]

Schechter's well-known statement that higher criticism was higher anti-Semitism was part of a speech he gave at a dinner honoring Kauf-man Kohler, who had just become president of the Hebrew Union College. At one point in this speech, Schechter accused the critics of taking the Bible away from the Jews and minimizing the Jewish contri-bution to mankind: "The Bible is our sole raison d'être, and it is just this which the higher anti-Semitism is seeking to destroy, denying all our claims for the past, and leaving us without hope for the future."[7] In another speech, Schechter attacked Wellhausen head-on, not be-cause of his theories of composite authorship, but rather for his explicit anti-Semitism. In his well-known statement endorsing Zionism delivered in 1906, he quoted the following from Wellhausen: "The persistency of the [Jewish] race may, of course, prove a harder thing to overcome than Spinoza has supposed; but nevertheless, he will be found to have spoken truly in declaring that the so-called emancipation of the Jews must inevitably lead to the extinction of Judaism wherever the process is extended beyond the political to the social sphere."[8]

Schechter's statements on biblical criticism as head of the Seminary were much more conservative than before his arrival in America. Even in his more extreme condemnations, he seemed to be more concerned with the denigration of Mosaic religion than with source theory per se. Nonetheless, on the verge of hiring Israel Friedlaender for the Seminary faculty, he stipulated to Friedlaender that even if he accepted the critical view of the Pentateuch, he was not to teach it.[9] Schechter set the curricular policy for the Rabbinical School, continued by Adler and Finkelstein, which excluded the systematic scientific study of the Pentateuch.

Other faculty members, though they readily applied the tools of historical scholarship to postbiblical tradition, were hesitant to apply this method to the Bible. Louis Ginzberg, the leading member of the faculty, took an ambiguous position on the origin of Pentateuchal Judaism. In his article on law codes in the *Jewish Encyclopedia*, Ginzberg stated that "the laws [in Exodus 21–23:19] originated a long time prior to the date at which the code was committed to writing." He went on to say that "the Deuteronomic Code, notwithstanding its many peculiarities, cannot properly be designated as a new code; it represents rather a revised and improved edition of the Book of the Covenant, made in conformity with the new ideas of the time." The great Talmudist reportedly regretted having written the *Jewish Encyclopedia* article.[10]

In a number of public statements, Ginzberg clearly and unambiguously condemned biblical criticism. In an article published in 1922 entitled "Bible Interpretation: The Jewish Attitude," Ginzberg was quoted as saying, "The philosophic premises [of biblical criticism] exclude a divine ordering of the universe and deny the possibility of God appearing to man. Consequently the theory of creation must be regarded as a myth; theophanies in any form are impossible and revelation is assumed not to be an historical fact. With all these assumptions Judaism is in entire disagreement."[11]

Kaplan's early doubts regarding traditional Judaism centered on his understanding of the Bible, particularly the matter of biblical miracles.[12] Arnold B. Ehrlich, a Bible scholar who frequented the Kaplan household at the time, was a primary force in molding his attitudes: "[Ehrlich] taught me to penetrate through the vast layers of traditional commentaries to the rock-bottom original intent of the biblical authors. In doing so, he undermined my belief in the Mosaic authorship of the Torah and in the historicity of miracles." [13]

Ehrlich, who was working on a Bible commentary, consulted Kaplan's father about the way certain biblical terms were used in the Talmud. He shared his insights and discoveries with the Kaplans. The young Kaplan absorbed these ideas and argued with his classmates at the Seminary about Ehrlich's theories.

Ehrlich was a rather eccentric man whose work, although not generally well known, is still valued by Bible scholars. [14] He came to the United States in 1875 but was never able to secure a teaching position with a Jewish institution because, while in Germany, he had worked with Franz Delitzsch on a Hebrew translation of the New Testament that was to be used for missionary purposes. Bible scholar Harry Orlinsky described Ehrlich as an "utterly egocentric personality . . . never in doubt that he was absolutely right in his understanding of the preserved Hebrew text [and] if he could not solve a difficulty, it was because the difficulty was insolvable." [15] The point is also illustrated by an epigram Ehrlich quoted from a medieval Muslim writer on the title page of his commentary *Mikra Kiphshuto: The Bible according to Its Literal Meaning.* The epigram reads, "He who has the truth is the majority, even if he is alone." The title page also contains a dating of the volume not in the Jewish or Christian mode but counting from the Declaration of Independence. It may be that Ehrlich, in his stubborn independence of mind and in his love for America, served as a role model for the young Kaplan.

Ehrlich wrote his commentary in Hebrew because he was intent on bringing to Jews the significant results of modern biblical criticism. He was a "master of the Hebrew language [and] his emendations were consistently of superior quality to those proposed by the vast majority of his contemporaries but they were too frequently quite unnecessary, and purely conjectural, rarely based on a sound understanding of the versions." [16]

In his introduction, Ehrlich explained that he was a man "of little faith," so that when the evidence was transparent he could face the fact that parts of the Pentateuch come from different periods sometimes hundreds of years apart. Relatively unconcerned with tracing the different documents through the Pentateuch, he did note their existence. He maintained that although the patriarchs believed in one God who was all-powerful, they did not deny the existence of other gods. He also assumed that because the story of the golden calf was not mentioned by the prophets, it was postexilic. He hypothesized that both the priestly code and the Book of Deuteronomy were "very late." Although tending toward secularism, Ehrlich gave clear evidence of his great love for the Jewish people and of his feeling that they have a unique mission to perform in bringing the message of the Torah to the world.[17]

Kaplan readily accepted multiple authorship of the Bible and the results of biblical criticism, since for him the Bible's main theme was the groping of the Jews as a collectivity for meaning and values. He believed that some parts of the Pentateuch were postexilic in origin and that these "facts" did not in any way impair Jewish life or undermine the centrality and importance of the Torah. In his 1914 article "The Supremacy of the Torah," he maintained that biblical criticism did not in any way weaken the authority of the scriptures.[18] Rather than answering the critics, Kaplan simply set them aside. For him, the status of the Torah did not derive from its origin but from its place in the history of the Jewish people. Whether or not it was to remain supreme in the future depended on the compelling force of the ideas in the Torah. If the Torah's authority could be maintained in this functional way, then no statement about its origin would be threatening. Function was compelling; origin was not.

Even at this early stage in his life, while still traditional in many of his views, Kaplan sought the means of reconciling old loyalties with new discoveries: "Traditional belief as to the origin of the Torah is not the sole support of its supremacy. If this is found to give way, the one derived from its having rendered Israel the instrument of divine revelation is no less effective in maintaining its preeminence."[19]

Kaplan was vigorously attacked in the Jewish press because of his acceptance of biblical criticism, despite his repeated statements that he upheld the Torah's supremacy. He was called a heretic, and there were demands that he resign from the Seminary because he could no longer teach traditional Judaism. According to one paper, "Professor Kaplan by denying that God has given the Torah to Israel and also that the belief in the Messiah is fallacious has destroyed the most solid foundations of the traditional faith." The organized Orthodox rabbinate convened a special meeting at one point in order to condemn Kaplan and his followers, whom they called "the half-Orthodox." From time to time, Kaplan did receive letters of support for his position,[20] but from his colleagues at the Seminary and from the leaders of the Conservative movement, he encountered either cold acceptance or open hostility.

In accepting the composite authorship of the Pentateuch, Kaplan had to face the problem of revelation. Here, as with other issues, his explanation was functional in nature. If the Torah is a composite document, then obviously it was not totally revealed to Moses. The Torah, however, remains divine in " a derivative way." It comes from God in the sense that "it represents the embodiment in Jewish life of ultimate moral and spiritual forces, the divine character of which reason is ready to affirm, [and] in no way conflicts with the results of modern biblical studies, and on the contrary is rather confirmed by them." The Torah is to be considered eternal in Kaplan's view, even though it is not directly revealed by God. For the Torah to be eternal means that it "must never cease functioning as a standard in Jewish life." The continued application takes place through reinterpretation (*derash*), which reveals the secondary meaning of the holy text. This secondary meaning changes from age to age as people relate the text to their own particular experiences.[21]

Kaplan, always concerned with continuity in Judaism, wanted to be sure that his theory of interpretation did not legitimize arbitrary changes in the meaning of basic concepts. Central concepts, such as revelation, must not be altered beyond recognition. A basic continuity of identity must be preserved, linking present interpretations with those of the past. This identity did not require "sameness of doctrine" but "constancy of ratio between experience on the one hand and Judaism's reaction toward experience on the other." If a person can find beliefs that engender the same reactions that traditional beliefs engendered, then there is obviously the continuity of identity that Kaplan was seeking. Thus, he dismissed the allegorical method of interpretation wherein the simple or primary meaning is completely erased. Following the allegorical method, usually identified with Philo, "the facts disappear entirely, the unities of character and incident [are] entirely ignored, and the entire content turned upside down."[22]

It is clear that Kaplan did not treat tradition lightly, nor was he attempting simply to change ancient notions into modern ones. His method, a type of demythologizing, was thus a translation or rendering of a thought from one system into another. If the belief embodied in a mythic system has been adequately translated, we should upon adopting the translation hold attitudes analogous to the ancients and see implications for our thought and behavior analogous to theirs without the necessity of adopting identical ideas. Calling such an interpretation functional meant that the implications and the behavior that flow from the reinterpretation should be similar, even though the content might look very different.

The concept of translation as a description of Kaplan's method allows for a pluralistic image of biblical interpretation. Just as a statement may be translated into many languages, so with the archaic beliefs we are discussing. Kaplan's translation into modern terms is thus no less valid intrinsically than the translation of biblical thought into Maimonides' Aristotelian system. At the same time, we can still measure the adequacy of these different translations to ascertain the degree to which they give a faithful rendering of the original. We would look at Maimonides' translation to see whether key notions function the same way in his system as they did in the original. One advantage of this notion of interpretation is that it is not necessary to choose between a traditional translation and a contemporary one, because both may function equally well under different circumstances. After all, rabbinic interpretation (*midrash*) is as much a translation as is our own rendering.

Kaplan's functional interpretation is not a facile criticism of traditional thought by modern values but rather an attempt to restore the traditional in a way that is genuinely operative. His critics are mistaken when they accuse him of a slavish acceptance of contemporary values. One critic, reacting against what he considered Kaplan's one-sidedness, stated that Judaism should not "capitulate to a scientific naturalistic imperialism but [there should be] a mutually active critique of Judaism by these values and conversely of these values by Judaism."[23] It will become clear that this "mutually active critique" is precisely what Kaplan was striving for in his work on the Bible.

Kaplan used the Bible as a point of departure in everything he wrote. It is surprising that nowhere in the great corpus of Kaplan's published works do we find a systematic exposition of the Pentateuch, in either its narrative or its legal portions.[24]

Kaplan never presented himself as a Bible scholar. His knowledge of ancient Near Eastern non-Jewish languages and literatures was limited and derived mostly from secondary sources. Acquainted with the discoveries of archaeologists, he had no deep interest or expertise in this area. His insecurity in Bible studies may explain his failure to deal with this area systematically in his published works. His value as a biblical interpreter derives from shrewd intuitions and keen insights, as well as from his talent as a preacher. Making the text relevant was his ultimate, but not his sole, purpose.

Kaplan had specific ideas about how the biblical mind functioned and believed that the ancients frequently were not able to deal with their own subjective states but constantly felt impelled to objectify and reify their feelings: "The ancients, with their limited self knowledge, could not regard their inner drives as subjective experience. Whatever inner force was beyond their control was to them as much of an objective and external fact as the things they saw around them. Like the external world the irresistible inner promptings of the heart or the will could not, they thought, but come from some deity."[25]

Kaplan is not unique in viewing biblical statements as projections. Among Jewish thinkers, however, he was rare in holding this view and was notably imaginative in furnishing examples. Commenting on the Garden of Eden story, he noted that "God's keen disappointment in creation is, in fact, Israel's resentment at the way in which the human being often spoils God's beautiful world."[26] In commenting on the story of Jacob's encounter with the angel, he pointed out that an encounter with demons was well within the limits of propriety to ancient Israelites. He gave a modern interpretation rather than dismissing this as a piece of superstition, explaining the ancient belief in demons as a crude way of accounting for the unconscious and the uncontrollable forces in human nature. He then added: "The latest outbreak of the demonic forces in the world that left Israel limping is very much in need of being countered by the faith that Israel will not only survive but come away from the tragic experience with renewed strength and blessing."[27] Here is Kaplan's Jacob wrestling with the angel.

Another aspect of biblical thinking that drew Kaplan's attention was the tendency to project ideals backward in time rather than forward as we might today. The Garden of Eden story is easily seen in this light, but Kaplan also applied the principle to the actions of the patriarchs. The ideal of the Jewish people was obedience to God's will. No matter how difficult life was, Jews believed it was incumbent upon them to maintain their trust in God. It was natural for the Jews, according to Kaplan, to see the progenitor of the race as fulfilling the ideal toward which they were working. Thus, in Abraham, "the task for which Israel lived met with fulfillment." He was tested and tried as the Jewish people were tested, but Abraham remained obedient and faithful; his descendants did not always do as well.

Once the ideal is projected back to the patriarchs, it becomes part of the justification for Israel's selection. Israelite leaders obviously perceived the masses as constantly falling short of the ideal. Why, then, was Israel selected? Israel was chosen because the ideal had already been fulfilled in Abraham. The *brit* (covenant) is God's promise to Abraham and his descendants that they would prosper and possess the land; they, in turn, were to obey God's will. This was the way the relationship between God and Israel was supposed to function. The Israelites projected the ideal relationship back into the past and then used the story of the patriarchs as a guide for interpreting the events of their own time: "Whatever befell Israel was interpreted consciously or subconsciously in terms of the experiences of the ancestors, experiences of trial, questioning, moving toward the prescribed goal and deviating from it, frustration, defeat, rescue, and fulfillment. No matter how far Israel would go astray or how near their great expectations bordered on extinction, the law of history or, in the language of the Torah, the covenant God made with the Patriarchs would bring Israel back into their destined course."[28]

Another dilemma in biblical interpretation is that certain matters were problems for Jews in biblical times but not now, and vice versa. For example, Kaplan maintained that in biblical times Jews were not troubled about God having an image. It was only in later times that the mental conception one forms of God became an object of concern.[29] To contemporary man, the fact of death is a given, and life after death is highly problematic. To the biblical mind, it was the opposite; hence, it was necessary to explain the phenomenon of death (one of the functions of the Eden story). Regarding Eve's curse in Genesis 3:16, Kaplan explained, "To the ancient mind the pangs of childbirth appeared unnatural and could be accounted for only on the ground of some primeval curse. The same is true of woman's willing subjection to man."[30]

The reification conspicuous in the Bible presents difficulties. Kaplan suggested a number of ways to understand the attitude that underlies the objectifications we find in the text. We can, for example, turn key noun forms into adjectival forms and then search for the quality or qualities that have been objectified in a particular entity. This predicate thinking, useful in theology, functions well in Kaplan's interpretation of the Torah.

His translations are bound up with his views on God and salvation. In addition to turning the noun into an adjective, it is important to articulate the meaning of the adjective in terms of some recognizable experience: "Divine is therefore whatever possesses the quality of furthering man's perfection or salvation. Torah-like is whatever possesses the quality of rendering the Jewish people aware of its function to further the process of man's perfection or salvation. Israel-like is the people that identifies itself with that process.[31]

Statements about God, Israel, or the Torah thus should be taken as describing not particular entities but rather the extent to which any element of experience is divine, Torah-like, or Israel-like. Applying this mode of interpretation to the Psalms, Kaplan translated the verse "The teaching of the Lord is perfect, restoring the soul" into "That which furthers salvation must be for us the will of God."[32]

Here is probably the clearest statement of Kaplan's openness and universalism. According to this mode of interpretation, salvation and the means to attain it may be found almost anywhere. Thus, not only is the Torah the "word of God," but any text that aids in restoring the soul must be considered divine. His universalism is at times wholly without boundaries. His willingness to embrace non-Jews as the carriers of religious ideals is also clearly implied in this predicate thinking. Kaplan's interpretation of Israel results in the startling recommendation that the Covenant ought to be dissolved. "The teaching that Israel is God's chosen people should mean that God's chosen people is any people that is consciously dedicated to the purpose of furthering the perfection or salvation of man." [33]

Kaplan's earliest biblical concerns centered around miracles. He was not predisposed to accept the suspension of the natural order as recorded in the Hebrew scriptures, pointing out that in the song of Moses (Exodus 15:1–8) the event of crossing the Red Sea seems to have a rather natural tone. Pharaoh and his chariots were drowned in the sea by a sudden storm, which is described in colorful metaphors by the poet. This poem, which is older than the prose portion that accompanies it, was taken literally, and the poetic images were turned into facts. The poet had written, "The floods stood straight like a wall" (Exodus 15:8). To the poet, the God of Israel can influence natural phenomena so as to aid his people: "I will sing to the Lord, for He has triumphed gloriously; horse and driver He has hurled into the sea" (Exodus 15:1). To the prose writer, "the God of Israel is the creator of the world who can remake and unmake it at Will." [34]

According to Kaplan, the plagues associated with the Exodus were perceived by the ancient Israelites as evidence of a struggle between God (Yahweh) and Pharaoh, who represented the sun god. Yahweh had to prove himself as much to the Israelites as to Pharaoh. Yahweh is portrayed here as the great warrior. Kaplan made no attempt to deal with the historical reality behind the legendary exaggerations. For Kaplan, the ancient Israelite belief in these miracles was an indication of "the great intuitive awareness that they owed to that power [Yahweh] their capacity to throw off the yoke of the nation that oppressed them." Then follows a sentence in the manuscript that Kaplan crossed out but that should be restored, for it is the final stage in the demythologizing process: "It means that the mental and social energies in man which give rise to various human societies such as tribes, cities, nations, or the United Nations are the most divine manifestations of the power that makes for man's salvation." [35]

There is no evidence that Kaplan ever wrestled with the historicity of the legends of Genesis or the narrative of Exodus. It may be that the distinction drawn by Ahad Ha-Am between historical truth (what people believe) and archaeological truth (what scientific analysis supports) solved the problem of historicity for Kaplan at an early date. Ahad Ha-Am believed that even if archaeological evidence should contradict what people believe about Moses, he would nonetheless continue to be an important historical personage. The force of his image has a generative power all its own.[36]

Kaplan accepted the Pentateuch as a composite document and believed that the Torah was edited rather late. His early verse-by-verse commentary contains many allusions to the different sources behind the text. However, he was not particularly interested in unraveling the whole sequence and rarely spent time indicating which verses came from which sources.[37]

The message of the Torah according to Kaplan's interpretation may be summarized as follows: Israel has been selected to live according to God's will, which is the rule of law and justice. Those who live by force and aggression will perish. The belief that right must triumph over might is established for the Hebrews by seeing these principles actually operative in their proto-history. Man suffers because of his pride and arrogance. The Torah comes into the world in order to offer man the opportunity to reclaim himself. Man can recover his original state of perfection, and movement toward this goal is initiated by God through the Torah and Israel.

For Kaplan, the story of creation was not a scientific explanation or even a metaphysical statement but was rather soterical in nature – it pointed toward man's salvation. (*Soter* from the Greek word meaning "save.") We learn from Genesis that the world was created in accordance with God's purpose — the fulfillment of man both individually and collectively. To say that God created the world is to make a statement about the nature of the world and the way in which it will function if we obey God's will, which is the rule of law and justice. Sin and evil come, therefore, from man's arrogance and lust for power. Man's fall is caused by his "spirit of self-sufficiency, of willfulness, disobedience, and arrogance, which in classical literature is designated as hubris." The rebelliousness of mankind against God is prefigured in Adam, just as the obedience of Israel to God's will is prefigured in Abraham: "To presume to be a god means to lust for power and to recognize no law higher than one's own will." The sin of Noah's generation was its cold, calculating, destructive intent and not necessarily evil behavior.[38]

The sin of rebellion against God takes the form of aggression and violence. This is the case not only with the generation of Noah but also with those who attempted to build the Tower of Babel. The primary point, according to Kaplan, is that "the chief menace to the world comes from the unification of the forces of evil." Kaplan saw the division of mankind into many languages and many nations as a positive occurrence, for "is not the disregard of differences a form of imperialism which is bound to bring about the dictatorship of a dominant clique which comes to tyrannize over and exploit the multitudes whom it has rendered helpless?"[39]

Abraham, of all the patriarchs, is the clearest symbol of obedience to God. God's command to Abraham to sacrifice Isaac is the supreme test of trust in God and obedience to him. In the modern age, the notion of obedience is not in vogue. Yet it was clear to Kaplan that in Genesis obedience is a prime virtue: "For the ancients obedience to the will of God was the prime virtue. Adam lacked it, Abraham had it. In our own day, this virtue must mean the power to conform to that innermost nature of reality, the basic law of life, obedience to which brings salvation to man and defiance of which leads to disaster."

Kaplan differentiated between the image of the patriarchs presented by the rabbis and the picture that emerged from a careful reading of the text. For the rabbis, Abraham is the founder of a religion. Thus, in the *Midrash* we have the story of Abraham's rejection of his father's idolatry. For the Torah, however, he is the founder of a people. In the former, the focus is on Abraham; in the latter, it is on God:

> The Torah's main purpose is to tell the wondrous way in which Yahveh raised up a people unto Himself, using Abraham as His chief instrument. Abraham's virtue on the other hand, consists in willingly lending himself as Yahveh's instrument for that purpose, by obeying His command and displaying faith, in the face of obstacles and postponements. God does not merely intervene in the affairs of the patriarchs. He is not a deus ex machina. He is the prime mover of the events in their lives, and occupies, as it were, the center of the stage.

According to Kaplan, the legends about the patriarchs arose because they were perceived as symbolizing the people of Israel. This interpretation is emphasized throughout his detailed remarks on the patriarchal legends. Thus, the extraordinary births of both Isaac and Jacob are a reflection of Israelite belief in the unique status of the children of Israel. That uniqueness is concretized by projecting it back onto the patriarchs in the form of the special conditions of their birth.

Another central theme in the early narratives is the relation of the patriarchs to the land of Israel. These legends reflect the importance of the land to the Jewish people in terms of fulfilling their ultimate destiny. Thus, the Torah emerges as the charter of the Jews to their land, and these legends show that Israel cannot remain rootless and still fulfill its destiny. The Zionist thrust of this interpretation is clear; but, as we know, Kaplan was a man of two civilizations. It was natural for him, therefore, to emphasize the notion of rootedness not only with reference to Eretz Yisrael but also with reference to the lands in the Diaspora where the Jews happened to be living. The patriarchal legends teach us the value of rootedness and arise out of this value as a goal and ideal of the Jewish people.

Kaplan believed that the extant version of the Exodus story arose in the period of the early monarchy. Both the Pentateuch and the prophetic literature reflect the deep impression made on generations of Israelites by these accounts. But regarding the actual historical happenings, Kaplan, surprisingly, did not adopt an evolutionary view of Israelite monotheism but believed, like Yehezkel Kaufmann, that Mosaic religion as it emerged during the Exodus was completely novel: "Nor did it [Israelite religion] emerge from a long evolutionary process in which longheld beliefs and practices were shed, leaving behind a permanent residue associated with some god or gods. The religion of Israel came like a bolt out of the blue."

The deliverance from Egypt frequently was advanced as a reason for performing rituals and acting morally. Kaplan saw this process as analogous to Americans conducting (or being exhorted to conduct) their public affairs in the spirit of the Declaration of Independence. This is strange, for although Americans do frequently recall the Declaration of Independence, it is not as much a part of American consciousness as the Exodus was for traditional Jews, who recalled it every day in their prayers and blessings. The Exodus from Egypt is the central event of Israelite history and presents us with God as emancipator. The ancient Hebrews thus experienced godhood not only in relation to such qualities of life as truth or beauty but as manifested primarily in human association. Yahweh is expressed in the Israelite capacity to act together and to throw off oppressors.

Concerning Sinai, Kaplan pointed out that only a handful of references to this theophany occur in the prophets. Such a lack may indicate that the association of the giving of the law with Sinai is rather late. Kaplan did not doubt that the Israelites experienced a theophany of some nature at Sinai which perhaps had not been originally associated with the law. The event became historical because it "derives from historical connections and sets off fresh historical connections." Kaplan understood the Sinai event as a kind of shock, analogous to experiences in an individual's personal life that lead to a greater awareness. Although he did not discuss in detail the nature of the shock, he said that "miracles reflect the awareness of God's power as a result of crisis in the outer life of the people. Theophany reflects the awareness of God's will as a result of crisis in the inner life of the people."

The covenant itself is demythologized by Kaplan as that which God requires from the Israelites and which is necessary for them to function as a people and to fulfill their destiny. The laws of the Torah "constitute the behavior which is to Israel what natural law is to any physical or animate being, the distinctive fact that gives Israel its character and helps to maintain it in life."

In conclusion, Kaplan's interpretation of the Hebrew scriptures may be described as functional. He sought to translate archaic notions into contemporary terms and to resurrect the attitudes behind ancient mythifications so that the *Weltanschauung* developed by these attitudes might again be operative. Kaplan, in his longing for the wholeness behind the myths, was a rebel against modernity. He hoped to reconstruct a world in which values were not in conflict with facts and "hard" knowledge.

10

THE CENTRALITY OF ETHICS:
The Society for the Advancement of Judaism

Leaving the Jewish Center was not easy for Kaplan or for his followers. The thirty-five families who joined him had invested heavily in the center. They had advanced $136,825 in donations and loans
in order to construct the magnificent center building on West Eighty-
sixth Street. The same group stood ready, in January 1922, to contribute within one week's time an additional two hundred thousand
dollars, provided the center would come under their control. Judah
Magnes was called in to arbitrate, but nothing came of this proposal.
There was much anger and mud-slinging on both sides. Those who
stayed felt that the Kaplan faction was defaulting on its responsibilities,
while many of the Kaplan supporters were tired of the "mummified"
Judaism they associated with the center. On the fifteenth anniversary of
the founding of the Society for the Advancement of Judaism, Joe Levy,
an SAJ stalwart, put it this way: "It required idealism, strength of character and courage to give up a membership in such an institution and
to sacrifice individual investments of a substantial nature; and what's
more the strong friendships of many years standing [were] strained to
the breaking point."[1]

Renewal through fragmentation is a well-known feature of the religious life of many groups in the modern period. It is also an old Jewish
"custom" and is especially familiar in America. Yet the phenomenon is
no less dramatic and painful because it is recurrent. The Kaplan followers left their palatial home at the center and moved down the block to
41 West Eighty-sixth Street, a small private house once occupied by

George M. Cohan. Levy remembers their tremendous sense of liberation and exhilaration at their own first Sabbath service, a sense of becoming free — "at last our leader could give free utterance to a conception of Judaism compatible with our present day needs."

The great question, of course, is one of intent. Did Kaplan and his group want to duplicate the center under a more liberal guise, or did they in fact want to become the nucleus of a new movement, perhaps even a new denomination? Many simply sought a congregation with a rabbi who would serve their day-to-day needs. Kaplan, though clear on matters of ideology, was much more ambivalent when it came to organizational matters and to his own role in the congregation. He constantly vacillated between his desire to formulate an ideology and his need to be a rabbi and a teacher. Sometimes his philosophical proclivities and the rabbinic calling pulled him apart. He was much more the prophet than the priest. Instinctively his mind ran to envisioning the goal rather than cutting the proper pathways to get there. Not only did he function poorly as a priest, that is, as a caretaker and administrator, but often he impeded the work of his followers who sought to aid him in the priestly function.

At the outset there was very little disagreement about matters of ideology. The initial euphoria lasted for quite some time. At one of the earliest organizational meetings of the board, Kaplan declared that they should be dedicated to the advancement of Israel and the Torah "in the light of reason and common sense." The group would be neither Orthodox nor Reform and would embrace the "restoration of Israel's land" as the "ideal for which this synagogue will work." Israel was the means; universal peace and justice were the ends. The board could easily unite behind such lofty sentiments, but more practical matters engendered some discussion. They needed to decide, for example, on Kaplan's tenure. Many advocated granting him life tenure, although some believed that their movement should not be identified wholly with one person. Kaplan himself supported a five-year term, emphasizing that he did not want to start a new religion. Praise for their leader came easily and naturally at these initial meetings. Mrs. Lamport, the wife of one wealthy manufacturer who was to become very active in the congregation, wondered aloud whether the group was worthy of Kaplan's leadership. Kaplan demonstrated his values when he insisted that his total salary be donated to the synagogue. The board voiced discomfort with this plan, and the matter was tabled for subsequent deliberation.[2]

The key issue to emerge during the very first days of the SAJ was the matter of its identity. Concerning the name, for example, Kaplan first suggested the American Synagogue but then changed his mind. In suggesting the Society for the Advancement of Judaism, he maintained that the term *society* was more appropriate than *synagogue* because he hoped to establish "a group of communities . . . with large numbers of adherents and followers who were not limited to the local community." Kaplan thus seemed to be advocating a new movement, but this is by no means clear. A denomination would possess its own organizational structure and its own ideology. The SAJ in its early years seemed to maintain both but was nonetheless a synagogue as well. In later years, Kaplan always claimed that he desired to establish a school of thought and not a denomination, but the first decade of the SAJ shows that its real status remained unresolved.

One significant indication in the direction of a larger organization was the existence of different membership levels. There were to be regular members living in the neighborhood and attending synagogue, as well as members not living close to the synagogue who might occasionally attend special events. Then there would be those who for a small fee (twenty-five dollars) would be national members. These would be "members of the movement," as the board put it, people who supported the concept of the society. Kaplan was very sensitive on the issue and at one early meeting told his followers that they must be on guard lest they be seen merely as another congregation on the West Side of Manhattan. He therefore proposed that they open up their facilities to Zionist groups and to the general public for educational activities.[3] Soon enthusiastic supporters were establishing chapters around the city. Evelyn Garfiel, a staunch supporter, organized SAJ groups at Barnard and at Hunter. She also organized a group of working women on the Lower East Side to discuss contemporary problems.[4]

Considering the magnificence of the center building it was natural for some at the SAJ to think of constructing some permanent edifice of their own. Kaplan was hesitant. He believed strongly that if they erected a building, their identity as a congregation would be a foregone conclusion. After a board discussion, he confided the following to his diary:

> I warned against the danger of being diverted from our aim by taking up the problem of a building for the Society. Once we do that we are bound to shrink into a congregation interested in its own upkeep. I advocated organizing groups similar to our own in different parts of the city and of the country, and then having these groups form the party which will embrace the vast mass of our people who want to remain Jews but cannot affiliate with Orthodoxy because of its medievalism and with Reform because of its un-Jewishness. . . . I pray to

God that I be able to carry out at least some of the plans that I suggest and for which the SAJ is so ready with its support.[5]

Such language provides convincing evidence that Kaplan early on entertained the idea of establishing a new denomination of national dimensions.

Within a few years of the founding of the SAJ, a small network of chapters already existed. Rabbi Max Arzt, a former student of Kaplan's, organized a group in Scranton, Pennsylvania, after a visit and lecture from his mentor. The same process repeated itself in Cleveland with Solomon Goldman, in Chicago with Max Kadushin, in Hartford with Morris Silverman, in New Bedford, Massachusetts, at Manhattan Beach, and in Brooklyn. Once these chapters were established, it became necessary to reorganize the society in New York. In February 1925, it was proposed that the society be separated from the synagogue. The synagogue would have its own board and president, and the society would continue to carry on all its activities, lectures, and publications. It would take over all the activities except for the holding of services. The congregation on West Eighty-sixth Street would be called "The First Synagogue," perhaps along the lines of the First Church of the Christian Science movement.[6]

Amid all this activity a group of board members began to search the Eighty-sixth Street area for a suitable building. In January 1925, they bought one at 11-15 West Eighty-sixth. Although those who pushed for its acquisition did so in the interests of the synagogue, the subsequent publicity represented the building as the national headquarters of a new movement, which would work to "revitalize Judaism in America by making it function as a civilization in the everyday life of its adherents."[7] Those perceiving the SAJ as primarily a national organization were as powerful as those who wanted a congregation with its own home.

Kaplan edged in the direction of a new denomination by creating the rabbinical council of the SAJ. Support at the SAJ was sufficient for him to direct all his energy to the national scene. His closest colleagues stood ready despite disagreement over how much change they were willing to embrace. Yet, the moment having come, he could not seize it. He found it easier to speak in a radical way than act in a radical way. Unable to exploit the energies of his followers, he lacked the political savvy and the courage to create a new movement of his own. He found it easier to think in terms of ideology rather than organization. It was at this critical time in the late 1920s that he began to speak of the movement more as a school of thought than as a separate denomination.

Events at the SAJ during this period (1925–1929) took on a momentum of their own. The building needed to be refurbished, which fully absorbed the energies of the board. As the members grew increasingly involved with the physical plant and with synagogue activities, the national dimensions of their venture seemed to recede from the forefront of their consciousness. Kaplan vacillated. On the one hand, he became caught up in synagogue matters and in the pleasures and problems of being a rabbi. On the other hand, he continued to lament the fact that the SAJ was more a synagogue than the nucleus of a new denomination within the Jewish community.

Kaplan functioned well in formulating the goals of the SAJ and in creating an institution that continued the center idea but on a more modest level. The goal was a synagogue that would be much more than a place to study and to pray. It would be a "seven-day synagogue," in Rabbi Israel Levinthal's apt phrase. The SAJ was very much the center of the social life of its members, with its theater parties and dinner dances at fine hotels. Within its first two years, the SAJ raised almost ninety thousand dollars for Palestine, "beautified" the Sabbath and holiday services, had instituted a three-day-a-week school with more than a hundred children, published a book by Kaplan, and opened a regular adult education program.[8] All these activities were expressions of Kaplan's vision and were carried out in grand fashion.

The adult education, for example, was outstanding in both the range of content and the quality of speakers. In the course of the first year of the SAJ, Judah Magnes spoke on "The Jewish Conscience," Horace Kallen on "The Jewish Question and International Politics," and Samson Benderly on Palestine. The topics reflect not only Kaplan's ethical concerns (Judge Bernard Rosenblatt on "Jew and Arab in Palestine") but his involvement in issues of general significance (William Kilpatrick of Columbia University on "Education and Character"). Kaplan was overeager to present his congregants with lecturers. During the first year, he sometimes arranged two or three lectures in one week, and it quickly became apparent that this schedule was too heavy. Some of the lectures were poorly attended, and after the first year the number per week was cut back.

Though the number of lectures was reduced, he continued to engage first-rate people. Shalom Spiegel, the great Hebrew savant who came to teach at the Seminary in 1929, was hired by Kaplan to give a number of courses at the SAJ. He spoke on biblical themes in Renaissance art as well as on the Bible as interpreted by Rembrandt. Later that same year, he also gave a series of twelve lectures on modern Hebrew literature which became the subject of his famous book *Hebrew Reborn*, published in 1930. The adult education lectures also reflected Kaplan's interest in women's issues with a survey on women's history entitled "The Five Ages of the Jewish Woman — A Historical Survey of the Cultural Development of Jewish Women."[9]

Kaplan's interest in art, evident in the Spiegel lecture series, led to the hiring of a very talented young woman, Tamima Gezari. Gezari originally had been Kaplan's student at the Teachers' Institute. A few years after her graduation, he asked her to teach art education at the Seminary. In the early 1930s, Kaplan suggested that Gezari paint a mural for the SAJ on the subject of "the Old and the New Palestine." This mural, which portrayed the *Halutzim* in the act of building up the land, stirred considerable controversy within the congregation. The opposition came not from anti-Zionist sentiments but rather from a few traditional individuals who found the giant mural offensive because it violated the Second Commandment.[10]

Kaplan's commitment to a wider vision of Judaism also found expression in the place of music at the synagogue. Cantor Nathanson, an outstanding cantor, was engaged at an early point. The synagogue choir sang regularly at Sabbath morning services, and Jewish music was a prominent feature of the adult education programming, with an original musical selection preceding each lecture. For example, when Israel Chipkin, the registrar at the Teachers' Institute, lectured on Jewish education in November 1929, he was preceded by a musical program presented by the Hebrew Arts Ensemble playing the music of Ernest Bloch.

Another common format was the dinner-dance combined with a lecture. Such an affair was held at the Savoy Plaza Hotel on November 19, 1931. This particular evening featured a lecture by Kaplan on Eugene O'Neill's "Mourning Becomes Electra" and a novel by Joseph Roth with Job as its subject. Although the evening was primarily a social event, Kaplan took the lecture seriously and attempted to articulate the essential differences between the Hebrew and the Greek views of life. He attended many such affairs, but never enjoyed the small talk and the socializing. No doubt there were some among the audience who didn't appreciate serious themes at a dinner-dance and were as uncomfortable with his lecture as he was with their chatter.

One of the more innovative ventures in the early years was Kaplan's effort to create a board of arbitration. In traditional Jewish communities, the rabbinical court, or *Bet-Din*, functioned in several ways. It dealt with conflicts involving marriages and divorces and other matters of personal status, and it also functioned as a small claims court in arbitrating disputes. In 1925, Kaplan recommended that a board of arbitration be established at the SAJ. It would have seven members and would arbitrate disputes between parties that consented to accept its authority. According to the laws of New York State, any dispute could be submitted to arbitration, with the written decision being "binding and irrevocable" under the law. This experiment was a significant attempt to reconstruct a traditional Jewish institution (the rabbinical court) and place it within a modern context. When Kaplan presented this proposal to the board, he described it as "a concrete embodiment of the ethical concerns of the Society." Unfortunately, we have no records of how the board functioned or the kind of disputes it considered.

The SAJ was no ordinary congregation and Kaplan no ordinary rabbi, as is well illustrated by the *SAJ Bulletin*. Every congregation has its publications announcing events, with remarks from the rabbi and perhaps a column written by a member, and so on. At the SAJ, the bulletin started off rather modestly and eventually developed into a printed journal called the *SAJ Review*; it had the same format as the *Reconstructionist Magazine* which succeeded it. From the beginning, Kaplan contributed heavily, of course, writing not only the editorials but also regular articles on every aspect of Jewish life. He paraphrased and interpreted the *Midrash* (a series in 1924 and 1925), instituted a regular section that contained selections from rabbinic literature ("an anthology of rabbinic lore"), and also wrote a "History of Judaism as Reflected in Its Literature" (September 1927–February 1928). Articles also appeared by Shalom Spiegel, Simon Greenberg, and Louis Finkelstein. These men were all young at the time, and Kaplan was eager to give their literary and philosophical efforts a significant exposure.[11]

From its inception, the SAJ was involved in Zionist affairs. Kaplan invited Chaim Weizmann to the congregation to speak whenever the Zionist leader came to America, and Weizmann was made an honorary member of the congregation. The SAJ led the other West Side congregations in raising money for Zionist causes and was intensively active in the Inter-Congregational Committee of the West Side which was formed to raise money for Palestine. The coalition sponsored dinners at the Astor Hotel which were heavily attended by SAJ members. One of the most interesting Zionist projects of the SAJ was its support of the Hebrew periodical *Ha-Shiloah*. This major Hebrew literary journal, originally edited by Ahad Ha-Am and later by Joseph Klausner, was having difficulties. Through his Zionist contacts, Kaplan learned that the journal needed money and persuaded a group of SAJ members to underwrite its continued publication. The board proudly asserted that in 1924, it had increased the subscriptions from four hundred to six hundred and that the journal was largely financed by the SAJ membership.[12] Although most SAJ members could read Hebrew and came from traditional backgrounds, only a few could actually understand the articles written in the journal. They backed *Ha-Shiloah* in the conviction that Hebrew and Hebrew culture were a significant part of Jewish life. Their support reflected their deep need to feel some involvement with Hebrew culture.

The most significant aspect of life at the SAJ during its early years was Kaplan himself. He could never really speak his mind at the center. Theoretically free to say whatever he wanted, in reality he always felt constrained by the Orthodox atmosphere. Although he had expressed much of his thinking at the center, it was not until he came to the SAJ that he fully elaborated the more radical implications of his thought. Week after week he articulated all of the major assumptions that were to characterize his system. His conceptualization was brilliant in its clarity and logical structure. Although he published a number of short works during this period, the primary vehicle for his ideology was the Sabbath morning sermon. Kaplan overwhelmed the congregation with his sincerity, his passion and the persuasiveness of his message.[13]

At the core of Kaplan's thinking was his belief that a primary function of Judaism was to promote ethical behavior. He invited the board to his house in early October 1922 and tried to persuade them that ethics ought to be the congregation's primary concern. It was clear that ethics was as basic to his thinking as the idea of "Judaism as a Civilization." In line with this emphasis, he suggested to the group that the name of the society be changed to the Jewish Ethical Culture Society. When asked how this group would differ from the Ethical Culture Society, Kaplan launched a long tirade against the Ethical Culture Society and charged that it lured Jews away from the Jewish people. His opposition to Felix Adler's group was at least in part a result of feeling threatened, for the philosophy of Ethical Culture was in fact very attractive to him. But Kaplan believed that "loyalty was the essence of virtue," and thus Felix Adler was being extremely unethical in abandoning the Jewish people. The Jewish Ethical Culture Society would be different from Adler's group because it would stress the individual's loyalty to the Jewish people and the building of a center in Palestine as a corollary of the ethical devotion. When the board members wanted a shorthand way to explain these views, they were told to describe it simply as ethical Judaism.[14]

One of the first publishing projects of the new society was a little book that explained the aims of the SAJ. It focused on ethics and was referred to as the *Blue Book*. This title may have been an oblique reference to the social register, which was also called the *Blue Book*. The book began by outlining the nature of the SAJ and emphasized the ethical elements in its identity:

> The Society for the Advancement of Judaism is a religious fellowship of Jewish men and women who want Judaism to act as an ethical influence in their everyday life.
>
> Most people associate Judaism with dogmas which are either self-evident or unacceptable, and with ceremonies which are honored more in the breach than in the observance.
>
> They ought to know better. They ought to know that Judaism once embraced the whole of life; that it consisted of a language, a literature, a code of laws, an ethical system, a community life, and a public opinion — that it was, in fact, a whole civilization.

According to the *Blue Book*, group deliberation and group study were the primary means of attaining the society's ethical aims. Prayer was included but was of less concern. Kaplan, ever the teacher, seemed to have unlimited faith in the power of the word. He assumed that behavior was deliberate and rational. "If the purpose of religion be to develop ethical personality," the *Blue Book* explained, "it can do so only by encouraging thought." Kaplan proposed that individuals within the synagogue should deliberate together on the real ethical conflicts they faced, and through this "cooperative thinking" they would develop the internal processes that would lead to more ethical conduct. In a rather naive classroom way, the *Blue Book* stated that "the essence of all right doing is to weigh consequences. Nothing is so likely to cultivate that habit as the exchange of ideas on the art of living."

Kaplan's proposal for influencing the ethical behavior of his congregation was to formulate with them a code for their own personal behavior through a series of meetings. The code would deal with business, political, and social activities as well as relations with non-Jews. There is no record of the code's details. Here, as in the case of the arbitration board, Kaplan was attempting to integrate the principles of traditional Jewish life into a nontraditional setting. The *Shulhan Arukh* and other Jewish codes had served as guides of the past but were not fully relevant or used by the non-Orthodox community of the present. The *Musar* (ethics) movement of Eastern European Jewry also served as a model for Kaplan's ethical program. The idea of a code of behavior (as opposed to a catechism of beliefs) was a particularly Jewish mode of dealing with the central problem of religious ethics.[15]

◆

Traditionally, religion had a strong ethical function. The formation of a virtuous character has always been one of the primary functions of religion. In the United States, many liberals have ceased to see religion as discipline and moved toward a more broad-minded position, viewing it as contributing toward self-realization, self-discovery and liberation. Kaplan also believed that religion enabled the individual to function optimally; but in addition, it fostered good character and self-control.[16]

Kaplan's ethical position may be understood as a reinterpretation of the traditional concept of God's sovereignty or kingship. He interpreted the concept of sovereignty to mean that needs and wants are not ultimate but must be subsumed under some higher law than the law of self-gratification. To do this is to accept the sovereignty of God. Real atheism is the "conscious belief that life and what it brings to us are ours to do with as we please." Kaplan spoke directly and powerfully to the inner conflict between the urge to be free and the need to live productively in society. He believed in forging ahead to ever higher levels of self-realization without abandoning the sense of responsibility. He rejected the notion that the "indulgence of the natural impulses is the only means to the realization and development of the individual." Some radicals maintain that all conventions stifle the natural instincts toward genuine goodness and creativity: "This view of the natural impulses surrounds them with the romantic halo as suppressed, victimized by the moral claims. This view identifies all morality with artificial conventions which, by hindering the satisfactions of the appetites, prevent the realization of one's true personality."[17]

Kaplan made these statements in the 1920s, when considerable emphasis was being placed on the individual pursuit of pleasure and tradition and conventionality seemed like restraints. A man of his time, he was ready to overthrow the traditional when it did not make sense and he never strayed from his belief in self-realization as the primary goal of man. But regarding ethics and morals, he remained the staunch defender of religion's traditional role. These two directions, apparently contradictory, were always united in Kaplan's mind. "Religion's main business," he wrote, "is to guide us in the art of living which is another name for the art of mutual adjustments that make for more

effective self-realization in each individual and more efficient cooperation among individuals and collectivities."[18] Cooperation and self-
realization went hand in hand.

Given the overthrow of traditional theology as a basis for virtue and
character, what did Kaplan put in its place to help encourage self-denial
and restraint? This question goes to the very heart of religious ethics
and poses particularly deep problems for the liberal theologian. At
times Kaplan recognized that rational arguments were insufficient to
motivate self-denying behavior and to inspire individuals to overcome
their narrow self-interest. So what was needed was a contemporary
substitute for the belief that the commandments come from God. In
the past, faith alone provided a sufficient basis for achieving "altruism,
generosity and holiness." In the modern world, where tradition is weak,
Kaplan suggested looking to faith in the value of the human personality.
Such a faith does not arise from fear or from the rigidities of habitual
opinions but from conviction. The very existence of altruistic individuals who look to the needs of others before their own should in and of
itself become the basis of our own altruistic and self-denying impulses:
"The human personality when it is honest, courageous and forgetful of
self is the strongest and most tangible evidence of the reality of God."[19]

Kaplan's rationale for altruism was weak; he knew some other
source of "commandingness" of the *Mitzvah* and the moral rule must
be found. He believed that individuals can sometimes be moved to self-
denial through community pressure. Traditional societies exert strong
pressures on individual members because the collective will is so clear
and united. Kaplan, the apostle of liberty and freedom, lamented the
passing of the institutions that expressed the collective will. He was in
fact quite far from the democratic individualism some ascribe to him.
"Throughout the centuries, wherever the Jews were scattered, they
lived in communities that were able to a large extent to enforce their
will upon the individual. If Judaism is on the wane it is because there is
no possibility of resorting to the collective mind or the collective will,
thus showing that the Jewish people are disintegrating."[20]

These thoughts about community coercion surface throughout
Kaplan's writings. He clarified his views when he dealt with the Catholic church. He admired the cohesiveness and the unity of the church
which helped it to withstand disintegrating forces of secularization in
the modern period. Indeed, he sometimes felt that the church could
serve as a model for the Jewish community.

The Catholics have, of course, an incomparably stronger bond of
unity which is reinforced by all the prestige, authority and skill in or-

ganization and education characteristic of the Church of Rome. They still operate with a powerfully cohesive force, a force whose decline in Jewish life has created the present problem of Judaism. The Catholic Church is the outstanding visible Church, possessing visible and tangible manifestations of its international solidarity . . . because visibility and tangibility are essential to help any group spirit alive, we Jews should strive to achieve a community status which is analogous to that of the Catholic Church.[21]

Kaplan's idea of calling a constitutional convention of the Jewish people emerged from his beliefs about the effectiveness of the collective will. These ideas were never picked up by the Reconstructionist movement, but they nonetheless represent an essential aspect of Kaplan. He deeply longed for the unity that had characterized an earlier period.

In a sense, Kaplan's desire was to circumvent one of the basic facts of American life, a novum in Jewish history — voluntarism. In the past, Jews had never had a choice about whether or not they were going to be Jewish. Anti-Semitism existed in the United States, but it seemed far less lethal than what many Eastern European Jews had experienced in the lands of their birth. All ethnic and religious immigrant communities felt strong pressures to integrate into American society. The basic question that faced committed Jews was whether or not the Jewish community would survive the freedom offered by America. Subcultural groupings in America are associational in structure, and there is "little external or internal compulsion to join or affiliate with the Jewish community." Kaplan proposed reintroducing elements of the traditional European Jewish communal structure into the American landscape while creating a substantially new kind of structure appropriate in an American context.[22]

The Jewish community in America was fatally flawed, he asserted, because it was based on organizations, primarily synagogues that were not compulsory. When financial problems arose, support of the Jewish communal organizations weakened. He believed that if the Jews were to remain a people in America, a significant measure of "involuntarism" must be introduced. In *Judaism as a Civilization*, he stated: "A person is a member of a nation not by choice, but by virtue of the pressure of the cultural group into which he is born. That pressure is exerted in the first instance through the family. If nationhood has played a useful part in the evolution of the race, it has been due, in no small degree, to this involuntarism which characterizes it. If, then, Jewish nationhood is to function in the Diaspora, its principal manifestation must be this very element of involuntarism characteristic of national life."[23]

Kaplan proposed a communal structure in which the overall councils or federations or *Kehillot* would not be merely fund-raising organizations. They would be quasi-governmental structures in the sense that they would "control" all other organizations. A Jew could not belong to any Jewish organization unless he or she was first a member of the community, the federation. A constitution would outline who could belong to the Jewish community (*Kehillah*) and what the obligations of each member would be.

> These might include . . . agreement to marry within the faith, or to proselytize the non-Jewish partner to a marriage, agreement to provide for such Jewish instruction as the community may deem necessary, willingness to pay such communal taxes for Jewish purposes as the community may require. In turn, the member may then claim such privileges as permission to worship in any of the community's synagogues, religious education for his children, religious services in celebration of *Brith Milah*, *Bar Mitzvah*, marriage, burial in a Jewish cemetery and with Jewish rites. All these services would have to be denied to non-members.[24]

Kaplan was not advocating the reintroduction of the New York *Kehillah*; he wanted to carry its policies much farther.

Nevertheless, Kaplan remained a genuine pluralist. His communal structure would include every kind of Jewish organization, both religious and secular, as well as all varieties of Jewish denominations from the most sectarian of the Orthodox to the most liberal of the Reform. The *Kehillah* would pass "laws" that would govern the qualifications for rabbis, cantors, teachers, social workers, and so on. These laws "would authorize courts for adjusting violations of its rules and arbitrating conflicts for which no law exists." He also advocated that Jewish law be reintroduced in the very sensitive area of ritual. Congregations of whatever stripe would set their own rules for their members. In the case of the Orthodox, the traditional canons would be in force. In the case of the more liberal groups, each would have to devise its own laws concerning how much of the old would be kept and what new rituals might be created.

Thus, Kaplan desired the reinstitution of Jewish law within the context of a democratic polity. His ideology would take the Jewish community back to the pre-emancipation model of organization, or at least to the European model of the early nineteenth century. Certainly the emancipation dethroned Jewish law. Although the term *Jewish law* continues to be in wide use, it is only in Israel that the *Halakhah* really has the force of law, meaning compulsion. In American society, as in all contemporary democratic societies, it is natural that religious organizations must be voluntary. Yet Kaplan's idea that the Jews constitute themselves a special kind of religious polity is not in and of itself illegal in America. It is not undemocratic, either. At every point, the rules that shall govern the Jewish community as a whole would emerge from representative bodies constituted by members. Kaplan advocated that Jewish law be reintroduced in the center of Jewish life. With the law would come courts and some kind of sanctions. Kaplan, the most famous excommunicant of modern times, seemed on the verge of declaring that the new *Kehillah* might expel people who did not conform to its basic requirements.

The whole scheme appears bizarre, a throwback to the repressive structure of Jewish life that had all but disappeared since the emancipation. It sacrificed a considerable degree of freedom to regain a remnant of the order that existed in former times. Preserving the Jewish people entailed the strengthening of the collective consensus of Jews as Jews. Kaplan proposed reinstating the "sovereignty" of the community as a significant force in Jewish life, as opposed to the sovereignty of the "autonomous individual." [25] This would increase the power of the community at the expense of the individual. Kaplan was ready to accept such limitations as the price of survival. He believed that democracy and freedom had to be limited if there was to be real community among Jews. Community was primary for Kaplan, not freedom.

Kaplan the innovator, the rejector of tradition, is only one aspect of this complex personality. He was very straitlaced in his moral convictions and often expressed contempt for those who lacked proper discipline. Tradition helped individuals in this direction: "We must not overlook the fact . . . that at the bottom of all veneration for tradition is the sense of continuity to human life which gives moral perspective to the life of the individual." Kaplan believed that it is a person's spiritual heritage that keeps him or her from falling "into sheer animalism." [26] Thus, tradition has a restraining and mellowing influence on the individual.

Although a thoroughgoing modernist himself, Kaplan had a keen sense of the destructive aspects of modernism. The tides of secularism had brought American Jews a deeper understanding of themselves and their environment, but eroded their sense of the numinous and the transcendent. Previous generations managed to sustain their sense of wonder and sensitivity to the divine presence. In America, they had become blasé: "It is this lack of zest which has secularized our lives, which has taken God out of our days. In asserting the sovereignty of

God, we refuse to accept such secularism as final. We are determined to recover the attitude of reverence, to recognize that there are things in life which we must approach in a spirit of piety." [27]

◆

The failure of the SAJ to develop into a new denomination may be blamed at once on Kaplan himself and on outside events. A new denomination would entail the creation of a national leadership fully dedicated to the SAJ ideals. Such a leadership would be primarily rabbinical and would have to create its own rabbinical school in order to train the next generation of rabbis devoted to the Kaplan ideology. In order to create this school, Kaplan obviously would have to leave the Jewish Theological Seminary, for there was no way in which the Seminary would become the bearer of his philosophy. This abandonment of the Seminary was simply a step Kaplan could never take.

The story of Kaplan's resignations from the Seminary and his negotiations with the Jewish Institute of Religion and the Hebrew Union College has never been fully told. [28] His ultimate decision not to leave the Seminary was fateful in terms of both his career and the destiny of the Reconstructionist movement. [29]

Rabbi Stephen Wise, founder of the Jewish Institute of Religion, and Kaplan were well suited to each other. Each displayed different strengths. Both were dedicated to Jewish cultural nationalism from the very beginning of the Zionist movement. Throughout their lives, these rabbinical leaders were also deeply involved in controversial social causes. Furthermore, they respected each other. In his autobiography, Wise described Kaplan as "one of the finest minds of the American Jewish community," and the Kaplan journal frequently refers to Wise with high regard. Kaplan was eminent as a theologian, philosopher, and teacher; Wise was strong as a social activist and organizer. They were close philosophically. As Wise once wrote to Solomon Goldman, "He [Kaplan], you and I are very nearly of one mind. There is no fundamental or unbridgeable gulf between us. We are bent upon doing the same thing." It may be that Wise did not want to become president of JIR himself because he knew that he was neither "an original thinker nor a productive scholar." [30] The combination of Kaplan the thinker and Wise the activist would have been formidable.

Wise considered Kaplan for the position of president of the institution from its very inception. "I went to see Wise," wrote Kaplan, two years before the JIR opened, "and after a few interviews with him we seemed to feel that ultimately he might get the funds for a rabbinical training school of which I would be given charge." Two years later, Wise, in writing to Kaplan, mentioned the fact that he had invited Kaplan to be a cofounder of the institution, but Kaplan refused.[31]

The Jewish Institute of Religion formally opened in the fall of 1922. In the spring of that year, Wise was making contacts in order to assemble a faculty, and he approached Kaplan about a position as a member of the teaching staff. It took Kaplan little more than two weeks to refuse Wise's offer. In declining, Kaplan made it clear that he might want to renew negotiations at some future time should conditions at the Seminary become intolerable. Both men realized the importance of the event. Kaplan, while still thinking about the offer, asked himself, "Will I have the courage to cross the Rubicon of my career?" Wise, in responding to Kaplan's refusal, wrote sympathetically:

> You will forgive me for saying by way of record that I believe it would have been better for you to have reached the decision to come to us, and joined with us in the founding of the Jewish Institute of Religion — better from the viewpoint of the Jewish cause and better I truly believe from your own viewpoint. I use the term your own viewpoint. I need hardly say that I am not thinking of your gain or advantage in a low sense, but I am thinking of the opportunity that I would have coveted bringing to you — namely, teaching under the most favorable auspices — that is to say in the spirit of freedom and of cooperation and of eager appreciation. The Institute would have welcomed and cherished your service.[32]

In his journal, Kaplan recorded a number of reasons for his refusal to join Wise. The SAJ had only been organized a few months before, and Kaplan was worried that the organization might fold if he were to associate himself with Wise and thereby brand himself as "extremely radical" and "heterodox." Kaplan was also concerned about the Teachers' Institute and feared that if he left it, the institute would be reduced to the "training of Sunday School teachers." After he told a delegation from the JIR board of trustees that he could not accept their offer, he castigated himself for his own ambivalence: "I am apparently doomed to go through life like Hamlet, a victim of weak will and indecision, knowing full well what I ought to do to be of greatest service to the Jewish cause, yet held back by fears and scruples that a truly strong man would have swept away as so many cobwebs." Kaplan continued to consider the offer long after he had declined it. In December 1922, Wise arranged a reception for more than one hundred Jewish leaders to welcome Felix Perles and Ismar Elbogen to the JIR. George Foote Moore of Harvard and Arthur C. McGiffert, president of Union Theological Seminary, along with Kaplan, were asked to make a few welcoming remarks. Kaplan at first refused, because Wise had asked him to speak for "Jewish Scholarship in America," and Kaplan felt that for him, scholarship was "nothing more than a suppressed wish." He finally accepted. When he rose to speak, perhaps overawed by the august group before him, Kaplan momentarily forgot what he was going to say and felt that he made a fool of himself. His reluctance to strike out with a new institution was partly due to his own insecurity: "My failure on so important an occasion has been preying on my mind. Perhaps it is a blessing in disguise. It will once and for all teach me to recognize my limitations, and stop the negotiations between Wise and myself which have done me spiritually more harm than good."[33]

The possibility of teaching in a hospitable atmosphere, however, continued to tempt him. In February 1923, Wise invited Kaplan to participate in a summer session for "younger men in the Jewish ministry" which the JIR was sponsoring. The schedule would include courses on *Pirke Avot* and on Pharisaism by R. Travers Herford, a series of lectures on "Sources and Development of Jewish Philosophy" by Harry Wolfson, and a lecture by Kaplan on "The Psychology of the Jewish Religion." Kaplan felt obliged to refuse because he believed his colleagues at the Seminary would interpret his association with the JIR as an act of disloyalty.[34]

As it turned out, he was invited by Weizmann to the Zionist Congress at Carlsbad to be held July 1923. On board the steamer going to Europe, he met Judge Julian W. Mack, who helped Wise organize the JIR and who worked with him in a number of other Jewish causes. One day, while sitting on deck, Mack turned to Kaplan and asked him point blank whether or not he was still interested in joining the faculty of the JIR. Kaplan was taken aback by the directness of the question, but fearful that his one chance of being "emancipated from the hostile atmosphere of the Seminary" would slip away, he authorized Mack to cable Wise that he would accept the position. Wise wired back immediately: "If Kaplan ready we are pleased offer him chair Religious Education and Homiletics."[35]

When Kaplan returned from the conference, where he had delivered an address on education in Palestine in Hebrew, he was dismayed to learn about the Adler correspondence published in *Idishe Licht*. (See chapter 8.) He renewed his negotiations with Wise, but again he hesitated. He heard that the institute was not yet really on its feet and that lecturers came and went without staying on as permanent members of the faculty. Then one Friday, the Kaplans invited Benderly to dinner and afterward took a long walk along Central Park West. Benderly, a longtime friend and a major figure in Jewish education, suggested to Kaplan that indeed he should resign, but rather than accepting a position with Wise, he ought to "consolidate the element that is neither Orthodox nor Reform into a third party." Kaplan was intrigued by the idea, and immediately after the Sabbath was over he hurried to see Wise, to show him the letter of resignation he had drawn up and to tell him of his new plan. Wise was disappointed, of course, but his graciousness impressed Kaplan and was further evidence of Wise's great respect.[36]

Kaplan, however, never submitted the letter of resignation to Adler. He consulted members of the board at the SAJ, and they all agreed that he should write Adler asking him to explain the statements he'd made to S. A. Israel, but should not resign. In the letter he finally wrote, Kaplan outlined his duties at the Seminary including teaching *Midrash*, religion, and ethics as well as homiletics, and asked Adler how he could ever write that he did nothing more than teach students how to construct a sermon. In response Adler explained that there were deep disagreements between himself and Kaplan. A believer in academic freedom, Adler felt nonetheless that a seminary was not like other institutions of higher learning: "How far this [academic freedom] applies in a theological seminary which teaches subjects that are bound to be treated subjectively, in which faith, tradition, even inherited prejudice if you please, must have a part is a subject we have never discussed but which probably ought to be discussed either between us or with the entire faculty." Adler attempted to convince Kaplan that his primary purpose was to make it clear that Kaplan's views did not dominate the Seminary or represent its official position on theological matters. He concluded his letter on a conciliatory note: "We have all been personal friends and we must continue to be but I think we are civilized enough to recognize and even to discuss our differences without destroying our friendships. This is more important for us to reconcile than a chance remark of mine in a letter." Kaplan was satisfied with Adler's reply.[37]

During the next few years, the JIR grew and prospered while Kaplan and Wise continued their very cordial relationship. Although many eminent men came to teach briefly at JIR, the mainstays of the faculty were Henry Slonimsky and Chaim Tchernowitz. Slonimsky, the teacher of philosophy who remained at the school until his retirement in 1952, and Tchernowitz, the Talmudist, both came into conflict with Kaplan in the late 1930s and 1940s. Writing in 1955 to Carl Herman Voss, the author of a number of books about Wise, Kaplan said that one of his reasons for not going to JIR was the hostility toward him of some members of the JIR faculty.[38]

When David Neumark, professor of philosophy at Hebrew Union College, died in 1924, feelers were put out to determine if Kaplan would be interested in the position. Kaplan responded positively and met with Julian Morgenstern, president of HUC, when the latter was in New York. Morgenstern first offered Kaplan a professorship of education, which Kaplan refused, fearing it would involve administrative work as well as teaching. Morgenstern then offered to create a special position for Kaplan somewhere "between the domains of Jewish Theology and Jewish Philosophy," as Morgenstern put it. Kaplan was also interviewed by Dr. Samuel Schulman, rabbi of Temple Beth-El, which later merged with Temple Emanu-El, the most prestigious Reform congregation in the United States. The two men spoke frankly about Kaplan's theology, and Schulman went away assuring Kaplan he would be at home at HUC and would even "bring a great deal of Jewishness to the college." Although the negotiations seemed to be going well, the offer was withdrawn. Morgenstern, in writing to Kaplan, did not spell out the details; he wrote cryptically, "I have very reluctantly come to the conclusion that we are still too far apart in our envisaging of Judaism's problem and in the solution of it which we would offer, to permit me to do that which my own personal feeling makes me desire strongly to do."[39]

Throughout this period, Kaplan threw himself vigorously into his work. He published a number of articles in the *Menorah Journal*, finished a manuscript on rabbinic theology which was later incorporated into *Judaism as a Civilization*, wrote pieces for the *SAJ Review* about a wide variety of subjects, worked with the SAJ, delivered lecturers to congregations on the East Coast as well as in the Midwest, taught rabbinical students, directed the Teachers' Institute, and was active in the Zionist Organization of America. Kaplan's unhappiness at the Seminary festered under the surface, so when Shalom Dov Ber Maximon resigned his position on the JIR faculty to become registrar, Kaplan again approached Wise about a faculty position. Wise was overjoyed. He told Kaplan he would do everything in his power to satisfy him: "Kaplan, you will be the first man on the faculty for whose sake students will join our institution." Kaplan, however, was concerned about his title. Slonimsky taught philosophy and ethics, and Kaplan was afraid their teaching might overlap. He insisted that his title be "Professor of the Philosophy of Judaism." The faculty did not agree to this title but nonetheless voted unanimously to invite him to join them. All parties at the JIR were concerned about proper timing. They did not want to invite Kaplan formally until after his resignation from the Seminary had been accepted.[40]

Although the players were those of 1922 and 1923 (Kaplan, Wise, JIR board, SAJ board, and Adler), the 1927 script was quite different. This time, Kaplan convinced the SAJ board of the wisdom of his move, and on January 19, 1927, he sent his resignation to Adler, who was then in Philadelphia. In his letter, Kaplan briefly explained his reasons. Since 1920, he had felt the opposition "bore down on me quite heavily. As a consequence I have gotten myself into a state of mind which is by no means conducive to such creative work as I would like to do in the field of Judaism." He therefore felt it necessary to resign his position as both professor of homiletics and principal of the Teachers' Institute. Adler's reply that he would make no attempt to dissuade Kaplan from his decision came as a surprise. Adler assumed it to be a "matured judgment" since he had not consulted Adler in making the decision. And when Marshall heard about the resignation, he wrote to Adler, "This is a matter which requires much delicacy in handling. It is quite a belated proceeding, which might well have taken place five years ago. It would have saved us from much embarrassment and would have simplified our recent negotiations with the Yeshiva, which I am persuaded were, at least unconsciously, affected by the peculiar attitude of Dr. Kaplan."[41]

Kaplan felt constrained to write again to Adler regarding academic freedom, which Adler had maintained was in force at the Seminary: "The question with me is not whether I could freely teach the practice and principles that differentiate Conservative Judaism from Reform. That is self-understood. The real question is whether I would be permitted to teach and practice with equal freedom those principles wherein Conservative Judaism differs from Orthodoxy."[42] Kaplan perceived a decided tendency at the Seminary to identify itself with Orthodoxy, as indicated by the serious consideration of merger with Yeshiva University.

When the word got out that Kaplan had resigned, he was inundated with letters from people at the Seminary imploring him to reconsider his resignation. The faculty of the Teachers' Institute wrote that they were "staggered" by the news and could not conceive of going on without Kaplan's "inspiration and guidance." But it was the students at the Rabbinical School who most effectively expressed the contribution he made to them and to the Seminary. In a letter to Adler authored by Milton Steinberg, the president of the student body, the sentiments of the students were eloquently stated:

> There is preeminently one man among our teachers who is responsible for what faith, and courage, and vision we may lay claim to. It is from him that we have acquired the hardihood to go on in a difficult and discouraging cause, for it is he who has given the Judaism we are expected to teach the content and vitality we have elsewhere sought in vain. He made the cause a creative venture, when it was otherwise a pursuit without purpose and without clarity. We have seen in him that clear and simple passion for spiritual honesty which we believe is the first desideratum in American Jewish life. And if we, his students, have learned something of that spiritual honesty our debt is to him. He has taught us devotion and given us things worthy of devotion when we had almost lost the faith that these were anywhere to be discovered. His example has given us to understand that creative spiritual activity was still possible in Jewish life and his was an example we have been sadly in need of. Preeminently our teacher and guide, we feel that the departure of Professor Kaplan will leave us utterly divorced from the things most worth learning, without the guidance toward those values which we believe Conservative Judaism ought to conserve and create.[43]

Kaplan was deeply moved by their expressions of appreciation and their apprehension at his departure. In late February, the Executive Committee of the Rabbinical Assembly passed a resolution stating that the resignation was "most unfortunate" and the Rabbinical Assembly "should put forth every effort within reason to obviate it." The students implored Adler to give Kaplan assurances that he would have freedom to speak his mind both in and out of the Seminary. The Executive Committee of the Rabbinical Assembly met with Kaplan and then put pressure on Adler to retain him. Kaplan's daughter Judith remembers distinctly the events of this time and recalls that Kaplan "was flattered like crazy into staying on at the Seminary. The delegations used to arrive at the house all day long and all night. The doorbell kept ringing with people from the Rabbinical Assembly and from the United Synagogue and from all sorts of places. They came pouring in. I remember the house was never our own."[44]

Finally, Adler contacted Kaplan and tried to dissuade him from leaving the Seminary. Kaplan was impressed by Adler's concern. So distressed was he by these events, said Adler, that he was unable to sleep.

Adler told Kaplan that negotiations with the yeshiva had been broken off, so there was nothing for Kaplan to fear on that score. He also assured Kaplan that the Seminary was not committed to Orthodoxy but to a "maximum program on the Jewish mode of life." Adler said nothing substantially new in this two-hour meeting; Kaplan reacted solely to his attitude.

Kaplan decided immediately to withdraw his resignation. When Kaplan told Wise of his decision, Wise was disappointed but once again accepted Kaplan's decision with grace and understanding. Wise confided the depth of his frustration to Judge Mack: "I feel very blue about the whole business. The truth is that we have no one in the faculty of his dimensions. . . . I have no bitterness or anger in my heart against him. I like him too much, but I am mighty sorry." Kaplan later recorded in his journal, "If in the course of a year or so I would accomplish one-tenth of what [Wise] hoped for from me, he would have me appointed to the presidency of the JIR." It should be noted, however, that the negotiations at this point were not for the presidency but for a faculty position and that Kaplan remarked in his journal that presidencies and deanships didn't really interest him. There is no doubt, however, that Kaplan was flattered by Wise's high expectations.[45]

There were psychological and political dimensions to Kaplan's decision to remain at the Seminary. Still experiencing self-doubts at this point in his career, he was fearful of completely severing his relations with the institution. Despite all the criticism he received, the Seminary had been his primary base of operations for many years. He came there in November, 1893, when he was admitted into the preparatory class at the age of twelve and a half. The Seminary was "family" and it embodied the ties with his traditional past. It represented a loving if demanding parent, and he was reluctant to leave "home."[46]

There were reasons that might be classified as partly ideological and partly political. Over the years, a significant number of men in the Rabbinical Assembly had become followers of Kaplan and were generally recognized as the forces on the left pushing in the direction of greater change. Kaplan wrote of his resignation that the only reason that swayed him was offered by Simon Greenberg, who maintained that without Kaplan the liberal forces in the Seminary clientele would be fatally weakened. Mack, among others, also believed that Kaplan, by getting assurances from Adler, had achieved a real victory for liberalism and academic freedom.[47]

Later in his life, Kaplan believed that his decision to remain at the Seminary was a wise one. He maintained that Reconstructionist ideology was not completely worked out, and had he gone to the JIR and become encumbered by administrative duties, he might never have developed his thought as fully as he did.

Indeed, in the 1920s, Kaplan began to chart a new course in both the method and the content of his ideology. Some, like Ginzberg, who adhered to the more traditional theories of scholarship, were threatened by his more pragmatic emphasis and his use of the new social sciences. The Seminary faculty felt uncomfortable with his criticism of Orthodox Judaism. Yet to remove Kaplan would have contributed to the forces of schism and undermined the coalition of diverse points of view that characterized the Conservative movement.

Kaplan was perceived by Seminary leaders as a divisive force in the American Jewish community. Finkelstein has said that he did everything he could to stop the spread of Reconstructionism precisely to prevent disunity. Perhaps the same forces were influencing Kaplan. He believed as passionately as anyone that divisiveness weakened; although he was always ready to speak out, he was reluctant to exacerbate the fragmentation within the Jewish community.

Kaplan's inability to leave the Seminary is part of the larger problem of Reconstructionism as a separate denomination. As Kaplan's thought began to crystallize throughout the 1920s, it was becoming obvious to many of his followers that the only way to implement the Kaplan ideology was outside the confines of the Seminary. Paralleling Kaplan's struggle regarding his transfer to the JIR was another struggle among the Kaplan disciples over whether or not they should sever their ties with the Seminary and begin a new denomination.

One step would have been to begin the organization of interested congregations into a separate group outside the framework of the United Synagogue and the Rabbinical Assembly. Some members of Kaplan's inner circle in the late 1920s advocated disassociation from the Rabbinical Assembly. It was Kaplan who kept his young radical followers from moving out of the Seminary orbit.

At the Rabbinical Assembly convention in 1926, he convened a group of his followers and proposed organizing them into a Rabbinical Council of the SAJ. Among those present were Max Kadushin, Solomon Goldman, Simon Greenberg, and Moses Hadas. The word quickly spread, and others voiced their willingness to join: Max Arzt, Morris Silverman, and Louis Levitsky. When Finkelstein heard about these meetings, he fumed and raged. He seemed pacified, however, after Kaplan assured him during a lengthy conversation that the group had no intention of breaking away from the Rabbinical Assembly. Kaplan further assured Finkelstein that no one would be admitted to the council who was not also a member of the Rabbinical Assembly.[48] It was obvious that there was within the Conservative rabbinate a significant number of men who believed in Kaplan and were willing to follow his lead. But where was he going and what risks was he willing to take?

Max Kadushin, who at that time was in Chicago, seemed to have been the closest to advocating an open break with the Seminary. "The source of the weakness has been the Seminary where everything given us had to be diluted, except your own material which also was not of the desired strength. . . . If our group will possess a program of action prompted by a realistic approach to our intellectual and spiritual difficulties, we can make an adjustment that will have the most far-reaching effects."[49] Herman Rubenovitz, who had convened the New England caucus of the liberal Rabbinical Assembly men, suggested that a letter be circulated to selected members asking them to join in organizing the liberal forces. Kaplan replied that such a letter would be considered an "insurrectionary act." He wanted to work with a "minimum of machinery" but admitted that "our desire to keep the United Synagogue intact places us in a difficult position; yet we must make a sincere effort not to do anything that might be prejudicial to its interests." Kadushin, on the other hand, stated that "if the United Synagogue and the RA see fit to sever us from their organization, we shall be in a much stronger position than if we were to withdraw of our own volition and form a separate party."[50]

Kaplan apparently made up his mind in the spring of 1927 not to withdraw from the Seminary. Having withdrawn his resignation from the faculty, he refused to take any steps that would constitute a clear break with the Conservative movement. Finkelstein was running scared but had much less to fear than he knew. The basic issue confronting the Rabbinical Assembly convention at Asbury Park that year was the unity and direction of the movement. Israel Goldstein spoke of the need for the Conservative movement to define itself more clearly so as to justify its existence as a third party. In response, Jacob Kohn raised a more fundamental question. "Is it true," he asked the assembled rabbinical leaders, "that we constitute a third party or that we want to be known as such?"[51] It is easy to forget that many still viewed the Conservative movement as the American expression of traditional Judaism and not as a separate movement. The hope was that eventually Orthodoxy would fade away and the Conservative movement would be considered the legitimate heir to the Jewish tradition.

Much of the discussion at the convention centered around the status of Jewish law and possibilities for change. Herman Rubenovitz, in a letter to Kaplan that spring, advocated that the liberal forces push for "modification of the Sabbath laws, revision of ritual, an interpretation of the Bible in harmony with liberal ideas and changes in the status of women in the synagogue." At the convention itself, Ginzberg and Kaplan argued over modes of change in the past and the desirability of change in the present. Ginzberg, rigorously conservative in his interpretation of the law, headed the Law Committee of the United Synagogue. Clearly, if the liberals were to implement their program, it would be necessary to gain some input into the procedure for legal change.

For a number of years, the idea had been bandied about that the Law Committee be transferred from the United Synagogue to the Rabbinical Assembly. Kaplan favored this move but wanted to be sure that it would not be dominated by the Orthodox elements within the assembly. At the same time, he was aware that the liberals were too weak to gain control. He was therefore very willing to accept the compromise proposed — that the new committee be composed of four Conservatives, four liberals, and two rabbis who were neutral. Kaplan also proposed that the new body merely respond to the legal question posed and that it possess no authority over the members.[52] The resolution establishing the committee was ambiguously worded so that all could be satisfied. The text runs as follows:

> Be it resolved that a committee of ten be appointed representing the various tendencies in the Rabbinical Assembly to act in an advisory capacity to the members of the Assembly in matters of religious and legal procedure. This committee shall have power to receive questions from Rabbis, to discuss the same with them and with one another. Where a decision is unanimous it shall be issued as an authoritative opinion of the Rabbinical Assembly; otherwise the committee shall put forward the majority as well as the dissenting opinions to the inquirer.[53]

In October 1927, Rubenovitz, Goldman, Kohn, and Kaplan were nominated to the committee.

The year 1927 marks a turning point in the history of the Conservative movement, particularly with respect to its ever-ambivalent liberal wing. Through the creation of the Law Committee, Kaplan's hopes were raised that he might yet effect significant changes. He wanted to remain with the movement because the parameters of its philosophy had not yet been fixed. There was a realistic basis to the prospect that Conservative Judaism might yet be reconstructed.

Kaplan was superb at formulating new directions in a whole host of areas but failed miserably when it came to taking action. He lacked the initiative to leave the Seminary or to supply a meaningful "political" solution to his coterie of young followers. He was his own worst enemy. Nonetheless, his ideological boldness forced his enemies to think through their own positions on the ultimate questions. He significantly influenced the students at the Seminary, the rabbis in the field, and the lay leaders in their synagogues.

11

SPIRITUALIZED INTELLIGENCE:
Living and Praying at the SAJ

For Mordecai Kaplan, the art of living together or living ethically was the central goal of every culture and civilization. In 1923 and 1924, the concept of civilization and more particularly of Judaism as a civilization was the primary theme of many of Kaplan's sermons at the Society for the Advancement of Judaism. To characterize Judaism as a civilization was to escape from the narrow identification of Judaism as a religion. Many Jews who were swept away by the ethos of their time had come to identify religion with superstition and with the most repressive aspects of the past. Kaplan's appeal began with a recognition of the very negative attitude most people had toward religion. Younger Jews identified religion with the foreignness of their parents and the restricted life they'd left behind in Europe. Although in other contexts Kaplan defined religion quite carefully, in his sermons he endorsed the popular attitude that religion had very little meaning for people in modern times. "Religion," he once told the congregation, "was an empty term which might refer to almost anything. It is almost as difficult to say what religion means as it is to fix the limits of a mist in windy weather. There is no human belief or practice that we might not designate as religion." Moreover, it was not religion that distinguished the Jew, for the liberal Jews had much more in common with liberal Christians than with Jews who were fundamentalists.[1]

At times, a total pessimism regarding the future of the Jewish people dominated his thinking. Neither liberal Jews nor fundamentalists could aid the Jewish people in their fight for survival. He was critical of both these groups and often said so from the pulpit. He portrayed the Orthodox as rigid and intolerant, giving priority to the ceremonial over the ethical. He insisted that they frequently became "ruthless and unscrupulous" in their dealings with the business world. Reform Jews, on the other hand, wanted to disassociate themselves from three thousand years of Jewish nationhood and would turn Judaism into a religious philosophy: "Philosophy fails as a bond of unity because of its static character . . . that which influences the conduct of people is not this or that philosophy, but the civilization into which one is born; the complex of relationships and the sum of habits and ideals resulting from those relationships into which one's lot is cast when he comes into the world."[2]

Often in those years, Kaplan felt he had to face the fact that it was not Jewish civilization but American civilization into which most Jews were born and in which they primarily lived. In moods of despair, he felt that Judaism as a civilization had no real future in America no matter what anyone did. What, then, were the options? Short of emigrating to Palestine, a possibility he rejected, the sole option seemed to be a complete shift of gears and context. He thought of changing the main thrust of his program and advocating a religion of American civilization rather than the notion of Judaism as a civilization. Slow progress at the SAJ persuaded him that perhaps he was asking too much of his members. Perhaps the only way truly to influence the ethical behavior of his constituents was to "utilize contemporary American needs to develop such spiritual values as might enable us to meet those needs in a rational and humane way." In fantasizing about this change of direction, he thought he would turn the SAJ into "the Society for the Advancement of the Religion of America." In his own life, he would cease to advocate the Jewish religion as the primary carrier of ethical and spiritual ideals. It seemed clear to him that Jews were abandoning their Judaism, and even those who continued to support Jewish institutions did so in a most perfunctory way. "The more I work," he thought, "the less hope I have of seeing Judaism take root in this country."

Kaplan was advocating a form of civil religion — general American culture would become the primary carrier of religious values. Insofar as he was concerned, the primary ethical values that originally appeared in the Jewish context could be transferred easily to American culture. In this new scheme American people would become the people of God. "After all God wants to choose America as the instrument of his will no less than he wanted Israel of old to act as an instrument of this kind." America could become the new Israel if it were only shown the way.

"Would to God," he wished, "that I were granted the opportunity to serve the American people by demonstrating even in a small way that it can become chosen of God as Israel of old was chosen, and even on a more comprehensive and significant scale."

At times like this, his attachment to America was a more profound emotion than the hope that the Jewish people might reconstruct itself in the land of Israel. He felt that to migrate to Palestine at this point would be "to die in a losing battle with the worst obscurantism in the world." In his mind, the life in Palestine was associated with the prevalence of Orthodox Jews or hide-bound Zionists, whereas life in America was associated with freedom, democracy, and all the values he cherished. Nonetheless, such moods passed, and he continued to see the Jewish people and Jewish civilization as the primary focus of his life and work.

To call Judaism a civilization rather than a revelation from God seemed to diminish it to the mere equivalent of the many cultures that exist in the world. Kaplan vacillated on this matter, sometimes stating that Judaism was no more than the "language and culture" of the Jews in the same sense that everyone belongs to a group and has a social and a religious heritage. At other times, he emphasized the distinctiveness of Jewish civilization, maintaining that it was both universal and national at the same time. Christianity as a civilization had failed, he believed, because it tried to be universal and denied the element of nationality. In Judaism, the universal is expressed through the national. "We must lift the specific interests of the group to the level of ideals that make for justice and peace." Civilization thereby becomes the primary means that embody the ethical life. The goal of Jewish civilization, according to Kaplan, was the "unification of mankind and the full need of personality to each individual human being." In these twin goals of the unity of mankind and the full development of each individual, he felt he had incorporated the primary ideals that constituted the ethical life.[3]

To maintain that Judaism was a civilization rather than a religion carried certain implications that were quite radical. Saying from the pulpit that "we have no beliefs that are fixed, no dogmas which may become the center of a new 'Orthodoxy'" is one of the most radical statements a rabbi can make. This is truly to accept the implications of Nietzsche's assertion that God is dead. If Judaism is a civilization, and a living civilization, then obviously it changes constantly, and no one belief or dogma can be permanent. Particularly in modern times, Kaplan believed people must learn to live without the finalities. "We have learned to regard no truth as finished and final. Whatever the teaching be and whoever its authority, it can never be above further research and inquiry. Such an attitude toward truth is entirely unthinkable with regard to any teaching which is believed to come directly from God."[4]

If the teachings of the Torah do not come directly from God, if they are not supernatural in their origin, then they must be reclassified. Kaplan's conception of God, though never very clear, nonetheless precluded the belief that the *Mitzvot* were divinely ordained laws. If he thought of God as "the living universe," as he said in 1926, then obviously God could not command the Jews what to eat or what to wear or how to celebrate the Sabbaths and festivals. The commandments, he explained, were customs and folkways that persisted long after their original reason for being instituted had ceased: "They are the slowly formed social habits which are peculiar to our people." It remained to be seen whether the *Mitzvot* could continue to inspire the loyalty and reverence of the Jews if they were thought of as merely the customs and folkways of the Jewish people rather than as divine commandments. Kaplan pointed out that Americans are strongly bound by social conventions although they never consider them divine in a supernatural sense. He dismissed the supernatural as an explanation but always insisted that aspects of the natural world were divine and deserved reverence: "To say that the natural world order cannot evoke a sense of mystery is to say that there is nothing of the divine in it. We cannot be in the presence of great character, intelligence or heroism without feeling that we are in the presence of something divine." The same may be said for the *Mitzvot* which command justice and aid the individual in leading an ethical life. Kaplan would say that the commandments were divine not in the sense that they come from God but in the sense that they help the Jewish people in the constant struggle to transcend themselves.[5]

◆

Kaplan sought to bring his message not only to the members of his congregation but to Jews all over the country. He traveled regularly to Jewish communities on the East Coast and in the Midwest and spoke to large crowds wherever he went. In addition to his speaking tours, he became widely known through the publication of *A New Approach to Jewish Life* which appeared in 1924. This small publication reiterated the major themes regarding Jewish civilization recounted above. Articles on *A New Approach* appeared in Jewish newspapers around the country — Indianapolis, Baltimore, Denver, and San Antonio, to name a few. The reception was almost uniformly enthusiastic. One writer lauded Kaplan as a "fearless" critic of established leaders both Orthodox and Reform. Another praised him for his reinterpretation of the concept of Torah and for having written the Jewish *Dance of Life*. Israel Zangwill endorsed Kaplan wholeheartedly when he said that *A New Approach* "in its fearlessness and fervor [is] one of the noblest utterances that has come from an American Rabbi."[6] *A New Approach* represents a more popular side of Kaplan than is found in some of his other writings. Whereas in the *Menorah Journal* his analysis was directed principally to intellectuals; this pamphlet represented a more broadly based appeal. There is little theology in *A New Approach* and no discussion of how the social sciences should be used to understand Judaism. Kaplan, instead, advocated a revitalization of Judaism through Torah, understood as lifelong moral education, through the resurrection of Hebrew as a living language, and through the rebuilding of Palestine as the guarantor of the Jewish future.

He had a vision of the synagogue as an institution that needed to be expanded in order to carry the burden of Judaism as a civilization. Although the synagogue would include many kinds of activities in its new form as a Jewish center, religious services would remain the foundation for expressing and reinforcing ethical values. What the synagogue services needed most in order to function ethically was authenticity. All aspects of the services and the rabbi should reflect genuinely and honestly the values of the group. Kaplan had little use for prayers or rituals that were empty of content. His obsession with honesty was reflected in everything he did. Especially in connection with religious matters, he felt that people are often dishonest because of a misguided sense of respect for the past.

Kaplan's need for authenticity surely stemmed from deep psychological roots as well. He had become estranged from the religion of his parents. Having come so far from where he began, it was essential that he not deny what he thought or felt. His rebellion was justified only if he continued to be honest in religious matters. It would have been difficult and painful for him to reject his past and yet not be true to his own hard-won beliefs. His ideological stand had cost him dearly; he had to be the person he seemed to be.[7]

This had important implications for Kaplan's attitude toward the synagogue and toward prayer. Praying was a way of expressing beliefs, and, as a dedicated rationalist, he wanted his prayers to express his commitments. He regarded prayers as if they were theological statements. If the statement did not correspond to his beliefs, it had to be changed or dropped. Within the circle of his colleagues and within the Conservative movement in general, those who were unhappy with the content of the prayers preferred to reinterpret the traditional text rather than reconstruct it. Kaplan considered this hypocritical, saying one thing but meaning another. His need to harmonize the text and his beliefs led him to make more radical changes than any of his colleagues or most of his former students would even have contemplated.

Shortly after the establishment of the SAJ, the board charged him to "beautify" the service, omitting or altering particular prayers that did not represent the SAJ ideology. Theoretically, these changes then would be submitted to the board for approval. At the very least, the board would be kept informed. As events developed, the congregation seemed to accept most of the changes Kaplan recommended without voicing much opposition. The initial changes in the liturgy reflected the basic tenets that became operative in all of Kaplan's later prayerbooks. The first and perhaps the most essential task was to eliminate references to the chosenness of the Jewish people. Kaplan preached against this idea from the pulpit and sought to eradicate it from one particular prayer (*Aleinu*) in which a set of phrases implying Israel's separateness and perhaps even superiority was dropped and another traditional verse emphasizing the special qualities of the Torah was substituted. The original version read, "We praise God, that he has not made us like the nations of the world, nor set us up as other peoples of the earth not making our portion as theirs nor our destiny as that of the multitudes." The revised portion reads, "We praise God, who has given us the Torah of truth and planted eternal life within us." [8]

It is difficult to document the exact date for the dropping of the phrase denoting Israel's chosenness (*asher bachar banu*), which occurs a number of times in the service, most prominently in the blessing for the Torah. The phrase "who has brought us near to your service" (*asher kervanu le-avodato*), again a traditional formulation, was eventually inserted into the first Torah blessing in place of the chosenness phrase. When the Reconstructionist Prayerbook was finally published in 1945, there was some opposition to these changes even within the SAJ itself. One gentleman withdrew from the congregation; others insisted on using the traditional formulation (*asher bachar banu*) when they were called up to the Torah. [9]

Kaplan also changed other formulations he felt were not fitting for the modern age. In the 1920s, he substituted an alternative Sephardic rendering in one prayer (*ain kelohenu*) for a phrase that referred to the sacrifices. Eventually, all references to the sacrifices were dropped, as were references to the resurrection of the dead. In the *Amidah* prayer, for example, he took out the reference to God as one who "revives the dead" (*mehaye ha-maytim*) and substituted the phrase from the high holiday liturgy describing God as one who "in love remembers his creatures for life."

Wherever possible, he substituted one traditional phrase for another, believing that he was not treating the text lightly or simply inserting his own philosophy into the liturgy. In the Torah service, when the scrolls are lifted up after the reading, the traditional rendering is, "this is the Torah which Moses set before the children of Israel by the word of the Lord through Moses." Because Kaplan accepted many parts of the Torah as being post-Mosaic and in any case did not believe in the divine origin of the Torah, he could not accept this phrase. In its place, he substituted a well-known phrase from the liturgy itself: "This Torah is a tree of life to those who hold fast to it; and of them that uphold it, everyone is rendered happy."

In time, he became more bold, eliminating the whole section of the *Shemah* (Deuteronomy 11:13–21) which seemed to connect the reward of abundant rain to the performance of the commandments. He was vehemently opposed to the magical or theurgic view of nature implied in this passage. At first, in the early 1930s, there is evidence that he simply left it out, but in the Sabbath prayerbook he substituted a few verses from Deuteronomy 28 that are less magical in tone. These verses read, "If you truly give heed to the voice of the Lord your God, by being careful to observe all his commandments which I am giving you this day, then all these blessings will come upon you. Blessed will you be in the city . . ." Even in the newly selected passage, Kaplan left out a phrase that referred to Israel's superior status as a reward for faithful observance of the commandments ("The Lord your God will set you high above all the nations of the earth").[10]

One of the most interesting of the early changes was made in the *Kol Nidre* prayer, recited at the beginning of the service on *Erev Yom Kippur* and considered one of the most sacred moments of the whole year. The prayer itself, however, is problematical on a number of counts. Its origin is obscure, but it was probably composed in the late Amoraic or early Geonic periods (600–800 c.e.). It states that all vows, obligations, and oaths made during the coming year shall be abolished and annulled. Most commentators hasten to point out that the vows referred to here concern only man's relationship to God and have nothing to do with ordinary contracts. The prayer has had opponents as far back as the Geonic period. In modern times, it was dropped for a long time by the Reformists and by Samson Raphael Hirsch as well. Over the centuries, anti-Semites have pointed to it as evidence that the Jews are treacherous and untrustworthy. Kaplan disliked the prayer because he considered the legal formulas, which constitute its essence, to have little real connection with the important spiritual and ethical themes of the high holiday season. He first thought of eliminating the text of *Kol Nidre* altogether. In August 1922, he invited Louis Finkelstein and his wife, Carmel, over to his house and mentioned the possibility of eliminating the *Kol Nidre* prayer and substituting a poem by Luzzatto while retaining the traditional melody. Finkelstein adamantly opposed the idea, fearing that such an action would lead to the abrogation of other prayers. Kaplan responded by saying that he "regarded sincerity in prayer as superior to all other considerations" and that he couldn't see how people could be sincere or spiritually uplifted by the contents of this prayer. He noted in his diary that Finkelstein remained obdurate, although Carmel Finkelstein seemed to agree with him. Unmoved by Finkelstein's opposition, Kaplan decided to retain the prayer only because of a conversation he had with his Seminary colleague Moshe Levine. Levine was a noted Hebraist and one of the few men on the Seminary faculty whom Kaplan liked and respected. Levine argued along the same lines as Finkelstein, but Kaplan was convinced more by Levine's "fine character," as Kaplan put it, than by the arguments he put forth.[11]

Kaplan finally did delete the *Kol Nidre* a number of years later, although, as mentioned, he retained the tune. Instead of the Luzzatto poem (it is not known which one he had in mind), he decided to insert Psalm 130. This very moving prayer is a call, indeed a crying out for forgiveness, and stresses the unworthiness of the penitent as he stands before God. It reads in part:

> A Song of Ascents
>> Out of the depths I call You, O Lord.
>> O Lord, listen to my cry:
>> let Your ears be attentive
>> to my plea for mercy.
> If you keep accounts of sins, O Lord,
>> Lord, who will survive?
> Yours is the power to forgive
>> so that You may be held in awe.

Kaplan noted that there was little resistance in the congregation, even from such traditionalists as Sol Lamport. The small degree of perceptible opposition came from nonmembers who rented seats for the holidays. Having spent thirty minutes defending the change, he was quite pleased that everyone seemed willing to go along with him.

By the time the next Yom Kippur rolled around, people were beginning to have second thoughts about the *Kol Nidre* matter. Many SAJ members had been discussing it at their summer resorts, and in early September a number of individuals approached Kaplan and voiced dissatisfaction with the change. Congregational stalwarts such as Joe Levy and Jacob Klein attempted to convince him that it was a mistake. Levy told him he had stirred up a hornets' nest and that he, Levy, was very upset. Kaplan was furious, which often occurred when he had to deal with the officers of his synagogue. He immediately convened a board meeting so he could inform everyone that he would not conduct the services or preach on Yom Kippur. By the time the meeting took place, he had calmed down considerably and was ready to reason with his *Baale Batim* (congregational leaders). Some of the board members put forth very moving pleas for retaining the prayer. Klein spoke of how good he felt at *Kol Nidre* because his conscience was relieved of all responsibility for pledges of money and volunteer work that he had made hastily but had not fulfilled. In a spirit of compromise, Kaplan offered the majority at the meeting and those in the congregation the alternative of saying the traditional prayer silently while the cantor would chant Psalm 130.[12]

This set of circumstances was quite revealing. Theoretically, Kaplan held that the synagogue should meet the needs of its members and be conducted in a democratic manner. On many issues (e.g., the place of women) where Kaplan felt one way (in favor of change) and the congregation felt another, he yielded to their wishes. Often, though, he could be adamant, as in the case of the *Kol Nidre*. The issue seemed to him so clear and the congregants so ignorant that he was impervious to their arguments.

On the eve of Yom Kippur, one of the Jewish newspapers called him and asked about the *Kol Nidre*. For a moment, he hesitated but then decided to relate fully what he was going to do. The opportunity was too good to pass up. Besides, he thoroughly enjoyed the role of crusader against the rigid traditionalism of the Orthodox. As he put it in his journal: "At first I refused, but then I thought to myself, 'why not use this opportunity to drive another nail into the coffin of Orthodoxy by exposing its senseless sentimentalism.'" No one enjoyed righteous indignation as much as Kaplan.

Even his mother got into the act. Writing to her son on the occasion of his daughter Selma's bas mitzvah, Anna Kaplan wished the family all the best and then proceeded to mention an article in the *SAJ*

Review that she did not like. Taking this tack led her to think of other things she did not like, including the *Kol Nidre*. "You are destroying Judaism," she wrote. "Do you understand what you are doing to yourself? I will not tell you what you are doing to me and maybe to your father in his grave. . . . I am too weak now I cannot write more. Be well and happy with your family. [signed] Your mother."[13]

Although Kaplan felt the *Kol Nidre* upheaval was a tempest in a teapot, he also recognized there was an important principal at stake. "In gathering for Yom Kippur," he stated in the *Jewish Daily Bulletin*, we want to voice "our sense of life's complexities and failures and our consequent dependence upon God for guidance and courage." The *Kol Nidre* was completely inappropriate for this purpose. Moreover, "if thinking men and women" are to be loyal Jews, such changes will have to be made. The *American Hebrew* hailed Kaplan's goal "to eliminate from Judaism 'all those elements which cannot stand the test of spiritualized intelligence.'" They also correctly pointed out that Reform synagogues long ago had eliminated the "dry legalistic *Kol Nidre*," and they were happy with his attempt to bring some vitality into "spiritually ossified New York." It may be that much of the criticism of Kaplan came from those who identified him with the Jewish Theological Seminary and its president, Cyrus Adler, as representative voices of traditional Judaism. An editorial in one Yiddish newspaper called on the Seminary to openly declare that it was no different from Hebrew Union College and that its faculty had fully abandoned the ideals of Solomon Schechter. If the Seminary was not willing to make such a declaration, then Kaplan should be fired immediately, because "he had no place on the faculty" of an institution that stood for traditional Judaism.[14]

Although Kaplan continued to oppose the *Kol Nidre*, sustained pressure from the congregation caused him to reconsider in subsequent years. Jacob Klein wrote him a letter in September 1930, saying in a very moving way that he simply missed the prayer and did not believe people felt themselves released from their obligations by its recitation. What finally changed Kaplan's mind was correspondence he had with Judah David Eisenstein in that same year (1930). Ira Eisenstein had become executive director of the SAJ, and his grandfather told him that he was disturbed by Kaplan's elimination of the *Kol Nidre*. Ira Eisenstein suggested that he write to Kaplan about it and attempt to change his mind. The elder Eisenstein wrote a long letter pointing to the origins of the prayer and its original meaning. Kaplan, who was acquainted with all the Talmudic material in Eisenstein's letter, wrote back that he was opposed to the *Kol Nidre* precisely because it had become so important to people and because it was regarded as a prayer when in reality it was no more than a juridical formula. Kaplan asserted that the undue significance attached to the *Kol Nidre* was idolatrous, which he defined in this case as "attaching undue sanctity to objects that in themselves have no significance." What won Kaplan over apparently was Eisenstein's interpretation that indeed the *Kol Nidre* did refer to vows and oaths between man and man and not to vows between man and God. In Eisenstein's words:

> The Kol Nidre was instituted as a prologue before our prayers on Yom Kippur in order to absolve all vows and oaths foolishly and in anger hastily annunciated to break up a relationship with a friend even to separate a son from a father, as was the case mentioned in the *Mishnah*. [In that situation a man] vowed not to eat at the table with his son at the wedding of his daughter, and many other examples of personal affliction which tend to create discord and hatred in the family and in society as enumerated in *Masseket Nedarim*. All such vows and oaths are made null and void by a simple process invented by our Talmudic rabbis, in order to make the road clear for forgiveness and good will to all for the coming year.

Though tenacious and stubborn, Kaplan prided himself on being rational. He was impressed with Eisenstein's explanation and thanked him for giving him the "actual purpose" of the *Kol Nidre*. Kaplan said he would reconsider, and if he became convinced, he would reinstate the prayer. He did reinstate the text but with a change that reflects Eisenstein's arguments. The amended *Kol Nidre* reads (italicized portions added):

> All vows, bonds, devotions, promises, obligations, penalties and oaths, wherewith we have vowed, sworn, devoted and bound ourselves, to take effect from this Day of Atonement unto the next day of atonement (may it come unto us for good), *so as to estrange ourselves from those who have offended us or to give pain to those who have angered us*, they shall be absolved, released, annulled, made void and of none [*sic*] more effect. These our vows, *and these only*, shall not be vows; these our bonds, and *these only*, shall not be bonds; these our oaths, and *these only*, shall not be oaths.[15]

Kaplan's willingness to alter classical texts is more strikingly illustrated by a small booklet the SAJ published in 1922. It was entitled *Selections from the Psalms for Responsive Reading*. Although the word *selections* does indeed appear in the title, it is nonetheless quite surprising to find a psalm entitled "A Prayer for Courage in Time of Trouble." The psalm in question is the twenty-third. The text runs to the words "Thy rod and thy staff they comfort me," and then the next line is "Into thy hand I commit my spirit, thou hast redeemed me O Lord." These "outside" readings were undoubtedly used for the Sabbath services and were introduced from many sources. In one Yom Kippur service, Kaplan included selections from the work of Harry Emerson Fosdick. He was particularly fond of Fosdick's *The Meaning of Faith*. This small book was meant to be read on a daily basis and contained selections from the scriptures in addition to excerpts from the sermons of such men as Theodore Parker, Ralph Waldo Emerson, and Henry Ward Beecher. Kaplan freely admitted that he introduced readings from Christian writers while removing any references to Jesus.[16]

Although Kaplan was radical in his vision and in his willingness to alter the liturgy, he was not extreme in his methods. At the SAJ, he tried new liturgies but no new formats. He conducted the services as the rabbi. The congregation was seated before and below the *Bimah* (stage), as is the case in most synagogues. The service consisted of prayers, readings, sermons, and music. He presented a new way of understanding but not an alternative model of spirituality.[17] His most daring innovation was the reformulation of the content of the prayers.

One of the most novel prayers Kaplan introduced was a piece called "The Thirteen Wants." He composed this prayer in February 1926 for the dedication of the SAJ's new quarters. He obviously had in mind the thirteen principles of faith formulated by Maimonides and believed that it was no longer possible or even desirable to have a set of abstract principles that all Jews should accept. But it was possible to agree on goals or, as he put it, "to agree as to what differences in our lives the fact of being Jewish should make." When "The Thirteen Wants" were inserted in the Sabbath prayerbook, they were called "The Criteria of Jewish Loyalty":

1. We want Judaism to help us overcome temptation, doubt and discouragement.
2. We want Judaism to imbue us with a sense of responsibility for the righteous use of the blessings wherewith God endows us.
3. We want the Jew so to be trusted that his yea will be taken as yea, and his nay as nay.
4. We want to learn how to utilize our leisure to best advantage physically, intellectually, and spiritually.
5. We want the Jewish home to live up to its traditional standards of virtue and piety.

6. We want the Jewish upbringing of our children to further their moral and spiritual growth, and to enable them to accept with joy their heritage as Jews.

7. We want the synagogue to enable us to worship God in sincerity and in truth.

8. We want our religious traditions to be interpreted in terms of understandable experience and to be made relevant to our present-day needs.

9. We want to participate in the upbuilding of *Eretz Yisrael* as a means to the renaissance of the Jewish spirit.

10. We want Judaism to find rich, manifold and ever new expression in philosophy, in letters, and in the arts.

11. We want all forms of Jewish organization to make for spiritual purpose and ethical endeavor.

12. We want the unity of Israel throughout the world to be fostered through mutual help in time of need, and through cooperation in the furtherance of Judaism at all times.

13. We want Judaism to function as a potent influence for justice, freedom and peace in the life of men and nations.

It is difficult to say which of the thirteen wants was most important to Kaplan personally, but number seven certainly would rank high on the list. Sincerity and authenticity were indispensable not only in the act of praying but in the other aspects of Kaplan's life as well. As a rabbi, he frequently found himself in situations that made him uncomfortable because he could not speak honestly. Most people come to terms with these moments; Kaplan never really did.

For example, he was ambivalent about eulogies. As a matter of policy, funerals were never held at the SAJ. Kaplan was determined not to turn the synagogue into a funeral parlor. When asked to conduct a funeral, he always complied if his schedule allowed it, but frequently the deceased person was someone he had known. Severe critic that he was, with himself as well as others, there were few individuals he could genuinely respect. If the deceased were someone who had been sufficiently "socially or spiritually minded," Kaplan had no trouble in delivering a eulogy. But his world, like all others, was filled with the imperfect people who were friends and family, and his discomfort therefore was constant. In one case, he thought he could extricate himself by composing a kind of prayer that would help the mourners to "transmute the loss of the departed into a spiritually energizing force." He was happy with his effort, but the prayer was probably of little real help to those mourners who needed to hear about the person they lost and to experience their grief.[18]

Family members report that in general Kaplan did not feel comfortable with pastoral duties. On one occasion, a member of the SAJ asked Kaplan to pray for her sick child. To his rationalist mentality this meant that "we are still living in the age of the medicine man." Yet he was not so cruel or insensitive as to tell the family what he really felt. He finally decided that the best solution was to let the matter drift, but felt he was compromising himself by not telling the parents what he really thought.[19]

Although genuinely concerned about his congregants' personal problems, Kaplan did not enjoy personal counseling. When the matter concerned religious or ideological issues, however, he was much more comfortable. On one occasion a Miss Bentwich who was visiting from England came to see him. She was the sister of Louis Finkelstein's wife, Carmel, the sister of Israel Friedlaender's wife, Lilian Ruth, and also the sister of Norman Bentwich, the scholar and biographer of Solomon Schechter. Miss Bentwich was staying with the Finkelsteins and was severely distressed because of the "inordinate scrupulosity" of the household religious observance, which she found quite oppressive. She was not a religious person, finding observance in general burdensome, and yet she wanted to find some way to relate to Jewish life. Kaplan was glad to offer her a new understanding of religion so that she might relate affirmatively and flexibly to Jewish law.[20]

The commitment to flexibility that he shared with Miss Bentwich was an ideal Kaplan sought to embody in all his religious behavior. He refused to be shackled by Jewish religious law or by empty formalities. Yet dealing with religious law was stressful for him because his reason and logic frequently were at war with his old habits. Sometimes his position was far more radical than that of his congregation and he had difficulties instituting the changes he wanted.

In 1924, Rabbi Barnett Brickner, who had been graduated from Hebrew Union College but who had also studied with Kaplan, came to see him. In the course of their conversation, Brickner mentioned that he had abolished the second day of the festivals in his congregation without any opposition. Kaplan told Brickner that he approved of the move "with all my heart . . . not because I believe that any spiritual gain would result from it, but I would feel that my own practice would conform more to my theory than it does at present." Kaplan continued to be unhappy with the second day, especially around the high holidays and Succoth. He complained that there were too many services and too many heavy dinners and too little of the religious and the spiritual. At one point, he proposed to some members of the SAJ board that he would eliminate the second day if they would pledge themselves in writing to proper observance of the first day. Nothing came of the proposal, even though some in the congregation agreed with him. The SAJ was a member of the United Synagogue, and eliminating second days might have caused Kaplan much grief and conflict with his Seminary colleagues. He also considered shifting all Jewish holidays to the nearest Sunday, when he realized how well attended Passover services were when the *Yom Tov* (holiday) fell on a Sunday. When it fell during the week some of his colleagues complained that they had to call off services because they were unable to assemble a *minyon* (quorum).[21]

From the period of his studies at Columbia with sociologist Franklin Giddings, Kaplan had come to see the commandments of the Torah more as local Israelite custom than as God-given laws. Yet his own religious behavior changed slowly. With respect to daily prayer, it is clear that he *davened* (prayed) regularly until the early 1930s. At this time, he still felt guilty if he missed a few days and felt that he should "not permit himself the laxity." As time went on, he seems to have dropped the habit of daily prayer but not the habit of putting on his *tallis* and *tefillin* (phylacteries) in the morning. Ira Eisenstein reports that in 1940, when the Eisensteins and the Kaplans spent the summer at the Jersey shore, Kaplan would get up every morning, don his *tallis* and *tefillin*, and sometimes, instead of praying, he would read from Ahad Ha-Am or John Dewey. Eisenstein observed him doing this not once but many times.

With respect to the Sabbath, the pattern was the same: very slow change. Here, though, Kaplan's overall behavior changed less than in the case of daily prayer. He continued to observe the Sabbath prohibitions even though he did take certain liberties in the early 1920s. Sometimes the liberties were minor, but they are nonetheless significant. He was inconsistent about writing; sometimes he did write on the Sabbath, and sometimes he was tempted to but didn't. He noted in his diary in December 1928 that while taking a walk on the Sabbath, he had some thoughts about the place of Palestine in Jewish life, but out of "regard for the traditional prohibition," he did not write them down. He thought, nonetheless, "what a senseless thing this prohibition of writing on the Sabbath! How much more sensible it would have been to prohibit preaching on the Sabbath." Sometimes, however, his needs won out over the voices of his past.

He was in the habit of preparing his sermons late on Friday nights, and this practice certainly involved writing on the Sabbath. One particular incident shows him entangled in his inconsistencies. It was Friday night, and he was in his study working on his sermon. Apparently, his daughters did not yet know that he sometimes wrote on the Sabbath.

*Kaplan at the Jersey Shore, 1931. (Courtesy Had-
assah K. Musher.)*

*Lena Kaplan at the Jersey Shore, 1931. (Courtesy
Hadassah K. Musher.)*

Kaplan mowing the lawn, 1931. (Courtesy Hadassah K. Musher.)

Selma came in, and Kaplan hastily put down his pen and started rustling papers, hoping she had not seen him writing. Afterward, he finished working on the sermon, and then wrote up this embarrassing incident in his journal.[22]

Kaplan kept a kosher home, with two sets of dishes. According to family tradition, when the Kaplans went to Italy in the summer of 1922, they ate nothing but sardines during most of the trip. The family vacationed at the Jersey shore most summers and always took two complete sets of dishes and pots with them. As he was the rabbi of the SAJ, it was natural for members to discuss *kashrut* with him. In March 1922, he spoke with a congregant who was considering making her house kosher and wanted Kaplan's opinion. After explaining that he kept a kosher home, Kaplan gave her a justification of *kashrut* but admitted that he found it difficult to defend the custom. It was obviously a defense against assimilation, he told her, but if in some way it proved "socially harmful, it is the duty of those who assume leadership to insist on its elimination." The key question was whether these prohibitions would prevent many Jews from becoming identified with the Jewish community. Kaplan thought not, but he was not optimistic about the future. "There can be no question that sooner or later Judaism will have to get along without dietary laws." Where people have the choice, in their homes, they should observe *kashrut*, but in the home of a gentile, "they should not be expected to abstain from *trefa* meat in the rabbinic sense."

Kaplan's thoughts on *kashrut* are quite revealing. Obviously he felt comfortable eating only kosher food both in his home and outside. Yet he still needed to question the subject and consider it from a logical point of view. His ambivalence and his rationalism come through strongly here. "I realize that if it were not for the environment in which I move, I would probably have given it up as an obsolete institution. But then again might I not have given up more besides. Is it, after all, so wrong to be the product of one's environment? Of course, if the traditional belief or institution is socially harmful it . . . would be my duty to urge its abrogation. But I cannot see wherein I am less broadminded or universal in my outlook because I have all my life abstained from *trefa* food. It seems to me that with the present lack of Jewish content nothing could be more fatal than to break down the principal fence against assimilation." [23]

By any definition except the most rigorously *halakhic* (according to Jewish law), Kaplan must be considered a deeply religious man. Because of his rationalism and rejection of traditional supernaturalism, one might mistakenly think that he lacked piety and spirituality in the accepted meanings of these terms. Nothing could be farther from the truth. Many who knew Kaplan and attended services at the SAJ have commented on the fervor with which he *davened*. Praying, for Kaplan, was as natural as thinking. Indeed, he makes just that comparison at one point: "To say, 'I believe in praying' sounds to me as absurd as to say, 'I believe in thinking.' The question whether prayer is effective is only a special form of the question whether thought is effective." So to pray was to find thoughts that would express one's beliefs, one's ideals, one's longings, and one's pain. Looking at prayer as expressive of one's deepest emotions led Kaplan to the conclusion that the *Siddur* was too restrictive: "Unfortunately we Jews have limited prayer to the deadening routine of reciting the few meager passages which go to make up our official prayerbook." [24]

In his search for meaningful texts, he frequently introduced readings from outside sources and composed prayers of his own. Despite the fact that he edited many prayerbooks and wrote many prayers, people today rarely think of him as a writer of religious poetry. He was always trying his hand at composing prayers to which the rational modern person could relate. One of his better efforts which never found its way into print is the following:

> O God . . . Thou art eternal—the life of all that live, the love of all that love. Thou art the courage of those who conquer adversity. Thou art the health of those who overcome sickness. Thou art the hope of those who sleep in the dust. Thou art holy, and those who strive after holiness know to worship thee.

This piece and the one below sound very much like examples of a practice Kaplan once advocated in a conversation with Louis Finkelstein. He proposed that essays or paragraphs that expressed a particular theological concept be turned into poetic form and used as prayers. The prayers here, which are from one of Kaplan's notebooks, sound like the results of just such an exercise.

> We Behold thee . . .
> We acclaim thee O God who dids't make thyself known to our fathers.
> We behold thee in the infinite forces that bind the Universe and in the loving-kindness of the human heart. Thou art in all and all is in thee.
> In thee live the good deeds of our fathers—to us their children may thy love bring redemption. Lead us. Help us. Save us. [25]

These prayers illustrate another aspect of Kaplan's attitude and philosophy: his dedication to fighting the magical attitude in religion and in prayer. Such an attitude is reflected in the belief that one can pray to a God who will change the world to conform to one's wishes. It might entail bringing rain or health or defeating one's enemy. For some, it is very difficult to revise such a concept of prayer because it flows so naturally out of needfulness. The above selections serve to illustrate a nonmagical or, as Kaplan would put it, a nontheurgic type of prayer. Nevertheless, the prayerbooks Kaplan edited in a later period and the liturgical material he used in the 1920s and 1930s continued for the most part to use the conventional prayer form in addressing God as "you" or "thou." If God did not interfere in the natural processes of the world and was essentially a power or a force, then obviously God could not be directly addressed. Given Kaplan's concern for authenticity, it is surprising that he was not troubled by this inconsistency. There are only a few efforts to change the basic form of the prayers from an address to God. At a later point, he confronted the problem, but his answer, though interesting, resolves nothing: "In what terms can we address God. We cannot do so in terms of scientific or philosophical abstractions, like process or energy, any more than we ordinarily use such terms in thinking about ourselves. Nobody would think of saying: those processes in relation to my body which make for my personality are hungry. One would say quite simply: I am hungry. . . . For similar reasons, we address God in prayer as *thou*."

Kaplan demonstrated his attitude toward prayer by consistently opening his classes at the Seminary with a prayer. He was the only faculty person who did this. The prayers changed from time to time. At one point, for example, he used the verses from the paragraph preceding the *Shemah* on Sabbath morning. The text, which he recited with the class in Hebrew, runs as follows: "O [Lord] put it into our hearts to understand, to discern, to attend, learn and teach, to heed, to do and to fulfill in love all the words of instruction in thy Torah."[26]

The religious life of Mordecai Kaplan must be evaluated not only by his observance of rituals and his habits of personal piety but also by his attitudes and policies concerning matters of personal status such as marriage, divorce, and conversion. In the early 1930s, two of his congregants at the SAJ came to him for a Jewish divorce. He sent the couple to the rabbinical *Bet Din* (court) at the Jewish Theological Seminary and attended the proceedings himself. He found the divorce action "dismal and unimpressive." He was perfectly aware that the couple involved did not really take the Jewish divorce seriously and were only complying with the rite pro forma. He felt it was quite anachronistic "in the manner of ancient formalities which are as much in place today as knee breeches and powdered wigs." Witnessing the divorce reminded him again that in the *halakhah* the woman "had hardly any rights of her own" and could "never divorce but only be the divorcee." As far as we know, he took no steps toward instituting new divorce procedures, perhaps because, here again, he was a member of the United Synagogue and the Rabbinical Assembly and significant changes would have meant an open break with these bodies.

He was also cautious about conversion. While still at the center, Kaplan conducted the conversion of a young woman adhering more or less to the *halakhah*. He had two rabbinic colleagues testify to the immersion which took place in the pool at the center. A number of years later (1926), however, he arranged to accept the testimony of female witnesses to an immersion while still having two rabbis act as the *Bet Din* (court) to accept the convert. Kaplan believed he would have no trouble finding two rabbis to act on these terms, but it is not known whether he ever did.[27]

Despite common knowledge that Kaplan did not himself adhere strictly to the law, he became a source for "legal" decisions. When a Conservative rabbi had a question (*She-aylah*), he would ordinarily turn to the Seminary's Law Committee, which at this time was dominated by Professor Louis Ginzberg. When it did not seem appropriate to ask Ginzberg, the more liberal members in the Rabbinic Assembly asked Kaplan's advice. Morris Silverman, leader of a Hartford congregation, supported and admired Kaplan. Silverman's congregation was having some stained-glass windows designed in 1927, and there was a dispute over whether or not it would be appropriate to have the human form as part of the stained glass in the synagogue. Since Kaplan commissioned a mural at the SAJ a few years later, his answer is predictable. "There is no reason at the present time," he wrote Silverman, "for excluding the human form from being depicted in stained glass provided it does not represent the Deity or any specific personage whether hero, prophet or sage." His traditional upbringing always lurked in the background, which may explain why he had to qualify his "permission."[28]

Some of Kaplan's most significant departures from traditional norms concerned the role of women. During his tenure at the center, he openly supported the women's suffrage amendment from his pulpit. At the same time, men and women were still seated separately at center services. Separate seating was considered the hallmark of the traditional synagogue, and members of the center were Orthodox. The center leadership insisted on the separate seating. After the opening of the SAJ, men and women continued to be seated separately. In 1922, the SAJ was quartered in a brownstone at 41 West Eighty-sixth Street lacking galleries or partitions, where the seating was obviously intimate. Nonetheless, several members opposed mixed seating. They warned Kaplan that if the SAJ changed to mixed seating, the congregation would definitely be identified as Reform and they would resist such a move. The congregants were willing to follow their leader, but change had to suit their own rhythm as well as Kaplan's.[29]

The SAJ high holiday services in 1922 were held on the Upper West Side in a large hall with mixed seating. We do not know how Kaplan got his way but apparently the old guard did not oppose him. He was particularly pleased with the new arrangement, because with the whole family seated together there was less talking during services. "I succeeded in doing away with the continual conversation and disinterestedness in the service that have always marred the services over which I had the good or ill fortune to preside." Nonetheless, he was still unhappy with the lack of attentiveness, and during the *Kol Nidre* service on Yom Kippur he lost his temper and scolded the congregation. This reproach displeased many congregants, including Kaplan's mother-in-law, who did not hesitate to let him know how she felt. Kaplan listened to her complaints with the proper respect. "I acted as a model son-in-law," he thought, and "listened to all she had to say — and she had a good deal to say about her wisdom and foresight in getting all her nine children — God bless them — to be good Jews and marrying them all off successfully. Therefore, I ought to give heed to her advice and not permit men and women to sit together at the SAJ House during services, and to control my temper in the pulpit. I was noncommittal on the former, and on the latter I promised her that next Yom Kippur I would demonstrate to her how even tempered I can be." [30]

The most interesting innovation concerning women occurred a month or so after the opening of the SAJ, with the bas mitzvah of Kaplan's daughter, Judith. In his later life, Kaplan was fond of saying that he had four reasons for instituting the bas mitzvah ceremony: his four daughters, Judith, Hadassah, Naomi, and Selma. The idea for such a ceremony must have been germinating in Kaplan's mind for quite a long time. At a United Synagogue convention in 1918, he raised the issue of equality for women in the synagogue, but he made no concrete suggestions and the discussion never went anywhere. After Judith's twelfth birthday, Kaplan began to think about doing something appropriate for the occasion. Her bas mitzvah was celebrated on the eighteenth day of Adar 5682, which corresponds to March 18, 1922, when she was twelve and a half. A simple announcement in the SAJ Bulletin invited everyone in the congregation to a meal afterward. There is no record of any opposition within the congregation, but Kaplan did have his difficulties. Before the event, there was considerable resistance from his mother and mother-in-law. Judith many years later recalled the following conversation between them. "'In-law,' said my mother's mother, 'Talk to your son. Tell him not to do this thing.' '*Machateineste* [In-law],' said Grandma Kaplan, 'you know a son doesn't listen to his mother. You talk to your daughter. Tell her to tell him not to do this thing!'" The grandmothers did not prevail, and the event proceeded as planned. As Judith recalls, her father did not decide exactly what she was to do until the night before. "Everything was in readiness except the procedure itself. On Friday night, after Shabbat dinner, Father took me into his study and had me read aloud the blessings which precede and succeed the Torah readings. How severely he corrected my diction. . . . He then selected a passage from the weekly portion . . . which I practiced reading in both Hebrew and English."[31]

The services took place on the first floor of the SAJ House, as they called George M. Cohan's converted brownstone, with the men seated in the front and the women seated behind. Judith had to sit up front with the men, "away from the cozy protection of mother and sisters." Strictly speaking, Judith's bas mitzvah was not what it would have been if she were a male. Judith was called forward to recite the Torah blessings and read a portion from the weekly *sidrah* (Bible portion). Kaplan himself read the blessings for the portion from the Prophets and the *Haftarah* (prophetic selection) itself. Although the ceremony was not fully equal to its male counterpart, the bas mitzvah was born, and, as Judith put it, "no thunder sounded, no lightning struck . . . and the rest of the day was all rejoicing." This first small step did not mean full equality for women, even at the SAJ. It took more than twenty years for women to be called regularly to the Torah. The SAJ thus stood in the anomalous situation of having many bas mitzvahs but no women who were ever again called up to the Torah. In the matter of calling women to the Torah, Kaplan chose to follow his flock rather than to act on his conscience.

Kaplan's attitude toward his congregation was complex. He was grateful for the continuous opportunity of expressing and developing his ideas but, there were many aspects of congregational life that irritated him. The SAJ members were devoted to Kaplan and frequently thought of him as "the great man." Yet they expected him to minister to their needs and were annoyed when he did not meet their expectations. Sometimes the members wanted to "use" the rabbi. One congregational leader was hosting a dinner for his workers; without explicitly stating so, he expected Kaplan to sing his praises as an employer. Kaplan took umbrage at being placed in this situation and his pent-up anger surfaced as he wrote about it in his diary: "J.L., my most ardent supporter, wants me to tell his working men what an idealist he is. . . . I can understand his wanting me to boast [for] him. But what I cannot understand and forgive is his resentment and retaliation because I have no inclination to prostitute myself, or rather my calling to his vanity. . . . The SAJ suddenly became to me an unclean thing. I wanted to get as far away from it as possible."[32]

Kaplan's fury with the congregation sometimes erupted during a sermon. These explosions were produced by the depth of his convictions, the intensity of his desire to win over his congregants, and his

ever-smoldering anger at not having changed their lives in any significant way. One *Shavuot* (Feast of Weeks), for example, the topic of his
sermon was "Can the Torah Become a Power?" He became so heated
in his delivery and "raged and thumped" with such vigor that his hand
hurt him all day.

Kaplan was rarely cool and detached; more often he was irascible
and impatient. Those who never encountered him directly might think
his intellectual rationalism would be reflected in his personality, but
nothing could be farther from the truth. Harry Libowitz, a member of
the synagogue board, told Kaplan that such blowups nullified the effect
of what he said. Lena Kaplan felt that the strain stemmed from her
husband's relationships with congregational members, particularly "his
own irritability and his inability to handle the members properly." And
indeed, the "great man" often seemed somewhat petulant and uncompromising. He frequently had a hidden agenda and did not relish dealing with the *Baale Batim* (the movers and shakers) with whom he had to
compromise.[33]

The SAJ members, however, were not much different from other
Jews of their time. They were for the most part well-to-do middle-class
Jews who had made some money (some of them a great deal of money)
and had moved up to the newly fashionable Upper West Side. The
attendance at services on the Sabbath was good, though sometimes dis-
appointing to Kaplan. One Sabbath, he had prepared a sermon on the
importance of leisure in the twentieth century and decided not to give
it because the attendance was so poor — 110, including quite a few nonmembers. He went into a fit of depression and regretted not having left
the SAJ before 1925 when the building was purchased. A suggestion
that he talk about plays and current books rather than the portion of
the week depressed him even further. Doubtless many rabbis would
have been happy in those years to have a congregation of more than a
hundred people on an ordinary Sabbath morning.

The upper-class status of the congregation was reflected in the
dinner-dances they scheduled whenever they could, which were always
held at first class hotels in the city. One such affair was held at the Hotel
Astor to celebrate the second anniversary of the SAJ. Four hundred
fifty people attended. Kaplan dealt poorly with such occasions because
he was not at ease with small talk. At his table the conversation turned
to golf, and he was "bored to death." He was irritated by the young
people's insistence on dancing between the courses, which he found
frivolous. There were many speeches, including one by Kaplan, and
everyone other than the rabbi seemed to think the affair a great success.[34]

At times, of course, he was buoyed up by public celebration. In January 1930, he celebrated twenty-five years in the rabbinate and was honored at an SAJ dinner with seven hundred people attending. Although such affairs were merely gestures, the size of the turnout was a measure of Kaplan's popularity. The truth of the matter, as Kaplan noted in his journal, was that the dinner had been arranged in order to increase the SAJ membership and that the idea of honoring him arose in the search for a viable pretext. Kaplan spoke for thirty-five minutes, satisfied with his delivery and with the content of the speech. He thanked God, "the giver of life and the source of all that makes life worthwhile," and expressed his gratitude to all those who helped him to take advantage of the opportunities and the blessings he enjoyed. He thanked his friends but noted in the privacy of his diary that he was difficult to work with and therefore didn't have too many friends. Nonetheless, he valued those he had because of their high hopes for him. This aspect of friendship was well expressed by his teacher Felix Adler, who wrote: "He is my friend who sees me as I might be, sees the standards which it is in me to live up to and by his relentlessly expectant eyes helps me to live up to them."

This particular celebration was unusual because Kaplan actually enjoyed himself. More often his mood was one of despair. He thought frequently of leaving the SAJ altogether, so scant seemed the progress toward implementing his ideas. He was not being paid for his services as a rabbi and thus had no financial incentive for staying on. In February 1929, he told the president of the SAJ that he was leaving in order to work on his writing and to implement his program through rabbis, teachers, and social workers rather than through a congregation. He confided to his diary that perhaps he had been expecting too much of the SAJ members. They were *Amcha*, a word that refers to the bulk of the Jewish people, and perhaps they just didn't measure up to his expectations.[35]

Kaplan's impulse to walk away from the SAJ was constant, not unlike his urges at the Seminary. His sense that he was not realizing his program oppressed him severely. But the source of his unhappiness is to be sought not in the objective conditions of the SAJ but within himself as a person. He was plagued by a sense of his own inadequacy, often feeling that his reach far exceeded his grasp. This perception was expressed in the diary not once but many times. As noted previously, he felt deficient when he compared himself to his colleagues at the Seminary. Although he was perfectly at ease in reading and writing Hebrew, he did not trust himself to speak publicly in Hebrew without much preparation. Even a minor faux pas in public where Hebrew was concerned troubled him deeply. He repeatedly expressed self-disgust because he had not produced a major publication. Throughout the 1920s, he published constantly in the *SAJ Review*, the *Menorah Journal*, and elsewhere, but the only book he produced was the slim (seventy pages) volume entitled *A New Approach to the Problem of Judaism*. He was approaching midlife and had not yet published a significant work. Then, too, he found writing difficult and undermining. Working on the book that was to become his magnum opus, he experienced continuous frustration: "The task of beating into shape the substance of the book on Judaism as a civilization is not only taking up all my spare time, but makes me feel how deficient I am in the mental qualities necessary to clear and effective writing. There is no end to the number of times I have to rewrite a passage before it expresses what I have in mind."[36]

Yet Kaplan's unhappiness was too pervasive to stem from a single aspect of his life. It was, in a sense, built into the very structure of his mind and his personality.

Several key insights of Karen Horney in her analysis of personality shed light on Kaplan's inner conflicts and on the structure of his psyche. Horney points out that people frequently construct an idealized image of themselves because they reject a realistic sense of the self with all its limitations and deficiencies. If they focus on the gap between the real sense of the self and their idealized image, they will constantly criticize themselves, always aware of how far short they are of their ideal. Sometimes, however, the individual, though aware of the distance from his or her idealized image, tends to identify with it. Regarding intelligence or power or some creative gift, the person comes to believe he or she is the ideal he or she has created. Such an identification with the ideal does not help one to grow but rather substitutes for realistic self-confidence and realistic pride. The idealized image serves to remove any sense of conflict, and so it is held to quite tenaciously. Some of the most accomplished individuals are frequently those who work the hardest at implementing the idealized image. The closer people believe they approximate their ideals, the more difficult it is for them to accept their own limitations.

Kaplan's idealized self-image revolved around his belief that it was his particular destiny to find a way to reconstruct Judaism, harmonizing it with life in the modern world and thus enabling the Jewish people to survive as Jews. The Jewish people became the center of his concern and his primary burden. The contrast between the real live Jews in his congregation and "the Jewish people" in his mind posed a genuine problem for him. He was tormented by the conflict between the image of Israel as "a people" whom he wanted to save and the particular Jews

Kaplan family in the early 1930s. From left: *Naomi Kaplan, Lena Kaplan, Ira Eisenstein, Judith
Kaplan, Mordecai Kaplan, Selma Kaplan, Hadassah Kaplan. (Courtesy RRC.)*

whom he couldn't stand. The conflict was revealed vividly in a diary
entry in 1924. He was upset by a particular board meeting of the SAJ
and wondered once again whether he should leave the institution. He
was disappointed with the members' lackadaisical spirit and with the
fact that "they were not ready to make any sacrifices in time or money."
The services were poorly attended, and the adult programs "were not
entertaining enough for them . . . they were worm-eaten with bore-
dom." Before he could even finish these thoughts, he shifted his mind
to the ideal and felt much better. The diary entry continued in the next
paragraph: "on the other hand, whenever I get the chance to concentrate on the problem of Judaism as a civilization, I see more and more
light, I am beginning to find a workable formula for Judaism in the
Diaspora."[37]

Thinking about the ideal comforted him, but often it exacerbated
his real-life problems. Because he desparately wanted to "save the Jewish people," the small gains in his congregation counted for very little.
The members of the SAJ attended regularly in decent numbers and
gave substantial amounts of money to the congregation, considering
that they had recently contributed a large sum for the center building.
They treated Kaplan as "the great man" and were very respectful. Yet

he continued to be unhappy with them. They were ordinary business-men and their families, whom he believed lacked spiritual depth. Some-times his feelings of disgust found their way into his sermons, as when he expostulated at length on the difference between the rabbinic "love of Israel" and the attitude of Moses, Elijah, and Isaiah, who were ever ready to hand in their resignations.[38]

The contrast between the ordinariness of the everyday and the ab-stract majestic level on which Kaplan's mind worked began to tarnish the ideal itself. As the rabbi of a congregation, he suffered a particular distress because he was always talking about the ultimate issues and the way things should be. The individuals in front of him never measured up, and he couldn't keep himself sufficiently rooted in present reality to see the small victories. His despair with the congregation led him to doubt his whole grand enterprise. This did not happen very often, but the pessimistic thoughts were never far from the surface: "My Jewish consciousness acts like an exposed nerve of a tooth. It gives me no rest. It often throws me into a fit of blues. Instead of making me experience the reality of God my Jewish consciousness often leads me to despair of mankind in general and of the Jews in particular. These last few days have again been days of torment and ordeal."

In this same diary passage, Kaplan called himself "a veritable Don Quixote," beguiled by the hope that he can protect and preserve Juda-ism. The mask of Don Quixote fit him well. He was constantly mistak-ing what was in front of him. Instead of seeing a mere discussion group or a meeting, he saw an opportunity to save the modern Jew. Instead of seeing a person opposing his ideas, he saw the forces of traditionalism arrayed against him. Like Don Quixote, he was divorced from imme-diate reality. He never was happy with half the loaf. Engaged in a great cosmic battle, he constantly feared he was losing ground. Many indi-viduals envision their activities in terms of some grand scheme, but they do not allow the vision to supplant the present reality. The ultimate indictment comes from Kaplan himself: "Beguiled by the delusion that I can help to render Judaism permanent or even temporarily safe, I fight against windmills which always worst me. That is why I am the knight of the long face, always grumpy, always in bad humor."[39]

Although constantly tormented by his doubts, he never succumbed to them. He was revitalized by the urgency of his mission and his ulti-mate faith in his message. It would be a serious mistake to take Kaplan's characterization of himself in a mood of depression as the whole mea-sure of the man. The truth is that his efforts to solve the problems of the modern Jew were of profound significance. Without vision, there is no progress, but that vision is sometimes very costly to its possessor.

12

RELIGIOUS NATIONALISM:

Weizmann and the Zionist Organization of America

Zionism occupied a central place in Kaplan's ideology. Throughout his life, he believed that the Jewish people needed to normalize their condition. Only with a land of their own could the Jews survive and prosper and again become a vital force on the world's stage. If Judaism was the religious civilization of the Jewish people, it followed that it would be fully and completely realized only in the Jewish homeland of Zion. At the same time, Kaplan's Zionism was a soft Zionism. He believed that the Diaspora was a permanent part of the Jewish condition and that Jews could live secure and creative lives outside a Jewish center.

Kaplan was a significant force in Americanizing the Zionist commitment. Like Horace Kallen, the leading exponent of American ethnic pluralism, and Louis Brandeis, Kaplan viewed Zionism and American life as perfectly compatible. Brandeis by his very association with the Zionist movement helped to make it respectable. Kaplan was one of the primary ideologists behind the process of Americanizing Zionism and also succeeded in articulating the religious dimensions of the Zionist dream. Kaplan's writings and, more importantly, his lecturing throughout the country from 1915 onward contributed substantially to the Zionist cause. His stature within the Zionist movement is reflected in the fact that when the Hebrew University was opened in 1925, the Zionist Organization of America chose him to represent it at the ceremonies. Although he was involved organizationally with the ZOA from time to time, his contribution lies not in his activity but in his formulations and ideology. Kaplan's particular approach never made his audiences feel uncomfortable about living in America rather than in Palestine. Listening to him, one might almost feel that Zion could exist in America as well as Palestine. He, of course, was not the only one who felt this way. Israel Friedlaender and Judah Magnes were both dedicated nationalists who shared his love for Zion and for America.[1]

Kaplan was inspired chiefly by the cultural Zionism of Ahad Ha-Am, whose essays he had read when he was still an adolescent. Seventy years later, he dedicated one of his last books to the memory of Ahad Ha-Am, who had revealed to him "the spiritual reality of the Jewish people" and had shown that "the meaning of God and the Torah can be properly understood only in relation to that central reality."[2] Ahad Ha-Am's death in 1927 called forth Kaplan's admiration for his teacher, whom he eulogized as having inaugurated a new era in Jewish history because of his humanistic reconstruction of Judaism. He perceived him as rejecting both a vulgar secularism on the one hand and a blind traditionalism on the other.[3]

Ahad Ha-Am (Asher Ginzberg) was born in the Kiev province of Russia in 1856 and died in Tel Aviv in 1927. He helped change the thought of a whole generation of Jewish thinkers and leaders. Theodor Herzl roused the world to the need for a safe and secure place for the body of the Jewish people. Ahad Ha-Am, Herzl's most important critic, awakened the Jews to the possibility of their spiritual regeneration. He understood that the collective redemption of the Jewish people was a process, not an event, and therefore would come about only with the gradual transformation of the heart and soul of the Jewish masses.

Ahad Ha-Am had believed that the greatness of the Jews lay not in their having been chosen by God but in their own creative genius. Flowing from the national will, this creative ability forged the primary direction of Jewish civilization throughout the ages. According to Ahad Ha-Am, God was not the principal agent in the life of the Jewish people; this role fell to the Jewish people themselves. The distinctiveness of the national Jewish will lay in the realm of morals and ethics. At the heart of the Jewish spirit was a deep social concern and an emphasis on the social responsibility of the individual. The national creative energy could not function when Jews lived under pressures to imitate the accomplishments of their non-Jewish neighbors. Only if a way was found to renew the national spirit could this assimilation be prevented.[4] The basic beliefs of Ahad Ha-Am were perhaps best summed up by a young Jewish scholar named Harry Wolfson, who wrote in the

American Hebrew in 1906: "There is a distinct Jewish spirit which is still active, and it is for the good of humanity that this spirit continue to be active. Palestine must become the center of the Jewish spirit; without a center this spirit will be extinguished. Palestine must become the center of the Jewish spirit before it becomes the center of Jewish life."[5]

Although Kaplan is credited by some as being Ahad Ha-Am's leading disciple, he nonetheless seriously departed from his mentor. Ahad Ha-Am was not deeply concerned about theology or about the ways theological commitments could be concretized in the ritual of the everyday. As a result, Kaplan felt that an Ahad Ha-Amian approach to Jewish life was severely limited. It is important to keep in mind that Kaplan and Ahad Ha-Am were reacting to different environments. Responding to the early Zionists who saw the solution to the Jewish problem in the transfer of Jews to the Holy Land, Ahad Ha-Am was not one of the so-called practical Zionists. Kaplan, on the other hand, was reacting to Orthodox and Reform Jews who viewed the Jewish problem as a matter of religious belief rather than as the actual state of the Jewish people or their collective consciousness. The different contexts altered the thrust of the message in each case. Ahad Ha-Am was perhaps the necessary but not sufficient condition for Kaplan's ideology and its emphasis on Jewish peoplehood. Kaplan began with Ahad Ha-Am but transcended him in significant ways.

The primary area of divergence between Kaplan and his teacher concerned religion. Kaplan, for all his insistence that Judaism was not a matter of belief but of peoplehood, remained intensely involved in religion. He believed that religion, given the proper interpretation, was essential to human fulfillment. Kaplan's lifelong struggle to lend new meaning to the concept of God was thoroughly alien to Ahad Ha-Am's approach to Jewish problems. For Ahad Ha-Am, God was dead; he had no interest in restoring basic theological assumptions to a central place in Jewish life. The "secular rabbi," as Asher Ginzberg was sometimes called, was not hostile to those who still found meaning in the observance of *mitzvot*. But neither was he interested in reconstructing the ritual system so that it could function again in a pivotal way for Jews. For Kaplan, the synagogue was central to the revitalization of the Jewish people. It was the institution that would be the key to Jewish revival. In its expanded form of the Jewish center, it would be the carrier of the new Jewish consciousness. For Ahad Ha-Am, the synagogue was a relic of the past and could perform no vital function in the renascence of the Jews.[6]

Kaplan would agree with his teacher that religion was but one of the forms of culture if the word *civilization* were substituted for *culture*.

However, he was much more confident about the part religion would play in Jewish survival. Kaplan resented his mentor's lack of understanding of religion. The cultural Zionism of Ahad Ha-Am and his conception of Judaism were disconcerting to Kaplan because they were "wanting in a basic appreciation of religion" and of religious longings.[7]

In one particular case, Kaplan used Ahad Ha-Am's approach but transferred it to the theological realm in a very novel fashion. In "The God Idea in Judaism," published in the 1930s, he began by outlining the main points of Ahad Ha-Am's essay on Moses. The essay distinguished between the historical Moses whose existence and character could be established or questioned by historical research and the image of Moses as it had functioned in the Jewish tradition. Even if it could be shown that Moses did not exist historically, "it is an indisputable fact that the idea of Moses figured prominently in the Jewish consciousness for centuries." Proceeding from this proposition, Ahad Ha-Am argued that this "Moses idea" answered some basic need of the Jewish people. He concluded that Jews ought to preserve the image of Moses no matter what the facts are because it has functioned in such a significant way and can continue to function in this way (as a metaphor for the passion for righteousness).

Applying this scheme to the God idea, Kaplan suggested that even if God did not exist, there was no denying that the concept of God had played a key role in the life of the Jewish people and answered a deep human need. This need is the quest for salvation or self-fulfillment. Just as the Jews should retain the Moses image, so should they retain the belief in God: "No attempt at ordering life can be complete without that nexus of truths which are symbolized by the God idea. No less important than holding those truths is the knowledge that human nature at its best has always sensed them. . . . If the Jews surrendered the spiritual leverage which the God idea afforded them, they would exhibit a mental inflexibility and moral obtuseness that would disqualify them for survival as a people."[8]

Whether or not a person is a Zionist will be determined by his or her attitude toward the land of Israel and its place in the life of the Jewish people. For Ahad Ha-Am, Zion is the center, but a center implies a periphery or in this case the Diaspora. Ahad Ha-Am believed there would always be Jewish communities outside the land of Israel, but their vitality and their Jewish character would be deeply dependent on the life-giving forces of Zion. Living in the Diaspora was a last resort for Jews, an expedient that would always be necessary but not really desirable. Kaplan's position on these issues must be understood within the context of American Zionism and his early attitudes about the Zionist enterprise.

American Zionism has always been primarily philanthropic. Even the most dedicated Zionist leaders had the feeling that America was different from other parts of the exile and that the Jews were not likely to have to flee persecution from the "*Goldene Medina.*" Early Zionist trendsetters such as Gustav Gottheil and Jacob De Hass were faithful disciples of Theodor Herzl, but most American Jewish leaders who embraced Zionism were loyal to Ahad Ha-Am. Solomon Schechter, Judah Magnes, Israel Friedlaender, Henrietta Szold, and Horace Kallen all were profoundly influenced by cultural Zionism. For them, Zionism was a way of revitalizing the Jewish people and stemming the tide of assimilation. Palestine would be a haven for the oppressed, but these devoted Americans did not feel oppressed. The most important person in this group was Israel Friedlaender, who, despite his early demise, exerted a significant influence over the ideology and organization of American Zionism. Friedlaender was one of the primary interpreters of Ahad Ha-Am on the American scene. In Friedlaender's interpretation, Zionism becomes a spiritual revival, whether in the Diaspora or in Zion, with the primary emphasis on Jewish culture. The political problems of the Jews could be solved in a number of different ways, the most important first step toward a solution being to get them out of Russia. Like most other American Zionists, Friedlaender did not negate the future of the Diaspora. He looked for ways to bring together the diverse factions of American Jewry by advocating a synthesis of "Zionism plus Diaspora, Palestine plus America" and religion plus nationalism.[9] The question of his hopes for American Jewry remain disputed, however, with some scholars believing that he was pessimistic about the possibility of a real creative Judaism in America and others believing that his position was closer to that of Dubnov, who saw the centers of Jewish life as coequal with a Palestinian community.[10]

Horace Kallen stands out above all others in his striking similarity to the philosophical approach of Kaplan. Even Kallen's biography resembles Kaplan's. Born in 1882 in a town in Silesia, then part of Germany, but now in Poland, he came to America at a young age and settled in Boston with his family. He attended the public schools and eventually studied at Harvard, where he ultimately received a doctorate in philosophy. Alienated from his father, a rabbi, throughout his life, Kallen did achieve a reconciliation at the end but he did not sit *shiva* or recite the *kaddish*.

Kallen was alienated not only from his father but from Judaism as well. Eventually, he did return to the fold, but not in a religious sense.

As one scholar put it, Kallen "did not return to his father or his father's religion, but to the Jewish heritage of culture, thought, and values, and to the feeling of membership in the Jewish people, to a lively sensitivity to the Jewish being and the Jewish experience."[11] Kallen is known primarily for his doctrine of cultural pluralism. He passionately believed that the Jews would not be free until they were free as Jews. Democracy did not mean sameness but the "union of the different." The image he put forward was not the metaphor of the melting pot but that of the orchestra, where each instrument (i.e., ethnic group) retains its identity and contributes to the harmony of the whole. If people are truly free, they will turn out to be different, and diversity enriches everyone. For Kallen, Judaism was a living culture which constantly changed because it was alive. Zionism was a logical extension of his belief in the right of the Jews to a separate group life. He did not think of Zion as primarily an answer to persecution but as an opportunity to revive the Hebraic spirit. Kallen certainly had a significant impact on Brandeis and was an important factor in the latter's "conversion" to Zionism.

Kallen and Kaplan were both schooled in the same pragmatic tradition and drew heavily on William James and Josiah Royce. Both were later confirmed in their ideas by the writings of John Dewey. They were thoroughly American and were dedicated to the ideals of Jefferson and the American enlightenment. Both believed in the freedom of individuals to live in a society that fostered diversity and pluralism. They were committed Zionists. Yet there were differences. Kaplan was a rabbi and a religious man and sought throughout his life to relate his ideals to his theological commitments. In this search, he was concerned with the theological implications of his primary categories. Although their assumptions were similar, they diverged significantly in the elaboration of their ideas. One misunderstands Kaplan completely if one merely equates him with essentially secular thinkers like Kallen.

Kaplan's Zionism was complex and ambivalent. Palestine was not the focus of his thinking; his focus was Judaism as a civilization. This idea was the basic organizing principle from which all else was derived. Judaism was not a religion or a set of beliefs, but a way of life. Understanding and implementing this idea would ensure the survival of the Jewish people. Having said this, it remained possible to conclude the argument in one of two ways. One could say that the only place where Judaism could function as a civilization was Palestine. Or one could recognize that the Diaspora would always exist and, therefore, the greatest need was to develop strategies that would allow Jews to maintain their identity in the lands of the dispersion. Although these may appear to be mutually exclusive positions, Kaplan affirmed them both in equal measure. He maintained that Palestine was the only place where an original Jewish civilization could flourish and also looked primarily to the dispersed communities of the Jewish people for the re-emergence of genuine ethnic-religious societies where Jews would live in two civilizations. There are, in other words, two Kaplans insofar as Zionism is concerned – a Palestinocentric Zionist and a Diaspora nationalist, the latter being more attuned to life in America.

Kaplan's commitment to Zionism, whether Palestine- or Diaspora-oriented, was evident early in his career and was rooted in a strong sense of ethnic identification with the Jewish people. He observed the desire of recent immigrants to assimilate into the larger American society and present themselves as members of a group that expressed universal ethical and moral values. They did not want to emphasize their distinctive past or their present ethnic bonds. Kaplan and other Zionist Jews, however, believed in group life as central to being a Jew. There was nothing wrong with being particularistic in one's thought or religion. "Do not be afraid of tribalism in religion," he wrote in his diary in December 1906."Viewed more deeply," he went on, "tribalism is the very law of religion. For so viewed tribalism means a certain definite conception of God peculiar to a race, nation or section of the world's population." [12]

"The Jews are a nation," the young rabbi preached in 1903. "Palestine and Judaism are as inseparable as the positive and negative in electricity or the north and south pole in the magnet." The implication here is that the "transformation of Jewish life" can take place only by means of a rebuilt Palestine. In his first book, Kaplan clearly seemed to argue that Jewish civilization would survive ultimately only in Palestine: "If what we want is that those who will be known as Jews should enrich the world with their ideas, their ideals, and their example, and do so not only as individuals but collectively, . . . then it is futile to expect that kind of Judaism ever to thrive in the Diaspora, either here or elsewhere." In the Diaspora, Jews who desire to live fully realize that they are in "*Golus*" and that "life at its best [is] an abnormality." If a land is free, the spiritual dilemma of Jews is worse yet because they lose their individuality in trying to "speak as the non-Jew speaks and think as the non-Jew thinks."

In these moods of nationalist assertiveness, Kaplan showed his readiness to dismiss the ideas of those like Simon Dubnov or Horace Kallen who emphasized the importance and the possibilities of Jewish survival in the Diaspora. According to Kaplan, social and cultural autonomy in the Diaspora was a dream that was "as little possible as that the sun should rise in the west." [13]

At the same time and often in the same document, he would contradict himself and take a stand that appeared inconsistent with the
Palestinocentric position. In the 1924 work being quoted here, he
went on to discuss the meaning of Torah as lifelong moral education without the slightest implication that such education necessarily had to take
place in a Jewish commonwealth. This "softer" kind of Zionism centered on nationalism as the "fellow feeling" of the Jews and stood in
opposition to "a proud chauvinism or a mere national braggadocio."
The Jews are one nation or one people whether they are willing to
admit it or not, he maintained. But being one people does not require
them to live in one land. The survival of the Jews as a people depends
on their will to live as a collectivity, in other words on the quality of
their collective consciousness. Jewish consciousness in this soft Zionism may flourish wherever Jews live. Kaplan believed that the Jews
would survive as a civilization or perish as a religion. He repeatedly
explained how to cultivate the collective consciousness of the Jews and
to foster their fellow feeling. First and foremost, he pointed to the elements that bind the Jews or any national group together, such as a common language and a common historical memory. He advocated the
study of the Hebrew language as the key element to Jewish identity at
every opportunity. "The Hebrew language would be cultivated not
only for synagogue responses," he wrote in the *Menorah Journal*, "but
as the medium of expression for a regenerated Israel and as the tangible
evidence in the Diaspora of the collective mind of the Jewish people." [14]
The value of studying the Jewish past, so that every Jew might retain
a sense of collective biography, was the leitmotif of all Kaplan's educational endeavors. The deepened collective consciousness that would
result from this emphasis on language and a sense of the past would
institutionally be located primarily in the expanded synagogue — the
synagogue center. Here the symbols, language, and ceremonies that
articulated the collective consciousness would be conserved and nur-
tured. The synagogue center would be the principal vehicle of Jewish
consciousness until the establishment of a center of Jewish civilization
in Palestine. [15]

Whenever Kaplan gave a general exposition of his ideology, he always mentioned Palestine but more often as a necessary courtesy rather
than a serious proposition. The specific implications of Palestine as a
center are never spelled out. After mentioning Palestine, he usually returned to describing how Jewish consciousness could be enhanced in
the communities of the Diaspora. He postponed the question of Palestine, saying that "Until Jews will acquire a center of national life [in
Palestine] it is necessary to establish Jewish centers in the Diaspora." It

is difficult to know whether Kaplan is referring here to Jewish communities of the Diaspora that would become centers or to synagogues that would be expanded. My feeling is that it is to the latter. It should be noted that Kaplan's softer Zionism is very close to the ideology of Simon Dubnov, despite explicit statements from Kaplan dismissing Dubnov's "Diaspora nationalism."

The establishment of a viable Jewish center of Jewish civilization in Palestine sometimes seemed to be in the very distant millennialist future. "The real Zionist platform," Kaplan wrote less than a year before the Balfour declaration, "is not the one formulated in the Basle program, but the prayer in our ritual which reads, 'Let our eyes behold thy return to Zion.'"[16]

Kaplan's profound ambivalence about Palestine appeared most vividly in connection with his children. He felt caught in a bind because in his heart of hearts he had grave doubts that the Zionist enterprise would ever bear fruit. He brought up his daughter Judith to be a "lover of Zion," but when he discovered the depth of her enthusiasm, he was distressed. He wanted her to think of her own future and in a moment of panic began feeding her anti-Zionist propaganda. "I thought that the arguments against Zionism would shake her faith in Palestine," he confided to his journal in this moment of doubt. "Instead she seemed as ardent in her faith as before. Of course, it is too soon to judge."[17]

◆

Though rarely active in the actual operations of the Zionist organization, Kaplan had significant involvement with the organized Zionist movement in American. The American movement was always in need of some way to interpret itself to the American Jewish community so that American Jews would perceive Zionism not as threat to their status but as a complement to their patriotism. Kaplan's role in this regard was notable even though his involvement in Zionist affairs was generally precipitated by special circumstances or crisis (the Brandeis-Weizmann controversy) or around some great event (the dedication of the Hebrew University). For a short time at the end of the 1920s, he had a position with the National Executive Committee of the ZOA.

Zionism in America has always leaned toward the "soft" variety. The American Jewish community had been "Israeli-ized," it has never been "Zionized." Jews support the state of Israel but never took Zion as the center of their lives. Zionism in America was never a response to a perceived present or future threat but grew out of a sense that the Jews (other Jews) needed a refuge from oppression. Indeed, both Zionism and emigrating to America were a response to the desperate need of European Jewry for safety and freedom from persecution. The movement was slow in starting but grew significantly during World War I, when the European Jewish communities were cut off from each other and were in a state of confusion and disarray. Louis Brandeis's control of the movement during the war was crucial because he facilitated the Americanization of the movement. Appealing strongly to Eastern European Jews who desperately wanted to be Americanized, the Brandeis period witnessed a phenomenal growth in the movement. (12,000 in 1914, 176,000 in 1919).[18] Brandeis said nothing new, but his synthesis of Americanism and Zionism was appealing and noteworthy. He perceived Zionism as a progressive idea because it allowed Jews more freedom, freedom to go to their own land if they chose to and freedom to build a model democratic society. For many American Jews, he helped transform Zionism from its emphasis on blood ties to the concept of "philanthropic Zionism."

For Zionists, the most important event of the war years was the Balfour declaration (November 2, 1917). Kaplan was truly moved and felt that a new Jewish holiday to be called *Yom Ha-Geulah*, the Day of Redemption, should be declared in honor of the achievement. Weizmann hoped Brandeis would support the Balfour declaration publicly, but Brandeis did not feel he could because of his position on the Supreme Court. At that point, the United States was not yet at war with Turkey. Nonetheless, Brandeis, along with Stephen Wise, worked behind the scenes to win Woodrow Wilson's endorsement of the declaration. The endorsement finally came two years after the event.

With the ending of the war in 1918, the Federation of American Zionists, which was an organization of Zionist organizations, became the Zionist Organization of America, an organization of individuals. Under the old structure, the central Zionist organization lacked influence over the individuals who belonged to the local Zionist lodges. With the new arrangement, Brandeis hoped to create a more efficient operation. Little did he know that he was soon to lose power completely when Weizmann's American supporters would take over the Zionist Organization of America.

The great drama of "Pinsk versus Washington" (Weizmann vs. Brandeis) dominated domestic Zionist politics throughout the spring and summer of 1920, and Kaplan was drawn in no less than other dedicated leaders. Ben Halpern has called the conflict between Weizmann and Brandeis "The Clash of Heroes," which indeed it was. For Chaim Weizmann, the war years were characterized by feverish activity and many victories. There was, of course, the Balfour declaration, which was a great personal triumph for him. He also worked hard at the peace conference and later at San Remo lobbying for the interests of the *Yishuv*.

Weizmann and the Boston patrician clashed over fundamental issues. Brandeis apparently believed that with the Balfour declaration the political phase of the Zionist cause had come to an end, and now it was time to concentrate on building up the *Yishuv* economically. He envisioned a decentralized World Zionist Organization and a Palestinian economic foundation (*Keren Hayesod*) which would be organized in such a way that it would be more efficient than the money-raising activities of the past. Brandeis hoped that American contributors would retain more control over their contributions. Weizmann advocated a centralized World Zionist Organization and a *Keren Hayesod* clearly under the control of the world body. When Weizmann arrived in New York on April 2, 1921, and set up an American division of the *Keren Hayesod*, it was a declaration of war against the Brandeis forces. The conflict came to a head at a meeting in Cleveland during the summer of 1921, with the Weizmann forces winning complete control of the Zionist Organization of America.

For once, Kaplan was at the center of a political conflict. He had some correspondence with Weizmann; a deep mutual respect existed between the two men. Shortly after Weizmann's arrival, Kaplan visited him on a Sabbath afternoon in his room at the Commodore Hotel. Kaplan's strategy to adjudicate the issues dividing Brandeis and Weizmann was to set up an impartial commission. Kaplan was rather naive perhaps, but Weizmann did not give him an absolute no and said he would confer with his staff about it. Kaplan went away quite impressed with the man and thinking very negatively about Brandeis. "What does Louis Brandeis know of Judaism to understand Zionism?" he thought to himself after the meeting. "But we are so much flattered when we see one of these half Jews take an interest in Judaism that we at once put him at the helm and there our trouble begins."[19]

Kaplan spoke to a small group of Zionist friends about his idea for a commission. They were positively disposed, and the group (including Benderly, Unterberg, and a few others) set about making the arrangements for a meeting. In the course of these conversations, it becomes clear that Kaplan was critical not only of the Brandeis camp but of Weizmann as well. At times, he was swayed by those who perceived Weizmann and his supporters as a "self-appointed oligarchy." Kaplan felt that giving the money raised for *Keren Hayesod* to a corporation organized by Weizmann was an "affront" to the American Zionist community.

The conference Kaplan organized finally took place on May 19 with about thirty-five people in attendance. Benderly did most of the work. It was only one of a great many occasions on which the two sides met, but it was one of the most critical public confrontations. The primary speakers were Weizmann and Ussishkin on the one side and Judge Mack and Felix Frankfurter on the other. The meeting began at three-thirty in the afternoon and ended about midnight. Charges were hurled back and forth.[20] Weizmann stated his conviction that there was an "impassable gulf" between himself and the American Zionist leadership. He felt that the issue was a matter of commitment and that when the chips were down the ultimate loyalties of the present leadership would be to America and not to a Jewish community in Palestine.

Kaplan and some of those present still hoped to engineer a compromise, not wanting to face the fact that the split was already irreparable. A committee was appointed to bring back a compromise plan on which the both sides might agree. They first went to see Mack, who would not be moved and insisted that the ZOA have the right to raise money on its own. When they went to see Weizmann, he was just as adamant. The scene was quite moving, especially for Kaplan:

> Weizmann berated the leaders of the ZOA as obstructionists. Finally in a very dramatic way Weizmann appealed to us as real Jews to help him against these obstructionists instead of acting as impartial judges meting out judgment. He actually wept when he spoke of how he was sacrificing himself for the movement. He had nothing else in the world to live for. He addressed himself to me in particular. When I shook hands with him as I was about to leave he kissed me.

As they left the meeting, Benderly saw that Kaplan had been won over by Weizmann's emotional appeal and proceeded to feed him some very negative stories about how Weizmann had acted in meetings with Brandeis. At this point, a disgusted Kaplan was ready to withdraw from the whole affair.

Kaplan nonetheless was convinced by his friends to intervene one more time to facilitate a solution. They decided to visit Brandeis in Washington in order to urge him to withdraw from the Supreme Court and give all his time to the Zionist movement. Such a plan tells us more about the group and about Kaplan than about the controversy. It was almost as if their solution to the controversy was to make Brandeis like Weizmann — a fully devoted twenty-four-hour-a-day Zionist. In the group going to see Brandeis were Benderly, Judge Rosalsky, Sam Lamport, and a few others from the center. As they were about to arrive in the capital, the group realized there was no consensus on exactly how to convince Brandeis of their plan, and indeed there was no consensus on their basic assumptions. Turning to Kaplan to formulate the principles that united them, they asked him to speak for the group. They basically saw themselves as representing no organization or faction but as a handful of concerned synagogue Jews who were dedicated Zionists and at the same time recognized their indebtedness to America. This type of Americanized Zionism was widespread, and they felt that it would certainly appeal to Brandeis.

They arrived at the Brandeis home precisely at nine A.M. When he spoke, Kaplan emphasized the importance of maintaining the "authority and integrity" of the World Zionist Organization, but at the same time the WZO was not to be considered as an end in itself. Certain implications flowed from these premises, Kaplan explained. "Being only a means to an end, the WZO must not take the attitude that loyalty to it is not merely a means of administrative efficiency but qualification for being a full-fledged Jew. We regard such an attitude as productive of a type of Jewish chauvinism that might compromise our position in the countries of our adoption." They were clearly taking a stand against the threat they perceived from the imperialist direction of the Weizmann camp. At the same time, Weizmann and the WZO were obviously vital. In order to be sure that the WZO remained in its place, however, it was necessary for the American Zionists to strengthen themselves, and this would entail Brandeis giving his full time and energy to the Zionist cause. Brandeis explained that the setting of overall policies was his most important function, and he would continue to exercise this role without changing his relationship to the Zionist Organization. "He stated that he gave all of his leisure time to Zionism. More he could not do. He did not care to come before mass meetings, for he was of the conviction that the time for mass meetings was over, and that no good could come out of them." [21] Brandeis urged the group to put their thoughts before their fellow Zionists at the upcoming Zionist conference in Cleveland.

Kaplan apparently never seriously considered going to Cleveland. It was perhaps a reflection of his belief that the matter of Brandeis's resignation and loss of power was already decided, or perhaps he just was not interested enough in the political infighting that might take place at the meeting. He had an opportunity here to be part of the concrete political process where ideas were turned into reality. He could not or would not work on this level. He continued to vacillate between support for a Brandeis-type Zionism and his great personal affinity for Weizmann. He felt loyalty to Weizmann but believed that

Europeans did not really understand America. He also feared the "chauvinism" of hard-line Zionists. In this situation, as in many others, Kaplan functioned as the innocent ideologue trying to keep the different sides together rather than as the hard-headed politician.

In order to evaluate the rather complex nature of Kaplan's Zionism, we need to understand that he repeatedly turned down opportunities to settle in Palestine. One such occasion arose during the Weizmann-Brandeis conflict, when Weizmann asked Kaplan whether he would be interested in serving on the International Commission which supervised the holy places. The commission was to consist of two Jews, two Christians, and two Muslims. Kaplan mentioned the proposal only once in his diary and apparently gave the matter no further thought. His complete unwillingness to consider Weizmann's proposal seriously is all the more surprising given the fact that it was precisely at this juncture (in May and June 1921) that he was having deep public conflicts with the center board. One would think he might have welcomed an opportunity to begin completely anew.

On the same occasion, Weizmann also asked Kaplan whether he would serve on the *Keren Hayesod* advisory board. Kaplan agreed. He then noted in his diary that he was going to spend the summer with his family at the Jersey shore.

During the next few years, Kaplan kept in touch with Weizmann. When the Zionist leader came to America again in the spring of 1923 to raise money, Kaplan was ready to help him at every turn. He organized the congregations of the West Side with the goal of raising one hundred thousand dollars for *Keren Hayesod*. The SAJ pledged to contribute twenty-five thousand dollars. On *Shavuot* (Pentecost), at a study session the SAJ organized, Weizmann rose and spoke about "Judaism as a Civilization" and its unique character. Kaplan was obviously deeply moved, especially when the group voted to make Weizmann an honorary member of the congregation. The only one who was unhappy was Kaplan's mother-in-law, who complained that she saw Weizmann writing on the holiday and thought it was wrong.[22]

Weizmann thought highly of Kaplan and encouraged him to attend the Zionist congress that summer in Carlsbad. Kaplan appreciated the invitation but hesitated to accept it, "more out of inertia than any definite reason." When it became clear that the congregation would be willing to defray the cost and the official invitation came, he decided to accept.

In June, Kaplan journeyed to Baltimore to attend a Zionist meeting. He wandered into a session of the *Histadruth Ivrith* (Hebrew Society) which was taking place at the same time as the Zionist meeting.

Reception for Chaim Weizmann by Intercongrega-
tional Committee of the West Side, Hotel Astor,
May 1923. Kaplan and Weizmann are seated at
the head table. (Courtesy RRC.)

The speaker acknowledged the distinguished visitor standing in the back of the room, and everyone applauded. Kaplan was flattered by the recognition but was worried lest he be asked to speak extemporaneously in Hebrew. In the end, he was only called upon to take a bow. His discomfort with speaking extemporaneously in Hebrew before a knowledgeable audience did not deter him from preparing his speech in Hebrew for the Carlsbad congress. Or perhaps his experience in Baltimore made him feel that it was a matter of self-respect to give the Carlsbad address in Hebrew.

Although Kaplan had no interest in committee politics, he understood that the real decisions were not made at large public conventions. He contemplated the Zionist congress with considerable cynicism, observing that "the entire procedure of a convention is all prearranged and the noise and the speeches are merely for display purposes." The Thirteenth Zionist Congress was to take place at the beginning of August. The British mandate in Palestine had only recently been established, and the Zionist Organization executive had been empowered as the "Jewish Agency" that would deal with the mandatory government. The proposal came up that there should be non-Zionists in the Jewish Agency so that it would truly represent the Jewish people. This issue deeply divided the delegates to the congress and was only settled in the late 1920s when the Jewish Agency was reorganized.

Carlsbad was a famous health resort not far from Prague, situated in the Sudetenland. It had a sizable Jewish community with a synagogue that could seat two thousand. People came from all over Europe to take the cure. It was well known for its mineral waters that were reputed to be particularly good for digestive diseases. Kaplan knew many people at the congress. Some had come from the Jewish Center, some were old "friends" from Kehilath Jeshurun like Harry Fischel, the philanthropist Kaplan referred to as the "Champion Jewish Vulgarian of the United States." He had just returned from Palestine, where he had attended the dedication of a house he had donated for Chief Rabbi Kook. Kaplan recorded with some revulsion that Fischel's name was inscribed on the house, "and all for a paltry $25,000." Here again, Kaplan failed to see what was in front of him. Fischel was not the incarnation of evil but just a wealthy Jew who wanted his name on a building.

Kaplan did not take advantage of the Carlsbad spa and its health-giving waters. Neither did he arrive at the congress with any expectation of influencing the course of its events. While waiting for the congress to begin, however, he did not waste time. In a series of meetings with Ussishkin, he and Sol Lamport undertook to gather SAJ support for the prestigious literary journal *Ha-Shiloach*. The Hebrew journal had fallen on hard times, and Kaplan was happy to lend a hand to help this important cultural enterprise. He enjoyed feeling that he was giving some concrete reality to his notion of Judaism as total civilization. He also managed to visit Prague, the home of Franz Kafka. It is an interesting coincidence that just at this time Kafka was becoming excited about the possibility of immigrating to Palestine. It is unlikely that Kaplan had ever heard of Kafka, and the places that drew him were probably the medieval synagogue, called the Altneuschul, and the old Jewish cemetery nearby.[23]

Kaplan attended some of the committee meetings at the congress, but these held no real interest for him. Contemptuous of the political process, he noted, "There was nothing exalting or uplifting about any of its sessions. On the contrary. It was a tug of war for power. It was natural, human and ordinary. " It did not inspire him at all. At the congress, he delivered his speech in Hebrew but felt that it did not make much of an impression, most people being more excited about Weizmann's statement scheduled for later on that evening. As a matter of fact, there was so much noise while Kaplan was speaking that few people could hear what he said. He spoke about education in Palestine, emphasizing the importance of the Hebrew University. He had worked hard on the address and was proud that he had finally delivered a major speech in Hebrew. "I am grateful," he wrote in his diary, "that I at least came off without disgrace which I might have suffered, if I had not taken care to write out the address."[24]

Kaplan proved to be more impressive at Carlsbad than he realized. Within a year of the congress, in the spring of 1925, he received an invitation from the prominent American Zionist Louis Lipsky to speak on behalf of the Zionist Organization of America at the dedication ceremonies for the Hebrew University. American Zionists felt themselves rather like poor relations insofar as Jewish culture and education were concerned. Europe and Palestine had their Jewish scholars and writers and the American Zionists were happy to be able to claim a person like Kaplan, who was known to the Zionist leadership and who could acquit himself well both in English and in Hebrew, despite his insecurities. For his part, Kaplan had long been a supporter of the Hebrew University and was pleased to have the chance to speak at the opening exercises.

Great occasions often intensify insecurities, and such was the case with Kaplan. He felt at the time that someone more scholarly than he should have been accorded the honor of speaking on such an auspicious occasion: "I pass among the laity for a great scholar and therefore am accorded an honor which I feel should have been bestowed upon someone far more deserving than I am."[25] During February and early March 1925, there were weeks of feverish preparations. He was granted permission for a leave from the Seminary and was gratified when Adler asked him to represent the institution at the exercises. His students were genuinely sad that he would be gone for the rest of the semester. The SAJ arranged a dinner for him at the Hotel Astor with some three hundred people in attendance, where Weizmann and Lipsky both spoke, praising Kaplan as "one of the greatest scholars in America." Kaplan took the praise lightly, realizing that people always exaggerate on such occasions, and noted later that he even forgot to thank Weizmann and Lipsky for their remarks. A large contingent from the SAJ came down to the ship to bid him farewell, presenting him with many gifts and tokens of their affection.

Onboard ship, Kaplan kept to himself. He had never found it easy to socialize, and in any case he wanted to work on his speech. Also on board, Weizmann "worked" the prospective donors to the *Keren Hayesod* or other Zionist causes. When the two men found time to socialize,

Kaplan sans *beard at the Zionist Congress at Carls-bad, 1923. (Courtesy RRC.)*

Kaplan seemed to bring out the religious side of Weizmann, who more than once expressed his belief that there was a divine providence directing the course of events in Palestine. As Weizmann spoke about his experiences regarding the mandate and the San Remo conference, Kaplan was thinking that these events of deliverance would certainly make more uplifting reading than the Book of Esther which they had just finished reciting aboard ship for the Purim holiday. Weizmann also reminisced about Herzl, whom he described as a simple man (*Tam* was the Hebrew word) who did not understand the Russian Jews and perceived them as wild and uncivilized. Weizmann was relaxed with Kaplan and did not play the role of the diplomat or the leader. Kaplan greatly admired Weizmann and eagerly showed him the outline of his speech.

In London, Kaplan visited his old friend Joseph Hertz, the first Seminary graduate. Hertz, though cordial, felt he must play the role of chief rabbi when greeting Kaplan, and dressed in the special square hat of his office to receive him. They spoke about the Hebrew University and some of the conflicts between Magnes and his various committees. Magnes wanted to hire some "experts" who lacked the usual academic credentials. One name that arose in this connection was that of the historian Joseph Klausner. Hertz also bragged that Lord Balfour had once heard him preach and compared him to the archbishop of Canterbury.

The small group of Zionists continued on their odyssey to the Holy Land and to the celebration of the first Jewish university. When their ship arrived at Naples, they were greeted by a group of young Italian Jews who came on board to express to Weizmann their happiness with the founding of the university. They spoke Italian, and Weizmann answered them in French. Kaplan was very moved by the whole scene and couldn't keep the tears back. But, of course, he was an emotional man, and there would be many times on this trip when he cried. When they all sang *Hatikvah* in a very soft voice, he was profoundly affected. In writing to his wife, Lena, about such ineffable experiences, Kaplan reminded her that when he felt something very strongly he always became mute.

As they sailed away from Naples, Weizmann looked out over the Mediterranean and said to Kaplan, "in less than 100 years this will be a Jewish lake" (just as the Romans had called it *Mare Nostrum*). Kaplan was startled and disturbed by such imperialistic Zionism. He was ever the idealogue, and ethical nationhood was at the core of his belief system regarding Jewish civilization.

After docking at Naples, the ship also stopped briefly in Egypt. Kaplan rushed to visit the pyramids and the Sphinx. When they arrived in the Holy Land, he was completely overwhelmed. On the train to Jerusalem, there were many stops where groups of young people greeted Weizmann, and again Kaplan was moved to tears.

A week or so elapsed before the opening ceremonies, with Kaplan using the time to tour the sights. Magnes greeted him warmly and took him on a tour of the Old City. Many sites were closed, however, because of the Arab strike protesting Balfour's visit. Kaplan explored Jerusalem and the outlying areas, visiting Jericho, Bethlehem, Hevron, and the Cave of Machpelah (traditionally identified as the tomb of the patriarchs). He also enjoyed the Hebrew ambience, trying to speak Hebrew whenever he could. "I am so steeped in the Hebrew," he wrote home to Lena, "that I find it almost painful to think in English." A young Seminary rabbinical student named Simon Greenberg helped him to make touring arrangements and then accompanied him to the Wailing Wall. It was Greenberg's impression that Kaplan was uncomfortable at the Wall: "Kaplan could get no inspiration there. He was too far removed from the religion of the pious . . . with their kissing of the stones. He was very obviously disappointed and left after a short stay." In order to say the evening prayers, they went to a nearby synagogue named for Rabbi Judah the Hasid.[26] Kaplan enjoyed the traditional synagogues he visited, especially one established outside the Old City by an American who had been associated with the Young Israel movement. He noticed that the men seemed to concentrate on their prayers and talked little. They all sang together, and Kaplan happily recorded that they did not spit on the floor as he had seen elsewhere. He looked for signs of religious renewal and concluded that the regeneration he hoped for would not take place in Jerusalem but rather in the new collective settlements. He was reminded of the lack of religious commitment back home when he met a man from the Jewish Center who had spent ten days in Paris and only a few days in Palestine. "Such are our Jews," thought Kaplan, "who pray three times a day that the *Shekhinah* [presence of God] should return to Zion."[27]

The official opening of the Hebrew University was a turning point in the transformation of the Jewish people. Chaim Nahman Bialik, the poet laureate of the Jewish people, perhaps most eloquently captured the spirit of the occasion when he said: "today Israel has lit on Mount Scopus the first candle of the renewal of its spiritual light; today a foundation has been laid for Jerusalem the Sublime. For thousands of years we Jews were enslaved, suppressed and persecuted, but here in the Kingdom of the Spirit, Jewry has always been a free and strong citizenry." As the day of the ceremony approached, the city filled up with Jewish leaders from all over Europe. Even more color was added to the occasion by the rumor that Lord Balfour was going to convert to Judaism. Balfour had received a tumultuous welcome as he rode from Jaffa to Jerusalem on the railroad. The crowds were especially large at Rishon Le-zion, where masses of people gathered to greet him. "Jerusalem is full these days with high and mighty ones from the world over," Simon Greenberg noted in his diary. "You can't turn without rubbing shoulders with some 'professor or Herr Doctor.'" The young rabbinical student was sure that many would not find a place for themselves and would return "disgruntled, disappointed and angry."

The amphitheater on Mount Scopus could accommodate two thousand, but four times that number appeared. As one journalist observed, it was as if all of Israel was gathered to Jerusalem for the opening of the university. God seemed to smile on the gathering as a strong morning wind subsided by the time the ceremonies began at three P.M. Rabbi Kook was the first to speak. Kook had been roundly criticized by his traditional rabbinical colleagues for accepting the invitation to offer the opening prayer at the ceremonies. When the moment finally came, he grew so passionate that he spoke for much longer than anyone expected, and, of course, no one could tell the chief rabbi to sit down.[28] His remarks reflected his messianic consciousness in that he viewed this occasion, with Jews from all over the world united on Mount Scopus, as the beginning of the in-gathering of the exiles.

The day was clear and brilliant as the choir sang from the Psalms in Hebrew, "The Heavens Declare the Glory of God." When Balfour, the handsome elder statesman, rose to speak, dressed in his academic robes, the whole mass of people rose with him and their cheering could not be silenced. Kaplan recorded that Balfour spoke for forty minutes without notes and without hesitation. In his address, Balfour pointed out that from the "very spot where they stood on Mount Scopus they could see where the Children of Israel entered the Promised Land." He reported that he had mentioned this fact to a friend, who said, "it was from this hill that the Roman destroyer of Jerusalem conducted the siege which brought to an end that great chapter of the Jewish people." On a more contemporary note, he spoke of the significance of a Jewish university for world culture. He singled out Einstein, Henri Bergson, and Sigmund Freud for having made particularly significant contributions to mankind.[29]

Kaplan spoke a number of times during that week. When he greeted his fellow Jews as a representative of American Zionists, he pointed to the crisis of American Jewry in the wake of the change in the immigration laws in 1924. These new laws severed the Jews in America from the main body of Jewry in Europe. "The immigration helped to keep alive whatever of Judaism the early settlers brought to America and now that our spiritual source is shut off, Zionism becomes the greatest hope for the spiritual renewal of the Jewish people."[30]

At one event later in the week, Kaplan was introduced by Judah Magnes, the head of the new institution and his old colleague. Simon Greenberg recalled the introduction many years later. Said Magnes: "I am a person who believes that a Jew can live a full life anywhere in the world and I live in Jerusalem. Here is a person who believes that a Jew can live a full life only in the Land of Israel and he lives in New York." Magnes was well acquainted with Kaplan and his writings and certainly sensed the ambivalence of his Zionist agenda.[31]

There was perforce much hyperbole during the next few days, despite Bialik's injunction that "the sacredness and the solemnity of this moment forbid us to desecrate it or abuse it by exaggeration." Everyone who spoke perceived the events from a cosmic point of view — including Kaplan. In one speech, Kaplan compared the Hebrew University to the academy at Yavneh after the destruction of Jerusalem. Just as the Yavnean academy came to symbolize the transformation of the Jewish people and was a key element in its rebirth, so the university would help to create the new Jewish civilization of the twentieth century. It would be a primary factor in solving the problem of Israel's adjustment to the modern world. That adjustment centered on "assimilating the method of science and the spirit of democracy without surrendering Israel's unique character." The creative process of forging a new Jewish civilization would be anchored at and symbolized by the Hebrew University. The opening of the university had thus a religious as well as a spiritual character. The university would be the prime mover in creating a Judaism synonymous with humanism: "Not only a new Judaism but a new Jew whose mental and moral integrity will serve as a standard to Diaspora Jewry." The university would thus play an integral part in Jewish rebirth which was by its nature a spiritual event: "The reawakening of the Jewish people is Israel's *Shekinah* demanding to be given a place in human life. In establishing the University, the Jews are yielding once more to the spiritual urge expressed in the divine command, 'Let them make me a sanctuary that I may dwell among them.'" The historic character of the Jewish people was to use their "unity for the purpose of making evident the reality of the spiritual," which it was doing again, according to Kaplan, through the establishment of the university.

Kaplan's remarks further attest to his religious and spiritual sensibilities. The university was the truest expression of Judaism as a civilization. Given Kaplan's preference for study over prayer in the synagogue, it is not surprising that he would regard a Jewish academic institution as the heart of Jewish civilization in the modern period. A university of Judaism would be the logical modern successor to the academy and the yeshiva. Because the Hebrew University would house both scientists and humanists, most of whom would also be Jewish, it was inevitable that the basic elements of Jewish civilization would be an ongoing and central concern. The Hebrew University would become the hub, the *axis mundi*, of the Jewish universe. The university thus is lifted to a new level and becomes numinous and spiritual.

The trip to Palestine in 1925 was Kaplan's first visit to the land of Israel, and so he spent about a month traveling and touring the Holy Land, visiting many of the new settlements in a "hay wagon without hay." He was very impressed with the "pioneer courage and determination of the settlers which was all the more amazing considering the life of the Jewish people over the centuries." Sometimes he was accompanied by the Gamorans, a couple who were heavily involved in American Jewish education and who were interviewing as many of the old settlers as they could in order to record their stories about the early days of settlement in the 1880s. He also arranged to be in Safed for the special celebrations of L'ag B'omer.[32] In Haifa, he visited a well-known artist and wanted to buy some paintings but would not talk price because it was the Sabbath.

In the course of his stay, Kaplan was approached by the Zionist executive committee and asked whether he would be willing to take charge of the educational system in Palestine. He wrote to Lena about it, saying that the offer was "tempting," but apparently turned it down without further consideration. As a reason for declining, he mentioned the new buildings of the SAJ which would "broaden" the appeal of the society. He seemed to forget how upset he had been with the prospect of the SAJ getting its own building ("since that would tie up their energies in an unproductive way"). His refusal even to consider the offer is significant. It was perhaps unreasonable to expect Kaplan, a man in his mid-forties with four young children, to pick himself up and emigrate to Palestine. Yet, considering the opportunities he had, one cannot help but notice the inconsistencies between his words and his actions. He seemed to be genuinely unhappy at the SAJ, so much so that he might have at least fantasized about the possibility of living in Palestine, just as he had contemplated leaving the Seminary and joining Wise at the Jewish Institute of Religion. Kaplan exhibited his inertia once again and this time did not even seem to feel the struggle. Having mentioned the job offer to Lena, he wrote that he was "counting the Omer with genuine impatience," for in seventeen days he would start on his return trip.[33]

Kaplan returned from Palestine all fired up about the importance of the *Yishuv* (the Jewish community in Palestine) and the necessity of supporting it. He saw the *Yishuv* as a center for pilgrimage and revitalization. "Every Jew should go to Palestine," he said (apparently meaning a visit, not to settle), and "every institution of learning should consider a trip to Palestine as its most important course."[34] Kaplan's commitment, though limited, was very real.

Given his consistent support of Zionism, it is not surprising that Zionist leaders continued to seek Kaplan's involvement in the movement's leadership. They did succeed in pressuring him to become active, but his interest lasted only a short time. His activity turned out to be productive for the organization and showed at least that his distaste for politics in the institutions in which he lived was not due to lack of ability.

◆

The Zionist Organization of America was considerably weakened in the late 1920s. After Weizmann's triumph at Cleveland in 1921 and

Kaplan on a donkey near Rishon Le-Zion during his visit to Palestine for the opening of the Hebrew University, 1925. (Courtesy Hadassah K. Musher.)

the exodus of Brandeis and his chief supporters, the organization was left in the care of Louis Lipsky, a dedicated Zionist and journalist. American Jews of the second generation were preoccupied at this time with moving out of the immigrant neighborhoods, climbing the socio-economic ladder, and building large synagogues as a symbol of their new prosperity and status. The Zionist organization concentrated almost exclusively on fund-raising, with the result that businessmen replaced the intellectuals. Zionism, formerly a hotly debated issue in Jewish circles, was rendered almost innocuous when it was presented as philanthropy. Lipsky was unable to prevent the erosion of Zionist

Kaplan at Kfar Nahum during his visit in 1925.
(Courtesy Judith K. Eisenstein.)

enthusiasm. By 1930, the membership in the Zionist Organization of America had slipped to about thirteen thousand. The only bright light in the Zionist firmament was the Hadassah, which in 1930 could boast about forty-four thousand members. Hadassah was formally affiliated with the ZOA but retained control of its own funds. In addition to the membership problem, Lipsky was apparently unskilled in the use of the organization's funds.

In desperation, Lipsky sought an infusion of fresh blood. There were individuals who were clearly identified with the "cause" yet remained always on the sidelines. Kaplan was such a person, and in 1927 Lipsky attempted to lure him as a member of the Administrative Committee of the ZOA. Kaplan did not usually attend the ZOA conventions, and so he was elected in absentia. In a crisis situation, it is always easier to shift the responsibility to someone who is not there. Shemarya Levin optimistically cabled the following to Weizmann from the meeting in Atlantic City: "attack various directions failed . . . Lipsky policies overwhelmingly endorsed . . . executive machinery approved new administration includes Henrietta Szold, [Judge] Rosalsky,

Mordecai Kaplan." But when Kaplan received the formal invitation from Lipsky, he turned it down. Quite politely but not very honestly, he said that he had always cherished the hope of working inside the Zionist organization instead of outside it but that he could not afford the time in light of his many commitments. Kaplan recorded his real feelings a few months latter when Lipsky came to see him about finding someone to replace him on the Administrative Committee. "There are enough necessary evils I have to do with," he thought, "without being dragged into the necessary evil of Zionist politics." He was relieved that he had not been tempted to succumb to the pressures exerted upon him.[35]

Apparently the pressure to get involved continued, for in spring of 1928, Kaplan helped to organized a "peace group," the goal being to bring some order into the ZOA by reconciling the contending factions. The peace group included Emanuel Neumann, Julius Wechsler, and Rabbi David de Sola Pool, among others. With the Lipsky administration slipping, it was inevitable that Mack and Brandeis would resume the Zionist leadership. By June, everyone was preparing for the next Zionist convention. Kaplan and his friends attempted to put together a compromise whereby Mack could reenter the ZOA administration without thereby displacing the Lipsky faction. All parties agreed that Lipsky would not be elected president, that Mack would serve on the Administrative Committee but would also decline to serve as president, and that the central organs of the ZOA would contain people from both factions.

In the midst of these very sensitive negotiations, in which Kaplan played a central role, he received a frantic telegram from Weizmann. The telegram voiced Weizmann's fear of a Zionist administration in America that would be "hostile to World Zionist policies" and would actually "wish overthrow of the whole Zionist structure." Weizmann emphasized his confidence in Kaplan, stressing that the responsibility and interests of the Zionist organization rested with him. Kaplan cabled him back reassuringly that Lipsky would have to go but that Kaplan and the peace committee were firmly committed to "uphold World Zionist policies and agency."[36]

At the convention in early July, Kaplan was in the center of a feverish round of activity. Working out a solution was one thing, but having it voted in was another. He was constantly running from one caucus to another, the maneuvering and the arguments becoming ever more complex and heated. At one point, he actually changed his hotel room because he was afraid of personal attack from some diehard Lipsky supporters who were very unhappy with the peace plan. Nevertheless, he seemed to enjoy it all. When he addressed the convention, he realized that he would have to be somewhat vague on the details in order not to alienate those who might oppose him. As a result of the convention, Lipsky remained nominal head of the Executive Board but was not elected head of the smaller but more powerful Administrative Committee. The convention had neglected, however, to elect a chairman for the Administrative Committee. They probably knew by this time that Kaplan would not be interested, but in September Lipsky came to see him about the matter. Kaplan realized that the time was crucial for the Zionists because of the negotiations to enlarge the Jewish Agency to include non-Zionists. Louis Marshall, a key figure in these negotiations, would have found it more congenial to work with Kaplan than with others. He considered accepting Lipsky's proposal because he was disgusted with his congregants at the SAJ. The high holidays had occurred early that year, and many of the SAJ members remained at their summer vacation homes. He thought perhaps that the members at the ZOA were at least more committed than these apathetic congregants. Kaplan was nonetheless unsure about what to do. He was torn between his desire to write and his sense that perhaps he could be of genuine service at an important moment in Zionist history. For once, he decided to accept the challenge and moved from the world of words to the world of action.[37]

Kaplan set right to work on the United Palestine Appeal drive that was then being organized. At the same time he restated his conviction in the news release announcing his election to the committee, that the ZOA was not just a money-raising organization but worked also on "higher levels." Kaplan was more political and less honest here than he usually was. When he addressed the Executive Committee of the ZOA in October, he attempted to raise the Zionist enterprise to a more elevated status and to relate it to the spiritual concerns of American Jews: "The permanent function of the Zionist movement should be to act as Palestine's spiritual agent in the Diaspora. The logic of Palestine applied to our life is that Judaism must be lived as a civilization, and that the Jew must learn to express himself creatively in all the forms of life of a civilization." Kaplan had placed himself very much in the Schechter tradition in which Zionism was considered as a way of strengthening the Jewish community in the Diaspora and as a way of getting Jews involved so they would not assimilate. To this idea, Kaplan added his own formulation that Judaism as a civilization would be an ongoing and vital entity both in the United States and in Palestine. The national character of the Jewish homeland would be extended to Judaism in the Diaspora. The goal of Zionism was "the transformation of Jewish life by means of a rebuilt Palestine," but the meaning of this for Americans had a special character: "The logic of Palestine applied to our life is that Judaism must be lived as a Civilization."[38]

Kaplan realized that his service as head of the Administrative Committee would have a significant symbolic value. Because of his work on the peace committee, he would be perceived as an agent of reconciliation, and indeed he tried to work toward this end. With respect to Hadassah, for example, he wanted to involve it in a more intimate relationship with the Zionist Organization and hoped it would become less independent. Kaplan believed that a separate organizational structure, even if devoted to a particular area, was a duplication of effort. "I must get those women into line," he wrote in his journal soon after he assumed his new position on the committee. In both speeches and publications, Kaplan tried to articulate a deeper understanding of the role of the ZOA. In a speech in Cleveland, for example, he attempted to explain the meaning of an enlarged Jewish Agency. He saw the expansion of the Jewish Agency as essential to the Zionist cause and the third and last stage in the evolution of Zionism. The first stage was self-emancipation (Pinsker), the second stage was political recognition (Herzl), and the third stage was the gathering of resources to accomplish self-emancipation (Weizmann). There was a large crowd of two hundred to four hundred people in Cleveland, and in Pittsburgh the week before there had been seven hundred present. Some of his strong supporters, such as Alex Dushkin, Solomon Goldman, and Barnett Brickner, had come to Cleveland along with the poet Tchernichowski.[39]

Kaplan was comfortable when giving prepared speeches, but sometimes he got himself into awkward situations. In November, for example, there was a large Zionist dinner for Weizmann at the Waldorf Astoria. Kaplan came late, hoping he would not be called upon, but was asked to speak soon after he entered the room. He disliked talking without a text, and even though his remarks were brief, he felt he was less gracious than the speakers who followed. He also felt awkward about socializing and forgot the names of a number of people he knew well. He didn't sleep well that night and only felt better after he read his remarks in the morning Yiddish paper, where they sounded "passable."[40]

In terms of political strategies, Kaplan attempted to use some of the ploys that had become habitual with him at the SAJ. At one meeting of the Administrative Committee, he was upset with a particular vote and walked out of the room. When he returned a few minutes later, there was a revote in progress which turned out to be much more to his liking. Kaplan walked out of innumerable meetings at the SAJ and was always threatening to resign. In considering this particular situation, he thought, "I should have used other tactics. A show of temper should be resorted to only as a very last measure."

On a rather cold day in February 1929, Kaplan and Benderly were walking down Broadway after a conference with the head of Teachers College at Columbia. They were talking about Kaplan's position with the Zionist organization. Benderly, a strong supporter of Kaplan, said he thought Kaplan had a tremendous opportunity. Under his leadership, the Zionist Organization could be turned from being exclusively a fund-raising organization to being an "instrument of developing Jewish life and culture in the Diaspora." Kaplan was flattered by the idea but was in conflict about retaining his position of leadership. His desire to write was always pulling at him, and he regretted that he had not yet produced any major work. His distaste for the public political arena got the best of him, and in the late spring he decided to resign. He did not stay long enough to make a lasting impact on the organization.[41] It was a road not taken, for there existed the possibility that Kaplan's particular brand of spiritual Zionism would have become the focus of the Zionist Organization of America and that the ZOA would have become the vehicle to unify American Jews (replacing the Reconstructionist movement in terms of Kaplan's efforts) and encourage their creation of a Jewish civilization both in the United States and in Palestine.[42]

Abba Hillel Silver once referred to Kaplan as a timid liberal. We do not know the exact context of these remarks or the particular matter the well-known rabbi was referring to. Nonetheless, Kaplan took it as an apt description. Convictions were never a problem with Kaplan; courage sometimes was. He was never lacking for ideas, and in the spring of 1929, he came up with a proposal for the reorganization of the ZOA. Such a reorganization, however, would have demanded much effort on his part and more political activity than he was used to. This one instance in which he finally did assume a political presence in the ZOA lasted only for a short time. In June 1929, he submitted his resignation to the Zionist executive, citing the need to work on his writing. The creative work was important, of course, but there were other issues as well. It also may be that Kaplan wanted to stay firmly esconced in the synagogue and the study where the realities of the world did not impinge. As in other instances, he himself gives us the clues to a deeper understanding of his actions. In talking with a friend about his plans for the reorganization, Kaplan said, "I am a man who deliberately draws a circle within which he decides to operate with his affirmative values and categories of thought, and beyond which he refuses to budge because it is a territory not meant for the habitation of the human mind."[43]

He did not attend the ZOA convention in July 1929 and felt guilty about it. He had sent in his speech containing his proposals for reorganization, fully aware, of course, that any hope of implementation depended on his being there in person and actively lobbying the delegates. He nevertheless followed the Jewish press, eagerly looking for some signs that the speech read to the delegates would make an impact. The speech went unnoticed. His reaction revealed his ambivalence. On the one hand, he felt that had he devoted himself to the project he could really turn the Zionist Organization around and could rescue it from the "deep rut" it was in. On the other hand, he felt that the writing he was doing was much more important than political activity. He realized, however, that he had always expended a good deal of effort "keeping away from public activity" and thought he would get much more done if he could easily devote himself to his book on Judaism as a civilization. Ultimately, of course, the man of words won out over the man of action. Working on the book, however, did not eliminate the conflict. There were other voices inside his head telling him that it would be much easier to get involved in the political activity than in the "lonely" work of writing chapter after chapter of the book.[44]

13

THE CLIMAX:

Judaism as a Civilization and After

For Kaplan, the publication of *Judaism as a Civilization* was the crowning achievement of his career. Little did he know that he would live yet another half-century and produce a series of works spelling out the details of his ideology. The last attempt at some kind of theological synthesis by an American Jew had been Kaufman Kohler's *Jewish Theology*, published in 1918. Kaplan's opus was on a much grander scale, providing an analysis of the ways Judaism had been affected by modernism and how it might be reconstructed. Although he was a prolific writer, Kaplan almost seemed to have exhausted his creativity in articles for the *SAJ Review* and was depressed that he had not produced one notable work.

The writing and publication of his magnum opus was motivated by his need to create some summary expression of his thought, the precipitating event being a contest sponsored by Julius Rosenwald, the president of Sears Roebuck and Company. In the late 1920s, Elisha Friedman, a Wall Street investment banker and an acquaintance of Kaplan, wrote an article suggesting that laymen donate money to a contest for scholars who would write about the place of Judaism in modern society. Rosenwald wrote Friedman that he was ready to offer ten thousand dollars for the prize in such a contest. In April 1929, a meeting was held at the City Club in New York to formulate the rules for the contest. The assemblage was an august "ecumenical" gathering including Leo Jung, the Orthodox rabbi at the Jewish Center, Rabbi

David de Sola Pool of the Spanish and Portugese Synagogue, Samson Benderly, Alexander Dushkin, Morris Waldman, Executive Secretary of the American Jewish Committee, and Dr. Julian Morgenstern, President of Hebrew Union College, among others. The general statement of purpose for the contest essays was issued a few months later: "For the fullest spiritual development of the individual Jew and the most effective functioning of the Jewish community in America, how can Judaism best adjust itself to and influence modern life with respect to (a) beliefs and theories; (b) institutions: the home, the synagogue, the school and other communal agencies; and (c) Jewish education; for the child, the youth and the adult?"[1]

The contest closed on April 15, 1931, with sixty-two submissions, half of them one hundred pages or more in length. Samson Benderly was appointed executive secretary of the contest, and seven judges were assembled. They included two Orthodox, three Reform, and two Zionists, all leaders in the Jewish community.[2] Kaplan submitted *Judaism as a Civilization* to the contest. His competitors (he did not know who they were) included his erstwhile colleague and supporter Rabbi Eugene Kohn; the writer and editor of the *Morgen Journal*, Peter Wiernik; his brother-in-law Rabbi Phineas Israeli; and noted rabbi and author Louis Newman. To ensure impartial judgments, the contestants assumed pseudonyms: Kaplan was "Ben Israel," Wiernik was "Stevedore," and Mary Blum from Chicago called herself "Dreamer of the Ghetto." Although many came from the large urban centers, others were obscure and lived in little-known but colorful places (Belflower, California; Corsicana, Texas; and one entry who listed his address as YMCA, Alton, Illinois).

It was expected that the decision would be rendered a few months after the contest closed and the contest results published before the end of 1931. As it happened, the decision was arrived at more than two years after the essays were submitted. Kaplan took the contest seriously, considering it an indication of how his ideas were being accepted. "It won't be long and I shall know whether my conception of Judaism has a fighting chance or not," he thought in February 1933. The contest was so much on his mind that it prevented him from concentrating on his work.[3]

Despite the fact that Benderly, Kaplan's devoted friend, supervised the contest, Kaplan was ignorant about the facts concerning other submissions until the very end. Kaplan contacted him frequently in the spring of 1933, but Benderly, a man of principle, informed his friend of the contest progress only in general terms. Yet Kaplan felt supported by Benderly and realized his friend was in a delicate position.

There were few people Kaplan felt really close to; his sense of isolation remained always on the periphery of his consciousness. He thought of himself as "lonely, repressed and uneasy," and at such moments his thoughts inevitably turned to his friend — "Thank God I have Benderly," he wrote in his journal. "In spite of all that I may have said in the pages of this journal in disparagement of him I still love and admire him."[4]

The delay in the decision stemmed from the strong disagreement about Kaplan's essay, though, of course, it is not certain that the judges knew it was written by Kaplan. He was among the finalists from the beginning. Dr. Harry Friedenwald, a judge and a well-known Zionist figure, appreciated Kaplan's work the most. He had read Kaplan's first essays in the *Menorah Journal* and was excited about the submission. "I regard it as one of the ablest and most profound studies that I have read in many years," he wrote to Benderly. Holding an opposing view was the lawyer Leo Huhner, a traditional Conservative Jew. Believing none of the essays worthy of the prize, he also opposed the money being divided among the top submissions. He was afraid that the ideas of the recipient of the prize would become the "standard held out by the American Jew to the gentile world." For him, "the essay by 'Ben Israel' [Kaplan's pseudonym] eliminates Judaism as a religion. . . . In discarding revelation, the Torah and its laws and festivals, the writer is certainly not representative of Orthodox or Conservative Judaism." Furthermore, Reform Judaism was presented as a failure, and Huhner believed the essay contained few practical suggestions for implementing the author's ideology. Another judge, Irving Lehman, was more appreciative of Kaplan, believing that the essay was "scholarly, thoughtful and sincere," and yet he, too, deemed it to have serious weaknesses: "The suggestions of a program show such an entire lack of understanding of the attitude of American Jews of all groups, and such disregard of practical considerations as to be almost entirely valueless." Lehman was right in the sense that Kaplan excelled at creating schemes and solutions but his proposals were not always applicable to the world as it really works. Nathan Isaacs, an Orthodox professor at Harvard Law School, agreed with Huhner but thought the prize should be awarded to the essay anyway, with a proviso that winning did not constitute approval by the judges of the sentiments expressed. Because of these disagreements, the judges decided to divide the money among the top three essays, with the largest sum going to Kaplan. They did not publicize the names of the recipients and asked the winners not to mention the contest if they published their works. Kaplan received thirty-five hundred dollars, Rabbi Lee Levinger (an author who directed the Hillel at the University of Ohio) received fifteen hundred dollars, and Rabbi Eugene Kohn received one thousand dollars.[5]

Kaplan immediately gave the money to Macmillan and Company to publish his manuscript. The first edition of *Judaism as a Civilization*, fifteen hundred copies, came out in May 1934; Kaplan received six hundred fifty of them. A second printing in 1935 consisted of one thousand copies; Kaplan bought five hundred. Thus, only a few copies of this classic of American Jewish ideology existed until it was republished in the 1950s. Kaplan would stipulate to a congregation that he was ready to speak without fee if they agreed to buy a certain number of copies of his book, which he would send them.[6]

Kaplan dedicated the book to his father, though he certainly knew that Israel Kaplan would have been distressed with much of its contents. The dedication, written in a florid Hebrew style many years after the elder Kaplan's death, suggests that Kaplan still yearned for his father's approval and confirmation.[7]

Kaplan supporters and critics alike learned a great deal from reading his magnum opus. *Judaism as a Civilization* was a unique creation in the field of Jewish thought. It carefully examined the existing religious movements within American Jewish society and found them wanting. Kaplan developed new ways of thinking about God, Israel, and the Torah that radically departed from traditional opinions and were completely within the context of twentieth-century thought. He created a new paradigm regarding the nature of Judaism for both his supporters and his detractors. To formulate a radical conceptual shift requires enormous imagination and creativity; individuals are bonded to their primary categories of thought and highly resistant to change. After Kaplan there was a new way to think about Judaism and its relationship to the Jewish people. Jewish nationalism had existed before, but no one, including Ahad Ha-Am, had defined Judaism in terms of peoplehood and at the same time concentrated on a reworking of the religious aspects of Jewish civilization in terms of contemporary categories of thought. Dedicated American Jews, struggling to make sense out of their lives in America, welcomed Kaplan's teachings with profound enthusiasm and gratitude.

In a 1935 review, Henry Rosenthal, a rabbi and professor of philosophy and a former Kaplan student, neatly summarized the content of the book. According to Kaplan, the Jewish heritage, including the belief in God, must be reinterpreted so that it will be consistent with the intellectual outlook of the twentieth century. The Torah, which is Jewish civilization in practice, must be given a new functional interpretation. Jewish nationhood, which is the core of Jewish civilization, must be made at least as appealing as any kind of territorial nationalism, and it must show how it serves the international community. Palestine must be established as a cultural center of Jewish nationhood along with life in the Diaspora, which should be organized around communities as the basic unit, not synagogues. Part of the reinterpretation of Judaism is to show the ways in which Jewish rituals are no longer laws but function as folkways that enrich Jewish life. In the ethical sphere, Jewish law must be brought to bear on the achievement of economic justice. Jewish education must serve not only to integrate Jewish life but also to transmit the values of the Jewish people in particular and of democracy in general.[8]

Historians of Jewish thought, in considering Kaplan and the creative theologians who came after him, maintain that there was no theology in America before Abraham Joshua Heschel and Martin Buber in the 1950s, that Americans were pragmatic and uninterested in theological questions. These scholars are correct in characterizing Kaplan's work as not strictly within the philosophical or the theological tradition; some have called it an ideology — a word Kaplan himself used. Scholars ordinarily consider ideologies to be merely programmatic and lacking analysis or depth on theological issues. Such a view fails to appreciate the scope of Kaplan's thought, reducing it to sociological theorizing. In fact the quest for the divine dominated Kaplan's thinking throughout his life, transcending the confines of the pragmatic and the sociological.[9]

Kaplan's ultimate goal was to find a way to reinterpret the belief in God so that the divine could continue to function in modern Jewish life. The process of reinterpretation represented a deep personal need for him; it was not merely an abstract philosophical question. Obsessed by the necessity to make the God idea effective, he emphasized that the process could begin only after the individual shed the theurgic (magical) aspects of traditional belief and disengaged from the "mass of traditional lore."[10] Such a need for reconstruction revealed his own lifelong struggle with the supreme theological questions.

Kaplan's theological formulations were elusive, reflecting the fact that he was more comfortable thinking about how the God idea functioned than about the nature of the deity. He nonetheless offered a direction for belief about the ultimate in characterizing God as the "cosmic life urge" which displayed itself in the human strivings for justice and freedom. Kaplan the immanentist never considered it a reduction of God to see divine qualities manifest in the human struggle for self-enhancement. If the universe has divinity, and it surely does according to Kaplan, then the more exalted self is the universe expressing that divinity. It has taken a billion years for the universe to produce a human being that could say "I" and could think in terms of the transcendent categories of righteousness and redemption. Personality thus becomes an expression of divinity within the universe.[11]

Kaplan's theology was criticized from all sides. Orthodox opposition was vehemently expressed through the monthly *Jewish Forum*, among other places, where a series appears in the fall of 1934. Rabbi Aaron Rosmarin led the assault with an article entitled "Whither the Jewish Theological Seminary." After a judicious sampling of statements from Morais, Schechter, Ginzberg, and Adler, the author concluded not unfairly that the avowed purpose of the Seminary and the United Synagogue was to further traditional Judaism. Rosmarin then dealt with Kaplan and "his student" Louis Finkelstein to show how the Seminary had strayed from the goals of the founding fathers and had rejected Conservative Judaism. He branded Kaplan's recent work as dangerous to the Jewish people and authoritarian in its own right, laying down the new rule that "There is no God and Kaplan is his prophet" (actually a quotation from another review). Most threatening to the writer was Kaplan's denial of the central belief in Jewish chosenness, a dogma Kaplan viewed as extremely harmful.[12] Rosmarin was particularly disturbed by the linkage Kaplan, as a good social scientist, continually tried to establish between primary Israelite beliefs and the pagan environment in which Judaism first appeared. For Kaplan, who rarely committed the genetic fallacy, it was not origin that mattered but function. The author angrily quoted Kaplan's assertion that after the Israelites entered the promised land, they "retained the survivals of animism. They had their sacred trees, sacred waters, sacred stones and mountains." Although the author presented these key ideas accurately, he did not introduce the context or analysis that explained Kaplan's position. There were times, moreover, when he ascribed views to Kaplan that were the exact opposite of what was presented, such as when he asserted that Kaplan advocated intermarriage. This distortion so outraged Rabbi David de Sola Pool that he took the time to answer the charge in the next issue of the journal: "[Kaplan's] provocative book invites dissent at so many points that there is no need to descend to criticisms which seem strangely indistinguishable from a complete perversion of his teachings." Kaplan's critics never knew that in the original manuscript of his work, he had advocated that the Sabbath be switched to Sunday; this most heterodox of recommendations was dropped after Ira Eisenstein and others strongly urged its removal.[13]

From the left, Kaplan was attacked in a more gentle way by no less than Julian Morgenstern, the president of Hebrew Union College.

Though he judged the work as "thoughtful and stimulating" and praised Kaplan as "a man whom I respect greatly for his deep sincerity, his Jewish loyalty and his idealism," Morgenstern made it abundantly clear that he rejected Kaplan's fundamental categories. He would have no part of what he called "racial nationalism," implying that Kaplan advocated a philosophy of "Jewish isolation." He believed that Judaism was a religion and American civilization was the only civilization he lived in. A rather well-known Reform leader, Rabbi Samuel Schulman, addressing the Central Conference of American Rabbis in 1935, added another significant dimension to the Reform critique when he employed the distinction between civilization and culture, a differentiation going back to the European sociological tradition. He claimed that civilization referred to things or externals, and culture to spiritual values. "Civilization has to do with the mastery of the environment. Culture is the expression of the spirit . . . and the inner life." Thus, it is their culture that differentiates one people from another, according to Schulman; the unique contributions of the Jewish people were in the realm of the spirit and not in the externals.

Ultimately, it was to the Seminary community that Kaplan's thought was significant — the most threatening and the most hopeful. His supporters were overjoyed with the publication of his work. Rabbi Henry Rosenthal rather fancifully thought people read Kaplan in order to refute him but went away preaching and practicing more than they cared to admit. Looking for reactions in the journals and newspapers of the time, one finds, however, fewer evaluations than might have been expected. *Judaism as a Civilization* was never reviewed in the *New York Times* or in the *Menorah Journal*. The *American Hebrew* in the 1930s was understandably more concerned with anti-Semitism in Europe, North Africa, and America than with the publication of books. Kaplan's early audience consisted largely of rabbis, educators, and social workers, a group that at this time was not large and the majority of whom had been Kaplan's students.[14]

The most representative Conservative appraisal came from Max Arzt, a rabbi from Scranton, who eventually returned to the seminary to serve for many years in various administrative capacities. Although Arzt considered himself a disciple, he objected, as did critics on the right and the left, to Kaplan's calling Judaism a civilization. It was the Jewish religion that differentiated the Jews from other nations, he said in 1935, and they are thereby a unique group "which defies classification in any existing category." Arzt resented Kaplan's implication that the Jews were not special or "chosen."

Arnold Eisen in his work on the intellectual history of this period has shown that Kaplan dominated the era, forcing Jewish leaders to take their stand either for or against him. Kaplan was enormously useful to all the Jews of the second generation. Many asked themselves, "Why remain Jewish?" Their religious leaders had to offer a compelling answer for those on the road to assimilation. Educated people often found that their beliefs concerning ethics and other ultimate issues were the same as those of others of their class and education. So what was the necessity for different religions? Why not just the dominant religion if there was to be any at all? Kaplan formulated the answer, which Arzt gladly quoted: "If progress means further complexity and differentiation, religion must be many to satisfy man's needs. Religion will be one and universal insofar as it will be identified more and more with the experience of life's momentousness and worthwhileness. It will be many and multiform insofar as different individuals and groups look to different sancta as symbols of life's worthwhileness."[15] To put the matter simply, the search to make life worthwhile is universal, but we differ in the manner in which we conduct that search.

Kaplan believed that the opposition to Judaism as a civilization was due to thinking about it only in terms of externals — quite ironic, considering the criticism he encountered. What they failed to appreciate, Kaplan believed, was that it was civilization that commanded a person's most basic loyalties. Civilization provides the unexamined assumptions about life and its meaning which influence a person's behavior more than abstract, professed belief. How we are raised is more important than what we study at school.

Arzt's objections highlight the weaknesses and problems of the Conservative movement with which Kaplan wrestled. In discussing the *Mitzvot* as customs rather than as laws, Arzt recognized that people are selective and do not observe all the *Mitzvot*. Though some laws will will be disregarded among even the most traditional (e.g., the commandment that each male was to write his own Torah scroll, Arzt pointed out), nonetheless, he maintained there was rarely a good reason for abrogating a specific law. Specific laws may require modification, but the concept of law remains inviolate and continues to be one of the cornerstones of Jewish life. The *Mitzvot* were laws, not custom, Arzt asserted.

Even those among the Seminary faculty who strongly opposed Kaplan read his book thoughtfully. Moses Hyamson (1862–1949), professor of codes at the Seminary and former judge *(dayyan)* of the London rabbinical court *(bet din)*, appreciated Kaplan's talents, but criticized him severely. Hyamson, a dedicated traditional Jew, found no reason to quarrel with Kaplan as a historian of Jewish thought. Kaplan was quite talented in this area, and even his critics appreciated his abilities.[16] Hyamson focused squarely on the key implications of Kaplan's radical antisupernaturalist view. When he saw "God idea," he asked, "and how do you pray to an idea?"[17] Hyamson also wondered about the solitary individual: "What about the person who loves his solitude and wants to live apart, seeking communion with the infinite." In his need to talk about the survival of the community, it is true that Kaplan did not always give such individuals their due. When Kaplan discussed the need for community structure and the deficiencies of the isolated single congregation, Hyamson had nothing but praise.

◆

In the everyday world of the 1930s, Americans including Jews were suffering hardship and deprivation. Depleted personal resources took their toll on Jewish institutions which depended so heavily on voluntary support. Kaplan felt the pinch directly when he had to cut the salaries of his faculty at the Teachers' Institute; the SAJ staff sometimes went for months without being paid. Under such circumstances the Jews were, understandably, strong supporters of Roosevelt and the New Deal. They also looked for other solutions, swelling the membership roles of radical groups — the many socialist sects and the Communist party. Irving Howe, literary critic and eloquent spokesman for the young radicals of that generation, captured the lure of socialist ideology in his autobiography: "Marxism advances a profoundly dramatic view of human experience. Its stress upon inevitable conflicts, apocalyptic climaxes, inevitable doom, and glorious futures gripped our imagination. We were always on the rim of heroism; the mockery we might suffer today would turn to glory tomorrow; our loyalty to principle would be rewarded by the grateful masses."[18] More than anything else, the struggle gave a sense of meaning and purpose.

In the late 1920s, Kaplan himself was drawn into the vortex of the socialist movement. Though its militant stand against religion and its anti-Zionism repelled him, he was, nonetheless, profoundly attracted to communism. He saw in it many parallels to prophetic thinking; both Marx and the Prophets denounced economic exploitation and argued that economic justice must be the primary component of ethical behavior. The prophets, however, did not exclude anyone from helping to usher in the new order; Kaplan believed that the middle class (where most Jews were) was indispensable in bringing about the socialist revo-

lution. "The middle class [i.e., the Jews] must realize their moral degradation and eliminate their exploitative behavior." Here, as in other
areas, he was pulled in two directions — two souls struggled within him:
"I shall call one Mordecai (the old Adam) and the other Menahem (the
regenerate me). Mordecai is a liberal bourgeois, Menahem is an out
and out Communist. Who am *I* in this business?"[19]

In Kaplan's own life, the drama was played out from the pulpit and
in the classroom. It was natural that his students at the Teachers' Institute should be attracted to the various radicalisms of the day. He was
sympathetic to their questioning; many at the Seminary even accused
him of aiding and abetting the students' socialist thinking. Just the opposite was the case. When Cyrus Adler passed a remark to Maurice
Karpf, director of the School of Jewish Social Work, about Kaplan's
being a radical himself, "Karpf informed him that he was mistaken
about me and that, on the contrary, I exerted 'a wholesome influence'
on them. Adler said he was pleased to hear that from him."[20] Adler had
known Kaplan since his student days and yet was always ready to believe the worst about him.

Kaplan's "wholesome influence" was felt not only at the Teachers'
Institute but also at the School for Jewish Social Work. This interesting
experiment was established in the early 1920s as the Training School
for Jewish Social Work and was part of the professionalization of the
field. Students took some of their professional courses at the New York
School of Social Work, with the Jewish courses being given at the Jewish school. Kaplan taught there on a regular basis, giving such courses
as "The Social and Religious Institutions of the Jew" and "Problems of
Adjustment to American Jewish Life." The students were caught up in
the social conflicts of the times and continually confronted him with
their radical ideologies. Through their questioning and through his
own attraction to communism, Kaplan was forced to deal directly with
the issue of how Judaism could help the individual overcome the social
evils of the day. Thus his work at the school was a significant factor in
the development of his philosophy as it appeared in *Judaism as a Civilization*.

The answers he gave the students emphasized the insufficiency of
humanistic values as the sole justification for dealing with social problems. Some kind of context larger than the human matrix was required
to inspire the devotion of the individual to the welfare of others. In a
1930 paper dealing with philanthropy, he suggested: "We cannot possibly remain content with making even human welfare the ultimate reason for giving of ourselves and of our means and energy to those with
whom fate has dealt unkindly. We must feel convinced or accept on

faith that service has its justification in the very nature of reality. Unless the universe be accepted as a meaningful totality in which our actions somehow count, no humanistic scheme of social improvement can ever arouse much enthusiasm or call forth much sacrifice."[21]

◆

Mordecai Kaplan was not only a teacher, a writer, a rabbi, and a teacher of rabbis, but he was also a husband and a father. His love for his wife was never in doubt, but family life was neither the center of his attention nor the focus of his energy. Lena Kaplan managed the house, took care of the finances, and tended to the children, thereby freeing him to devote himself to his many activities. They had financial difficulties because, although Kaplan taught at many institutions, he only took money from the Seminary.

Lena Kaplan was a fiercely caring person, extremely devoted to him, "peeling his grapes," the family reports. When he became interested in sculpting, she bought him clay for his various experiments, one of which turned out to be a rather striking bust of his father. She also frequently typed for him. He treasured her; the place she held in the family is illustrated by the lyrics to a song written on the occasion of Mordecai and Lena's twenty-fifth wedding anniversary by their daughter Judith and others of the Kaplan clan. The whole family gathered at the Kaplan home and sang together:

I Love to Lean on Lena

In time of strife, I need my wife
I always lean on Lena
In time of peace, my needs don't cease
I love to lean on Lena

She'll protect me from an importuning guest
Who is likely to become an awful pest
And when the text is troubling me
She'll bring cherries and hot tea
To restore to me my intellectual zest.

Refrain: In time of strife. . .

She'll lay out my tie and handkerchief and shirt
And she'll look behind my ears for dirt

Kaplan and his mother, late 1930s. (Courtesy RRC.)

And when homeward late I toddle
She'll become my artist's model
And assume a classic attitude and pert.

Refrain: In time of strife. . .

I adore to lean on Lena.

Lena Kaplan, the classic enabler, adored by the whole family, was a competent woman inside and outside the home. When Hadassah began in 1912, one of the first meetings was held in the Kaplan household, and Lena Kaplan served on the board of the organization in its early years. Active at the SAJ, she labored with the various committees and clubs. Kaplan consulted her on major decisions and often deferred to her. On the occasion of his fiftieth birthday, thinking back on his life, he wrote: "Despite my inability to read character, I was fortunate in getting a wife who possesses a character that is most ideally qualified to render our married life absolutely frictionless. I believe I would have

Bust of Israel Kaplan, which Mordecai Kaplan made. (Courtesy Dr. Naomi K. Wenner.)

Kaplan's father, Rabbi Israel Kaplan. (Courtesy Judith K. Eisenstein.)

gone to pieces if she had not afforded me the physical and mental peace that acts like oil on troubled waters. Having led a sheltered existence I have managed to take myself in hand as the years passed and have attained a certain degree of clarity and organization in my thinking."[22] Lena Kaplan, however, never became Kaplan's intellectual companion. In general, he lacked such companionship, which partly explains his sense of isolation, feelings of lonliness, and perhaps even his compulsive diary keeping.

Because Kaplan inaugurated the bat mitzvah and because of his early outspoken criticism of the inequality of women in traditional Judaism, he may be described as the father of the women's liberation movement in the Jewish community. His advocacy of the liberation of women owed much to the place women played in his own life. His mother, the mainstay of his childhood, thought the world of him and expected greatness from her son. His sister Sophie was perhaps his first Hebrew teacher — her knowledge and competence were evident to him throughout his life. Finally, the fact is that Kaplan had four daughters — Judith, Hadassah, Naomi, and Selma.[23]

Kaplan was determined that his daughters be well educated. Naomi and Selma attended the Fieldston School run by the Society for Ethical Culture. Kaplan had no hesitation in sending them to Fieldston, the teaching of Ethical Culture amounting to only one hour a week, hardly a significant part of the program. Despite his ambivalent feelings about Felix Adler, Kaplan, in his hyperbolic manner, described the speech Adler delivered at Selma's graduation as the most important lecture he had ever heard. His daughters naturally attended the Hebrew schools at the Jewish Center and at the SAJ, Judith going on to the Teachers' Institute to become an excellent Hebraist and a well-known expert in Jewish music.[24] Kaplan had mixed feelings about Naomi's attending medical school and becoming a psychiatrist; not inclined to appreciate Freud, Kaplan knew him primarily through his most insubstantial work, *Moses and Monotheism*. Naomi Wenner believes that in the course of time Kaplan became much more attracted to Frankl and the theory of Logotherapy than to Freud.

Warm and concerned but not demonstrative, Kaplan enjoyed the affection he received from his daughters. He kissed them infrequently until, having observed other fathers embrace their children at summer camp, they demanded it. He readily acceded to their demands. Hadassah Musher reports that his perfectionism manifested itself in his anxiety about the way she looked and the way she walked, which she found very oppressive at the time. On the other hand, his granddaughter Ann Eisenstein experienced "being unconditionally accepted — a kind of primitive loyalty and protectiveness toward the family" which certainly came as much from her grandmother as it did from her grandfather. However, grandparents are often more accepting of their grandchildren than their children. His daughters remember his passionate concern more than his unconditional acceptance.

Never a lighthearted person, Kaplan often seemed to bear the world and its problems on his shoulders. Yet he always had a sense of discovery — a new idea, a novel strategy, or an exciting project he would bring to the table. On one occasion he urged them to learn Esperanto. The day began for Kaplan with a cold shower and always included a long brisk walk down Central Park West or around the reservoir. By all family accounts, he was quite rigid in the routines of daily life — naps at certain times, fish before a speech, boiled milk with his postum, and so on. Changing religious ritual may have been easier for the founder of Reconstructionism than altering the habits of daily life. And, of course, there was his work. Kaplan seemed to work all the time. When Naomi Wenner was in medical school, she felt briefly competitive with him, but no matter how late she would stay up, his light was always on when she went to sleep. When Judith and Ira Eisenstein were courting, they would try to come home after Kaplan had retired for the evening — but they rarely succeeded.

The Kaplan daughters were an exuberant bunch. On one Sabbath afternoon at the Jersey shore, Naomi asked, "Can we take the car to the beach?" Kaplan was upset, answering sarcastically, "You can do whatever you want, but it's not my idea of spending a Sabbath afternoon." They all proceeded to barrage him with arguments until he "crumpled up," as he put it; they "demolished my defenses of the customary restrictions on the Sabbath and incidentally those of *kashrut*." His daughters would never have been so successful if Kaplan himself were not ambivalent about the *Halakhah*.[25] A similar incident concerned smoking. Israel Kaplan enjoyed cigars and smoked heavily; his son vowed that he would never take up the habit. Kaplan asked his daughters not to smoke, but he lost that fight — "the four smokestacks," he called them. While on a trip to Palestine in the 1930s, Naomi, twenty-two at the time, observed her father writing on the Sabbath. She very spitefully sat down next to him, lit up a cigarette, and said, "You make your rules, and I'll make mine."

Being the oldest, Judith occupied a privileged if somewhat onerous position.[26] She was a precocious child, reading at age two and a half and learning Hebrew at age four. She had a German nurse and learned to "chatter away" in German at an early age. Intending a more intellectual life for her, Kaplan did not approve of dolls for his eldest daughter. He frequently took her along with him to the library at Forty-second Street — a real treat, since she rode on the double-decker bus and was allowed to stay in the children's reading room. At a later point, he insisted that she summarize whatever she was reading — a demand that spoiled many a good book. She studied Hebrew privately with Max Kadushin because she was too advanced for classes at the Jewish Center and enjoyed writing plays and composing songs in Hebrew. "All this was not enough for my father," she later remarked, and so at age ten, she was started on intense study of *Chumash* and *Rashi*. Kaplan also went through a phase of thinking she should know the prayerbook more thoroughly and asked her to recite it for him daily, omitting the passages he eventually removed from the *Reconstructionist Siddur*. Her adolescent diary indicates that she attended a broad spectrum of plays, concerts, operas, and other cultural events in the city. She read very widely, never finding school a problem. As an exuberant thirteen-year-old, she wrote in her diary: "I find myself gaining courage in Latin, flying high in Math, gliding smoothly in English and hopping along merrily in German."

Nonetheless it was not easy being Mordecai Kaplan's daughter. Judith found her father demanding and became anxious about his approval. She occupied a special place in his mental and spiritual life as well as at the dinner table; he would discuss his ideas with Judith seated at his right hand while at the same time holding the hand of one of his other daughters who sat at his left. According to family legend, only Judith argued philosophical matters with her father. She concluded early in life that she was an atheist but was afraid to tell him. She resolved to give up praying but kept on pronouncing nonsense syllables in her prayers at night so her sister Hadassah would not reveal her secret. She finally summoned the courage, at about age eleven, to confront her father: "I expected a blast of wrath — whether God's or my father's I wasn't quite sure and it may have amounted to the same thing." Kaplan's reaction was philosophical — " What do you mean by God?" he queried. The lion did not roar this time. He went on to explain his belief, focusing on the elimination of supernaturalism and "the vision of a power within us that works toward a better life."

Conflicts between father and daughter were inevitable, but one particular incident betrays the unique relationship he had with Judith. A few months after her bat mitzvah, Kaplan discovered Judith's diary and proceeded to read it. When he came across a passage in which she referred to him as a despot, he was shocked — as if such angry and rebellious thoughts were not perfectly normal for a thirteen-year-old. He was deeply disturbed and recorded his reaction in his own diary, revealing his deep need for his daughter's approval and companionship: "She is only thirteen at present. Yet when upon a single occasion I crossed her will, she became so wrought up that she charged me in her diary with being a despot. There are a number of irrelevant charges she brings against me in what she says there — which fact leads me to believe that I am bound to be disappointed if I look forward to having in her an intellectual companion." A few weeks later, the question of diary keeping came up at dinner, and he asked Judith to bring her diary to the table. At first refusing, she finally brought it with the pages in question torn out. She told him she was ashamed of what she had written — no doubt, she was also angry at her father, having suspected that he read her very private reflections.[27]

For his part, Kaplan enjoyed sharing his thoughts with Judith, and when she was away he missed her companionship. During the summer of 1926, she attended summer camp. Kaplan wrote her about an article he had read in a scientific journal: "p.g. [please God] when you come back I shall read it with you, as I shall read many other books and articles which will do both of us a lot of good . . . [signed] with boundless love Your Pop."[28] She frequently became "involved in her own life," sometimes to the point where she lacked time for her father. After one particular outbreak at the dinner table, Kaplan, feeling injured, sat down and wrote: "I controlled myself and did not utter a single word in reply but I have been in low spirits ever since. The outbreak revealed to me how little Judith and I have in common, a fact which came home to me all the more as I reflected upon the way in which she avoids me almost surely for fear that I might ask her to read with me on any subject whatever. . . . I had hoped that when Judith would be grown up that I would renew my youth through her, that I would have in her a collaborator in my efforts to upbuild Jewish life. The vocation of teaching music places her in an excellent position to cooperate with me. Yet she doesn't show the slightest inclination to read, study or work on any project jointly with me."[29]

Kaplan's relationship with his daughter brings to mind other famous fathers and daughters. Anna Freud, for example, became an extension of her father in many ways. Not only did she enter the field of psychoanalysis but Freud analyzed his daughter, proposing that her recurrent dreams about a person being beaten be interpreted as a veiled wish to have sexual intercourse with him. He shared his research with her; eventually, she delivered some of his papers and represented him at many international congresses. Most importantly, she became his primary caretaker, clearly replacing her mother. Freud was aware of the fact that he clutched her for life support but could not control himself. In the early 1920s, Freud had a series of operations on his jaw which increased his dependence on Anna and cemented their relationship. If she ever had any thoughts of a life without her father, they were now given up. "You are right," Anna Freud wrote to Lou Andreas-Salome. "I would not leave him now under any circumstances."[30]

A strong parallel case could be made for Henrietta Szold, the founder of Hadassah, and her relationship with her father, Rabbi Benjamin Szold. She was his secretary-translator (Anna Freud had refused to be her father's secretary), his researcher, and his partner. When Szold first became editor of the Jewish Publication Society in her early thirties, she lived away from home for a few years. She never put down roots in Philadelphia, the home of the society: "It somehow or other seemed harder for me to go away today [from Baltimore] than ever before," she once wrote after visiting her parents. "I am afraid of myself. I do not think I have the courage to undertake this for another year. . . . I wanted to say once more before I go to bed tonight, that I have the best mother and father that ever God gave to anybody, and that I love them more than I can tell." She was in her early thirties when she wrote this.[31]

Judith Kaplan Eisenstein was luckier than Anna Freud and less dependent than Henrietta Szold. Being Kaplan's eldest, she certainly felt the weight of his expectation. She was brought up as a son, not prepared for the conventional female roles. Remaining close to Kaplan, she nonetheless pursued her own independent goals. Despite his expectations, there was no question but that she was going to go her own way. Even so, he derived much pleasure from her obvious competence and talent. In the course of time, she published important works in her own field, received her Ph.D., and became a well-known expert in Jewish music. She taught for many years at the Teachers' Institute, even though in financially difficult times she did not always receive a salary.

In the early 1930s Mordecai Kaplan's life changed significantly. Ira Eisenstein became his assistant, his son-in-law, and eventually his most loyal disciple. As Kaplan became increasingly involved in his writing, he sought to bring an assistant into the congregation. Eisenstein graduated from the Seminary in 1931 and became Kaplan's assistant at that time. He had been engrossed in working with Kaplan and the congregation during his years at the Seminary and was an increasingly frequent visitor at the Kaplan household. Ira adored Judith Kaplan from the very beginning. She, however, was involved in another relationship that culminated in a brief and unhappy marriage.[32] Ira was profoundly unhappy at the prospect of losing Judith, not knowing that within a short time he would have the opportunity himself of proposing marriage to her.

The marriage of Judith Kaplan and Ira Eisenstein a month after the publication of Kaplan's book was certainly a match "made in heaven." They shared much in common, including their love for music, resulting later in a host of collaborations.[33] During the courtship, father, daughter, and fiancé often would have discussions late into the night: "While these hours spent around his desk were among the most frustrating imaginable, they were also some of the most precious," Eisenstein later wrote. The triad was unique. Judith possessed a singular place in her father's life, and marrying Ira granted Kaplan more than he could have hoped for — she provided him with a son to carry on the family business in that age before women rabbis. Moreover, Ira became the intellectual companion Kaplan had always sought and a talented collaborator in reconstructing Jewish life. He would be a disciple, a son, and a friend all at once. Although it was never easy in the shadow of the great man, life with Kaplan was uniquely rewarding for Eisenstein. The excitement of being part of a grand project was everpresent. For Kaplan the marriage was an unmitigated blessing. Surprisingly, Kaplan never or rarely came between them. There was a bonding of each to each as well as all three together — the alliance was profound, permanent, and impenetrable.

◆

Eisenstein's coming to the SAJ reveals much about Kaplan and about the institution. In 1930, his executive director decided to become a rabbi and entered the Jewish Institute of Religion, thus forcing Kaplan to hire someone at once. Although he had considered others, Kaplan was happy to offer the position to Eisenstein. "It appears that he will accept the offer," Kaplan wrote in his journal. "This makes me extremely happy because I have the feeling that he will help me to enlarge the SAJ and in time take it over entirely and have it function in the spirit of Judaism as a modern spiritual civilization."[34]

Kaplan genuinely believed in the democratic process and advocated it for the synagogue, but his hiring of Eisenstein exposed his difficulty with acting on this principle. According to Eisenstein's account, Kaplan did not consult the board of the SAJ before he asked him to become the executive director. The members of the board knew Eisenstein, and the process of considering him would have been an easy one. As it turned out, Kaplan only asked the board to ratify his action, which

Members of the Kaplan family, 1950. From left:
Ira Eisenstein, Judith K. Eisenstein, Miriam Eisen-
stein, Lena R. Kaplan, and Mordecai Kaplan.
(Courtesy SAJ.)

embarrassed Eisenstein and angered the board. Eisenstein was outside
the room when they argued about the hiring. "Physically I was out of
the Library; actually I could hear almost every word that was spoken,
especially since the voices grew louder as the debate grew hotter. I
looked for some other place to wait, but the only choice was the stairs
leading to the lower floor. I felt that decency demanded I keep out of
earshot, but even on the stairs I could hear several members of the
Board angrily challenge Rabbi Kaplan's arbitrary and unilateral decision." The SAJ was having serious financial trouble, and the board
questioned the wisdom of taking on a new person at a considerable cost
(twenty-five hundred dollars). Kaplan, feeling himself backed against
the wall, threatened to resign; though more petulant than professional,
this ploy usually got him his way.

Kaplan also employed the same tactic with Eisenstein himself. A
short time after he accepted the SAJ position, Eisenstein was offered a
full rabbinical post at the much larger congregation of Mishkan Tefila
in Boston at six thousand dollars a year. He had already served there as
rabbi for the high holidays and enjoyed the power and authority of the
appointment. As he put it many years later: "At the SAJ they thought of
me as a kid. At Mishkan Tefila I was already honored as a rabbi." Eisenstein felt he had to present Kaplan with his dilemma. Riding on the
New York subway, they discussed the matter. Kaplan again employed
the strategy of threatening resignation, and again it worked. Eisenstein
was taken by surprise: "of course it was entirely up to me but, if I

decided to accept [Mishkan Tefila] he would immediately resign from the SAJ and propose that it be liquidated."

A year after Eisenstein had accepted the position of executive director he was appointed assistant rabbi (or assistant leader, as he was called). There was again opposition from the board, primarily economic in nature, but Kaplan carried the day and was delighted: "They sent committees to confer with me and to urge me to try to get along without him, but I would not think of giving in to them, because I realize fully his [Eisenstein's] worth to the SAJ. . . . Fortunately I permitted nothing to swerve me from my purpose to have him associated with me in guiding the destinies of the SAJ." [35]

The style of the SAJ changed little over the years and might be better understood through a comparison with the *Havurot* of today. *Havurot*, small fellowship groups, conduct religious life in a manner that has recently become emblematic of many Reconstructionist synagogues. The *Havurah*, or fellowship, movement grew out of the counterculture of the 1960s and 1970s. Members meet for prayer in small, face-to-face egalitarian clusters. Many are leaderless. In others, the leader (rabbi) self-consciously attempts to relate to the group in a nonauthoritarian manner. The *Havurot* often maintain their ties to the past by using traditional texts in their prayers but then reinterpreting them in forums that almost invariably accompanied the service. As Riv-Ellen Prell remarked in a recent, insightful, study, they have altered the aesthetics (the form) of their prayers in order to express their individuality but have retained the established content. Invariably informal, there is "an increased sense of self" that emerges from the continual soul stretching and "God wrestling" that goes on at prayer times. [36]

The SAJ expressed the dissenting ideology of an earlier era. The content of the prayers was changed quite drastically, but the "aesthetics," to use Prell's concept, remained completely traditional. Indeed, other than the change in the language of the liturgy, the SAJ was almost indistinguishable from other synagogues within the Conservative movement. Kaplan and Eisenstein were the sources of authority who stood in front of the congregation on a *bimah* (stage) led the service and preached the sermons. For Kaplan, the modern temper and contemporary consciousness were expressed by the changes in the language of the prayers. Forums or discussions were rarely held in the synagogue during services. Kaplan's ideology of religious functionalism constituted for many committed Jews of the 1920s and 1930s the counterculture of that era; additionally, Kaplan helped prepare the way for the later counterculture.

As rabbi of the SAJ, Kaplan functioned in a variety of roles. Dr. David Teutsch of the Reconstructionist Rabbinical College has delineated the several capacities by which we can classify a rabbi depending on how much emphasis he accorded a particular function. The first function is the pastor-counselor function. In the ordinary course of events, people turn to the rabbi at times of crisis. All seminaries today include courses in pastoral psychology, a relatively recent innovation. For Kaplan, the pastoral demands at the SAJ were an intrusion he disliked and tried to avoid whenever possible. After spending more than an hour with one woman from the congregation, he was quite disgusted: "Thus does the SAJ intrude itself into my life directly and indirectly as a nuisance and as a problem."

In addition to being a counselor, the rabbi is also an administrator who runs an institution, sits on committees, and is involved in an endless round of meetings and deliberations. At the SAJ, Kaplan was involved in the administration of the synagogue in only a peripheral way. Such activities did not interest him, and he attended meetings only when he was compelled to. The rabbi also has a sacerdotal function: he officiates and becomes the actualizer of key rituals in the lives of his congregants. Kaplan did officiate at services, of course, but declined whenever possible to perform other kinds of rituals. As a matter of policy, funerals were never held at the SAJ; he performed marriages and funerals for his congregation when he had no choice, but he never found this aspect of the rabbinical life fulfilling.

Kaplan felt most at home in the teaching function of the rabbi. His sermons were invariably based on the reading of the week and dealt with primary religious and ethical issues. Week after week and year after year, he developed his ideology from the pulpit. His rather ordinary congregation became outstanding in the course of time because of the continuous teaching received from Kaplan. To this day, listening to Kaplan congregants of that era discuss Jewish issues, one hears the eloquent resonances of Kaplan himself.

The rabbi also has a prophetic function. He speaks out on moral and ethical issues and exhorts his congregants to pursue the exalted path of social and economic justice. Some rabbis are able to stir their listeners, to move them deeply, to lift them to a higher level of consciousness and insight. In his prophetic capacity, the rabbi is prone to think in extremes rather than engage in cool, reasoned analysis. Kaplan, the prophet of renewal, was certainly a charismatic leader. Especially in the breadth of his social vision and in his capacity to motivate and inspire others Kaplan's talents appeared to be limitless.

Prophets are lonely, but those around Kaplan never understood how lonely he was. Perhaps it had to do with the rabbinical role itself. Whitehead defined religion as what people did with their solitariness, but for Kaplan religion flourished only within a social context: "Solitariness may be as essential to the life of the spirit as sleep is for the recuperation of physical energy," Kaplan wrote, "but the time to experience the reality of God is when we are in the midst of those who are kindred to us in soul by reason of common hopes and common difficulties." The Psalmist understood intuitively that there was comfort in the sanctuary (a public place); according to Kaplan, the rabbis said straight out that "those who study the Torah entirely by themselves condemn themselves to sterility and frustration." The rabbis demanded that a person have a *Haver* (friend, colleague, partner) because one must be with others when in the pursuit of "spiritual attainment." Likewise, monks desire solitude but always within the general framework of a spiritual community. The modern rabbi suffers from loneliness in a special way. Kaplan was obviously talking about himself when he gave an analysis of the rabbi's spiritual needs and his essential loneliness: "Spiritually speaking we are never so alone as when we are busy with the round of our duties of preaching, teaching, attending meetings, making calls, officiating at various functions." His experience of being a rabbi was that he gave much more than he received and that the giving did not replenish his energy but only drained him of his strength. It is remarkable that he never ceased his workaholic schedule until he was well into his nineties.[37]

◆

As a direct result of his magnum opus and the attention it received, Kaplan and his followers launched a lively biweekly publication on topics of current interest to serve as a forum to disseminate their views. The first number of the *Reconstructionist* appears in January 1935 under Kaplan's editorship with the aid of Ira Eisenstein. Though small in terms of the number of pages, the journal became a notable forum for the exchange of opinions. As a matter of policy, Kaplan solicited articles from a broad spectrum of Jewish thinkers, and, particularly in its early years, the most original minds in the Jewish community published here.

Kaplan experimented on other fronts as well. The SAJ was a ready forum for ritual innovation, where he constantly tried new approaches. One of the most significant examples of his willingness to experiment is *The New Haggadah*, which Kaplan, Eisenstein, and Rabbi Eugene Kohn published in 1941. It is difficult for us in this age of feminist

Haggadahs and ecological seders to appreciate the impact of the Reconstructionist Haggadah. Many were shocked and offended because
of what was omitted (the ten plagues), what was changed (the language
of the *kiddish*, where references to chosenness were removed), and what
was inserted (historical portions on Moses, which are not found in the
traditional Haggadah). Almost immediately, Kaplan's outraged colleagues at the Seminary wrote him a ten-page letter detailing their pro-
tests. For the moment, however, they were not yet ready to go public
with their opposition.

Dismayed but not deterred by opposition, Kaplan continued to
work on other projects, the most important being the Reconstructionist *Sabbath Prayer Book*, which was published by the Reconstructionist
Foundation in 1945. The introduction to the prayer book described the
many beliefs of traditional Judaism that Kaplan felt were no longer accepted by Jews. Again he and his disciples deleted, revised, and added
material to create a new prayer book that reflected what Jews actually
believed. The opposition to the *Sabbath Prayer Book* was zealous, potent, and immediate. Not hesitating to criticize him publicly this time,
the senior professors at the Seminary (Ginzberg, Marx, and Lieberman) completely disassociated themselves from this heretical venture.
They believed that the liturgical changes he inaugurated went entirely
beyond the pale. Within a month of the publication of the *Sabbath
Prayer Book*, The Union of Orthodox Rabbis of the United States and
Canada issued a ban (*herem*) against Kaplan. In the *New York Times* it
was reported that his prayer book was burned during the *herem* ceremony at the Hotel McAlpin in New York City.[38]

Although Kaplan retired as dean of the Teachers' Institute in the
mid-1940s, he continued to teach at the Rabbinical School until 1963.
(Stories were circulated that some of his colleagues refused to speak to
him after the *herem*.) As years passed and the shock of his *Prayer Book*
faded, it appeared that finally his colleagues were beginning to appreciate him. His ideas for a University of Judaism were finally implemented in the late 1940s when he made a number of trips to the West
Coast to aid in the actual setting up of the University in Los Angeles.
Continuing his activity within the Conservative movement, he hoped
that Reconstructionism would be officially declared the left wing of
Conservative Judaism.

In 1949, at the age of sixty-seven, Kaplan published *The Future of
the American Jew*. This major work reiterated his basic approach, but
more importantly it spelled out his mature thinking on the idea of a
chosen people, the nature of religion, Jewish law, the status of women,
and the way in which a reconstructed Judaism understood basic moral

A light moment at the Seminary, ca. 1950. From left: *Judah Goldin, Moshe Davis, Mordecai Kaplan, Hillel Bavli, Seymour Fox. (Courtesy Library of JTS.)*

and spiritual values. At a time when most people begin to think of retirement, Kaplan's energies seemed to increase. The 1950s and 1960s were years of great creativity for him. Continuing to publish frequently, he produced significant works on Zionism, the history of Judaism, and the demands of "Ethical Nationhood."[39]

In his determination not to be divisive, Kaplan preserved the Reconstructionist movement as a "school of thought" rather than as a denomination. Nonetheless, the Society for the Advancement of Judaism was not only a congregation but also the focus for groups or congregations who wanted to affiliate with the Reconstructionist philosophy. In 1954, the Federation of Reconstructionist Congregations and Fellowships[40] was organized. Over time the number of affiliates grew, but not until the late 1960s did the movement actually become a separate denomination. Many Kaplan followers had considered going denominational for a long time, but the man most responsible for this important development was Ira Eisenstein. In 1968, five years after Kaplan had retired from the JTS, the Reconstructionist Rabbinical College opened its doors in Philadelphia with Eisenstein as its first president. The institution reflected Kaplan's approach, with women absolutely equal in all respects and a curriculum devoting each successive year to a different phase of Jewish civilization (Biblical civilization the first year, Rabbinic the second, etc.)

The divisiveness created by a new denomination was a stumbling block to Kaplan, but the success of the new college was not. After Eisenstein's retirement, the new president, Ira Silverman, raised funds to move RRC to a beautiful campus in Wyncote, Pennsylvania, on the outskirts of Philadelphia. The Federation of Reconstructionist Congregations and Havurot grew apace, and in 1992 there were seventy affiliated groups with some fifty thousand members. One very striking feature of these institutions is the youth of the leadership. It is not surprising that innovative and experimental modes continue to be the hallmark of Reconstructionism. The ideology of Mordecai M. Kaplan has not yet become a tradition in need of reconstruction.

In many ways Mordecai Kaplan's life embodies the American Jewish experience of the first half of the twentieth century. He died in 1983 at the age of 102, having lived through the whole saga of the American Jew in our times. Arriving here as a boy, growing up in New York City, becoming thoroughly Americanized, he struggled to find ways of making Judaism compatible with the American experience and the modern temper.

CONCLUSION

In 1931, Kaplan's uniqueness was beautifully summed up by his friend and admirer Maurice Karpf; these remarks also may serve as a starting point for an assessment of Kaplan and his mission at the midpoint in his life: "While as you know, I have always thought well of [Kaplan] I have come to admire his intellectual virility as I never have before. We have also come to love him as a person of rare spiritual quality and one of those fortunate spirits that can live in a world of their own creation free from the sordidness and pettiness of everyday life and to live and function on their own plane and with their own ideals. . . . I have the feeling that Kaplan is much more valuable as Prophet than as a Priest and I think it will be up to others to serve or supply the Priests."[1]

From the very beginning of his career, Kaplan's strength and his weakness was his ability to live on the level of his ideology. His mind had its roots in the world of his father, which, despite his radicalism, Kaplan never completely abandoned. His rationalist-analytical temper and his obsession with ethical issues are both evident in the world of Lithuanian Jewry from which he came. Though thoroughly American-ized, he himself always lived in two civilizations. He was the *Talmid* and the *Rav* (the rabbi who studied) and the sociologist-become-theologian. His secular training enabled him to become the primary spiritual spokesperson for second-generation Jews in America who were torn between their need to relate to their past and their craving to be part of the land in which they were growing up.

Throughout his life, the Seminary was both Kaplan's salvation and the primary source of his suffering. It lifted him out of the obscurity of the congregational rabbinate and forced him to become a public figure and to develop his ideas systematically. The contrast between his floundering as an Orthodox rabbi and the confidence exhibited in the *Menorah Journal* articles he wrote a few years after leaving Kehilath Jeshurun is quite striking. As a public figure, he was appreciated from the beginning and spoke locally and nationally year after year, often for little or no money. At the same time, he constantly thought of leaving the Seminary because he felt unappreciated by his colleagues; he suffered from their rejection, though it was concealed by the civilities of politeness. The antagonism between Kaplan and Ginzberg, for example, was common knowledge to the Seminary community during the 1920s and 1930s. With the publication of *Judaism as a Civilization* and later the *New Haggadah*, grudging toleration gave way to attack.

Yet the Seminary was also his home, where he had "lived" since the year before his bar mitzvah. He was an excellent teacher of rabbis and despite all other problems was always appreciated by his students. Not all the rabbinical students agreed with him, but they all respected him. In describing the Seminary of those years, Professor Neil Gilman articulated Kaplan's preeminence among the students: "He alone integrated theology, ideology and program . . . there simply were no alternatives, not only at the Seminary but even elsewhere in the Jewish theological world; until the mid-fifties when Herberg and Heschel began to write and teach."[2] It is quite astonishing that future rabbis were never asked to think about religious issues except by Mordecai Kaplan. The Seminary faculty valued scholarship above all. Kaplan, himself a congregational rabbi, stood alone in his commitment to the congregational rabbinate.

Kaplan taught not only at the Seminary but also at Columbia and at the Jewish School for Social Work. Some sixty years after the events, one of his students from the Jewish School of Social Work remembered him vividly and described the class with Kaplan as "*the* academic experience of my life." This student, who attended the school from 1933 to 1935, continued: "The year we had with Kaplan was the year his magnum opus, *Judaism as a Civilization*, was published and of course we used it a lot. . . . He was a wonderful, stimulating teacher — his knowledge and understanding in so many fields, his insistence on straight, honest thinking (no bluffing or pretending allowed), a good sense of humor, etc."[3] In his opening address to the students of the Teachers' Institute in 1934, Kaplan stressed the importance of "their being intellectually and morally honest — honest with themselves as a condition of being honest with others."[4] Honesty was one of the cornerstones of his value system, and though he did not always reveal his thoughts, he was genuine and authentic in everything he said. There was no posturing or "seeming" (Buber's term) in the way he presented himself.

His work at the Seminary, including his administration of the Teachers' Institute, enabled him to become a primary force in the field of Jewish education in America. All the principal leaders of Jewish education who themselves were educated between 1910 and 1940 were students, if not disciples of Kaplan. He assembled an outstanding faculty at the Teachers' Institute and developed adult Jewish education (the Friedlaender classes) when serious study on a popular level was unknown at the time. Though the faculty respected him, he was critical of them because he regarded them as secular Hebraic nationalists who had little genuine understanding of religious issues. At the 1934 convocation of the Teachers' Institute, one of the distinguished Hebraists on the faculty irritated Kaplan because of his exaggerated nationalism. Zvi Scharfstein, Kaplan asserted, "sailed [sallied?] forth fascist fashion into the sea of sentimental nationalistic slush."[5]

Kaplan's commitment to Zionism began during his adolescence and remained a significant aspect of his worldview throughout his life. Indeed, one might describe his system as a species of religious Zionism. Nonetheless, though his Zionism was ever-present, it followed in the Schechter tradition, its chief goal being to provide a bulwark against assimilation. A geographic center in the land of Israel was absolutely necessary as part of the reconstitution of the Jewish people; the Diaspora would be a permanent feature of Jewish life. But statehood was not as important as peoplehood: "nationalism is not a political but a cultural concept," Kaplan asserted. "Its fundamental purpose is to humanize and civilize."[6] His belief that one could live in two civilizations obviously implied that Jewish life could be as fulfilling in the United States as in the land of Israel. Kaplan was primarily the ideologist of community concerned with the relationship of community to the ethical and theological realms.

Community had to be rooted in institutions, and in the United States the enhanced synagogue would become the embodiment of communal life, Kaplan believed. He helped establish the Jewish Center in New York City as an experiment in social engineering where Jews could anchor both their work life and their play. The center concept was copied very widely during the decade after its inception. Kaplan's tenure there was short, however, because his commitment to social justice antagonized many of his wealthy congregants. Although his sermons were never theologically radical, the publication of an article in the *Menorah Journal* in 1920 in which he fiercely attacked all forms of organized Judaism in America precipitated his departure from the center and the establishment of the SAJ.

At the same time as Kaplan was writing the 1920 article for the *Menorah Journal*, he was also cultivating a group of associates in the fascinating experiment of the Society for Jewish Renascence. The group consisted of rabbinical colleagues, a few faculty members from the Seminary who supported him, and other members of the New York Jewish leadership. It was an attempt to establish a third way of being Jewish in America, neither Orthodox nor Reform. A middle road was needed because the Seminary did not seem to represent a distinct ideology. Kaplan was at the helm of the enterprise, which is probably why it never succeeded. The time was ripe and the people were present, but Kaplan could not be depended on to lead his troops into action. He was a magnificent source of ideas and of engaging formulations; he had no flair for political activity and disappointed those who had come to depend on him. In 1920 and again some seven years later, his most ardent supporters were ready to abandon the Seminary and move out on their own. They waited only for the signal — but it never came. Kaplan was bound to the Seminary and to the formulation of his ideology and could not extricate himself from either enterprise. He was fundamentally ambivalent about creating a new denomination. Even though the SAJ was set up as the core of a new movement, not merely as a congregation, Kaplan held tenaciously to the assumption that fragmentation was fatal to Jewish life and must be avoided at all costs. The belief in unity, paradoxically enough, was the primary dogma of all those who opposed him and the spread of Reconstructionism. So he opted for the concept of a "school of thought" rather than a new denomination and proceeded with the formulation of his ideology. Kaplan could formulate and reformulate ad infinitum. It was his obsession and his ultimate pleasure. At times, the process seemed as important as the product; the search for solutions became an end in itself.

Yet the ideology Kaplan created, though it reflected his own ambivalence and the uncertainties of his generation, served the Jewish community well. He abhorred supernaturalism because it entailed a belief in magic and in miracles that violated natural law. But he was not a naturalist. He dismissed that term because it denoted an insufficient understanding of life in the universe. The scientific approach was the beginning of all knowledge but not the end. He believed in science but rejected scientism, science as a religion that elevates man and his mind to the pinnacle of creation, believing him to be self-sufficient in solving his problems. He accepted equality but perceived democracy as a serious threat to Judaism because it assumed the primacy of the individual and left little room for the life of the community. Even his harshest critics recognized that he was a true *ohev yisrael* (lover of Israel). Yet in the privacy of his own mind, he was often impatient with and alienated by the Jews he had to serve. Drawn into the vortex of the "Jewish problem" by fate and by choice, he was apprehensive about his daughter's interest in a life of service to the Jewish people. His pessimism seemed to be justified when the chairman of a program in Albany introduced him as having written the greatest book since "Spinoza's Guide to the Perplexed." Though his gloom was persistent, so was his natural energetic mode of being. He experienced enormous exhilaration when studying or teaching or attempting a new formulation — all of which were part of his daily life until the process of aging began to slow him down in his mid-nineties.

Kaplan's doubts about himself and his abilities never hindered his perpetual activity. Moreover, he concealed his anxiety with astonishing success. Ira Eisenstein, who lived with Kaplan for almost fifty years, was shocked to learn of Kaplan's lack of confidence as expressed in the diary. The public Kaplan appeared to be confident and bombastic, yet in the privacy of his own thoughts the great man often felt inadequate. A few months after the publication of *Judaism as a Civilization*, when he still did not find the long-awaited review of his book in the *New York Times*, he speculated that Cyrus Adler, a distant relative of the Sulzberger family, had arranged for the book not to be reviewed. Perhaps it was because of his poor writing ability, he thought, as he leafed through the journal: "I happened to look into one of the earlier volumes of this journal and noted the flatness and colorlessness of its contents, and became so disgusted with myself that I almost made up my mind not to continue with this journal. To aspire to higher standards of excellence and to be totally impotent to attain them is the most tragic aspect of human life. . . . With an inarticulate ancestry such as mine, with the worst kind of academic training to start me on my professional career, is it a wonder that I have to go through the tortures of the Laocoön before I organize my ideas, and the anguish of the deaf mute before I articulate them."[7] It is possible that the doubts served as a generating force, for he invariably felt that the formulation was not quite right. Before the ink was dry on his first great work, he was already writing the next.

His goal was ever before him. He wanted to help create a Jewish civilization that would be an integral part of the modern world and would allow Jews to take their Judaism for granted, to live without endless spiritual conflict and intellectual evasiveness. The emancipated Jew could take nothing for granted — as Kafka put it, "even the past had to be earned." Mordecai Kaplan spent his life in search of a past and a present that Jews, in a ceaselessly changing world, could call their own and honestly preserve without forfeiting their future.

SOURCES

ABBREVIATIONS

AJA — American Jewish Archives
AJHS— American Jewish Historical Society
HUC— Hebrew Union College
JIR — Jewish Institute of Religion
JTS — Jewish Theological Seminary
SAJ — Society for the Advancement of Judaism
RRC — Reconstructionist Rabbinical College

A NOTE ON THE KAPLAN PAPERS

Mordecai Kaplan kept a diary from the time he was in his early twenties. The diaries for 1904 to 1907 are in the Kaplan Archive at the Reconstructionist Rabbinical College in Wyncote, Pennsylvania. Kaplan's major diary begins in 1913. There are a total of twenty-seven volumes. The books are large accountant-type volumes and have about three hundred pages each. The original of the first twenty-five volumes, which I shall call the Kaplan journal, is at the Jewish Theological Seminary. The original of volumes 26 and 27 (from 1973 onward) are at the RRC. There is a microfilm of the first twenty-five volumes at the RRC, at the American Jewish Archives in Cincinnati, and at Hebrew Union College in Jerusalem. The Kaplan Archive at the RRC also houses Kaplan's correspondence, consisting of eight thousand pieces, fully catalogued. The Littauer Foundation, the Kaplan family, and a number of others have contributed toward the publication of the Kaplan journal, a project in process. Wayne State University Press will publish a condensation of the Kaplan journal in three volumes. A catalogue of the Kaplan correspondence assembled by Richard Libowitz may be found in *Jewish Civilization: Essays and Studies, Volume 2, Jewish Law, Honoring the One Hundredth Birthday of Rabbi Mordecai M. Kaplan*, ed. by Ronald A. Brauner, Philadelphia: Reconstructionist Rabbinical College, 1981. The rest of Kaplan's papers also are found at the Kaplan Archive but have not been catalogued.

NEWSPAPERS AND PERIODICALS

American Hebrew, 1886–1920
American Jewish Chronicle, New York, 1918
American Jewish Press, Minneapolis, 1924
Denver Jewish News, 1924
Hadoar, 1945
Ha-Levanon, 1882
Ha-Zefirah, 1882
Hebrew Standard, 1916–1921
Idishe Licht, 1923
Jewish Forum, 1920–1921
Jewish Record, San Antonio, Texas, 1925
Maccabbaean, 1909
Menorah Journal, 1915–1930
Morgen Journal [Yiddish], 1920–1921
New Era Illustrated Magazine, 1904–1906
New Palestine, 1925–1928
New York Herald Tribune, 1925
New York Times, 1916–1925
New Yorker Yidishe Zeitung, 1886
Proceedings of the Biennial Convention of the Jewish Theological Seminary Association,
    1888–1902
Proceedings of the Rabbinical Assembly of America
Reform Advocate, 1904
SAJ Bulletin
SAJ Review, 1923–1929
United Synagogue Recorder, 1920–1929
Yidishe Tagblat, 1927

ARCHIVES

American Jewish Archives, Cincinnati

Rabbi Hyman Enelow papers
Horace J. Kallen papers
Mordecai M. Kaplan papers
Louis Marshall papers
Jacob Schiff papers

American Jewish Historical Society, Waltham

Cyrus Adler papers
Bernard C. Ehrenreich papers
Society for the Advancement of Judaism Collection
Stephen Wise papers

Central Zionist Archives, Jerusalem

Normal Bentwich papers
Isaac Berkson papers
Jessie Sampter papers
Henrietta Szold papers

Columbia University, New York

Felix Adler papers
Franklin Giddings papers
Mordecai M. Kaplan master's thesis

Hadassah, New York

Henrietta Szold papers

Hebrew University, Central Archives for the History of the Jewish People, Jerusalem

Alexander Dushkin papers
Joseph Klausner papers
Judah L. Magnes papers

Jewish Theological Seminary, New York

Cyrus Adler papers
Max Arzt papers
Israel Friedlaender papers
Louis Ginzberg papers
Gustav Gottheil papers
Simon Greenberg papers
Charles I. Hoffman papers
Max Kadushin papers
Abraham J. Karp Collection
Jacob Kohn papers
Alexander Marx papers
Herman Rubenovitz papers
Solomon Schechter papers
Mayer Sulzberger correspondence
Henrietta Szold papers

Weizmann Institute, Rehovoth

Chaim Weizmann papers

Yeshiva University, New York

Institutional Synagogue Collection
Mordecai M. Kaplan papers

PRIVATE COLLECTIONS

Mordecai M. Kaplan papers in possession of Hadassah Musher
Minute books of Kehilath Jeshurun
Minute books of Society for the Advancement of Judaism
Samson Benderly Rosenwald Contest papers in possession of the author
Diary of Judith Kaplan Eisenstein in possession of Judith K. Eisenstein
Phineas Israeli papers in possession of Nathan Israeli

INTERVIEWS

Jacob Agus, May 1984
Rabbi Isadore Barnett, graduate of JTS, student of Kaplan, June 1988
Lisa Bernstein, niece of Lena Kaplan, March 1988
Gershon Chertoff, son of Paul Chertoff, July 1988
Mordecai Chertoff, son of Paul Chertoff, JTS faculty member, July 1988
Moshe Davis, January 1989
Samuel Dinin, former registrar of Teachers' Institute, September 1988
Judith Epstein, Kaplan congregant, April 1988
Louis Finkelstein, March 1974
H. L. Ginsberg, September 1988
Robert Gordis, April 1984
Simon Greenberg, March 1985
Ann Eisenstein, daughter of Ira and Judith Eisenstein, April 1990
Ira Eisenstein, 1973–1991
Judith Kaplan Eisenstein, 1973–1991
Myron Eisenstein, brother of Ira Eisenstein, and Ruth Eisenstein, April 1990
Mrs. Elitzur interviewer, "Transcript of Interview with Mordecai Kaplan," September 27, 1960, Institute for Contemporary Jewry, Oral History Project, Hebrew University
Selma Kaplan Goldman and Dr. Joseph Goldman, October 1986
Nathan Israeli, son of Phineas Israeli and Sophie Kaplan, September 1987
Max Kadushin, January 1974
Nathan Kallin, JTS graduate, June 1988
Louis Kaplan, scholar at Brandeis, April 1991
Judge Benjamin Wm. Mehlman, April 1990
David Musher, son of Hadassah and Sidney, and Ruth Musher, April 1991
Hadassah Kaplan Musher, 1985–1991
Sidney Musher, November 1985
Abigail Rosenthal, daughter of Henry Rosenthal, student and colleague of Kaplan, April 1990
Rabbi Ralph Simon, JTS graduate, September 1988
Naomi Kaplan Wenner and Charles Wenner, April 1975

NOTES

PREFACE

1. I am well aware that I am using this quotation in a somewhat different sense from the author.

2. Kaplan's full bibliography, which comes to some four hundred items, may be found in *The American Judaism of Mordecai Kaplan*, ed. by Emanuel S. Goldsmith, Mel Scult, and Robert Seltzer (New York: New York University Press, 1990), pp. 415–53.

3. Alexander Dushkin, *Living Bridges: Memoirs of an Educator* (Jerusalem: Keter Publishing House Ltd., 1975), p. 14.

4. I am indebted to Professor Louis Kaplan for this quotation.

CHAPTER 1

1. The *Gaon* is also referred to by the acronym *Ha Gra*, the *Gaon* Rabbi Eliyahu. The expression "unrelenting intellectuality" comes from the fine recent biography of Judah Leib Gordon by Michael Stanislawski, *For Whom Do I Toil? Judah Leib Gordon and the Crisis of Russian Jewry* (New York: Oxford University Press, 1988), p. 9. The specific material on Israel Kaplan is taken from interviews with Mordecai Kaplan or from the Kaplan diary entry for January 25, 1917, written a few days after Kaplan's father passed away.

2. For a full description of the Volozhin, and other yeshivas, see Samuel Mirsky, *Jewish Institutions of Higher Learning in Europe: Their Development and Destruction* [Hebrew] (New York: Ogen Publishing House of Histadruth Ivrith of America, 1956).

3. See Mirsky, p. 61, as well as the more general description in Gedalyahu Alon, "The Lithuanian Yeshivas," trans. by Sid Leiman in *The Jewish Expression*, ed. by Judah Goldin (New Haven: Yale University Press, 1976), pp. 452–69.

4. The connection between the *Haskalah* and Mordecai Kaplan is taken from the essay by Emanuel S. Goldsmith "Mordecai Kaplan and the Retrieval of the Haskalah," in *The American Judaism of Mordecai Kaplan*, ed. by Emanuel S. Goldsmith, Mel Scult, and Robert Seltzer, (New York: New York University Press, 1990). On Gordon, see Stanislawski, pp. 32ff.

5. The specific material on Israel Kaplan is derived from a number of sources. The most important is the Kaplan journal. Mordecai Kaplan wrote about his early life several times. The first published account was written in 1942: "The Influences That Have Shaped My Life," *The Reconstructionist* 8, no. 10 (June 1942). The second account is "The Heart of Wisdom," *The Reconstructionist* 17, no. 6 (May 1951). The other accounts are "The Way I Have Come," *Mordecai M. Kaplan: An Evaluation*, ed. by Ira Eisenstein and Eugene Kohn (New York: Jewish Reconstructionist Foundation, 1952), pp. 283–321; and "How to Live Creatively as a Jew," *Moments of Personal Discovery*, ed. by R. M. MacIver (New York and London: Harper and Brothers, for the Institute for Religious and Social Studies, 1952), pp. 93–104. In addition to these sources, I talked with Mordecai Kaplan about his early life in 1972–1974.

6. On the *Musar* movement and Israel Salanter, see the following, from which this account is drawn: Louis Ginzberg, "Rabbi Israel Salanter," *Students, Scholars and Saints* (Philadelphia: Jewish Publication Society, 1928); Hillel Goldberg, *Israel Salanter: Text, Structure, Idea: The Ethics and Theology of an Early Psychologist of the Unconscious* (New York: Ktav Publishing House, 1982). See also Hillel Goldberg's shorter treatment of Salanter in *Between Berlin and Slobodka: Jewish Transition Figures from Eastern Europe* (Hoboken, N.J.: Ktav Publishing House, 1989).

7. For a general account of Sventzian, see *Sefer Zikaron Le-esrim Ve-Shalosh Kehilot She-Nehrevu Be-Ezor Sventsian* [Sventzian Region Memorial Book of Twenty-three Jewish Communities], ed. by Shimon Kanc (Tel Aviv: Former Residents of Sventzian District in Israel, 1965). For a brief treatment of Reines, see Hayim Z. Reines, "Isaac Jacob Reines," *Jewish Leaders 1750–1940*, ed. by Leo Jung (New York: Bloch Publishing Co., 1953). This article tends to present Reines as more modern than he really was. A more objective and complete treatment is the Hebrew work by Geulah Bat-Yehudah, *'Eysh Ha-Meorot* [The Man of Light] (Jerusalem: Mossad Ha-Rav Kook, 1985).

8. See Kovarsky's article in *Ha-Levanon* (Paris, Mainz, London) 1882 no. 7: 52; and other material on Reines's proposals in *Ha-Zefirah* (Warsaw and Berlin) 1882, no. 29.

9. See article in *Ha-Zefirah* 1882, no. 29: 228.

10. The material here is taken from interviews with Kaplan in 1972–1974. For a fine treatment of Kaplan and his relationship with his mother in a wider context, see Carol Kessner, "Kaplan and the Role of Women in Judaism," Goldsmith, Scult, and Seltzer, pp. 335–57.

11. For the revision of the standard sequence of events, see, for example, Jonathan Frankel, *Prophecy and Politics: Socialism, Nationalism and the Russian Jews, 1862–1917* (New York: Cambridge University Press, 1981).

12. For the fire of Sventzian, see Kanc. For the earliest account of the Kaplan exodus, see Kaplan journal, January 30, 1917. The point about Hamburg comes from personal interviews with Kaplan.

13. The best general work on the Jews in New York is the classic by Moses Rischin, *The Promised City: New York's Jews 1870–1914* (Cambridge: Harvard University Press, 1964). For a critical evaluation of the condition of traditional Jewry in New York, see the work by Rabbi Moses Weinberger published in 1887. The book was written in Hebrew and has been translated recently as *People Walk on Their Heads: Moses Weinberger's Jews and Judaism in New York*, trans. by Jonathan Sarna (New York: Holmes & Meier Publishers, 1982). See the introduction by the translator for the point about democracy.

14. See *People Walk on Their Heads*, p. 16, for an analysis of the *kashrut* situation. See also the article in the Hebrew newspaper *Ha-Ivri* (New York), June 26, 1892.

15. Eisenstein is a fascinating character. See, for example, Lloyd P. Gartner, "From New York to Miedzyrecz: Immigrant Letters of Judah David Eisenstein, 1878–1880," *American Jewish Historical Quarterly* 52 (1963): 234–44. For mention of the Brooklyn Bridge and

the Statue of Liberty, see Judah David Eisenstein, *Ozar Zikhronothai* [autobiography and memoirs] (New York: by the author, 1929), p. 51. He notes that people who wanted to walk over the bridge were charged one penny. On the chief rabbi, see Abraham J. Karp, "New York Chooses a Chief Rabbi," *American Jewish Historical Quarterly*, (March 1955): 129–98. On the chief rabbi and Eisenstein and the whole situation of New York Jewry in the 1880s, see Jeffrey S. Gurock, *The Men and Women of Yeshiva: Higher Education, Orthodoxy, and American Judaism* (New York: Columbia University Press, 1988), chapter 2.

16. For the details of the *kashrut* situation, see *People Walk on Their Heads*, see chapter 2. On the charge that the chief rabbi was being used for money-raising alone, see *American Hebrew*, January 11, 1889. With the passage of time, even the most dedicated members of the Orthodox community were able to recognize the fiasco of Rabbi Jacob Joseph. See *Sefer Ha-Yovel Shel Agudath Ha-Rabbanim D'Artzot Ha-Brit VeKanada* [Jubilee Volume of the Union of Orthodox Rabbis of the United States and Canada] (New York: 1928), pp. 17ff. The most detailed version of the *kashrut* aspect of the story is found in Harold P. Gastwirt, *Fraud, Corruption and Holiness: The Controversy over the Supervision of Jewish Dietary Practice in New York City 1881–1940* (Port Washington, N.Y.: Kennikat Press, 1974).

17. The most extensive account by Kaplan is contained in the Kaplan journal, October 28, 1914. The quotation regarding the standards of Orthodox rabbis is found in the journal entry of January 17, 1929.

18. Kaplan's bar mitzvah invitation, which is found among his papers, refers to him as Max. Material on the change of names comes from interviews with Kaplan in 1972. The bulletins at City College also refer to him as Mark, and some relatives I interviewed still referred to him as Uncle Mark.

19. For a history of Jewish education in New York, see Jeremiah Berman, "Jewish Education in New York City 1860–1890," *Yivo Annual of Jewish Social Science* 9: 247–75. See also Steven Brumberg, *Going to America, Going to School: The Jewish Immigrant Public School Encounter in Turn-of-the-Century New York City* (New York: Praeger, 1986).

20. The material on Abraham Cahan comes from the dissertation of Gilbert Klaperman, "The Beginnings of Yeshivah University – The First Jewish University in America" (Yeshiva University, 1955). Klaperman cites the article in *Yidishes Tageblat*, July 27, 1888, which refers to Cahan. The fourteen-year-old is also mentioned by Klaperman. Kaplan arrived two years after Cahan left.

21. Morris Raphael Cohen, *A Dreamer's Journey: The Autobiography of Morris Raphael Cohen* (Glencoe, Ill.: Free Press, 1949), p. 69. Cohen mentions Kaplan as his classmate in a letter to Alexander Dushkin, a professor of education at the Hebrew University and a former student of Kaplan's. Cohen was apparently in Palestine in 1938 and was writing to Dushkin to thank him for a dinner that was arranged in Cohen's honor. Kaplan was mentioned in the course of the letter; he was at the Hebrew University at the time. Morris Raphael Cohen to Alexander Dushkin, May 24, 1938, Alexander Dushkin Papers, Hebrew University, Jewish National and University Library, Archives of the Jewish People.

22. Mordecai Kaplan, "Influences," p. 29.

23. For a full account of City College, see Sherry Gorelick, *City College and the Jewish Poor: Education in New York 1880–1924* (New York: Schocken Books, 1982), part I. Quotation on higher education, Gorelick, p. 62. For the more conventional picture of City College, see Irving Howe, *A Margin of Hope: An Intellectual Biography* (New York: Harcourt Brace Jovanovich, 1982).

24. The merit rolls are found at the New York Public Library, as are the college registers for the years 1896–1899. In his senior year, Kaplan is listed as fifty-second in the class, with Morris R. Cohen holding his own at thirty-third. It is perhaps significant that many dropped out, for the class size was down to 133. Julius Greenstone, a lifelong friend of Kaplan who also became an important figure in the Jewish community, is listed as number 68. Kaplan

is listed in the 1896 register as Mark and in 1899 as Mordecai. In 1895, he is listed as living at 736 Lexington Avenue, which is the address of the old seminary. For his memory of his college years, see the Kaplan journal for August 9, 1926.

25. For the history of Reform Judaism, see Michael A. Meyer, *Response to Modernity: A History of the Reform Movement in Judaism* (New York: Oxford University Press, 1988). A very good summary is Moshe Davis, "Jewish Religious Life and Institutions in America," *The Jews: Their History, Culture and Religion*, 3rd edition, ed. by Louis Finkelstein (Philadelphia: Jewish Publication Society, 1960), Vol. 1, pp. 488–588.

26. For the Pittsburgh Platform, see *American Hebrew*, January 29, 1886, p. 178.

27. *American Hebrew*, January 15, 1886. See the biography of Rabbi Kohut's wife for a similar explanation: Rebekah Kohut, *My Portion* (New York: Thomas Seltzer, 1925), p. 85. Also see J. D. Eisenstein, "On the Establishment of the New Seminary," *New Yorker Yidishe Zeitung*, 1886; also found in *Ozar Zichronothai, Autobiography and Memoirs: A Diary of Important Jewish Events since My Arrival in New York in 1872 with a View Backward to the First Jewish Settlement in 1654* [Hebrew] (New York: J. D. Eisenstein, 1929), pp. 206–11.

28. For an in-depth study of the rabbinate in America that contains important material on the Seminary founders, see Jeffrey S. Gurock, "Resisters and Accommodators: Varieties of Orthodox Rabbis in America, 1886–1983," *American Jewish Archives* 35 (November 1983): 100–188. The conceptualization in this paragraph is drawn largely from Gurock.

29. *American Hebrew*, January 7, 1887, contains a report on the first class. See also *Proceedings of the First Biennial Convention of the Jewish Theological Association Held in the City of New York* (1888), p. 17. The quotation is from Alexander Kohut and is found in *American Hebrew*, January 7, 1887.

30. *American Hebrew*, February 4, 1887. On morning classes, see *American Hebrew*, January 27, 1889.

31. Personal interview with Kaplan, June 1972.

32. For the statement by Morais, see *American Hebrew*, February 19, 1886. The *American Hebrew* very much reflected the interests of the founders. The stories mentioned are found in *American Hebrew*, March 18, 1887.

33. For material on Morais, see Henry Samuel Morais, "Sabato Morais: A Memoir," reprinted from *Proceedings of the Sixth Biennial Convention of the Jewish Theological Association Held in the City of New York* (1898), p. 9. Cyrus Adler eulogized Morais, his teacher, as an excellent linguist in Italian, Spanish, and Hebrew: Cyrus Adler papers, Jewish Theological Seminary of America, box 8, "Notes for a Speech on Death of Morais." See also Joseph H. Hertz, "Sabato Morais: A Pupil's Tribute," *The Jewish Theological Seminary Semi-Centennial Volume*, ed. by Cyrus Adler (New York: Jewish Theological Seminary, 1939), p. 48. See also in that volume Henry P. Mendes, "The Beginnings of the Seminary," pp. 37ff. On the opening ceremonies of the seminary, where Morais arrived from Philadelphia when the ceremonies were about to conclude, see *American Hebrew*, January 7, 1887. On Mendes, see David de Sola Pool, *H. Pereira Mendes: A Biography* (New York: n.p., 1938), p. 23; and Eugene Markowitz, "Henry Pereira Mendes: Architect of the Union of Orthodox Jewish Congregations of America," *The Jewish Experience in America: Selected Studies from the Publications of the American Jewish Historical Society, 1969*, ed. by Abraham J. Karp (Waltham, Mass.: American Jewish Historical Society, 1969), Vol. 5, p. 134. See also the unpublished thesis of Eugene Markowitz on Henry P. Mendes, on deposit at Yeshiva University. The only faculty person to receive a salary was Bernard Drachman. See his very detailed autobiography, Dr. Bernard Drachman, *The Unfailing Light: Memoirs of an American Rabbi* (New York: Rabbinical Council of America, 1948), p. 3. Unless otherwise noted, facts about Drachman are drawn from his autobiography.

34. The facts of Kaplan's early life, unless otherwise noted, are taken from a series of personal interviews. Life of C. E. Hillel Kauvar: *Autobiography*, American Jewish Archives. Five students denied admission in the first year: *American Hebrew*, January 21, 1887, p. 161.

35. Kaplan remembered Greenstone being five years older than himself. *Who's Who in American Jewry* (New York: Jewish Biographical Bureau, 1926), p. 233, lists him as born in 1873, which would have made him eight years older than Kaplan. Kaplan also remembered being in some classes with Greenstone at the Seminary although Greenstone finished in 1900 and Kaplan in 1902. Greenstone later moved to Philadelphia, taught at Gratz, eventually became the principal, and is most well known for his work *The Messiah Idea in Jewish History* (Philadelphia: Jewish Publication Society, 1906); on Greenstone and progress, see *American Hebrew*, February 16, 1900.

36. Julius H. Greenstone, "Reminiscences of the Old Seminary Days," *United Synagogue Recorder* 6, no. 4 (October 1926): 9. Greenstone mentions that the dormitory was on the third floor. According to another opinion, the third floor contained a room used for a synagogue plus offices, and the second floor had a library and reading room. See Joseph B. Abrahams, "The Buildings of the Old Seminary," *The Jewish Theological Seminary Semi-Centennial Volume*. Phineas Israeli married Sophie Kaplan.

37. For Morais's report, see *Proceedings of the Fourth Biennial Convention of the Jewish Theological Seminary Association Held in the City of New York* (1894), p. 26. On the teaching of secular subjects, *Proceedings*, see p. 6. The *Semi-Centennial Volume* lists George Sternberg as "Instructor of Latin, Greek and German, 1892–1894," as well as Joseph Jacobs, who functioned as registrar and as "Professor of English Literature and Rhetoric, 1906–1913."

38. Mordecai Kaplan to Rabbi Bernard C. Ehrenreich, September 13, 1945, Ehrenreich papers, American Jewish Historical Society. In this letter to Ehrenreich, Kaplan mentions that Ehrenreich was right about Kaplan's nickname. Unfortunately, Ehrenreich's letter in which he mentions the nickname has not survived in the Kaplan papers.

39. Steven Siegel, the archivist of the 92nd Street Y, brought the matter of the neighborhood to my attention. One of the books in Kaplan's library which is now at the Reconstructionist Rabbinical College (RRC) has a bookplate from the Maimonides Library of B'nai B'rith. The B'nai B'rith office is mentioned by Deborah Dash Moore in *B'nai B'rith and the Challenge of Ethnic Leadership* (Albany: State University of New York Press, 1981). The early Seminary bulletins listed names and addresses of students.

40. Ehrlich is mentioned in every autobiographical piece Kaplan ever wrote. The quotation here comes from Greenstone, "Reminiscences," p. 9.

41. Mordecai M. Kaplan, "The Way I Have Come," *Mordecai M. Kaplan: An Evaluation*, ed. by Ira Eisenstein and Eugene Kohn (New York: Jewish Reconstructionist Foundation, 1952), p. 290. For a fuller discussion of Ehrlich, see chapter 9 herein. Sossnitz was described in his obituary as "well-known among all the *Maskilim* in this city as an original thinker and a scientist." He was born in Russia, had a traditional education, and, for a number of years, was assistant editor of *Ha-Zefirah*. This Hebrew journal included articles on scientific subjects. When he came to New York, he worked at the Astor Library and later became a Hebrew school principal; *American Hebrew*, March 4, 1910, p. 466. He also contributed a number of articles to the *Jewish Encyclopedia*.

42. Gilbert Klaperman, *The Beginnings of Yeshiva University*, unpublished dissertation, Yeshiva University, June 1955. Klaperman is not completely correct, because the Seminary did hold public examinations of its students from time to time, as was the custom. Whether or not the Seminary did slight particular visitors, however, is difficult to say.

43. On public examinations, see Greenstone, "Reminiscences." See also the announcements that public examinations would be held in *American Hebrew*, May 10, 1889, p. 1; and *American Hebrew*, September 15, 1899, p. 580: "Visitors will be invited to suggest any portion of the Talmud for sight reading." But Jaffe conducted the examinations. Thus, the Seminary assumed a middle position between keeping the examinations closed and allowing well-known European rabbis to do the examining.

44. The remark about Talmud in English in *Ha-Ivri*, December 18, 1896, quoted in Klaperman's dissertation, p. 84; on Yiddish, in *American Hebrew*, November 11, 1887.

45. Eisenstein on the Orthodox and reformers: Judah David Eisenstein, "The Establishment of the New Seminary" [Hebrew], originally appeared in Yiddish as a newspaper article, republished in Eisenstein's memoirs, *Zikhronathai*, p. 207. On each one making his own law: *Zikhronathai*, pp. 208–9. Knowledge but no faith cited in Klaperman, *Beginnings*, 79–86.

46. Blumenthal on training rabbis: *Proceedings of the First Biennial Convention*, p. 10. Blumenthal on culture and refinement: *Proceedings of the Second Biennial Convention of the Theological Seminary Association held in New York* (1890), pp. 7, 9. Kaplan on the rights of the minority: *American Hebrew*, November 24, 1899, p. 87. Kaplan on Saul: *American Hebrew*, January 11, 1901, p. 164. Treasurer of the literary society: *American Hebrew*, February 28, 1902, p. 465.

47. The week of Kaplan's sermon: *American Hebrew*, April 5, 1901. Kaplan speaking at the memorial service: *American Hebrew*, March 14, 1902, p. 521.

48. The sermon, written in Kaplan's hand, is on deposit at the Reconstructionist Rabbinical College and has no title. I assume, however, because Kaplan's student sermon was delivered immediately after Passover, that this is in fact the student sermon. A note on the first page indicates that the sermon was delivered on Passover in 1901, at Orach Chayim Synagogue and at the Forsythe Street Synagogue. Kaplan was twenty when he gave this sermon.

49. See, for example, Kaplan, "The Way I Have Come."

CHAPTER 2

1. Although this chapter deals with the roots of Kaplan's thought, not all of the primary influences will be presented here. Ahad Ha-Am the Zionist thinker, for example, will be presented in the chapter on Zionism.

2. The figure for the student body is from Horace Coon, *Columbia: Colossus on the Hudson* (New York: E. P. Dutton and Co., 1947), p. 92. The point about the schools is in F. W. Boardman Jr., *Columbia: An American University in Peace and War* (New York: Columbia University Press, 1944), p. 13.

3. Coon, p. 91.

4. Boardman.

5. Coon, p. 105.

6. Mordecai M. Kaplan, Registration Book, Columbia University. At that time, each person had a little book which their instructors signed at the beginning and ending of each course. This booklet is among Kaplan's papers at the Reconstructionist Rabbinical College. We therefore know Kaplan's courses and his instructors for each year he was enrolled at Columbia.

7. The lecture notes that Adler prepared for this course are among his papers at Columbia University. Thus, we have access to the lectures Kaplan heard in one of his key courses at Columbia. They are in Felix Adler papers, box 100–1900E–1904B, Columbia University. Some of the course descriptions in the Columbia catalogue list the books required for the courses Kaplan took. By cross-checking the books in the course lists against the books from Kaplan's library at the Reconstructionist Rabbinical College, we are in a position to know for certain some of the books he read at this time. For example, there is an English translation of Kant's *Critique of Pure Reason*, published in 1900 and required for a course, "Philosophy of Kant and His Successors," which Kaplan took with Professor W. H. Sheldon from October 1901 to May 1902. On the inside cover of Kaplan's copy is his signature and after his name the letters "C.U." The book is underlined throughout, with many notes in the margins. Sheldon wrote a letter of recommendation for Kaplan in which he referred to Kaplan's summaries of Kant as "masterpieces of clearness and directness." Sheldon believed Kaplan's work showed "decided philosophic ability which ought to be cultivated." In Kaplan's library, there is also a copy of *The Religion of Duty* by Felix Adler in a 1905 edition which is heavily underlined.

8. Kaplan's master's thesis may be found at Columbia University. It runs to some ninety pages and is written in Kaplan's own hand.

9. Kaplan journal, December 5, 1906, Reconstructionist Rabbinical College.

10. John Herman Randall Jr., *The Making of the Modern Mind*, rev. ed. (Boston: Houghton Mifflin Co., 1940), p. 506.

11. Letter from Kaplan to the author, February 1974. Herbert Spencer died in 1903.

12. Letter from Herbert Spencer to J. A. Skelton, July 29, 1893, cited in J. D. Y. Peel, *Herbert Spencer: The Evolution of a Sociologist* (New York: Basic Books, 1971), p. 153.

13. Ibid., pp. 112–31.

14. For more on Ahad Ha-Am and Kaplan, see Meir Ben-Horin, "Ahad Ha-Am in Kaplan: Roads Crossing and Parting," *The American Judaism of Mordecai Kaplan*, ed. by Emanuel S. Goldsmith, Mel Scult, and Robert Seltzer (New York: New York University Press, 1990), pp. 221–33. We shall discuss Ahad Ha-Am more extensively below.

15. The meeting is recorded in Kaplan's journal, December 1906.

16. Richard Hofstadter, *Social Darwinism in American Thought 1865–1915* (Philadelphia: University of Pennsylvania Press, 1948), p. 157.

17. Franklin H. Giddings, *Principles of Sociology* (New York: Macmillan Co., 1903), pp. 225–26.

18. Franklin H. Giddings, *The Elements of Sociology* (New York: Macmillan Co., 1898), p. 6.

19. Ibid., p. 121.

20. Ibid., p. 139.

21. Giddings, *Principles*, p. 144.

22. Kaplan told me that he read Durkheim in English, and since Durkheim's classic work did not come out in English until 1915 (*The Elementary Forms of Religious Life* [London: George Allen and Unwin, 1915]), the date of Kaplan's reading is pushed beyond his graduate years. Kaplan began publishing a major series of articles in the *Menorah Journal* in 1915 in which the general outline of his philosophy is already in place (before he read Durkheim). I once asked scholar Jacob Agus about the matter of Durkheim and Kaplan. He told me that he asked Kaplan about precisely this matter in the late 1930s when he was working on his doctoral dissertation which became *Modern Philosophies of Judaism*. Agus said that in their initial conversation Kaplan told him that Durkheim was of negligible importance in molding his thought. Ten years later, Kaplan was saying and writing that Durkheim was the most important influence on him next to Ahad Ha-Am. It still may be the case that a comparison of Kaplan and Durkheim will be fruitful, but we must be clear about the matter of origins. There is also no evidence that Kaplan was influenced by Max Weber.

23. Giddings, *Principles*, p. 130.

24. Ibid., p. 154.

25. On society and the individual reaching full achievement: Giddings, *Principles*, pp. 306, 309. Optimistic appraisal of present conditions: *Principles*, p. 302.

26. Abraham J. Karp, "Solomon Schechter Comes to America," *American Jewish Historical Quarterly* 53 (1963), reprinted in *The American Jewish Experience in America*, ed. by Abraham J. Karp (Waltham, Mass.: American Jewish Historical Society, 1969), Vol. 5, pp. 111–30.

27. See very detailed multivolumed work from the *Geniza* on the Jewish communities of Egypt in Shlomo Dov Goitein, *A Mediterranean Society: The Jewish Communities of the Arab World as Portrayed in the Documents of the Cairo Geniza* (Berkeley: University of California Press, 1967).

28. Karp, "Solomon Schechter," p. 129.

29. *Yidishe Welt*, July 3, 1904, p. 4, as cited in Gilbert Klaperman, *The Early Years of Yeshivah University*, dissertation, Yeshiva University, p. 86.

30. Although Kaplan's diploma is dated 1902, he is still listed as a student in the 1903–4 register of the Seminary. He continued to attend classes at the seminary, particularly those of Schechter. Schechter summering at Tannersville: *American Hebrew*, June 27, 1902.

31. Details of this incident are from an interview with Kaplan in June 1972. For facts on Kaplan receiving a scholarship, see *American Hebrew*, November 6, 1903. On Elias Solomon, compare the Seminary registers for 1902 and 1904. He is listed as graduating in both.

32. See Seminary Register for 1903–4, where Kaplan and Henrietta Szold are listed as students. Szold was not a casual student but attended class regularly. Although no one thought she would receive a rabbinical degree, she was listed as a regular student in all the seminary attendance lists. In her diary, she relates Louis Ginzberg's feeling that she was the only one who understood what he was saying. Szold attended the seminary regularly for three years. See Mel Scult, "Hadassah Preludes — Henrietta Szold Rabbi," *Hadassah Magazine*, June–July 1990, pp. 23–24.

33. Quotation on nature from Kaplan journal, December 8, 1904. The original of this particular early diary is at the Reconstructionist Rabbinical College.

34. Kaplan journal, August 24, 1914.

35. For the details, see Bernard Drachman, *The Unfailing Light: Memoirs of an American Rabbi* (New York: Rabbinical Council of America, 1948), p. 199.

36. For an analysis of modern Orthodox rabbis including preaching, see Jenna Weissman Joselit, *New York's Jewish Jews: The Orthodox Community in the Interwar Years* (Bloomington: Indiana University Press, 1990), pp. 54–97.

37. Sermon notebook I, Reconstructionist Rabbinical College.

38. *American Hebrew*, May 22, 1903, p. 38.

39. The phrase "posthumous victories" comes from Emil Fackenheim. See, for example, his *God's Presence in History: Jewish Affirmations and Philosophical Reflections* (New York: Harper and Row, 1970). On the pogroms, see *The Voice of America on Kishineff*, ed. by Cyrus Adler (Philadelphia: Jewish Publication Society of America, 1904). Adler notes that the imperial government refused to receive the petition, and so it was never officially delivered. Kaplan's words are from Sermon notebook I.

40. *The Complete Diaries of Theodore Herzl*, ed. by Raphael Patai, trans. by Harry Zohn (New York: Herzl Press, 1960), Vol. 4, book 17, pp. 1547, 1548.

41. Kaplan journal, December 7, 1904.

42. See Gilbert Klaperman, *The Beginnings of Yeshiva University*, unpublished dissertation, Yeshiva University, p. 133.

43. See Harry Fischel, *Forty Years of Struggle for a Principle: The Biography of Harry Fischel*, ed. by Rabbi Herbert Goldstein (New York: Bloch Publishing Co., 1928). Goldstein studied with Kaplan at the Seminary and himself eventually became rabbi of Kehilath Jeshurun.

44. On the Ruskays and the Baums, see Lawrence W. Crohn, *We Remember: The Saga of the Baum-Webster Family Tree 1842–1964* (privately published), p. 25. I want to thank John Ruskay who made this family history available. He is now vice chancellor of the Jewish Theological Seminary and for a while served on the staff at the SAJ.

45. Kaplan journal, August 23, 1914, has details about the congregation. For the Orthodox context, see Joselit, *New York's Jewish Jews*.

46. The point about being fashionable and the remark about the dingy building are found in Kaplan journal, October 25, 1914.

47. Interview with Kaplan, 1972. In 1987, I gave a lecture at the West End Synagogue in New York City about Kaplan. This congregation includes the Kaplan family and many original members of the Society for the Advancement of Judaism. After my talk, in which I related the incident regarding the sermon notes, a little lady about ninety years old raised her hand and said that she had been at Kehilath Jeshurun as a child and she knew who stole the sermon notes of Rabbi Peikes. She refused to reveal the name of the culprit. The lady was Judith Epstein.

48. Defeat of motion to renew in the minute book of Kehilath Jeshurun, April 15, 1903. I am grateful to Rabbi Haskel Lookstein for allowing me to study the minute books, although

I do have the feeling that he and others connected with the congregation would rather forget that Kaplan was ever there. I had the same experience when I went to the Jewish Center (before the coming of Rabbi J. J. Schachter, who has been very helpful).

49. The text of the ad is taken from *American Hebrew*, May 22, 1903. Asher is mentioned in Kaplan's journal, August 23, 1914. Kaplan mentions Asher but does not say that Asher recommended him.

50. Minute books of Kehilath Jeshurun, November 1903, p. 28.

51. Letter from Kaplan to Joshua Jaffe, November 26, 1903, Kaplan papers at Reconstructionist Rabbinical College; minute books, April 3, 1904, p. 37; Kaplan journal, August 23, 1914. The by-laws of the congregation adopted in 1903 stated that "the Rabbi must possess the necessary certificate of *Hatoras Hora'ah* and must be able to deliver sermons and discourses in the English language"; Article XIII, Section 4, By-Laws of Kehilath Jeshurun. The use of the term *minister* may go back to England, where only the chief rabbi was "rabbi" and everyone else was "minister." My thanks to Jonathan Sarna for this point.

52. See Jeffrey Gurock, "Resisters and Accommodators," *American Jewish Archives*, November 1983, for a complete discussion of this issue.

53. I have not seen a copy of the complete text, but the circular is quoted in *American Hebrew*, June 14, 1904, and in the *Jewish Gazette*, May 6, 1904.

54. Eugene Markovitz, "Henry P. Mendes: Architect of the Union of Orthodox Jewish Congregations of America," *American Jewish Historical Quarterly* 55 (1966). Reprinted in Karp, *American Jewish Experience*, Vol. 5, pp. 130–49.

55. *Sefer Ha-Takanot Shel Agudath Ha Rabbanim Ha Orthodoksim B'Amerika*, [Constitution of the United Orthodox Rabbis of America], New York 5662, p.s.

56. *Sefer Ha-Yovel Shel Agudath Ha Rabbanim D'Artzot Ha-Brit Vekanada* [Jubilee Volume of the Union of Orthodox Rabbis of the United States and Canada] New York, 1928, p. 22.

57. For the story of the funeral, see Abraham Karp, "New York Chooses a Chief Rabbi," *American Jewish Historical Quarterly* 44 (1955); *The Jewish Encyclopedia* (New York: Funk and Wagnalls Co., 1905), Vol. 9, p. 2282. See also the account by Abraham Cahan in *Grandma Never Lived in America: The New Journalism of Abraham Cahan*, ed. by Moses Rischin (Bloomington: Indiana University Press, 1985), pp. 72–73.

58. *Jewish Gazette*, May 6, 1904. The quotation condemning Levinthal is in *American Hebrew*, June 14, 1904.

59. The quotation from Schechter is in the article by Meir Ben-Horin, "Solomon Schechter to Judge Mayer Sulzberger — Part II, Letters from the Seminary Period (1902–1915)," *Jewish Social Studies* 27 (April 1965): 80. Ben-Horin notes that he asked Kaplan about the letter. Kaplan wrote back, "I am quite sure that the Kaplan to whom Schechter refers in his letter to Judge Mayer Sulzberger was not Mordecai." Ben-Horin received this on December 10, 1965. In light of the facts presented here, however, it seems quite clear that Kaplan must have forgotten the incident when he wrote to Ben-Horin. In 1972, when I interviewed Kaplan, he told me there had been a ban issued by Bernard Levinthal, but he couldn't recall the details. The reconstruction of the incident is recent, and I did not have the opportunity to share it with Kaplan before he died. It is interesting to note that Israel Levinthal, Bernard Levinthal's son, attended the Seminary, graduated in 1910, and became a prominent Conservative rabbi. Kaplan related his memory of the elder Levinthal attending his son's graduation from the seminary in 1910. Kaplan found it somewhat incongruous, "Yet . . . the old Levinthal was present and delivered a prayer in Hebrew in which he uttered fulsome praise of Schechter and invoked God's protection over the Seminary." Kaplan journal, March 10, 1926.

60. On organization of the Talmud class, minutes of Kehilath Jeshurun, November 1, 1904. Judith Epstein, who had been a student in Kaplan's school at Kehilath Jeshurun, told of the fears of the students when I interviewed her in March 1988. She liked to tell a story about a Hanukkah celebration that Kaplan was preparing with the class in which her little friend

asked her whether she was scared of Rabbi Kaplan. She answered she was not scared always, adding that she was certainly "whistling in the dark." Judith Epstein later became a member of the SAJ and a strong Kaplan supporter for many years. On Kaplan at JTS and the terror some students felt, see chapter 8.

61. *American Hebrew*, July 8, 1904. See report of Herzl's death in *American Hebrew*, July 29, 1904, which also contains a report on the union's meeting and its resolution.

62. *American Hebrew*, July 29, 1904.

63. This story was related by Judith Epstein, March 1988.

64. Aaron Rothkoff, "The American Sojourns of Ridbaz: Religious Problems within the Immigrant Community," *American Jewish Historical Quarterly* 57 (June 1968): 557–73. *Ridbaz* was the Hebrew acronym used by Rabbi David of Slutsk.

65. Minutes of Kehilath Jeshurun, October 29, 1903, p. 27. The minutes do not clearly state the fate of the old building.

66. Cited in Rothkoff, "American Sojourns," p. 562.

67. Julie Miller of the Ratner Center at the Jewish Theological Seminary brought this document to my attention. It was found among the seminary files in Kaplan's hand and addressed to the congregation with the date Ellul 29/5664. Neither the newspaper accounts nor Kaplan's diary mention this statement. We cannot be certain that he sent it.

68. Interview with Kaplan, October 1972.

69. *American Hebrew*, September 30, 1904.

70. *American Hebrew*, October 7, 1904.

71. The Reform rabbi's comment in *The Reform Advocate*, December 3, 1904. Judah David Eisenstein, *Ozar Zikhronothai: Autobiography and Memoirs* [Hebrew] (New York, 1929), p. 108. There is also a picture of the *Slutsker Rav* there. Eisenstein comparing Kaplan to a fine piano: *American Hebrew*, December 9, 1904. Judith Kaplan, Mordecai's daughter and Ira Eisenstein's wife is a fine musician and a scholar of Jewish music.

72. *American Hebrew*, January 6, 1905.

73. *American Hebrew*, December 30, 1904.

74. Kaplan journal, December 7, 1904.

CHAPTER 3

1. Kaplan journal, December 2, 1906; November 23, 1906.

2. Kaplan journal, August 21, 1905.

3. Remarks about Adler's writings: Kaplan journal, June 6, 1905, and August 20, 1905. Kaplan offered an Ethical Culture scholarship: Kaplan journal, February 19, 1917. Kaplan thinking of joining Ethical Culture: Kaplan journal, July 2, 1916. For the opinion of Ira Eisenstein, see "Ethical Culture Sees It Through," *SAJ Review* 8, no. 16 (December 28, 1928): 2. Two of Kaplan's daughters attended the Fieldston School which was run by the Ethical Culture Society. The comment on Adler's speech about Geiger is in the *American Hebrew*, May 20, 1910.

4. The details of Adler's life, unless otherwise noted, are drawn from Benny Kraut, *From Reform to Ethical Culture: The Religious Evolution of Felix Adler* (Cincinnati: Hebrew Union College Press, 1979).

5. John Herman Randall, Jr., "The Department of Philosophy," *A History of the Faculty of Philosophy at Columbia* (New York: Columbia University Press, 1947), pp. 102–46.

6. Felix Adler, *The Religion of Duty* (New York: McClure Philips and Co., 1905), p. 4. This book is in Kaplan's library, as are the following by Adler: *Life and Destiny, or Thoughts from the Ethical Lectures of Felix Adler* (New York: McClure Philips and Co., 1903); *The Essentials of Spirituality* (New York: James Pott and Co., 1905); *The Reconstruction of the Spiritual Ideal* (New York: D. Appleton and Co., 1924); *The Ethical Philosophy of Life* (New York: D. Appleton and Co., 1927). Even though I quote particular statements, the importance of Adler is in his general approach and not in any one remark.

7. Adler, *The Religion of Duty*, p. 23; see also Adler, *Life and Destiny*, p. 25.

8. Adler, *Life and Destiny*, pp. 132–33.

9. Felix Adler papers, box 100–1900E–1904B, folder E, "Lectures for Course at Columbia, February 17, 1903." These lecture notes were typed out by Adler, and each session is dated. The course is Philosophy 18, "Political and Social Ethics," which we know Kaplan took because of his registration book and also from my conversations with Kaplan.

10. Kaplan journal, May 8, 1906.

11. Adler, *The Religion of Duty*, p. 42.

12. Ibid., p. 35.

13. Ibid., p. 37.

14. Ibid., pp. 39, 40.

15. Kaplan journal, August 17, 1905. I shall deal with Ahad Ha-Am extensively in chapter 9.

16. Matthew Arnold, *Literature and Dogma* (London: MacMillan and Co., 1892), p. ix.

17. Arguing with peers: interview with Kaplan, August 1972. Doubting Mosaic authorship: Mordecai M. Kaplan, Paper read at meeting of alumni at Tannersville, July 1912, Kaplan papers at Reconstructionist Rabbinical College.

18. Arnold, *Literature and Dogma*, p. 28.

19. The inner urge: Kaplan journal, July 20, 1927. The best that is in us: Kaplan journal, May 28, 1933. Men's needs: interview with Kaplan, August 1972.

20. For a comparison of Dewey and Kaplan, see Allen Lazaroff, "Kaplan and John Dewey," *The American Judaism of Mordecai M. Kaplan*, ed. by Emanuel S. Goldsmith, Mel Scult, and Robert Seltzer (New York: New York University Press, 1990), pp. 173–97. Lazaroff does not attempt to establish Dewey's influence on Kaplan but rather compares their systems.

21. As mentioned above, the thesis is written in Kaplan's hand and runs to ninety-five pages. It is entitled "The Ethical System of Henry Sidgwick" and was submitted on February 28, 1902. It can be found in the Rare Book Collection of Columbia University Butler Library. The thesis is referred to in *Columbia University — Master's Essays 1891–1917, Vol. I* (New York: Columbia University, 1917), p. 70.

22. For a more contemporary treatment of Sidgwick, see William C. Havard, *Henry Sidgwick and Later Utilitarian Philosophy* (Gainsville, Fla.: University of Florida Press, 1959).

23. I am indebted to Professor S. Daniel Breslauer of the University of Kansas for the references in this paragraph and for the general points being made. He was very generous with his thoughts about Sidgwick and Kaplan. The quotation regarding reward and punishment is found in J. B. Schneewind, *Sidgwick's Ethics and Victorian Moral Philosophy* (Oxford: Oxford University Press, 1977), p. 27. On Sidgwick's point about God's will, see Henry Sidgwick, *The Methods of Ethics* (Chicago: University of Chicago Press, 1972), p. 504. For the point about prayer, see Schneewind, p. 27.

24. For a discussion of theurgy or magic in prayer, see Mordecai Kaplan, *Judaism without Supernaturalism* (New York: Reconstructionist Press, 1958), pp. 38–40.

25. Mordecai M. Kaplan, *The Ethnical System of Henry Sidgwick*, unpublished master's thesis, Columbia University, p. 16.

26. Ibid.

27. Ibid., p. 92.

28. Kaplan mentioned the novel and stressed its importance in an interview in 1973. The comment about its import is by Richard Haggart, "Introduction," *The Way of All Flesh* (London: Penguin Books, 1986), p. 7.

29. See Jeffrey Gurock, "Resisters and Accommodators," *American Jewish Archives* 35 (November 1983), for a fuller treatment of Margolies in terms of acculturation. I have chosen to write Margolies's middle name with an S rather than a Z because it often appears this way in the press. The school in New York City, Ramaz, is named after him.

30. For the events connected with the strike, see Gilbert Klaperman, *The Story of Yeshiva University* (New York: Macmillan Co., 1969), pp. 97–99. Apparently, the issues were not

settled in 1905–6, because two years later the students went out on strike again. An agreement was reached after a very long negotiating session that took place at Kehilath Jeshurun on May 12, 1908. At this point, it was decided that the yeshivah should become an institute of "Torah and *Hokhma* [secular knowledge]" which would produce rabbis "according to the spirit of the times." Klaperman, p. 107.

31. Kaplan journal, May 8, 1906.

32. Kaplan journal, November 24, 1906.

33. Kaplan journal, December 8, 1904.

34. Reform or half-hearted cosmopolitanism: Kaplan journal, December 5, 1906. Reaction to Friedlaender: Kaplan journal, December 2, 1906. For a fuller comparison of Friedlaender's and Kaplan's views, see below. Kaplan and Friedlaender are also treated in an essay by Baila Shargel, "Kaplan and Israel Friedlaender: Expectation and Failure," Goldsmith, Scult, and Seltzer, pp. 94–122.

35. Since these remarks regarding the attack on the Jews were written in the Kaplan journal November 26, 1906, it could not be the famous attack by Police Commissioner Bingham which led to the founding of the Kehillah in 1910.

36. Kaplan's remarks on Nietzsche in Kaplan journal, December 2, 1906. The quotations are in German, and the translations are my own.

37. Kaplan journal, August 1, 1905; May 11, 1906; May 25, 1906.

38. Kaplan journal, May 7, 1905; August 23, 1905; November 1906.

39. Kaplan journal, August 23, 1905.

40. Interview with Kaplan, June 1972.

41. Minute book of Kehilath Jeshurun, November 1906, p. 83.

42. Kaplan journal, December 31, 1906; November 25, 1906; August 23, 1905.

43. The facts in connection with Lena Rubin Kaplan are based on interviews with the daughters of Rabbi Kaplan and with Judith Epstein, whose parents were members of Kehilath Jeshurun and who attended the congregational school when Kaplan was its head. Lisa Bernstein, a niece of Lena Kaplan, talked with me in March 1988 and was also extremely helpful.

44. Minutes of Kehilath Jeshurun, April 16, 1907, p. 97 for "rabbi" being crossed out.

45. A break between Reines and Israel Kaplan in a letter from Reines to Israel Kaplan, December 1908 [Hebrew]. The *Smicha* letter from Rabbi Reines is among Kaplan's papers. The congregational welcome in Minutes of Kehilath Jeshurun, October 18, 1908, 125.

46. Minutes of Kehilath Jeshurun, October 1909, p. 145.

CHAPTER 4

1. See "The Charter of the Seminary—Inaugural Address, Delivered November 20, 1902," *Seminary Addresses and Other Papers by Solomon Schechter* (New York: Burning Bush Press, 1959).

2. *American Hebrew*, June 3, 1910, for Schechter as Ram Dass. His capacity for anger: "Tribute of Dr. Solomon Solis-Cohen" [to Solomon Schechter], *Students Annual, Jewish Theological Seminary, May 1916* (New York: Jewish Theological Seminary, 1916), p. 59. Student with jokes ready: Moses J. Abels, "Teacher and Friend," *Students Annual*, 1916, p. 46. Sparkling conversation: Dr. Herman Abramowitz, "A True Jewish Scholar," *Students Annual*, 1916, p. 57. Schechter saying Kaplan was always serious: Kaplan journal, May 27, 1929.

3. Kaplan journal, December 15, 1927.

4. Drachman was valued by Schechter because of his "kosher English," Meir Ben-Horin, "Solomon Schechter to Judge Mayer Sulzberger: Part II, Letters from the Seminary Period 1902–1915," *Jewish Social Studies* 27 (April 1965): 76. Schechter on Mendes: Solomon Schechter to Cyrus Adler, March 26, 1902, Solomon Schechter papers, Jewish Theological Seminary. Drachman's bitterness about the Seminary: B. Drachman, *The Unfailing Light: Memoirs of an American Rabbi* (New York: Rabbinical Council of America, 1948), pp. 260–61;

his son, who edited this biography, noted Drachman's bitterness about being fired in 1909. The Seminary pleaded financial considerations, but this was a thin disguise. Schechter's negative evaluation: Solomon Schechter to Albert H. Jessel, August 5, 1912, Schechter papers, JTS. See also Jeffrey Gurock, "Resisters and Accommodators: Varieties of Orthodox Rabbis in America, 1886–1983," *American Jewish Archives* 35 (November 1983).

5. See Eli Ginzberg, *Keeper of the Law: Louis Ginzberg* (Philadelphia: Jewish Publication Society, 1966).

6. Kaplan journal, April 25, 1915.

7. On Friedlaender's appearance: Baila R. Shargel, *Israel Friedlaender and the Transformation of European Thought in America*, unpublished dissertation, Jewish Theological Seminary, 1982, p. 18. See her *Practical Dreamer: Israel Friedlaender and the Shaping of American Judaism* (New York: Jewish Theological Seminary, 1985) for a complete study of Friedlaender. On ignoring the Pentateuch: Kaplan, interview, June 1972. On Friedlaender's intentions: Israel Friedlaender to Solomon Schechter, August 7, 1903, as cited in Shargel, *Israel Friedlaender*, p. 38. For a comparison of Kaplan and Friedlaender, see Baila Shargel, "Kaplan and Friedlaender: Expectation and Failure," *The American Judaism of Mordecai Kaplan*, ed. Emanuel S. Goldsmith, Mel Scult, and Robert Seltzer (New York: New York University Press, 1990), pp. 94–122.

8. On registration, see *New Era Illustrated Magazine*, 4, no. 3, February 1904, p. 97. On downtown branch: Mordecai Kaplan, "The Teacher's Institute and Its Affiliated Departments," *The Jewish Theological Seminary of America: A Semi-Centennial Volume*, ed. by Cyrus Adler (New York: Jewish Theological Seminary, 1939), p. 122. Schechter's remark on location of the Seminary in Solomon Schechter to Cyrus Adler, May 22, 1907, Adler papers, American Jewish Historical Society. Schechter's report on the staff: "Report to Board of Trustees: April 26, 1908, by Solomon Schechter," in Marshall papers, box 20, American Jewish Archives.

9. On the committee, see Solomon Schechter to Adolphus Solomons, November 10, 1908, Schechter papers, JTS. On the Jewish Teachers College Fund, see Jacob H. Schiff to Louis Marshall, August 3, 1909, in Marshall papers, box 24, AJA. On the model school downtown, see Solomon Schechter to Adolphus Solomons, April 9, 1909, Schechter papers, JTS.

10. Adler's concern, in Cyrus Adler to Louis Marshall, May 6, 1909, Marshall papers, box 24, AJA. Kohn's refusal, in Solomon Schechter to Louis Marshall, June 17, 1909, Marshall papers, box 44, AJA. Before Schiff came up with the Teachers Fund, Schechter had offered the "Management of the Teachers Course" to Max Schloessinger. Schloessinger had been employed at Hebrew Union College and left in a dispute with Kaufman Kohler over the issue of Zionism. See Solomon Schechter to Louis Marshall, April 30, 1908, Marshall papers, box 44, AJA. Schloessinger refused the offer primarily because sufficient funds were not available to do the job right, he said; Max Schloessinger to Louis Marshall, May 22, 1908, Marshall papers, box 20, AJA.

11. For Henrietta Szold and Ginzberg, as well as her relationship with the Jewish Publication Society, see Jonathan Sarna, *JPS: The Americanization of Jewish Culture, 1888–1988* (Philadelphia: Jewish Publication Society, 1989).

12. Interview with Kaplan, June 1972.

13. "Speech Delivered to Seminary Alumni — June 1909," in Kaplan archive at Reconstructionist Rabbinical College. The speech can be found in published form as "Judaism and Nationality," *The Maccabaean* 17 (August 1909): 59–64. This article probably was Kaplan's first publication, although there is an M. Kaplan who is listed as a writer of some small articles in the *Jewish Encyclopedia*.

14. It is not really known whether Adler wrote negatively to Schechter. For the Schechter remark but not the Adler negative remark to which it is allegedly a response, see Moshe Davis, "Jewish Religious Life and Institutions in America," *The Jews — Their History, Culture and Religion*, ed. by Louis Finkelstein (New York: Harper and Brothers, 1949), Vol. 1, p. 537. That Schechter did consult Adler, see Solomon Schechter to Louis Marshall, June 17, 1909,

Marshall papers, box 44, AJA. This letter also contains the other details about the interview and Schechter's remark about Kaplan being strong. It is also probable that Adler heard Kaplan's speech, because he was on the same program; Charles Hoffman to Louis Marshall, December 28, 1909, Marshall papers, box 24, AJA. The program consisted of Solomon Schechter, who spoke on "Recent Hebrew Literature," Cyrus Adler on "The Part of the Alumni Association in the Promotion of Judaism in America," and Kaplan, whose speech was entitled "Nationalism as a Religious Dogma." At this meeting, Kaplan also was elected to the executive committee of the Alumni Association along with C. H. Kauvar, Jacob Kohn, and Julius Greenstone. See *American Hebrew*, June 11, 1909.

15. Solomon Schechter to Cyrus Adler, June 29, 1909, Schechter papers, JTS.

16. See Solomon Schechter to Louis Marshall, October 13, 1909, Marshall papers, box 44, AJA.

17. M. M. Kaplan, "The Teacher's Institute," *The Jewish Theological Seminary Semi-Centennial Volume*, ed. by Cyrus Adler (New York: Jewish Theological Seminary, 1939), p. 125; see also the announcement of Kaplan's appointment in *American Hebrew*, July 16, 1909. The Seminary paid no rent to the Uptown Talmud Torah and put the president of its board on the board of the Teachers College. It is clear that the arrangement was inadequate. See Solomon Schechter to Louis Marshall, August 2, 1909, Marshall papers, box 44, AJA. For more on the Uptown Talmud Torah, see Jeffrey S. Gurock, *When Harlem Was Jewish 1870–1930* (New York: Columbia University Press, 1979), pp. 98–110.

18. Harmon H. Goldstone and Martha Dalrymple, *A Guide to New York City's Landmarks and Historical Districts* (New York: Simon and Schuster, 1974), p. 149.

19. The Hebrew Technical Institute was a vocational high school for boys. See *Jewish Communal Register of New York City 1917–1918*, p. 657, for a description of the school and a picture of the building. The building still stands and is not part of New York University. The teachers had a library, an office, and a number of classrooms in the annex. Kaplan's brothers-in-law contributed six thousand dollars toward the purchase of books for the library. Kaplan journal, June 17, 1916.

20. Facts on Asher in Israel Goldstein, *A Century of Judaism in New York — Bnai Jeshurun 1825–1925, New York's Oldest Ashkenazi Congregation* (New York: Congregation Bnai Jeshurun, 1930), pp. 225–26. Some of the facts in this paragraph are from an interview with Kaplan, June 1972. The teaching of homiletics was a rather low priority at the Seminary, as evidenced by the fact that when Asher was sick, Schechter appointed two senior students to take his place. "Report of Solomon Schechter to the Board of Directors, November 21, 1909," Marshall papers, box 24, AJA.

21. For the full account of the club, see Moshe Davis, "Israel Friedlaender's Minute Book of the *Achavah* Club (1909–1912)," *Mordecai M. Kaplan Jubilee Volume — On the Occasion of His Seventieth Birthday, English Section* (New York: Jewish Theological Seminary, 1953), pp. 157–215. The Kaplan quotation is on p. 190.

22. Ibid., p. 185. Davis asserts that the idea for this speech came from Kaplan, but he offers no documentation. Davis interviewed Kaplan for his article, and it may be that Kaplan himself is the source.

23. For a more complete exposition of "national Judaism," see Deborah Dash Moore, "A New American Judaism," *Like All Nations? The Life and Legacy of Judah L. Magnes*, ed. by William M. Brinner and Moses Rischin (Albany: State University of New York Press, 1987), pp. 41–57. Kaplan's remark is in a letter to Phineas Israeli, January 31, 1909. I am grateful to Nathan Israeli, his son, for permission to quote from this letter.

24. Kaplan's remarks to Schechter: Mordecai Kaplan to Solomon Schechter, March 18, 1911, Solomon Schechter papers, JTS. See Israel Friedlaender to Solomon Schechter, November 3, 1910, Schechter papers, JTS.

25. *Shir Ha-Shirim Rabbah* mentioned in Kaplan journal, June 9, 1915. Hundreds of cards are among the Kaplan papers with verses from this Midrash. On Kaplan's hope of publication: Mordecai Kaplan to Louis Marshall, Marshall papers, Box 44, JTS. The Frankfurt

manuscript was lost, and according to Dr. Samuel Lachs, Kaplan's story of the manuscript is the only one in existence. In 1913, Kaplan wrote to Marshall asking for his help in securing a copy of a Vatican manuscript of *Shir Ha-Shirim Rabbah*. Kaplan thought Marshall might know the American ambassador in Rome who would help in getting a copy of it. The faculty at the Seminary knew of the Kaplan work and turned to him when they were interested in *Shir Ha-Shirim Rabbah*. In November 1940, for example, Louis Finkelstein, the president of the Seminary, wrote to Kaplan asking him about a particular phrase and the way it appeared in the Frankfurt manuscript. Louis Finkelstein to Mordecai Kaplan, November 25, 1940, Kaplan Archive, RRC.

26. Schechter's letter in the Kaplan journal, November 21, 1915. Kaplan's translation was one of the Schiff Classics published by the Jewish Publication Society: *Mesillat Yesharim — The Path of the Upright by Moses Hayim Luzzatto: A Critical Edition Provided with a Translation and Notes* by Mordecai M. Kaplan (Philadelphia: Jewish Publication Society, 1936). For more details on *Mesillat Yesharim*, see Jonathan Sarna, *JPS — The Americanization of Jewish Culture 1888–1988: A Centennial History of the Jewish Publication Society* (Philadelphia: Jewish Publication Society, 1989), pp. 157–58.

27. Kaplan related to me the matter of his becoming head of the Seminary in 1972. It may be, however, that he said this because of what he himself wrote in the journal, which is by no means clear. In his later life, Kaplan had the habit of reading over the journal, and so his memory is very heavily influenced by what he wrote, in this case on September 15, 1915. It is also quite clear that Ginzberg believed Schechter had him in mind. See Eli Ginzberg, *The Keeper of the Law: Louis Ginzberg* (Philadelphia: Jewish Publication Society, 1966), p. 133. In 1977, Eli Ginzberg wrote, "my father wanted to be Schechter's successor and resented the fact that he was not the choice of his colleagues or the Board." Eli Ginzberg, "The Seminary Family," *Perspectives on Jews and Judaism: Essays in Honor of Wolfe Kelman*, ed. by Arthur A. Chiel (New York: Rabbinical Assembly, 1978), p. 118. Ginzberg had become very close to Szold, who expected that they would marry. Ginzberg rejected Szold and married a woman he met on a trip abroad. Szold recorded her belief that because Ginzberg rejected her, Schechter came to feel that he was not worthy of the presidency of the seminary. In her words, "I always felt that he [Schechter] would not be pleased if came to pass that Ginzberg married me. Instead of which I now hear that he [Schechter] says that if he [Ginzberg] had married me the successorship to the seminary would have been settled so far as he [Schechter] was concerned. He as my husband would have been the choice. But not as things are now. With me he would have trusted him fully; without me and after his treatment of me he trusts him not at all. Momma said the same — 'not only has he lost you, he has lost the presidency as well.'" For the full story of Szold and Ginzberg, see Irving Fineman, *Woman of Valor: The Life of Henrietta Szold 1860–1945* (New York: Simon and Schuster, 1961). Friedlaender also believed he was passed over; see Shargel, *Israel Friedlaender*, p. 131.

28. Mordecai M. Kaplan, "The Influences That Have Shaped My Life," *Reconstructionist* 8 (June 26, 1942). Speech to the alumni, "Paper Read at Meeting of Alumni at Tannersville, July 1912," RRC. In an interview in 1972, Kaplan asserted that Schechter did not believe the Torah was given at Mount Sinai. When pressed for documentation, however, he gave none.

29. The paper on the Torah: Mordecai M. Kaplan, "The Supremacy of the Torah," *Students Annual of the Jewish Theological Seminary of America*, 1914, pp. 180–92. Remark on the students: Kaplan journal, August 23, 1914. Schechter's warning: Kaplan journal, June 9, 1915. Greenstone reaction to the article: Julius Greenstone to Mordecai Kaplan, July 8, 1914, Kaplan archive, RRC.

30. Mordecai M. Kaplan, "What Judaism Is Not," *Menorah Journal* 1 (October 1915): 208–16; "What Is Judaism?" *Menorah Journal* 1 (December 1915): 309–18. Schechter's remark to Kaplan is from an interview, June 1972.

31. Mordecai Kaplan to Alvin Johnson, April 30, 1933, Kaplan archives, RRC. The entry concerning the letter is in Kaplan journal, May 1, 1933. The full dedication is in Kaplan's book, *The Religion of Ethical Nationhood* (New York: Macmillan Co., 1970). It reads, "To

the memory of Ahad Ha-Am [Asher Ginzberg] who revealed to me the spiritual reality of the Jewish people, of Solomon Schechter who granted me the opportunity to transmit it to my students and of Louis Dembitz Brandeis, who pleaded for ethical nationhood in American life."

32. Kaplan fancied himself somewhat of an artist and sculpted a likeness of his father which is really quite good. During his last days in an old age home in Riverdale New York this sculpture and a picture of his father were two of his most prized possessions.

33. Friedlaender had gone on a fact-finding mission to Eastern Europe in 1919 for the Joint Distribution Committee. In July 1920, he was murdered in the Ukraine along with a rabbi and a social worker who were traveling with him.

34. On the Teachers' Institute generally, see M. M. Kaplan, "The Teachers Institute and Its Affiliated Departments," *Jewish Theological Seminary Semi-Centennial Volume.* For early figures on the Teachers' Institute, see letter from Solomon Schechter to Louis Marshall, October 13, 1909, in Marshall papers, box 44, AJA. See also Mordecai Kaplan, "The Teachers' Institute," *Students Annual of the Jewish Theological Seminary*, 1915, p. 62. Other teacher training schools established at the time were Teachers' Institute of Mizrachi (1917), the Baltimore Hebrew College (1919), and the Boston Hebrew Teachers' College (1921). Alexander Dushkin's *Jewish Education in New York City* (New York: Bureau of Jewish Education, 1918) is a very important source for this period. See also Cyrus Adler folder in Schiff papers, box 449, AJA, for annual reports. Material on the Friedlaender classes is found in Chipkin file of Kaplan letters at RRC, including a report entitled "Memorandum concerning the Israel Friedlaender Classes Prepared by Israel Chipkin, June 22, 1931," as well as a letter from Chipkin to Kaplan, January 20, 1928.

35. On the Seminary College and Leo Honor, see letter from Israel Chipkin to Kaplan, July 13, 1926, at RRC. Material on the matter of the budget from interview with Samuel Dinin, September 1988. Dinin was registrar of the Teachers' Institute for many years and taught education. The diploma matter is mentioned in a letter from Joseph Abrahams to Kaplan, April 19, 1932, at RRC. On the matter of the Teachers' Institute being detached from the Seminary, see *Bulletin of the Alumni Association of the Seminary College of Jewish Studies*, 75th-anniversary issue, 1984, "Professor Mordecai M. Kaplan 1880–1983," by Samuel Dinin.

36. See Kaplan journal, February 4, 1929, and February 11, 1929. The student would receive a bachelor of science degree from Columbia and a bachelor of Jewish pedagogy from the Seminary. This combined program also entailed supervised practice teaching. For more details, see Kaplan, "The Teachers Institute," pp. 137–38.

37. On Kaplan's change of title to dean, see Kaplan diary, October 20, 1930, where he expresses his feeling that it was an afterthought rather than a carefully considered gesture of honor. The Teachers' Institute student newspaper of the early 1930s was written in Hebrew with articles on modern Hebrew writers (at New York Public Library). Kaplan attributes the changeover to Hebrew to Moshe Levine. All classes were in English when the school began, and Hebrew was introduced over a number of years.

38. For Kaplan's Hebrew style, see, for example, his essays in *The Foundations of Jewish Education in America: A Collection of Essays to Mark the Thirty-fifth Anniversary of the Teachers Institute of the Jewish Theological Seminary of America* [Hebrew], ed. by Zvi Scharftein (New York: Teachers Institute, 1946). Kaplan has a general introductory essay on "The Goal of Jewish Education in America" and an essay on "The Teaching of *Tanakh* in Our Time." There is also an essay by Judith K. Eisenstein on "Music in Jewish Education." Kaplan taught in Hebrew at the Hebrew University from 1937–1939 and at this time also kept his diary in Hebrew. See Kaplan journal, September 1925, for opening exercises at Teachers' Institute in Hebrew. On Kaplan preparing by reading Hebrew and lack of courage to speak English, see Kaplan journal, December 16, 1928. For students complaining and switching to English plus Benderly's remark, see Kaplan journal, January 27, 1929. On Kaplan fantasizing about

creating a scandal, Kaplan journal, December 3, 1928. Bavli's remarks are in Hillel Bavli, *The Image of an Institution: Memoirs and Observations about the Teachers Institute of the Jewish Theological Seminary of America* [Hebrew] (New York: Teachers Institute, 1959), p. 19.

39. Interview with Samuel Dinin, September 1988. On Kaplan's depression over teaching of *Chumash*, see Kaplan journal, April 2, 1930.

40. For faculty, see bulletins of the Seminary for this period. See Dr. Albert Schoolman, "Leo Honor 1894–1956," *Jewish Education* 28 (fall 1957). On Israel Chipkin, see *Jewish Education* 27 (fall 1956), where the whole issue is devoted to him. For individual portraits of Moshe Levine and Ovsay, see Bavli, *The Image of an Institution.*

41. Regarding the heavy schedules, in 1935, Bavli taught twelve periods in the Teachers' Institute, six in the Seminary College, and six in Friedlaender classes; Halkin taught six in TI, 8 in the college, and six in Friedlaender classes. These figures are taken from class schedules in Dinin folder of Kaplan letters, RRC. On the matter of budget, Judith Eisenstein reports that in 1931 she did not receive any salary at all though she was teaching full-time; interview, October 1988. On having little patience with details: Kaplan journal, May 15, 1929. Kaplan on need for religion in Jewish schools: *Jewish Tribune*, July 4, 1930. On modern Hebrew literature without permanent values: Kaplan journal, January 14, 1929.

42. This analysis is Kaplan's and is drawn from Kaplan journal, May 1922.

43. On Magnes, see Arthur Goren, *New York Jews and the Quest for Community: The Kehillah Experiment 1908–1922* (New York: Columbia University Press, 1970), pp. 85, 248. More on Magnes may be found in the introduction in Arthur Goren, *Dissenter in Zion: From the Writings of Judah Magnes* (Cambridge: Harvard University Press, 1982).

44. Kaplan's remark about Magnes and the Seminary circle in "Transcript of Interview with Mordecai Kaplan," September 27, 1960, Elitzur, interviewer, Institute for Contemporary Jewry, Oral History Project, Hebrew University. Later in his career, Kaplan enjoyed discussing the Torah portion with a colleague or an ex-student on a regular basis. Magnes was among the earliest with whom Kaplan shared his thoughts. He may have been the earliest companion to join Kaplan on his walks around the Central Park Reservoir.

45. Theodore A. Bingham, "Foreign Criminals in New York," *North American Review* 188 (September 1908): 384–94, as cited in Goren, *New York Jews*, p. 25. All material on the *Kehillah* is drawn from Goren unless otherwise noted.

46. See minutes of Kehilath Jeshurun, February 4, 1909. The groups being represented are found in Goren, *New York Jews*, p. 49.

47. On Schechter and the executive committee, see Solomon Schechter to Louis Marshall, March 2, 1909, Marshall papers, box 44, AJA. On Schechter and the social workers, see Solomon Schechter to Cyrus Adler, January 14, 1910, Schechter papers, JTS.

48. *American Hebrew*, March 4, 1910.

49. Ibid., p. 459.

50. Goren, *New York Jews*, p. 88.

51. Nathan H. Winter, *Jewish Education in a Pluralist Society: Samson Benderly and Jewish Education in the United States* (New York: New York University Press, 1966), chapters 3 and 4.

52. Comments on Benderly in "From America," *Ha-Shiloah* 12 (July–December 1903), as cited in Winter, *Jewish Education*, p. 43. Many years later, Judah Magnes remembered reading about Benderly's efforts in *Ha-Shiloah* in 1903. See Benderly's "Life and Works – A Tribute from Dr. J. L. Magnes," *Jewish Education* 20 (Summer 1949): 4.

53. On the trustees of the bureau, see Magnes papers, P3/F 1-L:22, memo, April 1910, AJA. For Kaplan's remark on mutual need, see Mordecai M. Kaplan, "The Impact of Dr. Benderly's Personality," *Jewish Education* 20 (Summer 1949): 16. Kaplan's remark on Benderly and Ahad Ha-Am is also in this article.

54. The 1914 address is in *Jewish Theological Seminary, Students Annual*, 1915, p. 62. On the upgrading of the entrants, see Kaplan, "The Teachers Institute," p. 127.

55. Alexander M. Dushkin, *Living Bridges: Memoirs of an Educator* (Jerusalem: Keter Publishing House, 1975), pp. 9–10. The "Benderly boys" included Rebecca Aronson. Being called "boys" betrays the sexism of the period.

56. On Kaplan having little faith, see Kaplan journal, October 3, 1914. The members of the first group were Rebecca Aronson, who eventually married Barnett Brickner (who became a leading Reform rabbi); Isaac Berkson, an important theorist of Jewish education who became a professor of education at City College; Ben H. Birnbaum; Israel Chipkin, who became registrar at the Teachers' Institute, helped organize the American Association for Jewish Education, was director of Jewish Education Association of New York, and was editor of *Jewish Education;* and Alexander Dushkin, who was very active at the bureau, organized the journal *The Jewish Teacher*, taught and helped organize the Department of Education at the Hebrew University, was director of the Bureau of Jewish Education in Chicago, helped to found Hebrew Teachers College in Chicago, and was editor of *Jewish Education;* Leo Honor, who taught at Teachers' Institute, was director of the Board of Jewish Education in Chicago, and later became professor of education at Dropsie College in Philadelphia; Marvin Isaacs; Louis Prashker; and Ben Rosen. The names of those in the group are listed in Kaplan's pocket calendar for 1913, which is among his papers at RRC. The "ceaseless chatter" comment is from Alexander Dushkin, "The Personality of Samson Benderly – His Life and Influence," *Jewish Education* 20 (Summer 1949): 10. Benderly as the Hasidic *rebbe* is from Dushkin, *Living Bridges*, p. 12.

57. On Kaplan's great satisfaction with the Benderly boys, see Kaplan journal, October 4, 1914. "Good Jewish teachers" is from Samson Benderly, "The Problem of Jewish Education in New York City," *American Hebrew*, March 24, 1911, p. 605, as cited in Winter, *Jewish Education*, p. 55. Statement of aim of Jewish education is in "A Brief Summary of the Decisions Arrived at by the Thirty-One Conferences Held by the Talmud Torah Principals in New York, 1912, Bureau of Education," which appears as Appendix D in Winter, p. 212. On Conservative rabbis accusing Benderly, see Dushkin, *Living Bridges*, p. 19.

58. Kaplan journal, May 5, 1915.

59. Kaplan journal, October 4, 1914. Part of this appears in Kaplan's article in *Jewish Education* in 1949. Regarding the matter of doctorates from the first Benderly group, we may note the following publications based on Ph.D. dissertations: Alexander Dushkin, *Jewish Education in New York City* (New York: Bureau of Jewish Education, 1918); Isaac Berkson, *Theories of Americanization: A Critical Study* (New York: Columbia University, 1920).

60. For the Benderly report of May 1911, see Magnes papers, P3/F 1-L:23, AJA. The Benderly statement about expanding the Teachers' Institute is in report of February 8, 1911, Bureau of Jewish Education, Magnes papers, AJA. See exchange between Magnes and Schiff on Benderly's scheme for an educational fund. The total yearly budget Benderly requested was one hundred thousand dollars. Magnes asked Schiff to donate half the money on condition that Magnes come up with the rest. Schiff reacted quickly, asserting that it would take an endowment of two million dollars to generate such a yearly budget. The ever-generous Schiff was willing to donate ten thousand dollars a year for ten years to such a fund. See letters from J. L. Magnes to Jacob Schiff, March 9, 1911, and Jacob Schiff to J. L. Magnes, March 20, 1911, in Magnes papers, AJA. For Schechter's remark about the Teachers' Institute, see letter from Solomon Schechter to Louis Marshall, August 5, 1915, Marshall papers, Box 44, AJA.

61. Kaplan journal, May 27, 1915.

62. Goren, *New York Jews*, p. 105.

63. Mordecai M. Kaplan, "The Function of the Jewish School," *Jewish Teacher* 1, no. 1, pp. 9, 11, 12. Benderly created the Jewish Teachers Association of New York which published the journal *Jewish Teacher.* The journal was edited by Alexander Dushkin with Isaac Berkson serving as business manager and Kaplan, Julius Greenstone, and Harry Friedenwald as members of the advisory board. The journal appeared until 1924. In 1926, the National Council

for Jewish Education was organized. It consisted of school principals, executive heads of bureaus, and professors in teachers' colleges. In 1929, it began publishing *Jewish Education* with Alexander Dushkin as editor.

64. The day before Schechter died, Kaplan had a long talk with him. He was complaining that the Seminary receives little recognition from such as Warburg and that he is "afraid to invite lecturers on philanthropic matters because they inevitably stress their dissociation from the Seminary and what it stands for." Kaplan journal, November 18, 1915.

CHAPTER 5

1. See Moshe Davis, *The Emergence of Conservative Judaism: The Historical School in 19th Century America* (Philadelphia: Jewish Publication Society, 1963).

2. The account of the United Synagogue, unless otherwise noted, is based on the unpublished dissertation of Herbert Rosenblum, *The Founding of the United Synagogue of America, 1913*, Brandeis University, 1970. Schechter's being of two minds is a general deduction from all the evidence. For the remark about a separatist movement, see Cyrus Adler to Solomon Schechter, January 28, 1912, as cited in Rosenblum, p. 205. For the remark about detracting from the Seminary's authority, see Cyrus Adler to Solomon Schechter, February 2, 1912, Solomon Schechter papers, Jewish Theological Seminary.

3. For Kaplan's involvement, see the annual reports of the United Synagogue, 1913–1920. The incident with Hertz comes from an interview with the author, 1973.

4. For Adler on seating, see *Cyrus Adler — Selected Letters*, ed. Ira Robinson (Philadelphia: The Jewish Publication Society of America, 1985), vol. 1, Cyrus Adler to Morris Teller, September 24, 1916, p. 319. For a general discussion on separate seating, see Jonathan D. Sarna, "The Debate over Mixed Seating in the American Synagogue," *The American Synagogue: A Sanctuary Transformed*, ed. by Jack Wertheimer (Cambridge: Cambridge University Press, 1987), pp. 363–95.

5. For Schechter's remarks at the first convention, see *United Synagogue of America Report* 1, 1913, pp. 18, 19. For Schechter's remark to Magnes, see Solomon Schechter to Judah Magnes, July 12, 1911, Magnes papers, Central Archives for the History of the Jewish People, Hebrew University. Regarding the perception that the United Synagogue was Orthodox and Conservative at the same time, the *American Israelite*, January 1921, contains an article announcing that the United Synagogue had delegates "representing the Orthodox and Conservative elements of American Jewry"; *American Israelite* 67, January 13, 1921.

6. *Young Men's Hebrew Association, Fiftieth Anniversary Bulletin*, 1924; *YMHA Bulletin*, February 1913, p. 1; *YMHA Bulletin*, September 1913.

7. Report to the board, "Minutes of the Board of Directors of the YMHA," May 25, 1915, Reconstructionist Rabbinical College. Kaplan also invited well-known Reform rabbis to speak on Friday evenings. See invitation to Rabbi Hyman Enelow, Enelow Papers, American Jewish Archives. On the observant young men, see Kaplan journal, February 8, 1915.

8. Kaplan journal, March 4, 1915; October 21, 1914.

9. On forming a group: Mordecai Kaplan to Felix Warburg, November 1, 1913, Kaplan Archives, RRC. The article appeared in *YMHA Bulletin*, October 1914, p. 3. The article is unsigned, so we do not know whether the author is Kaplan. The sentiments do represent Kaplan's attitude.

10. *YMHA Bulletin*, February 1914, pp. 17, 18. This issue included a summary of the previous year's articles.

11. Horace Kallen's theories on cultural pluralism are exactly parallel to Kaplan's and were published at the same time. See, for example, Kallen's "Nationalist and the Hyphenated America," *Menorah Journal* 1 (April 1915): 779–86.

12. *YMHA Bulletin*, November 1913, p. 11. This issue records the attendance at the high holiday services run by Kaplan at about six hundred people. Quotations here are from

the text of the speech. It has no title, only "Spoken the Second Day of Rosh Hashona, September 10, 1915 at the YMHA Services," and is found in the Kaplan archive at RRC.

13. Kaplan journal, April 23, 1915. The formulation here (the power that makes for freedom) is, of course, familiar from Kaplan's later work, particularly *The Meaning of God in Modern Jewish Religion.*

14. Kaplan joined the board in February 1913. A full year before, Warburg had written to him about joining the board. For some reason, Kaplan hesitated. Felix Warburg to M. M. Kaplan, February 7, 1912; and Felix Warburg to M. M. Kaplan, February 24, 1913, RRC. During the first year, Kaplan attended meetings regularly, but then his attendance fell off. From 1916 to 1919, he attended a few times a year. See minutes of the Board of Directors of the YMHA, 1913–1919 in the YMHA archives.

15. Mordecai M. Kaplan to Felix Warburg, March 23, 1915, RRC.

16. Kaplan journal, April 23, 1915; January 26, 1915; November 4, 1914. The Straus family owned Macy's. Isidore Straus, an active member of the Jewish community, had perished on the *Titanic.* The losses of the family were also losses to the YMHA. In May 1912, the *YMHA Bulletin* noted the tragedy of the *Titanic* and the death of the prominent Jews aboard: Benjamin Guggenheim, Emil Tausig, George Rosenheim, and Isidore Straus. The story about the last few minutes was told in the bulletin: "The last boat was being launched with a place for Mrs. Straus. Because of his age, a place was offered to her husband. 'I'll stay with the other men. I'll not take a woman's place.' This decision brought his wife to his side and they perished together."

17. For an account of the dinner, see Kaplan journal, April 3, 1915. The name "Society for the Advancement of Judaism" seems to have been used at B'nai Jeshurun, the congregation Magnes was briefly associated with. See *American Hebrew*, February 10, 1911. He stayed at this congregation for a year or so and then apparently used the name SAJ for the organization Warburg headed.

18. *YMHA Bulletin*, February 1914, p. 31; Kaplan journal, April 20, 1915.

19. Kaplan journal, June 29, 1916. Lehman was one of the judges for the Rosenwald contest, with Kaplan's essay *Judaism as a Civilization* being in dispute among them. For the details, see chapter 13 herein.

20. See Hyman Goldstein, "A History of the Young Israel Movement," *Jewish Forum* 9 (December 1926): 529–32; and Rabbi David Warshaw, *A History of the Young Israel Movement 1912–1937*, unpublished master's essay, Bernard Revel Graduate School, 1974.

21. *American Hebrew*, January 19, 1913.

22. Goldstein, "A History," p. 530.

23. The 1926 account by Goldstein quoted above points to Friedlaender, "who used his every influence and gave unstintingly of his time and energy to the work of the organization; p. 532. Goldstein does not mention Kaplan, but this article appeared in an Orthodox journal in 1926, when Kaplan was already persona non grata in the Orthodox community. On the Endeavor Society, see references in Jeffrey Gurock, "Resisters and Accommodators: Varieties of Orthodox Rabbis in America, 1886–1983," *American Jewish Archives* 35 (November 1983): 169.

24. Jacob Schiff to Bernard Richards, January 31, 1916, Brandeis papers, as quoted in Melvin Urofsky, *American Zionism from Herzl to the Holocaust* (Garden City, N.Y.: Doubleday, 1975), p. 173.

25. Kaplan journal, July 18, 1916.

26. Mordecai Kaplan to Bernard Richards, November 12, 1920, Kaplan papers, American Jewish Archives. Adler's remark on the congress is in a letter from Cyrus Adler to Judge Mack, July 2, 1918, Schiff Papers, box 463, AJA.

27. Mordecai Kaplan to Dr. Harry Friedenwald, April 23, 1916, Kaplan papers, box 2523, AJA.

28. On the second generation, see Deborah Dash Moore, *At Home in America: Second Generation New York Jews* (New York: Columbia University Press, 1981), as well as Arnold M. Eisen on the intellectual history of American Jewry in the second and third generations, *The Chosen People in America* (Bloomington: Indiana University Press, 1983). The best work on the immigrants in New York is Moses Rischin, *The Promised City: New York's Jews 1870–1914* (New York: Corinth Books, 1964).

29. For some interesting parallels to Kaplan (e.g., Horace Kallen, Morris Raphael Cohen, and Lionel Trilling), see Susanne Klingenstein, *Jews in the American Academy 1900–1940: The Dynamics of Intellectual Assimilation* (New Haven: Yale University Press, 1991).

30. For the concept of latent and manifest function, see, for example, Robert K. Merton, *Social Theory and Social Structure* (Chicago: Free Press, 1957). On function as essence, see Kaplan journal, February 1917.

31. Center sermon, January 1920, RRC.

32. Mordecai Kaplan, "What Is Judaism," *Menorah Journal* 1 (December 1915): 309.

33. Center sermons, March 29, 1919, RRC. I am indebted to Barbara Gish for the general thrust of this paragraph.

34. For examples in which scholars ascribe influence to Dewey, see *Mordecai M. Kaplan: An Evaluation*, ed. by Ira Eisenstein and Eugene Kohn (New York: Jewish Reconstructionist Foundation, 1952), p. 19; articles on Kaplan in the *Encyclopedia Judaica*; and Charles S. Liebman, "Reconstructionism in American Life," *American Jewish Yearbook 1970* (New York: American Jewish Committee, 1970), p. 51. It is also quite interesting to note that Alan Lazaroff's recent study of Dewey and Kaplan compares and contrasts the two men but makes no attempt to establish Dewey's influence over Kaplan. See Allan Lazaroff, "John Dewey and Mordecai Kaplan," *The American Judaism of Mordecai Kaplan*, ed. by Emanuel Goldsmith, Mel Scult, and Robert Seltzer (New York: New York University Press, 1990), pp. 173–97. Dewey's books: *Democracy and Education* (1916), *Reconstruction in Philosophy* (1920), *Human Nature and Conduct* (1922), and *A Common Faith* (1934). On the group studying James: Kaplan journal, February 1915.

35. The manuscript "The Meaning of Religion" is in Kaplan's own hand and is among his private papers. The comment cited here is on p. 3, RRC.

36. "What Judaism Is Not," *Menorah Journal* 1 (October 1915): 215; Kaplan journal, August 1914; Mordecai M. Kaplan, "The Relation of Religion to Nationalism," *SAJ Review* 8 (October 1928): 22.

37. James, *Pragmatism and Four Essays from The Meaning of Truth* (New York: Meridian Books, 1955), p. 145.

38. Kaplan journal, January 26, 1914; *Menorah Journal* 1, p. 210.

39. James, *Pragmatism*, p. 59; letter to Henry Hurwitz, March 17, 1916, RRC. See parallel ideas of Israel Friedlaender in Baila Shargel, *Israel Friedlaender: Practical Dreamer* (New York: The Jewish Theological Seminary of America, 1985).

40. From notes for a course Kaplan gave at Columbia. The notes are entitled "Outline of Lectures of a Course Given at Teachers College," February 23, 1917, p. 5, Kaplan papers, RRC. On the moral order of the universe: Kaplan journal, December 8, 1905.

41. Alfred N. Whitehead, *Religion in the Making* (New York: World Publishing Co., 1960), p. 16. For a discussion of the individual and society, see Peter L. Berger, *Invitation to Sociology: A Humanistic Perspective* (Garden City, N.Y.: Doubleday and Co., 1963), p. 95.

42. Kaplan, "What Is Judaism," p. 316. The phrase *collective mind* does not come to Kaplan from Jung but is found in many other sources, including his teacher Franklin Giddings.

43. Mordecai Kaplan, "How May Judaism Be Saved," *Menorah Journal* 2 (February 1916): 43.

44. Kaplan journal, January 1916.
45. Mordecai M. Kaplan, "The Essence of Judaism," p. 5, manuscript at RRC.
46. Mordecai M. Kaplan, "The Synagogue and the Community," a 1932 speech, text at AJA.

CHAPTER 6

1. Kaplan's first major use of the term *civilization* in connection with Judaism was at the dedication of the center, March 24, 1918. Excerpts from his speech are found in *American Jewish Chronicle*, April 19, 1918. The article is entitled "Judaism as a Living Civilization." Contents of this article are discussed below. This article should not be confused with "The Jewish Center," *American Hebrew*, March 22, 1918, which is well known.

2. Harry Glucksman, "Tendencies in the Jewish Center Movement," *National Conference of Jewish Social Service, Proceedings* 1923, pp. 144–53, as reprinted in *Trends and Issues in Jewish Social Welfare in the United States: 1899–1958*, ed. by Robert Morris and Michael Freund (Philadelphia: Jewish Publication Society, 1966), pp. 225–30.

3. Kaplan journal, April 10, 1915.

4. Concerning Beth-Israel, see Tina Levitan, *Islands of Compassion: A History of the Jewish Hospitals of New York* (New York: Twayne Publishers, 1964), p. 92. On Kaplan not being concerned about particulars, see Kaplan journal, April 10, 1915.

5. Cohen and Christian Science: Kaplan journal, August 25, 1917. For Kaplan as observant, see, for example, Marc Lee Raphael, *Profiles in American Judaism: The Reform, Conservative, Orthodox and Reconstructionist Traditions in Historical Perspective* (San Francisco: Harper and Row Publishers, 1984), p. 179.

6. Facts on Rosalsky in Obituary, *New York Times*, May 12, 1936, p. 23; *Who's Who in American Jewry 1926* (New York: Jewish Biographical Bureau, 1927); Kaplan journal, April 21, 1918. For Schwartz, see *Who's Who 1926*.

7. Facts on Israel Unterberg in Obituary, *New York Times*, May 2, 1934; and *Who's Who in American Jewry 1926*. On the Lamports, see Obituary, *New York Times*, September 14, 1941; November 9, 1940; and Gilbert Klaperman, *The Story of Yeshiva University* (New York: Macmillan, 1969). For list of board members, see *Journal of Jewish Center*, April 12, 1918, p. 3. For the remark about the Lamports being star workers, see letter from Amelia Morganroth to Mordecai Kaplan, February 1920, RRC. Amelia Morganroth was on the center staff.

8. On consulting Margolies: Kaplan journal, March 2, 1918. Also interviews with Judith Kaplan Eisenstein, April 1986. The issue of mixed seating is brought up in Bernard Drachman's autobiography, where he discusses leaving the synagogue Beth Israel-Bikur Cholim: Bernard Drachman, *The Unfailing Light* (New York: Rabbinical Council of America, 1948), p. 197. The matter of synagogue suffrage being equal for men and for women is found in Kaplan journal, January 1917.

9. Kaplan journal, May 22, 1917.

10. Kaplan journal, August 29, 1917.

11. Material on Kaplan's leaving the profession from Kaplan journal, May 8, 1917. Kaplan also learned that Revel's brother-in-law wanted to give money to the seminary for scholarships so that students might study for traditional rabbinical ordination (*Hatraat Hora-ah*). He hoped, too, to see an Orthodox *rav* at the head of the Seminary and was apparently willing to give up to ten thousand dollars if this were done. Kaplan didn't know all the details, but he understood that the offer was never accepted.

12. *American Jewish Chronicle*, March 8, 1918, p. 491.

13. On the salary, see Kaplan journal, July 22, 1918. Kaplan's insistence with regard to the salary was not just a matter of the wartime atmosphere of sacrifice in 1918. At the SAJ, he also refused a salary, with the congregation paying only for his insurance.

14. *Journal of the Jewish Center*, April 26, 1918, p. 1. The articles in the center journal are unsigned.

15. The dedication is reported in *American Jewish Chronicle*, March 29, 1918.

16. For the general context of the modern Orthodox synagogue, see Joselit, *New York's Jewish Jews* (Bloomington: Indiana University Press, 1990), pp. 25–54.

17. Information on the school is very meager. See Kaplan journal, December 26, 1918. Interview with Judith Kaplan Eisenstein, May 1986. On Kadushin as disciple, see below.

18. Much later (1931), Judith was offered a job at the center as a teacher, but she turned it down. Information here from interviews with Naomi Kaplan Wenner and Judith Kaplan Eisenstein.

19. For Talmud class, see Kaplan journal, July 28, 1919. Bible class is mentioned in *Journal of the Jewish Center*, October 18, 1918, p. 3.

20. See letters from Amelia Morganroth to Mordecai M. Kaplan, RRC.

21. Notice of the parade from *American Hebrew*, April 30, 1920. Details of music from Judith Kaplan Eisenstein and from *Journal of the Jewish Center*, October 18, 1918, p. 2.

22. Wilson compared to Jacob and the angel in a sermon preached on November 23, 1918; Wilson compared to Abraham, October 19, 1918. Kaplan papers, RRC.

23. Sermon at center, November 30, 1918, RRC.

24. Sermon at center, September 29, 1918, RRC.

25. Enlarged definition of Zionism in center sermon, April 24, 1921, entitled "What Zionism Can Give to the Jew"; Zionism not chauvinism in center sermon, April 5, 1919, RRC.

26. Kaplan journal, December 29, 1918.

27. Center sermon, April 21, 1921; center sermon, April 21, 1921, RRC.

28. Center sermon, December 7, 1918. On mingling one's soul: M. M. Kaplan, "The Center and Civilization," *American Jewish Chronicle*, April 19, 1918.

29. *Journal of the Jewish Center*, November 8, 1918, p. 1; *Journal of the Jewish Center*, May 10, 1918, p. 3.

30. The sermon on the emancipation of women was delivered at the center on November 2, 1918. The concept of the chosenness of women is clearly in the text of the sermon, although the word *chosen* is not used there. The verse is from I Samuel 2:16. The translations from Genesis are from Everett Fox, *In the Beginning: A New English Rendition of the Book of Genesis* (New York: Schocken Books, 1983). The verse in Zachariah 4:6 expresses the same thought about power and was a favorite of Kaplan's, although he did not use it here: "Not by might nor by power but by My spirit, sayeth the Lord of Hosts."

31. The notion of the primacy of man as the image of God is found not only in Jewish sources but in Christian as well. It was a staple of sixteenth-century renaissance Platonists who saw man as a reflection of God and therefore worthy of love.

32. Harold M. Schulweis, "Predicate Theology: Feuerbach's Copernican Revolution," *Reconstructionist* 49 (June 1984): 3. For examples of predicate theology in Kaplan's early thought, see chapter 9. Kaplan journal entry, September 3, 1922.

33. Kaplan journal, March 3, 1926.

34. Mordecai M. Kaplan, "The Future of Judaism," *Menorah Journal* 2 (June 1916): 169. Kaplan's statement on mysticism is in Kaplan journal, February 13, 1929.

35. Statement on God as immanent in Kaplan journal, March 3, 1926.

36. From an unpublished manuscript in the Kaplan papers, "The Meaning of Religion," p. 251, RRC.

37. At the end of "The Meaning of Religion," there are some scattered undated sermon outlines. The quotation regarding the *Shekhinah* in *Galut* is from these pages.

38. Kaplan journal, August 31, 1917.

39. Kaplan, "The Meaning of Religion," p. 93.

40. God as helper in *Judaism as a Civilization* (New York: Macmillan, 1934), p. 400.

41. "God as helper . . ." in the *Meaning of Religion*, 37; "Cooperation is from the standpoint . . . ," ibid., 79; "benevolent energies . . . ," ibid., 36; to be at home in "the world . . . ," ibid., 39.

42. See, for example, "Kaplan's Approach to Metaphysics," by William Kaufman; and "Kaplan and Process Theology," by Jacob Staub. Both essays are found in *The American Judaism of Mordecai Kaplan*, ed. Emanuel S. Goldsmith, Mel Scult, and Robert Seltzer (New York: New York University Press, 1990).

43. Kaplan, "The Meaning of Religion," p. 19.

44. M. M. Kaplan, *Judaism in Transition* (New York: Behrman House, 1936), xiv; "The Meaning of Religion," p. 26 (Seeking God).

CHAPTER 7

1. The Rabbinical Assembly was organized in the 1920s by the Seminary and included all Conservative rabbis.

2. Herman H. Rubenovitz to Charles Hoffman, October 3, 1910, Hoffman Papers, Jewish Theological Seminary.

3. Kaplan journal, August 23, 1914. The next year, the meeting was held at Arverne (near the Rockaways), with Ginzberg talking on "The *Halachah* as a Source of History." For a later version of this talk, see Louis Ginzberg, "The Significance of the *Halachah* for Jewish History," *On Jewish Law and Lore* (Philadelphia: Jewish Publication Society, 1955). Schechter spoke on the "Function of the Rabbi."

4. Ginzberg's report, "Minutes of the Executive Council of the United Synagogue, April 1917," in Judah L. Magnes papers, 6/3/537, Central Archives for the History of the Jewish People, Hebrew University. Kaplan's remarks in *United Synagogue Report*, 1918, p. 46. See also Sidney Schwarz, *Law and Legitimacy: An Intellectual History of Conservative Judaism 1902–1973*, unpublished dissertation, Temple University, 1981. The members of the first Law Committee were not chosen from the young or from those adamant for change. Its first members were Louis Epstein, Herman Abramowitz, Abraham Hershman, and Alexander Marx. *United Synagogue Report 1919–1920*, p. 6.

5. The layman's comments quoted in a letter from Herman H. Rubenovitz to Jacob Kohn, January 27, 1928, Herman H. Rubenovitz papers, JTS. For the possibility that United Synagogue could be used as a vehicle for Conservative Judaism, see Jacob Kohn to H. H. Rubenovitz, April 14, 1919, in H. H. Rubenovitz and Mignon Rubenovitz, *The Waking Heart* (Cambridge, Mass.: N. Dame, 1967). For meeting about a third party, see Kaplan journal, December 29, 1918.

6. Kaplan journal, December 29, 1918.

7. Kohn's remark on Kaplan inertia in a letter to H. H. Rubenovitz, March 6, 1919, in Rubenovitz papers, JTS, and in *The Waking Heart*, p. 140. Kohn being overwhelmed by Kaplan speech in letter to Rubenovitz, *The Waking Heart*, p. 141. The speech mentioned here is of primary importance. It was published in the *Menorah Journal* in 1920 and will be discussed further below.

8. The June 9 letter is found in a number of places, including Kaplan's papers at RRC and Ginzberg's papers at JTS. Kaplan recorded the back-and-forth developments over the place of the meeting and his own reaction to Ginzberg in Kaplan diary, July 29, 1919. For Friedlaender's reaction, see Israel Friedlaender to Louis Ginzberg, June 13, 1919, Ginzberg papers, JTS. See Louis Ginzberg to M. M. Kaplan, June 13, 1919, Ginzberg papers, for the original of the letter refusing Seminary as a place of meeting. For Ginzberg's letter to Adler informing him of what was happening, see Louis Ginzberg to Cyrus Adler, June 20, 1919, Adler papers, JTS (not in Robinson). For the full text of the June 9 letter and a somewhat

different version of the whole incident, see Eli Ginzberg, *Keeper of the Law: Louis Ginzberg* (Philadelphia: Jewish Publication Society, 1966), pp. 148–49.

9. For Ginzberg's and Kaplan's remarks, see *Commencement Addresses, June 9, 1919*, by Sol. M. Strook, Professor Louis Ginzberg, Professor Mordecai M. Kaplan (New York: Jewish Theological Seminary, 1919). Ginzberg's remarks are on p. 18, Kaplan's on pp. 32–33.

10. Harry Cohen's remarks in letter to Morris Adler, September 7, 1955, Friedlaender papers, as originally cited in Baila Shargel, "Mordecai Kaplan and Israel Friedlaender: Expectation and Failure," *The American Judaism of Mordecai Kaplan*, ed. Emanuel S. Goldsmith, Mel Scult, and Robert M. Seltzer (New York: New York University Press, 1990). Kaplan's article in the *Menorah Journal* is certainly an expansion and reworking of the original speech, but we lack the original text. Citations from the article were published a year later in August 1920.

11. A typed transcript of the discussions of the second series of meetings on July 6 and 7, 1920, are at the RRC. The other participants are listed there. They include Solomon Lamport, Emanuel Newman, Morris Levine, Joshua Bloch, Bernard Richards, and Israel Unterberg. "Renascence" is the spelling originally adopted by the organization.

12. The quotations from the SJR meetings are all taken from the transcript of the proceedings. The members of the committee that first formulated these resolutions included Rubenovitz, Kaplan, Kadushin, and J. Kohn.

13. All the quotations here are from the SJR transcript. The file on the SJR also contains a letter from Kaplan to Elias Solomon, September 24, 1920. The remark by Finkelstein about the "mistake" of having joined the SJR is from a letter from L. Finkelstein to M. M. Kaplan, April 27, 1921, RRC. There is a form letter announcing fortnightly meetings of the SJR, December 3, 1920, H. H. Rubenovitz papers, JTS. Among Kaplan's papers are notes for speeches he presented to the group in 1920. The meetings apparently took place over a year or so. Again, another form letter says that the meetings of the society would be discontinued until further notice. A. G. Robinson (secretary) to Dear Friend, March 26, 1921, Magnes papers, Archives of the Jewish People, Hebrew University.

14. Jacob Kohn to H. H. Rubenovitz, August 31, 1921, Rubenovitz papers, JTS.

15. Julius Greenstone to M. M. Kaplan, October 10, 1920, Kaplan papers, AJA; Kaplan also received letters of support from former students when he was attacked in the Jewish press. David Aronson to M. M. Kaplan, January 18, 1921, Kaplan papers, AJA. Finkelstein remark in an interview with the author, 1977.

16. M. M. Kaplan, "A Program for the Reconstruction of Judaism," *Menorah Journal* 6 (August 1920): 183.

17. Ibid., p. 187.

18. Ibid., p. 189.

19. Ibid., pp. 190, 196, 195. On the Sabbath: Kaplan journal, December 19, 1918.

20. *Morgen Journal*, January 12, 1921, p. 1. The chairman of the meeting was M. S. Margolies, who was rabbi of Kehilath Jeshurun when Kaplan worked there from 1903 to 1909.

21. Editorial, *Jewish Forum* 2 (January 1921): 645, by B. Drachman. See also *Idishe Licht* 1 (June 1923), where H. Hirsch said that "though Orthodox in practice [Kaplan's] teachings are full of *Apikorsuth* [heresy]." The expression "wolf in sheep's clothing" was used in a sermon about Kaplan at the Seventieth Street Synagogue by Rabbi Henry Morais (the son of Sabato, the first president of the seminary). See letter from Kaplan to H. H. Rubenovitz, January 11, 1921, in H. H. Rubenovitz, *The Waking Heart* (Cambridge: Nathaniel Dame and Co., 1967), p. 59.

22. Leo Jung, "Orthodoxy Reform and Kaplanism," *Jewish Forum* 4 (JApril 1921): 7878–83.

23. Bernard Drachman, "An Examination of Professor Mordecai Kaplan's Views on Judaism," *Jewish Forum* 4 (February 1921): 721–31.

24. Kaplan is referring here to the meeting of the Union of Orthodox Rabbis mentioned above. "An Explanation by Professor M. Kaplan," *Morgen Journal*, January 16, 1921 (translated by M. Scult).

25. "Man the Standard of All Values," center sermon, October 25, 1919.

26. "Moral Bankruptcy of the Competitive System," center sermon, April 21, 1919. The same view is expressed in 1921 in a center sermon he entitled "Is Our Morale Crumbling." Kaplan notes he is called a Bolshevik in Kaplan journal, July 28, 1919. He calls Amos a Bolshevist in center sermon, April 12, 1919. Attack on luxury is in center sermon, September 14, 1918.

27. Original center sermon, November 9, 1918, on democracy versus bolshevism. Goldstein against radicalism in *American Hebrew*, January 30, 1920.

28. Kaplan journal, July 28, 1919.

29. Kaplan journal, August 14, 1918; on Louis Ginzburg's attitude, June 4, 1941; Shaw quotation, January 7, 1919.

30. Kaplan journal, August 14, 1918.

31. The letter from Anna Kaplan is at RRC. It is undated, but the contents make the approximate time clear.

32. The minutes of the meeting were professionally recorded. They are entitled "The Jewish Center Convention – February 9, 1921," and are found at RRC.

33. Max Kadushin and his relationship to Kaplan are discussed below. The school incident is recorded in Kaplan journal, May 5, 1921. Letter from Herman H. Rubenovitz to Kaplan, January 20, 1921, at RRC Kaplan asks for a leave: Kaplan to William Fischman, April 28, 1921, RRC.

34. Kaplan journal, May 12, 1921.

35. Kaplan to William Fischman, January 16, 1922, RRC.

36. Ike Phillips to Israel Unterberg, May 5, 1922, in Unterberg file at RRC. Interview with William Feinberg, 1973. Feinberg was very active at the center and was one of those who stayed.

37. Rabbi Louis Finkelstein related the incident about the delegation from the center coming to Adler. There is no way to corroborate the story. Interview with Finkelstein, March 1974. He said he thought Kaplan never knew of this incident.

38. Louis Kraft, "The Jewish Center Movement," *Mordecai M. Kaplan: An Evaluation*, ed. by Ira Eisenstein and Eugene Kohn (New York: Jewish Reconstructionist Foundation, 1952), pp. 119–35. Kraft's essay is based almost solely on Kaplan's own work, *The Future of the American Jew*, which came out in 1948.

39. For a study of the synagogues in Harlem, see Jeffrey Gurock, *When Harlem Was Jewish 1870–1930* (New York: Columbia University Press, 1979).

40. Mordecai M. Kaplan, "Outline of Remarks Made at the Laying of the Cornerstone of the Yorkville Jewish Institute, Sunday, May 16, 1915, 4 p.m.," RRC.

41. Kaplan's account in his journal, June 20, 1916; speech in *American Hebrew*, May 26, 1916.

42. It has often been asserted that the CJI was the creation of Mordecai Kaplan. The myth regarding Kaplan's part in creating the CJI comes from a number of sources. Oscar Janowsky in *The Jewish Welfare Board Survey* (New York: Dial Press, 1948), p. 244, makes it clear that he believes "that the ideological foundations of the present day Jewish Community Center were laid by Mordecai Kaplan was early as 1908." Although he uses the word *center*, he is referring to the CJI and not to the Jewish Center. His evidence is the work of Isaac Berkson, *Theories of Americanization* (New York: Columbia University, 1920), p. 187, who for a short time was himself director of the CJI. Berkson gives no hard evidence to back up his assertion that Kaplan conceived the idea for the CJI in 1908. In other words, Berkson believed the idea for the Institute came from Kaplan but had no good reason for asserting this. A careful reading of the minutes of Kehilath Jeshurun lead to the conclusion that the Talmud Torah that congregation sought to establish was a very modest affair and was not engineered

by Kaplan, who left Kehilath Jeshurun in 1908. There is no evidence that Kaplan laid out the program of the CJI. The very special organization of the institute flows much more from the work of Berkson himself, who was giving his teacher more credit than he deserved. Kaplan's remark about being uninvolved is in Kaplan journal, April 9, 1918.

43. On the Institutional Church, see James Hastings, ed., *Encyclopedia of Religion and Ethics* (New York: Charles Scribner's Sons, 1908–1927), s.v. "Institutional Church." Goldstein resented Kaplan from the time when he was a student of Kaplan's at the Seminary. It is quite ironic, therefore, that it was because of Kaplan that Goldstein entered the rabbinate. According to his biographer, Goldstein recorded in his diary that he had a "conversion experience" while listening to Kaplan preach at the funeral of Rabbi Asher, a Seminary professor who died in November 1909. See Aaron Reichel, *The Maverick Rabbi: Rabbi Herbert Goldstein and the Institutional Synagogue* (Virginia Beach: Donning Co., 1984), p. 44. Goldstein's statement ("My plea") in Herbert Goldstein, "The Institutional Synagogue" *Hebrew Standard* September 15, 1916.

44. Reichel, *The Maverick Rabbi*, p. 132.

45. A copy of the constitution of the Institutional Synagogue is found at Yeshiva University Archives in the Institutional Synagogue Collection. I am indebted to Dr. Roget Cohn for his gracious assistance. The other facts in this paragraph can be found in Reichel, *The Maverick Rabbi*. The synagogue published a bulletin called the *Institutional* which contains much useful material on the 1930s. The Institutional Synagogue building at 116th Street was later expanded to include six stories with a gymnasium and a pool as well as a large sanctuary. The building still stands and is now a church.

46. Kaplan made this statement at the dedication of the Jewish Center. The address may be found in Mordecai M. Kaplan, "Judaism as a Living Civilization," *American Jewish Chronicle*, April 19, 1918.

CHAPTER 8

1. Information on the graduation of Kaplan quotation are from *New York Times*, June 12, 1916. Schiff's reaction is in a letter from Jacob Schiff to Cyrus Adler, June 12, 1916; Adler's response is in Cyrus Adler to Jacob Schiff, June 15, 1916. Both letters are in the Schiff papers, box 449, Adler Folder, American Jewish Archives.

2. Adler's remarks on faculty: Kaplan journal, April 1924. Adler's remarks in *Jewish Exponent*, July 6, 192, and also in "The Standpoint of the Seminary," *Lectures, Selected Papers, Addresses by Cyrus Adler — Collected and Published by His Colleagues and Friends on the Occasion of his Seventieth Birthday, September 1, 193, with a Bibliography* (Philadelphia: privately printed, 1933), p. 261. Adler on mixed seating: Cyrus Adler to Solomon Goldman, *Adler Letters*, Vol. 2, March 27, 1925.

3. Sidney Schwarz, *Law and Legitimacy: An Intellectual History of Conservative Judaism 1902–1973*, Unpublished dissertation, Temple University, 1981, p. 114.

4. Cyrus Adler, "Non-Partisan Judaism," *Jewish Forum* 2 (September 1919); Cyrus Adler, "The Stand Point of the Seminary," *Lectures . . . by C. Adler*, p. 252; Cyrus Adler to *Hebrew Union College Monthly*, *Adler Letters*, Vol. 1, February 11, 1919. I am indebted to Jonathan Sarna for the insight that Adler was close to the Sephardic style.

5. Mordecai Kaplan, "The Function and Organization of the Synagogue," delivered to the United Synagogue, January 16, 1921, Reconstructionist Rabbinical College. Kaplan's diary also indicates that Adler attacked him at the convention when he delivered the paper; Kaplan journal, May 1921.

6. For the full text of Adler's reply to Kaplan on the synagogue speech, see Cyrus Adler to Kaplan, *Adler Letters*, Vol. 2, February 14, 1921. On the matter of "making noise" and its negative results, see letter to Jacob Schiff, *Adler Letters*, Vol. 2, June 15, 1920: "We have made a noise in the world of recent years in America and England and probably elsewhere far out of proportion to our numbers." Adler believed in quiet diplomacy.

7. Cyrus Adler to Mordecai M. Kaplan, *Adler Letters*, Vol. 2, September 21, 1923. Letters of S. A. Israel and Cyrus Adler reprinted in *Idishe Licht*, July 1923, p. 3. Regarding Kaplan and theology, Kaplan, of course, taught much more than how to construct a sermon. His guiding principle was that before he could teach men how to preach, they must have some idea of what they wanted to say. In his journal on December 25, 1923, he listed the content of his course in homiletics: 1919–1920, The Problem of Reinterpretation: Scripture and Rabbinic Writings; 1920–1921, Detailed Interpretation of Genesis; 1921–1922, The Jewish Sanctions for Some of the Current Religious and Ethical Concepts (freedom, nature, etc.). In addition to teaching homiletics, Kaplan also taught *Midrash*. It is quite ironic that Kaplan's homiletics students in the upper classes did not feel they were getting enough practice in the actual construction of sermons. Letters from Louis Levitsky to Kaplan, June 22, 1922, RRC. In a minor but revealing sidelight on the whole matter, when Adler set up examination committees for graduating rabbinical students, he had a committee on theology but Kaplan wasn't on it. In 1923, Ginzberg, Marx, and Hyamson were on a committee on theology, and Kaplan was on a general committee. Cyrus Adler to Israel Davidson, June 28, 1923, Davidson papers, Jewish Theological Seminary (not in *Adler Letters*). At an earlier point, Ginzberg was interested in teaching theology at the Seminary. See Cyrus Adler to Louis Ginzberg, *Adler Letters*, Vol. 2, July 1, 1920.

8. Kaplan journal, October 1925; December 1924; August 20, 1923. Kaplan's magnum opus, of course, was published in 1934. He had published a number of articles in the *Menorah Journal* and wrote steadily for the *SAJ Review* during the 1920s. See Kaplan's complete bibliography in *The American Judaism of Mordecai Kaplan*, ed. Emanuel Goldsmith, Mel Scult and Robert Seltzer (New York: New York University Press, 1990) Kaplan reacted somewhat jealously to Finkelstein's publication *Jewish Self-Government in the Middle Ages*, Kaplan journal, February 1925.

9. Kaplan journal, September 1924, September 1926, December 1927.

10. Kaplan journal, May 1927. Kaplan also refers to himself as "eaten up by ambition," September 1926. On need to do literary work, Kaplan journal, November 1927.

11. In a letter to Solomon Schechter asking for a raise, Ginzberg maintained that few works of Jewish scholarship were of "equal importance to Jewish learning as the three works of mine published by the Jewish Theological Seminary." (He was right!) Louis Ginzberg to Solomon Schechter, May 16, 1910, Adler papers, JTS (not in *Adler Letters*). Eli Ginzberg, *Keeper of the Law: Louis Ginzberg* (Philadelphia: Jewish Publication Society of America, 1966). Epstein's report, *United Synagogue of America and Women's League, Annual Reports*, 1919 and 1920, p. 91.

12. See Eli Ginzberg, "The Seminary Family: A View from My Parents' Home," *Perspective son Jews and Judaism: Essays in Honor of Wolfe Kelman*, ed. by Arthur A. Chiel (New York: Rabbinical Assembly, 1978). Ginzberg maintained that his father and Marx never had an argument and were very close even though they never called each other by their first names.

13. Ginzberg's most famous *responsum* related to the use of grape juice as a substitute for wine during the era of Prohibition: "Responsum on the Matter of Wine Which Is Kosher and That Which Is Not Fitting for the Mitzvah" [Hebrew], 1922, translated in *American Jewish Yearbook*, Vol. 5. My thanks to Jonathan Sarna for this reference. Speech by Ginzberg in Ginzberg folder in the Marx papers, where he deals with the matter of changes in the law; for remarks to United Synagogue in 1921, see *American Hebrew*, January 21, 1921.

14. The detailed description of the convention is found in Kaplan journal, July 7, 1927.

15. Ginzberg, *Keeper of the Law*, p. 138. In an interview, Finkelstein himself remembered the incident and believes that "even at that time there was difficulty in the faculty — this tension between Dr. Kaplan and Professor Ginzberg."

16. Kaplan journal, July 7, 1927. For a general discussion of the conflict described here, see Marshall Sklare, *Conservative Judaism: An American Religious Movement* (New York:

Schocken Books, 1972), pp. 159–99. On traditional scholarship as a mode of escape, see Kaplan journal, December 1923.

17. Kaplan journal, June 1926.

18. *Hebrew Standard*, January 7, 1921.

19. The fullest account of the possible merger is in Aaron Rothkoff, *Bernard Revel: Building of American Jewish Orthodoxy* (Philadelphia: Jewish Publication Society, 1972), pp. 94–115. On the yeshiva in general during this period, see Klaperman, *The Story of Yeshiva University*, pp. 149ff, and Jeffrey S. Gurock, *The Men and Women of Yeshiva* (New York: Columbia University Press, 1988). On the Seminary, see Cyrus Adler, *I Have Considered the Days* (Philadelphia: Jewish Publication Society, 1941), pp. 360ff. For information on Brush and his bequest, see *New York Times*, March 3, 1927, p. 14; and *The American Jewish Yearbook*, Vol. 30, 1928–1920, ed. by Harry Schneiderman (Philadelphia: Jewish Publication Society, 1929), p. 75. It was Mathilde Schechter who first interested Brush in the Seminary. See Hannah Marx, "An Appreciation of Mathilde Schechter," *Women's League Outlook* 9 (December 1938): 3. For the facts on Unterberg and the Teachers' Institute, see chapter 4 above. On Yeshiva University, see Jeffrey Gurock, *The Men and Women of Yeshiva: Higher Education, Orthodoxy and American Judaism* (New York, Columbia University Press, 1988).

20. Kaplan's report regarding N. Lamport and O. Rosalsky in Kaplan journal, June 27, 1925. Marshall's stand in L. Marshall to Cyrus Adler, December 29, 1925, as published in A. Rakeffet-Rothkoff, "The Attempt to Merge the Jewish Theological Seminary and Yeshiva College 1926–27," *Michael: On the History of the Jews in the Diaspora*, ed. by Lloyd P. Gartner (Tel Aviv: Diaspora Research Institute, 1975), p. 258.

21. Louis Marshall to Cyrus Adler, January 28, 1926, in Rakeffet-Rothkoff, *Michael*, p. 264.

22. See *Adler Letters*, Vol. 2, p. 123.

23. Finkelstein approved the idea in principle and suggested that the yeshivah give preparatory courses and *Hatarath Horoah* (advanced rabbinical ordination) and the Seminary continue to train preachers and ministers. Adler's position was uncertain. He seemed to have a vision of a total Jewish university that could also include Dropsie and the Training School for Jewish Social Workers. Needless to say, he saw himself as the head of such an institution and perhaps hesitated only because of all the administrative headaches involved not only in running such an institution but in creating it in the first place. Kaplan journal, March 10, 1926, records in detail the faculty meeting at which the merger was discussed.

24. Bernard Revel, "Seminary and Yeshiva" (unpublished, 1928), cited in Rothkoff, *Bernard Revel*, p. 112.

25. Mordecai M. Kaplan, *The Greater Judaism in the Making* (New York: Reconstructionist Press, 1960), p. 357.

26. For a full discussion of Kaplan and the Bible, see chapter 9.

27. Mordecai M. Kaplan, "The Scientific Basis for Adjustment of Judaism to Modern Life," *American Jewish Chronicle*, August 2, 1918, p. 304.

28. This quotation is the first entry in Kaplan's major journal and was the basis for a speech he was going to give at the Harvard Menorah Society; Kaplan journal, February 24, 1913. The most eminent critic to mistakenly believe Kaplan reduced religion to group process was Jacob Agus in *Modern Philosophies of Judaism* (New York: Behrman House, 1941). Kaplan's emphasis on the group does not come from Durkheim. See above, chapter 2.

29. This story is somewhat suspect because it is related by Kaplan, who was not there, but if it is not true it ought to be. See Kaplan journal, March 19, 1917. There was another such incident with Adler about ten years later, when David Goldstein, Milton Steinberg, and Henry Rosenthal sent to Adler with a twenty-page paper criticizing the curriculum. When Kaplan heard about it, he remarked, "It must have cut Adler to the quick." Kaplan journal, February 12, 1927.

30. See untitled speech by Louis Ginzberg, *United Synagogue Recorder*, July 1923, p. 10. Finkelstein's remark was in an interview with this author in 1974. Louis Ginzberg, "Judaism and Modern Thought," *United Synagogue Recorder*, October 1922, pp. 2–3.

31. Quotations here are from Kaplan, "The Scientific Basis."

32. As long as his father was alive, Kaplan studied Talmud with him regularly. Kadushin reported on the study group in an interview in January 1974. Kadushin's notes for the group which studied the social scientists is found among his papers. Apparently, there were two separate groups. In Kaplan's diary, he records that a group of students came to him in February 1917 and wanted more Talmud study. He began meeting regularly with them. This group included Mortimer Cohen, Solomon Goldman, and Max Kadushin, among others. They studied *Bava Basra*. Kadushin's notes indicate that the social science group began in October or November 1917 and continued throughout that academic year. In Kadushin's mind, fifty-eight years later the two groups coalesced into one. The point about two civilizations stands nonetheless.

33. The manuscript is found among Kaplan's papers and runs to about one hundred sixty typed pages. There is also a letter from Macmillan Co. in 1927 accepting for publication a manuscript entitled "The Ideology of the Rabbis." I do not know why this manuscript was never published.

34. Unless otherwise indicated, all quotations are from the manuscript entitled "The Ideology of the Rabbis."

35. I first read about this meeting in Kaplan's diary for September 12, 1926. It was a few years later that I came across the manuscript on rabbinic Ideology and realized that I had the very passages Kaplan and Ginzberg were discussing that evening. The point had to do with the relationship between the Days of the Messiah and the World to Come. Kaplan said that the manna was promised for the World to Come and that the World to Come succeeded the Messiah's time and that phenomena of a supernatural character would happen only in the World to Come. Ginzberg may have believed with Maimonides that the World to Come referred to immortality of the soul immediately after death. They looked up a passage in the *Mekhilta*, a rabbinic commentary that Kaplan felt proved his point, and they found that Kaplan was right, that the manna was to be again in the *Olam Ha Bah*. Kaplan derived considerable pleasure from his feeling that he won the argument. He does not mention the particular passage they looked up. He only mentions that they consulted the *Mekhilta* on the matter of the manna. The passage is probably *Mekhilta-de-R. Ishmael* (*Lauterbach*, Vol. II) *Massekhta Vayassah*, chapter V, p. 119.

36. Louis Ginzberg, "The Seminary and Jewish Scholarship," *United Synagogue Recorder*, October 1923.

37. "Mathilde Schechter Memoir" is found among the Schechter papers at JTS. For a more complete treatment, see Mel Scult, "The *Baale Boste* Reconsidered: The Life of Mathilde Roth Schechter," *Modern Judaism* (February 1987): 1–29. Schechter's remark to a friend is in a letter he wrote in 1885. It was never mailed and is in the Schechter papers. Kaplan's remark about Schechter is in Kaplan journal, February 4, 1917.

38. On dry as dust scholarship, see Kaplan journal, October 10, 1914. Neil Gilman's point may be found in *Proceedings of the Rabbinical Assembly 1986*, "Entering the Second Century – From Scholarship to the Rabbinate." Among Kaplan's papers are lists of students with remarks about the various religious beliefs of each one. On one particular list is the name of Seymour Siegel, who went on to become an important Jewish thinker in his own right. On his student questionnaire, Siegel indicated that he believed literally in ten of the thirteen principles of Maimonides. He did not believe in the return of the sacrificial cult or in the restoration of the Davidic dynasty. He believed literally in a personal Messiah. The episode involving the extra meetings of the students and Davidson is drawn from Kaplan journal, April 5, 1930.

39. The Hanukkah sermon on moral courage is in Kaplan journal, December 8, 1928. On Kaplan devoting himself fully to homiletics: Kaplan journal, January 4, 1929. On sermon outlines handed in late: Kaplan journal, May 29, 1930. The evaluation of Henry Rosenthal: Kaplan journal, April 4, 1929. Dr. Simon Noveck reports that Kaplan told him Henry Rosenthal and Milton Steinberg were the two best students he ever had. Rosenthal eventually became an academician and taught philosophy at Hunter College. I am grateful to his daughter Professor Abigail Rosenthal for allowing me to read the unpublished manuscript by her father which contained a biographical introduction on Rosenthal's life.

40. Interview with Louis Finkelstein, March 1974; with Robert Gordis, April 1984; with Max Kadushin, January 1974.

41. The *Midrash* material consists of typed class notes among Kaplan's papers at RRC. There are three manuscripts, two on *Bereshit Rabbah* and one on *Shir-Ha-Shirim Rabbah*. The Hebrew in these manuscripts is in Kaplan's hand; the English is typed.

42. Mordecai Kaplan, "Notes on *Bereshit Rabbah*," p. 3 (On Midrash Rabbah xv:6).

43. From an interview with Rabbi Nathan Kollin, a student of Kaplan's from the late 1920s.

44. Kaplan diary, January 16, 1929; December 18, 1929.

45. All the groups are mentioned in the Kaplan journal: 1912 group, June 19, 1915 (former RIETS students); 1914 group, January 27 (Alstat, Halper, Teller, Kohn, among others); 1915 group, February 20, 1915 (Bosniak, Burstein, Teller, Halpern, among others, studied James and Royce); 1917 group, February 22, 1917 (Goldman, Kadushin, Mortimer Cohen, Boroway, and Levy, among others, studied Baghot and McDougal); 1923 group, February 23, 1923, and Horowitz papers, box 25, folder 5, AJA. M. M. Kaplan to Henry Horowitz, January 24, 1923.

46. Friedrich Nietzsche, *Thus Spake Zarathustra*, trans. by Walter Kaufman (New York: Viking Press, 1966), p. 78.

47. Finkelstein interviews, March 1974. Finkelstein's remark about revelation and miracle in Kaplan diary, March 12, 1917. Kaplan's recording of a meeting with Finkelstein in 1920 when Finkelstein mentioned his desire to be a lawyer, in Kaplan notes at RRC. On the same paper, Kaplan notes that he was reading Buber's "*Von Geist des Judenthums*" at this point (1920). Finkelstein's 1929 comment in a letter to Kaplan, August 2, 1929, at RRC.

48. The walks around the reservoir were mentioned in interviews with Kaplan, Finkelstein, Kadushin, Dinin, and Ira Eisenstein. Finkelstein letter to Kaplan containing both the evidence of his guilt about delivering the same sermons and the feeling that Kaplan was dominating, Louis Finkelstein to M.M.K. April 25, 1921, at RRC. I found this letter purely by accident after Finkelstein had denied that Kaplan dominated him. Whether Finkelstein forgot how he felt or whether he was consciously distorting the truth when he talked with me, we shall never know. Kaplan journal, April 17, 1921. A photostat of Finkelstein's April 25 letter is also found in Kaplan papers, box 2325, AJA.

49. "Who is to blame for the strain . . . ," Kaplan journal, May 8, 1933. "Did everything to stop Reconstructionism . . . ," interview with Finkelstein, 1974. My thanks to Neil Gilman for relating the details of his interview with Finkelstein.

50. Most of the information in this paragraph is from a 1974 interview with Finkelstein. A few days before his death in 1987, Rabbi Ludwig Nadelman, at one time Kaplan's assistant, told me a very moving story about taking Finkelstein to visit Kaplan at the nursing home in Riverdale when Kaplan was near death. Kaplan usually spoke English, sometimes Hebrew, but on this occasion would speak to Finkelstein only in Yiddish.

51. On Kadushin, see Theodore Steinberg, *Max Kadushin — Scholar of Rabbinic Judaism: A Study of His Life and Work and Theory of Valuational Thought*, unpublished Dissertation, New York University, 1979. Kadushin as "his master's voice" is from an interview with Simon Greenberg, March 1985. On Kadushin's articles in the early 1920s, see Max Kadushin, "The

Function of the Synagogue and Center," *Jewish Center*, September 1923, pp. 6–11; and "The Place of the Center in American Jewish Life," *Jewish Center*, June 1926, pp. 11–17. For Kadushin's place in the Kaplan circle, see Kadushin file in Kaplan papers, RRC. For Kaplan's proposal to promote Kadushin to the SAJ, see Kaplan journal, May 15, 1929.

52. My thanks to Judith Kaplan Eisenstein for the information about Kadushin's wife.

53. See Steinberg, *Max Kadushin*, pp. 50ff, for explanation of distance between Kaplan and his disciple. Information here is also from an interview with Kadushin in 1974. For Kadushin's analysis, see his *Organic Thinking: A Study in Rabbinic Thought* (New York: Jewish Theological Seminary, 1938).

54. Details on Simon Greenberg from an interview in March 1985. Details on Gordis from interview in April 1984. In terms of personal impact, Simon Greenberg's letters to Kaplan are quite revealing. When the University of Judaism was established in the late 1940s, Kaplan and Greenberg actually lived together in the same room for a month. Knowing Kaplan in this way made a very deep impression on Greenberg, and he mentioned it with much feeling every time afterward that he wrote to Kaplan. For Steinberg, see Simon Noveck, *Milton Steinberg: Portrait of a Rabbi* (New York: KTAV Publishing House, 1978). The quotation about Levine and Kaplan is on p. 28. For the student letter to Adler about Kaplan in 1927, see below p. 274. The reconstructed class conversation comes from an interview with Rabbi Nathan Kollin, a classmate of Steinberg's. Eisenstein's remark about Steinberg and the SAJ is from an interview with Ira Eisenstein, September 1988. Steinberg took Kaplan's place as professor of homiletics when Kaplan was in Jerusalem from 1937 to 1939. See Milton Steinberg, *Proceedings of the Rabbinical Assembly*, 1949, pp. 376–377, where he castigates his teacher for the lack of a metaphysical base to his system. For a full treatment of Kaplan and Steinberg, see Simon Noveck, "Kaplan and Milton Steinberg: A Disciple's Agreements and Disagreements," *American Judaism*, pp. 140–70.

55. Much of this information on Eisenstein is from his autobiography, *Reconstructing Judaism: An Autobiography* (New York: Reconstructionist Press, 1986).

56. Letter from Ira Eisenstein to a Mr. Goldfarb, RRC. The letter is undated but seems to be related to Kaplan's twenty-fifth anniversary at the Teachers' Institute (1934). The other quotations here are from interviews with Eisenstein.

57. Both third-person diary entries are from the journal, December 18, 1928. I owe a large debt for the analysis here regarding words and things to stimulating conversations with my brother Professor Allen Scult of Drake University. Kaplan's statement that he wanted to change human nature is found in the minutes of the Jewish Reconstructionist Foundation, March 14, 1944. A statement about compromise, already quoted, is in Kaplan journal, December 29, 1918. The statement reads, in part, "I must admit that I am too dogmatic in my way and unless I could carry out my wishes to the full I would not be satisfied. . . . If I am to launch a spiritual venture I do not want to be hampered by a sense of yielding and compromise."

CHAPTER 9

1. For Kaplan's views on the Bible, see Mordecai M. Kaplan, *Judaism as a Civilization* (New York: Reconstructionist Press, 1934), index under "Bible." See also Kaplan, *The Future of the American Jew* (New York: Macmillan, 1948), "A New Educational Approach to the Bible," p. 23; and Kaplan, *A New Approach to the Problem of Judaism* (New York: Society for the Advancement of Judaism, 1924), "The Meaning of Torah."

2. Kaplan alternated in his homiletics course between an examination of some general religious problems and an examination of the Bible. In his journal, December 1923, he lists the following topics: 1916–1917, Detailed Examination of Genesis; 1917–1918, The Psychological and Sociological Aspect of the God Concept; 1919–1920, The Problem of Reinterpretation: Scripture and Rabbinic Writing; 1920–1921, Detailed Interpretation of Genesis.

3. Among Kaplan's papers is a typed outline of the lectures he gave in both these courses. There is also an abundance of other unpublished material. In his journal, he frequently summarized his sermons and public lectures. There are also two biblical commentaries in typescript; neither is dated or has a title. The first, which I call "The Early Commentary," was composed between 1910 and 1930. Both the quality of the paper and the typing indicate this early period. The second I call "The Torah and Salvation: A Modern Reinterpretation of the Bible" (Kaplan approved both these titles). It runs to about two hundred fifty pages and was composed in the late 1940s and early 1950s. Although in general I shall confine my remarks to the period before 1934, I intend to draw on the latter commentary in presenting Kaplan's analysis of the Bible.

4. Eugene Kohn, "Mordecai Kaplan as Exegete," *Mordecai M. Kaplan: An Evaluation*, ed. by Ira Eisenstein and Eugene Kohn (New York: Jewish Reconstructionist Foundation, 1952).

5. Ibid., p. 154.

6. See "Literary Suggestions," in *All the Writings of Ahad Ha-Am* (Jerusalem: Jewish Publishing House, 1953), p. 288. See also Kaufman Kohler, *Jewish Theology Systematically and Historically Considered* (New York: Macmillan, 1918), pp. 46–47; Harry M. Orlinsky, "Jewish Biblical Scholarship in America," *Jewish Quarterly Review* 45 (April 1955): 382.

7. Solomon Schechter, "Higher Criticism — Higher Anti-Semitism," *Seminary Addresses* (Cincinnati: Ark Publishing, 1915), p. 37.

8. Solomon Schechter, "Zionism — A Statement," *Seminary Addresses*, p. 94.

9. Mordecai Kaplan, interview, July 1972; also confirmed in an interview with Louis Finkelstein, April 1973. See also Mordecai M. Kaplan, *Judaism as a Civilization* (New York: Macmillan, 1934), p. 163, for a statement on Schechter and biblical criticism.

10. Louis Ginzberg, "Law Codes," *Jewish Encyclopedia*, Vol. 8 (New York: Funk and Wagnalls, 1906), p. 636. The truth about Ginzberg's attitude is that he was of two minds. His critical faculties told him that elements in the Pentateuchal codes were obviously not all Mosaic; yet his deep commitment to traditional Judaism and to the Jewish community led him to take strong public stands against biblical criticism. Before Ginzberg came to the Seminary, he was considered for a position by Isaac M. Wise at the Hebrew Union College. Wise never made it completely clear why he selected Henry Malter over Ginzberg. One graduate of the class of 1896 at Hebrew Union College heard from a friend who was on the board of governors at the time that Wise had been excited about Ginzberg but decided not to recommend his appointment after he heard that Ginzberg inclined favorably to the Wellhausen interpretation of the Pentateuch. See Harry H. Mayer, "What Price Conservatism? Louis Ginzberg and the Hebrew Union College," *American Jewish Archives*, Vol. 10, pp. 145ff.

11. Louis Ginzberg, "Bible Interpretation: The Jewish Attitude," *United Synagogue Recorder* 2 (July 1922): 2.

12. Kaplan, interview, July 1972.

13. Mordecai M. Kaplan, "The Way I Have Come," *Mordecai M. Kaplan*, ed. by Eisenstein and Kohn, p. 289.

14. See, for example, Harry M. Orlinsky, "Prolegomenon," in Arnold B. Ehrlich, *Mikra Kiphshuto: The Bible according to Its Literal Meaning* (New York: KTAV, 1966). Vol. 1 originally appeared in 1899 and dealt with the Pentateuch. Vols. 2 and 3 were published in 1900 and 1901, respectively, and dealt with the Prophets and Hagiographa.

15. Ibid., p. ix.

16. See Harry M. Orlinsky, "Jewish Biblical Scholarship in America," *Jewish Quarterly Review* 45 (April 1955): 386. It seemed to some scholars that Ehrlich sometimes changed the text almost as if he were correcting a student's composition, as, for example, his changing of the word *barah* (created) in Genesis 1:3 to *badah* (imagined or contemplated). Ehrlich seemed to spend his time elucidating what to other scholars might seem obvious. In Genesis 1:2, the most difficult word is *merahefet* (hovered) or perhaps *tohu va-vohu* (unformed and void).

Ehrlich, however, wrote more than half a page on the word *hay'etah* ("was") in the phrase "the earth was unformed and void." He attempted to show that the word *hay'etah* indicated an equivalence between the earth and the void, rather than an object that had a certain quality. Thus, the verse is intended to say (as the new Jewish Publication Society translation indicates), "the earth being unformed and void with darkness over the surface of the deep." To explain the deeper meaning of what seems obvious was Ehrlich's way and his strength.

17. Pentateuch from different periods: Ehrlich, *Mikra*, Vol. 1, p. xxxvi. Different documents: see, for example, his comment on the word *na'aseh* in Genesis 1:26, *Mikra*, Vol. 1, p. 3. For the existence of other gods, see his comment on Genesis 12:3, *Mikra*, Vol. 1, p. 32. Golden Calf post-exilic: his comment on Exodus 32:1, *Mikra*, Vol. 1, p. 198. Priestly code is late: Orlinsky, "Prolegomenon," p. xxviii. For evidence of his love for the Jewish people, see his comment on Genesis 12:3, in Ehrlich, *Mikra*, 1, 32.

18. Mordecai M. Kaplan, *The Supremacy of the Torah* (New York: Students' Annual of the Jewish Theological Seminary of America, 1914), p. 183. The same point was made to the Seminary alumni in 1912; the unpublished text is found among Kaplan's papers, "Paper Read to Meeting of Alumni" (Tannersville, N.Y., July 1912). Also in the notes for a course entitled "Interpretation of the Bible," which Kaplan gave at Columbia Teachers College in 1915–16, Kaplan papers. See also Mordecai Kaplan, *A New Approach to the Problem of Judaism* (1924; reprint New York: Society for the Advancement of Judaism, 1973), p. 28; and *Society for the Advancement of Judaism* 8 (February 1929): 17. Kaplan also alluded to his acceptance of biblical criticism in his series of articles in the *Menorah Journal* in 1915, 1916, and 1917. He makes the point also in Kaplan journal, December 1913 and March 1915.

19. Kaplan, *The Supremacy*, p. 186.

20. For example, in Kaplan's papers there is a letter from N. B. Ezra, dated November 5, 1926. Apparently, he was the editor of a traditional monthly journal in Shanghai. A review of Kaplan's *A New Approach to the Problem of Judaism* (1924) appeared in the journal, and Ezra requested more of Kaplan's writings, which he said "filled a very important need." Another letter from Abraham Van Son, a Dutch Jew, dated February 1, 1929, asks why Kaplan is called an "Epikorus," "since in Holland the rabbis do not consider higher criticism to be a threat." Letters are in the Kaplan Archives at the Reconstructionist Rabbinical College.

21. Quotations in this paragraph are from Kaplan's speech at Tannersville to the alumni. Kaplan's theory of the secondary meaning is close to Schechter's notion of *Klal Yisrael* and its importance in being the locus of authority. See Schechter, "Study of the Bible," *Studies in Judaism — Second Series* (Philadelphia: Jewish Publication Society, 1908), pp. 31–54.

22. Kaplan, speech at Tannersville.

23. See Steven Katz, "Mordecai M. Kaplan: A Philosophic Demurer," *Sh'ma: A Journal of Jewish Responsibility* 4 (November 1974): 157.

24. The two manuscripts on the Bible mentioned above and on which this account is based are quite different in character. The older one contains a verse commentary covering the first fifteen chapters of the book of Genesis. In addition to this verse commentary, there is an exposition of the themes in each weekly portion; the more recent work drops the verse commentary and contains comments on the whole Pentateuch according to the weekly *sidra*. Further sources of Kaplan's thought on the subject include an unpublished work entitled "The Meaning of Religion" and material from Kaplan's journal.

25. Kaplan, "Torah and Salvation," p. 74.

26. Kaplan, "Early Commentary," p. 29.

27. Kaplan, "Torah and Salvation," *Sidra Vayishlah*. (Much of the manuscript lacks pagination. It is divided according to the weekly readings, or *sidrot*. Pages and *sidrot* will be given where they occur.

28. Ibid., p. 63.

29. Kaplan, "Early Commentary," p. 31.

30. Ibid., p. 9.

31. Kaplan, "Torah and Salvation," p. 30.

32. Ibid., p. 3. Professor Avraham Holtz of the Jewish Theological Seminary reported Kaplan using this interpretation in class.

33. Ibid., p. 31. The technique of reversing theological statements is an old liberal ploy. The practice goes back to the nineteenth century and may have been used first by Ludwig Feuerbach. Many examples are found in John Dewey's *A Common Faith* (1934; reprint New Haven: Yale University Press, 1974). See, for example, "It is a claim of religions that they effect a generic and enduring change in attitude. I should like to turn the statement around and say that whenever this change takes place there is a definitely religious attitude" (p. 17). This book was originally published in 1934, the same year as Kaplan's *Judaism as a Civilization*. For the earliest example of adjectival thinking in Kaplan's work, see Kaplan journal, September 3, 1922.

34. Kaplan, "Torah and Salvation," *Sidra Beshalah*. Quotations here are from *The Torah: A New Translation* (Philadelphia: Jewish Publication Society, 1962).

35. Kaplan, "Torah and Salvation," *Sidra Bo*.

36. In 1972, I took my son Joshua to see Kaplan. Joshua was at that time about six years old. We had been discussing the Exodus, and I told him that the story of the plagues was only an exaggeration and that they did not really occur. "Why, then," he asked me, "did Pharaoh let the children of Israel go?" I could not answer his question. While we were visiting Kaplan, I encouraged Joshua to pose his question again. Kaplan, who was ninety-one at the time, gave a more radical answer than I would have considered. He told Joshua that Moses never asked Pharaoh to let the children of Israel go in the first place. The story of the meetings between Moses and Pharaoh — and, of course, the plagues — was fiction. What probably happened, he explained, is that the Israelites just fled. Being slaves, it would have made little sense for them, in the course of a rebellion, to ask permission to leave. Ahad Ha-Am's comment on historical truth is contained in his essay entitled "Moses." See Leon Simon, ed., *Essays, Letters, Memoirs: Ahad Ha-Am* (Oxford: East and West Library, 1946), pp. 102–16.

37. In his commentary from the late 1940s, there is a statement worth noting even though it is only a cryptic remark jotted on the side of a page. It reads, "J = Divinity in Israel, values of people-hood, law. E = Divinity in nature, values of creativity." The problem with this analysis is that Kaplan probably had in mind chapter 1 of Genesis as reflecting E. According to E. A. Speiser, however, most critics agree that chapter 1 is from P (priestly source) rather than from E (Elohist source). E has no part in telling the story of the primeval age. He enters when the narrative is well into the Abraham legends. While P seems to have some elements Kaplan is pointing to, it also relates to genealogy and other matters that militate against Kaplan's neat analysis. Speiser does point out that J tends to be more earthbound than E, being "led to interpose angels or dreams, or both, the Deity being regarded, it would seem, as too remote for personal intervention." We could retain Kaplan's analysis without tying it to a documentary framework by focusing on his statement that "God reveals himself in a two-fold capacity." See E. A. Speiser, ed., *Genesis* (Garden City, N.Y.: Doubleday and Co., 1964), introduction.

38. This summary is based on Kaplan, "Torah and Salvation."

39. Unless otherwise noted, all subsequent quotations from Kaplan are taken from "Torah and Salvation," which has very irregular pagination.

CHAPTER 10

1. Minutes of the Society for the Advancement of Judaism, January 24, 1922, contain the figures mentioned. The minutes state that thirty-five families left the center; other sources say twenty-two. Levy's remarks are from the text of a speech he gave on the fifteenth anniversary of the SAJ. This speech is contained in the SAJ papers at the American Jewish Historical Society.

2. Kaplan's statements of the goals: SAJ minutes, January 24, 1922; Mrs. Lamport's remark: SAJ minutes, January 31, 1922. On May 2, 1927, the board chairman called attention to the fact that Kaplan had never been paid and that the endowment insurance he asked for in place of a salary also had never been established. They passed a resolution to bring the insurance up to date.

3. Levels of membership: SAJ board minutes, February 7, 1922; opening up to Zionist groups: SAJ Board minutes, February 14, 1922.

4. *SAJ Bulletin*, February 16, 1923. Evelyn Garfiel eventually became Max Kadushin's wife.

5. Kaplan journal, September 28, 1923. See also December 16, 1924, where Kaplan reiterates his desire for a "chain of Societies."

6. For the establishment of the chapters, see SAJ board minutes for 1925, 1926, 1927, where these chapters are mentioned as they formed. The reorganization of the SAJ is discussed on February 2, 1925, but obviously it does not work because precisely the same matter is discussed three years later. See SAJ minutes, April 9, 1928.

7. *New York Herald Tribune*, March 22, 1925.

8. Israel Levinthal's remark is quoted by Deborah Dash Moore in "A Synagogue Center Grows in Brooklyn," *The American Synagogue: A Sanctuary Transformed*, ed. by Jack Wertheimer (New York: Cambridge University Press, 1987), pp. 277–327. Kaplan's book is entitled *New Approach to Judaism* and was republished in 1973 by Hartmore House, Bridgeport, Conn.

9. See *SAJ Bulletin* for 1922. This synagogue publication came out in mimeographed form. On small attendance at lectures, see SAJ board minutes, December 4, 1922. On Spiegel lectures and lectures on women's history, see bulletins for 1929 and 1930 in the SAJ collection at the American Jewish Historical Society. Other lectures in the early years included Salo Baron on "The State and the Jew," Sidney Hook on "The Marxian Philosophy of History," and Jacque Faitlovitch on the Falashas. See Kaplan journal, December 26, 1929. See preface in Spiegel's *Hebrew Reborn* for acknowledgment of his gratitude to SAJ.

10. See *The Art of Temima Gezari: Painting, Drawing and Sculpture*, ed. by Daniel Gezari. See also *Reconstructionist*, May 1935. The mural still may be viewed at the SAJ.

11. The arbitration board is mentioned in the SAJ board minutes for October 27, 1924, and in an article in *American Israelite*, April 2, 1925. The dinner-dance lecture is mentioned in an invitation to this event found among the SAJ papers at AJHS. The contents of Kaplan's speech are contained in his journal, November 29, 1931. Maurice Samuels spoke at the Hotel Delmonico on April 17, 1932, where the SAJ had a similar affair.

12. SAJ minutes, May 11, 1924.

13. Some think Kaplan did not measure up to someone like Stephen Wise as an orator. See Melvin I. Urofsky, *A Voice that Spoke for Justice: The Life and Times of Stephen S. Wise* (Albany: State University of New York Press, 1982), pp. 79–80.

14. Meeting with the board, Kaplan journal, October 13, 1922.

15. The title page of the *Blue Book* reads simply, "The Society for the Advancement of Judaism," with no author mentioned. It is set up in a question-and-answer format. I assume Kaplan wrote it. He is listed as the "Leader" of the society. The statement of aims is on p. 5, the statement about deliberation on p. 15. The Code of Practice is mentioned in a number of newspaper articles: *Denver Jewish News*, November 13, 1924; and *American Jewish Press* (Minneapolis), November 7, 1924. See SAJ papers at AJHS. For a discussion of the Musar movement, see chapter 1 above.

16. The background material and line of reasoning in this and the previous paragraph are based on an essay by Michael Novak, "Crime and Character," *This World*, Spring–Summer 1986, pp. 26–54.

17. Mordecai Kaplan, *The Meaning of Religion*, unpublished manuscript from the 1920s, RRC, p. 142.

18. Ibid., p. 124.

19. Ibid., p. 147.

20. M. M. Kaplan, sermon at the Jewish Center, March 1, 1919, RRC.

21. Remarks on the Catholic church in *Judaism as a Civilization* (New York: Macmillan, 1934), p. 77. The visibility of the church in *The Future of the American Jew* (New York: Macmillan, 1948), p. 99.

22. Daniel J. Elazar, *Community and Polity: The Organizational Dynamics of American Jewry* (Philadelphia: Jewish Publication Society, 1976), p. 12.

23. Kaplan, *Judaism as a Civilization*, pp. 292–93.

24. Kaplan, *The Future of the American Jew*, p. 395.

25. For a very pointed analysis of this key concept, see Eugene B. Borowitz, "The Autonomous Jewish Self," *Modern Judaism* (February 1984): pp. 39–55.

26. Kaplan, *The Meaning of Religion*, p. 122.

27. Ibid., p. 118.

28. See partial account in Parzen, *Architects of Conservative Judaism* (New York: Jonathan David, 1964), pp. 198ff.

29. The theory that Kaplan was offered the presidency of the Jewish Institute of Religion twice comes from Wise himself, who recorded this fact in his autobiography. Wise had Kaplan in mind for the presidency but never officially offered it to him. Stephen S. Wise, *Challenging Years: The Autobiography of Stephen S. Wise* (New York: G. P. Putnam's Sons, 1949), p. 136. Charles Liebman maintains that Kaplan was offered the presidency at least once, in 1927. See Charles Liebman, "Reconstructionism in American Jewish Life," *American Jewish Yearbook 1970* (New York: American Jewish Committee, 1970), p. 30.

30. For Kaplan as one of the finest minds, see Wise, *Challenging Years*, p. 136. Wise and Kaplan of one mind: S. S. Wise to Solomon Goldman, AJA, JIR collection. Wise sees himself as neither original thinker nor scholar: this is the judgment of Michael Meyer in "Kelal-Yisrael: The Jewish Institute of Religion," *Hebrew Union College — Jewish Institute of Religion at One Hundred Years*, ed. by Samuel Karff (Cincinnati: Hebrew Union College Press, 1976), p. 148.

31. Wise could get the funds: Kaplan journal, July 27, 1920. Wise recorded in 1927 that as far back as 1915, Kaplan came to him and told of his unhappiness at the Seminary. At that time, Kaplan considered becoming part of the Free Synagogue movement. See memo of a meeting, January 3, 1927, attended by Judge Mack, Wise, Kaplan, Dr. Kohut, written by Wise, in AJA, JIR collection. Wise invites Kaplan to be co-founder: Wise to Kaplan, July 26, 1923, American Jewish Historical Society, Kaplan file in Wise papers.

32. Kaplan hoping to renew negotiations in the future: Kaplan journal, May 5, 1922; courage to cross the Rubicon: Kaplan journal, April 27, 1922. Better for Kaplan to have come to the JIR: Stephen Wise to Kaplan, May 31, 1922, AJHS, Kaplan file in Wise papers.

33. Kaplan feels like Hamlet: Kaplan journal, April 1922. For the exchange before the meeting, see Wise to Kaplan, November 16, 1922; Kaplan to Wise, November 21, 1922; Wise to Kaplan, November 25, 1922, AJA, JIR collection. For Kaplan's reaction to the meeting and feeling like a failure, see Kaplan journal, December 7, 1922.

34. Wise to Kaplan, February 23, 1923; Kaplan to Wise, March 4, 1923, AJA, JIR collection.

35. Kaplan journal, July 1923.

36. Kaplan journal, September 1923. Wise expressed the same idea in 1927 when he told the JIR faculty that Kaplan "is the only man in the four Jewish seminaries in America who has created his own 'school.'" Extract of minutes of faculty meeting, January 12, 1927, AJA, JIR collection.

37. A rough draft of the Kaplan's letter of resignation is among his papers. The language is quite restrained but clearly shows his anger. It reads in part, "But inasmuch as you imply that if you were to know that I was teaching the knowledge of Judaism you would consider my membership in the Seminary faculty a source of embarrassment to the Seminary,

I cannot see how I can act otherwise than send you herewith my resignation as Professor of Homiletics and as Principal of the Teachers' Institute." The letter is unsigned, undated, and untitled, but it is in Kaplan's handwriting, and its contents clearly mark it as the resignation letter of 1923. Kaplan explaining what he in fact did in class: Mordecai M. Kaplan to Cyrus Adler, September 16, 1923, Kaplan papers, RRC; Adler saying we are all personal friends: Cyrus Adler to Mordecai Kaplan, September 21, 1923; Kaplan to Adler, September 24, 1923. Adler's letter may be found in *Cyrus Adler — Selected Letters* (Philadelphia: Jewish Publication Society, 1985) Vol. 2, p. 79.

38. Among those who taught briefly were Harry Wolfson, Salo Baron, George Foote Moore, David Yellin, and James Parkes. See Wise, *Challenging Years*, p. 133; Mordecai Kaplan to Carl H. Voss, January 23, 1955, AJHA, Kaplan file in Wise papers; For evidence that Slonimsky was interested in the deanship Wise had in mind for Kaplan, see Judge Mack to Wise, January 14, 1927, AJA, JIR collection.

39. Morgenstern offering: Kaplan journal, September 24, 1925; conversation with Schulman: Kaplan journal, November 1, 1925; Morgenstern can not make offer: Kaplan journal, December 15, 1925.

40. Kaplan would attract people: Kaplan journal, January 3, 1927. On January 3, 1927, Wise wrote, "I feel that [Kaplan's] coming now would do more than anything else to guarantee the stability, and humanely speaking, the perpetuity of the Jewish Institute of Religion"; memo of meeting of January 3, 1927, in Wise's study, AJA, JIR collection. Kaplan insists on his title: Memo re Kaplan, January 6, 1927, by Wise, AJA, JIR collection. Faculty agree to invite Kaplan: "Extract of Minutes of Executive Committee Meeting January 12, 1927, Re: Dr. Mordecai M. Kaplan," AJA, JIR collection. They want to invite him after he submits his resignation: "Extract of Minutes of Board of Trustees, February 8, 1927, Re: Dr. Mordecai M. Kaplan," AJA, JIR collection.

41. Resignation letter: Mordecai M. Kaplan to Cyrus Adler, January 19, 1927, RRC. Adler makes no attempt to dissuade Kaplan: Cyrus Adler to Mordecai Kaplan, January 26, 1927, RRC. Marshall's remark that it should have happened five years ago: Louis Marshall to Cyrus Adler, January 23, 1927, quoted in Aaron Rothkoff, *Bernard Revel: Builder of American Jewish Orthodoxy* (Philadelphia: Jewish Publication Society, 1972), p. 338.

42. Mordecai M. Kaplan to Cyrus Adler, January 31, 1927, RRC.

43. Note from the faculty of the Teachers' Institute faculty to Mordecai Kaplan, January 23, 1927, RRC. Rabbinical School students to Cyrus Adler, undated, RRC. This letter was composed by Milton Steinberg. My thanks to Simon Noveck for this piece of information.

44. Statement of Rabbinical Assembly Executive Committee, RRC. Present at the meeting were rabbis Drob, Finkelstein, Simon Greenberg, and Morris Silverman, among others. Kaplan remembered being impressed by the fact that Drob, the most Orthodox of the group, individually asked him to stay on. Interview with Kaplan, August 1972. See also Kaplan journal, February 23, 1927. Also reporting on the Rabbinical Assembly, Kaplan to Judge Mack, March 9, 1927, AJA, JIR collection. Interview with Judith Kaplan Eisenstein, July 1974.

45. Wise to Judge Mack, February 24, 1927, AJA, JIR collection. Kaplan journal, February 23, 1927. See also Judge Mack to Mordecai M. Kaplan, March 1, 1927, RRC.

46. Kaplan's letter to Carl H. Voss.

47. Simon Greenberg: Kaplan journal, February 23, 1927. Judge Mack's belief in the victory for the liberal forces: Judge Mack to Wise, March 1, 1927, AJA, JIR collection. The same point was made to the Executive Committee of the JIR board. See "Extract of Minutes of Executive Committee Meeting, March 9, 1927," AJA, JIR collection. For documentary evidence on the liberal wing of the Rabbinical Assembly, see Herman H. Rubenovitz and Mignon L. Rubenovitz, *The Waking Heart* (Cambridge: Nathaniel Dame and Co., 1967), pp. 73–84.

48. Kaplan journal, July 1926.

49. Kadushin to Mordecai Kaplan, March 1, 1927, RRC.

50. Letter ought to be circulated: Rubenovitz to Mordecai Kaplan, April 8, 1927, RRC. Minimum of machinery in letter: Kaplan to H. H. Rubenovitz, April 20, 1927, RRC. Max Kadushin to Mordecai Kaplan, May 6, 1927, RRC. Some of the letters from this period have been published in Herbert Rosenblum, "The Emergence of the Reconstructionist Movement," *Reconstructionist* 51 (May 1975): 4, 7–21. This article contains the correspondence that circulated among the key men: Kaplan, Kadushin, Goldman, Rubenovitz, and Eugene Kohn.

51. Kaplan journal, July 1927.

52. Rubenovitz to Kaplan, April 15, 1927, RRC.

53. Kaplan journal, July 1927.

CHAPTER 11

1. Sermon delivered at the SAJ, November 2, 1923, RRC.

2. Mordecai Kaplan, "Why Combat Fundamentalism," outline of a lecture delivered on February 15, 1924; "Why Is Judaism More Than a Philosophy," sermon at SAJ, November 9, 1923, RRC.

3. Sermon at SAJ, January 11, 1924; sermon at SAJ, September 23, 1922, RRC. The whole discussion on America as the civilization of choice is found in the journal, December 26, 1923.

4. "Is Judaism a Revelation or a Philosophy," sermon at SAJ, November 2, 1923, RRC.

5. "Fundamentalism vs. Modernism," lecture at SAJ, January 9, 1924; God as the living universe: Kaplan journal, February 18, 1926. When pushed, Kaplan might say that he believed in God as a transcendent being. He once explained that while he "believed in God as a transcendent Being," he could not conceive of that Being having any meaning for us except through and in terms of human experience." Kaplan journal, November 1, 1925.

6. *A New Approach to Jewish Life* has recently (1973) been reprinted for the Jewish Reconstructionist Foundation by Hartmore House of Bridgeport, Conn. This new edition contains an introduction by Jacob Neusner. Reviews of Kaplan's book are contained in *Jewish Courier*, Chicago, January 4, 1925; *Jewish Transcript*, Seattle, March 20, 1925 (which contains the quotation from Israel Zangwill); and others. These newspaper articles and scores of others are found in scrapbook 2 of the SAJ papers housed at the American Jewish Historical Society. Kaplan's trip in late 1927 and early 1928 was typical. He spoke at Chicago, Minneapolis, Detroit, and Syracuse. He also traveled abroad in 1923 to the Zionist Congress at Carlsbad, where he gave a paper, and in 1925 to the opening exercises of the Hebrew University, where, as the representative of the Zionist Organization of America, he delivered one of the dedication lectures.

7. The insights in this paragraph arose from conversations with Robert Seltzer of Hunter College and his own work on Simon Dubnov.

8. Although many of these changes were already found in the Reform Union Prayerbook, not all were introduced in the Hebrew text as Kaplan had done.

9. For a more complete treatment of the changes in the liturgy, see Ira Eisenstein, "Kaplan as Liturgist," *The American Judaism of Mordecai Kaplan*, ed. Emanuel S. Goldsmith, Mel Scult, and Robert Seltzer (New York: New York University Press, 1990). Eisenstein remembered the *Aleinu* change being there when he started to attend the SAJ in the late 1920s. The phrase for chosenness apparently was not taken out until the 1940s. Eisenstein remembered the details surrounding the official adoption of the prayerbook in 1945 by the SAJ; interview, July 1989. The new Reconstructionist Prayerbook, *Kol Haneshamah*, introduces a new formulation in the blessing over the wine (*Kiddush*). Instead of the chosenness phrase or Kaplan's 1945 version, it reads, "For you have called to us and set us apart to serve you." The commentary explains: "The version used here imagines a God who calls all

humanity and makes holy those who, like Israel, heed the call and engage in God's service." *Kol Haneshamah* (Wyncote, Pa: Reconstructionist Press, 1989), p. 128. The Union Prayerbook of 1940 retains the chosenness phrase in Hebrew but softens it in English.

10. When asked about the changes, Kaplan maintained that they were all early, 1920s, but in some cases I have not been able to document the specific date when a particular passage was removed—e.g., the resurrection of the dead. "This is the Torah" was dropped on Rosh Hashanah, 1926. On this particular Rosh Hashanah, Kaplan left out most of the psalms in the early part of the service (before *Borekhu*) because there was hardly anyone in the synagogue at that point. See Kaplan journal, September 12, 1926, for purposes of comparison. The Union Prayerbook used by Reform congregations simply dropped the last sentence of *Ein Keblohaynu* which referred to sacrifices. Concerning resurrection of the dead, it substituted the following for the reference in the *Amidah* prayer: "Who hast implanted within us eternal life." For all quotations from Kaplan's Sabbath service, see *Sabbath Prayerbook with Supplement Containing Prayers, Readings and Hymns and with a New Translation* (New York: Jewish Reconstructionist Foundation, 1945). For Reform practice, see *The Union Prayerbook for Jewish Worship* (New York: Central Conference of American Rabbis, 1940).

11. Conversation with Finkelstein and his wife: Kaplan journal, August 31, 1922; conversation with Moshe Levine: September 18, 1922.

12. Klein perhaps did not realize that the language of the *Kol Nidre* nullifies all vows from the *present* Yom Kippur until the *next* one.

13. The board meeting and the discussions with individual board members: Kaplan journal, September 30, 1927; October 19, 1927. Anna Kaplan to M. M. Kaplan, December 24, 1927, RRC.

14. *Jewish Daily Bulletin*, October 7, 1927; *American Hebrew*, October 14, 1927. For criticism of Kaplan, see *Yidisher Tagblat*, October 7, 1927.

15. Jacob Klein to Kaplan, September 20, 1930, RRC; Kaplan thinking of restoring the Kol Nidre and resolution by the Board that he should be supported in his stand: SAJ board minutes, September 30, 1929. The Eisenstein-Kaplan correspondence is found at the RRC. See also Ira Eisenstein, "Kaplan as Liturgist," *The American Judaism of Mordecai M. Kaplan*. I am grateful to Eisenstein for first pointing out the correspondence to me. The text of the amended *Kol Nidre* is taken from the *High Holiday Prayerbook, Vol. II, Prayers for Yom Kippur* (New York: Jewish Reconstructionist Foundation, 1948), p.3. I am also indebted to Professor Jakob Petuchowski for his help with *Kol Nidre*, especially a letter on June 14, 1984, in which he helped to put the *Kol Nidre* in historical perspective. After the altered *Kol Nidre* was reinstituted, Ira Eisenstein sent it to colleagues and friends for reactions. See Kallen papers, box 8, Folder 23, Ira Eisenstein to Horace Kallen, September 29, 1931, AJA.

16. *Selections from Psalms for Responsive Readings*, SAJ papers at AJHS. Kaplan adding H. E. Fosdick, see Kaplan journal, September 30, 1925.

17. This very important point about format is made by Neil Gillman in "Entering the Second Century: From Scholarship to the Rabbinate," *Proceedings of the Rabbinical Assembly of America* (New York: Rabbinical Assembly of America, 1986).

18. Difficulties with funerals in many places in Kaplan journal, e.g., October 1, 1932, where a plaque was being put up dedicated to the father of one of the members Kaplan knew was dishonest and exploitive in his business.

19. Kaplan journal, February 1924.

20. Miss Bentwich: Kaplan journal, May 20,1933. It may be interesting to note in terms of the relationships of the Seminary faculty that Professor Boaz Cohen was married to Israel Friedlaender's sister. (My thanks to Jonathan Sarna for this information.) Herbert Bentwich had nine children and it is impossible to identify which daughter visited Kaplan.

21. Moving holidays to Sunday: Kaplan journal, April 13, 1933; Second Days eliminated: Ira Eisenstein interview, 1989. The SAJ discussed the matter of eliminating second days endlessly and finally came to a decision in the early 1950s to restrict major holidays except Rosh Hashanah to one day. According to all accounts, Kaplan remained on the side-

lines and allowed the different factions in the congregation to fight it out. The same is the case concerning calling up women to the Torah on a regular basis, which was not instituted until the 1940s. My thanks to Myron Eisenstein for these details. Conversation with Brickner in Kaplan journal, September 17, 1924. Proposition to fully observe the first day in Kaplan journal, October 8, 1930.

22. Kaplan preparing sermons on Friday night: Kaplan journal, February 20, 1925; Selma Kaplan finds Kaplan writing on the Sabbath: Kaplan journal, September 21, 1934; Kaplan davonning daily and studying a *Blatt Gemorah:* Kaplan journal, July 3, 1925. We should note that Kaplan wore the four-fringed undergarment throughout his life. In his later life, he was fond of showing people the *tzizit* (tassles) of this undergarment (*arba kanfot*) which he had had dyed purple. Although today all *tzizit* are white, in ancient times they were purple (*tehelet*), which was supposed to symbolize the power of God. The Orthodox used to tell the story with great relish that all Kaplan's children wore *tzizit*. The story is not true, of course, because Kaplan had four daughters.

23. All the quotations on *Kashrut* are from Kaplan journal, March 28, 1922.

24. Kaplan journal, May 21, 1933.

25. There is the slight possibility that Kaplan did not author these prayers. He had the habit of copying prayers he liked into his notebooks and did not always indicate the author. In the case of the prayers cited here, there are many revisions, which probably indicate that he was writing them himself.

26. The translation is taken from *The Sabbath Prayerbook*, p. 116. The comment about addressing God is from *Questions Jews Ask* (New York: Reconstructionist Press, 1956), p. 104.

27. See Kaplan journal, February 15, 1933 for the divorce incident, and Kaplan journal, February 22, 1926, for the material on conversion. Strictly speaking, the immersion in the pool at the center was not *halakhic*, either. The woman wore a bathing suit, and the pool did not meet all the requirements of a *mikveh*.

28. Mordecai M. Kaplan to Rabbi Morris Silverman, April 27, 1927, RRC.

29. See Jonathan D. Sarna, "The Debate over Mixed Seating in the Synagogue," *The American Synagogue: A Sanctuary Transformed*, ed. by Jack Wertheimer (New York: Cambridge University Press, 1987), pp. 363–95.

30. Kaplan journal, October 2 and 3, 1922.

31. The account here is based primarily on Judith's memoir as published, "Judith Kaplan Eisenstein Becomes the First Bas Mitzvah 1921 [sic]," *Eyewitnesses to American Jewish History, Part IV, The American Jew 1915–1969*, ed. by Azriel Eisenberg, (New York: Union of American Hebrew Congregations, 1976), pp. 29–32. Both the Kaplan journal and the *SAJ Bulletin* confirm that the bas mitzvah was in March and not May, as Judith's account has it. When asked about this, Judith remembered that when she published her account, she asked her father about the date, and he apparently did not look in the journal and thus gave her the wrong day (May 5) and the wrong *Parsha*. He said it was *Kedoshim*, but again, according to the *SAJ Bulletin*, March 1922, it was *Ki Tissah*.

32. Kaplan journal, December 20, 1932.

33. Kaplan thumping on Shavout: Kaplan journal, May 19, 1926; Kaplan wrote about his wife after they had a fight over his behavior: Kaplan journal, December 29, 1924.

34. Sabbath morning with only a hundred: see Kaplan journal, March 16, 1926; dinner dance at the Hotel Astor: February 10, 1924. Difficulty in small talk and also dinner dance: May 22, 1922 in Kaplan journal.

35. Celebrating twenty-five years in the rabbinate: Kaplan journal, January 13, 1930. This passage includes the quotation "He is my friend . . ." which Kaplan ascribes to Felix Adler, but does not give the source. Quitting the SAJ, February 1, 1929, Kaplan was ordained in 1902 so actually it had been twenty-seven years in the rabbinate.

36. Difficulties in writing, Kaplan journal, December 11, 1930; his reach far exceeds his grasp, Kaplan journal, March 9, 1931.

37. Kaplan journal, December 14, 1924.

38. Kaplan journal, March 9, 1926.
39. Kaplan journal, March 16, 1926.

CHAPTER 12

1. For an in-depth study of Kaplan's Zionism in the period after *Judaism as a Civilization*, see Jack J. Cohen, "Reflections on Kaplan's Zionism," *The American Judaism of Mordecai Kaplan*, ed. Emanuel S. Goldsmith, Mel Scult, and Robert Seltzer (New York: New York University Press, 1990), pp. 401–15. For Friedlaender, see Shargel, *Practical Dreamer: Israel Friedlaender and the Shaping of American Judaism* (New York: Jewish Theological Seminary, 1985), especially chapter 9. On Judah Magnes, see *Like All Nations? The Life and Legacy of Judah Magnes*, ed. by William M. Brinner and Moses Rischin (Albany: State University of New York Press, 1987). On the relationship between Zionism and Americanism, see Deborah Dash Moore, "The New American Judaism," *Like All Nations*, pp. 41–57.

2. For the dedication to Ahad Ha-Am and to Schechter and Brandeis as well, see Mordecai M. Kaplan, *The Religion of Ethical Nationhood: Judaism's Contribution to World Peace* (New York: Macmillan Co., 1970). See also Kaplan's autobiographical statement "The Way I Have Come," in *Mordecai M. Kaplan: An Evaluation*, ed. by Ira Eisenstein and Eugene Kohn (New York: Jewish Reconstructionist Foundation, 1952), for tributes to Ahad Ha-Am. The second part of the quotation (on the meaning of God) comes from "The Way I Have Come," p. 298.

3. For Kaplan's comment on the occasion of Ahad Ha-Am's death, see *SAJ Review*, January 7, 1927, p. 2. In a telephone conversation with me in 1972, Kaplan expressed annoyance that so many considered the primary influences on him to be non-Jewish, whereas he felt it was Ahad Ha-Am who was the primary influence. The most important recent study of Ahad Ha-Am is *At the Crossroads: Essays on Ahad Ha-Am*, ed. by Jacques Kornberg (Albany: State University of New York Press, 1983).

4. See, for example, Ahad Ha-Am, "Ancestor Worship," *Essays, Letters, Memoirs: Ahad Ha-Am Translated from the Hebrew*, ed. by Leon Simon (Oxford: East and West Library, 1946).

5. These statements come from a letter Wolfson wrote to the *American Hebrew* after he heard a lecture by Horace Kallen. See *American Hebrew*, May 27, 1910.

6. For Ahad Ha-Am's doubts about the future of religion, see, for example, the letter he wrote to Israel Abrahams, March 30, 1913, in *Essays, Letters, Memoirs*, p. 270.

7. Kaplan journal, October 4, 1914. Ahad Ha-Am's discussion of traditional religious rigidity is found in "The People of the Book," *Essays, Letters, Memoirs*, pp. 58–64.

8. Kaplan's essay is "The God Idea in Judaism" and may be found in *The Jewish Reconstructionist Papers*, ed. by Mordecai M. Kaplan (New York: Behrman's Jewish Book House, 1936). The whole point of the connection with Ahad Ha-Am was suggested in an essay by Meir Ben Horin, "Ahad Ha-Am in Kaplan: Roads Crossing and Parting," *The American Judaism of Mordecai Kaplan*.

9. Israel Friedlaender's famous "Zionism plus Diaspora" statement is taken from the introduction to his book of essays *Past and Present: Selected Essays*, 2nd ed. (New York: Burning Bush Press, 1961), xxiii. In an unpublished version of some of these essays, Baila Shargel found the expression "religion and nationalism." See Shargel, *Practical Dreamer*, p. 161. For the relationship of Ahad Ha-Am to American Zionism, see Evyatar Friesel, "Ahad Ha-Amism in American Zionist Thought," in Kornberg, *At the Crossroads*, pp. 133–42.

10. Shargel cites Friedlaender's statement that "In the dispersion we can and must aim at the preservation of Judaism, at the adaptation of Judaism, but we scarcely dare hope for a creative Judaism," *Practical Dreamer*, p. 179. Friesel sees Friedlaender as very close to Dubnov; Kornberg, pp. 139–40.

11. Milton R. Konvitz, "Horace Meyer Kallen (1882–1974): In Praise of Hyphenation and Orchestration," *The Legacy of Horace M. Kallen*, ed. by Milton R. Konvitz (New York: Herzl Press, 1987), p. 17. The material in this section on Kallen is based mostly on Konvitz.

12. Kaplan journal, December 26, 1906.

13. The statement on the Jews as a nation is in Kaplan, sermon book II, 1903, RRC. The statement about the transformation of Jewish life and Palestine is found in an article by Kaplan in *New Palestine*, October 19, 1928. On *Galus* and its abnormality, see Kaplan, "Judaism and Nationality," *Maccabaean* 17 (August 1909): 63. The statement on Judaism as feasible only in Palestine is in Kaplan, *A New Approach to Jewish Life* (New York: The Society for the Advancement of Judaism, 1924; repr., Bridgeport Conn.: Hartmore House, 1973), p. 52. The statement about Dubnov and Kallen follows on p. 53.

14. Kaplan, "The Future of Judaism," *Menorah Journal*, June 1916, p. 171.

15. These thoughts are contained in an outline of conversations Kaplan had with the leaders of the Jewish Center. See Kaplan journal, August 31, 1917.

16. Kaplan, "The Future of Judaism," p. 171.

17. Kaplan journal, March 16, 1926.

18. For a detailed history of the Zionist movement in America, see Melvin Urofsky, *American Zionism from Herzl to the Holocaust* (Garden City, N.Y.: Anchor/Doubleday, 1975). The figures for membership are on p. 147. See also Naomi Cohen, *American Judaism and the Zionist Idea* (New York: KTAV, 1975).

19. Kaplan journal, April 1921. Unless otherwise indicated, the rest of the account is taken from the Kaplan journals.

20. For Mack's point of view, see Harry Barnard, *The Forging of an American Jew: The Life and Times of Julian W. Mack* (New York: Herzl Press, 1974).

21. Kaplan journal, June 16, 1921.

22. Kaplan journal, May 29, 1923.

23. For the full story of the sponsorship of the *Hebrew Journal*, see above p. 260. See Ernst Pawel, *The Nightmare of Reason: A Life of Franz Kafka* (New York: Random House, 1985).

24. Kaplan journal, August 19, 1923.

25. Kaplan journal, March 12, 1925 (aboard the S.S. *Olympic*).

26. Greenberg's remarks are included in his diary March 28, 1925, found in the Greenberg papers, Jewish Theological Seminary.

27. Kaplan journal, April 1, 1925. From the time Kaplan left New York, he kept the diary in Hebrew. I have translated the quotations from this period. Kaplan's remark to Lena in a letter dated April 1, 1925. I am grateful to Hadassah and the late Sidney Musher for allowing me to look at the letters from Kaplan to Lena from this period.

28. The details of the opening are taken from "The Palestine Bulletin," published in Jerusalem, April 3, 1925, Central Zionist Archives, A 209/145. See also *New Palestine*, April 8, 1925. Kook's speaking too long comes from an interview with Simon Greenberg, March 1985. Kook's remarks are recorded in a book published by the Hebrew University sometime after the event which includes many of the speeches of that first week: *The Hebrew University of Jerusalem — The Opening Exercises* (Jerusalem: Hebrew University, 1926). Referred to hereafter as *Opening Exercises*.

29. Details of the day in this paragraph are found in *The New Palestine*, April 8, 1925. The full text of Balfour's speech is found in *Opening Exercises*.

30. *Jewish Record*, San Antonio, Texas, April 24, 1925, contains the transcript of Kaplan's speech. See SAJ papers, box 2, AJHS.

31. Magnes's introduction to Kaplan's speech is from an interview with Simon Greenberg, March 1985.

32. L'ag B'omer is the thirty-third day of the counting of the Omer which begins on the second day of Passover and ends on Shevuot. (Feast of Weeks). The thirty-third day is a scholars' holiday because of the cessation of a plague during the second century. It is also the supposed anniversary of the death of Simon Bar Yochai, the author of the *Zohar*, according to the Kabbalists. On that date, the pious gather at the grave of Simon Bar Yochai in Meron which is near Safed. The celebration is famous. It is this celebration that Kaplan attended.

33. The details here are from Kaplan's letters to his wife, Lena. When Kaplan was at the Hebrew University from 1937 to 1939, there were more attempts to keep him there, but he refused all offers. Regarding his refusal to accept a teaching position at the Hebrew University in 1939, see letter from A. Frankl to Chaim Weizmann, January 23, 1939, Weizmann Archives, Weizmann Institute.

34. The statement here is from *Jewish Daily News*, June 28, 1925.

35. The details of the ZOA for this period can be found in Urofsky, *American Zionism*, chapter 9. S. Levin to Chaim Weizmann, June 30, 1927, Weizmann papers, Weizmann Institute. Kaplan statement about being dragged into Zionist politics in Kaplan journal, December 7, 1927.

36. Details, including the text of the telegram from Weizmann, are found in Kaplan journal, June 24, 1928.

37. The appointment was written up in the Jewish press in America and abroad. See *Jewish World*, London, September 27, 1928.

38. The press release announcing Kaplan's election is found in the papers of Henry Hurwitz, the editor of the *Menorah Journal* and a good friend of Kaplan's. It is dated September 14, 1928, and is found in box 25, folder 6, Hurwitz papers, American Jewish Archives. Kaplan's speech to the Zionist executive is found in *SAJ Review*, October 19, 1928. The quotations concerning the transformation of Jewish life are from *New Palestine*, October 19, 1928.

39. For Kaplan's article in *New Palestine*, see October 19, 1928, issue. Other details here are from the Kaplan journal for the fall of 1928. On Kaplan at the meeting in Cleveland, see *Jewish Independent of Cleveland*, January 4, 1929.

40. On the dinner, see *New York Times*, November 21, 1928; and Kaplan journal, same date.

41. The conversation between Kaplan and Benderly is in the Kaplan journal, February 4, 1929.

42. I am endebted to Deborah Dash Moore for this speculation, which seems a natural consequence of the subject of this discussion.

43. Kaplan journal, June 26, 1929.

44. Kaplan journal, July 3, 1929.

CHAPTER 13

1. Unless otherwise noted, all facts are taken from documents in the contest papers. I am very grateful to Rabbi Ira Eisenstein for giving me this valuable collection.

2. The judges and their affiliations were Lee K. Frankel, businessman, Reform; Elisha Friedman, economist, Zionist; Nathan Isaacs, professor at Harvard Law School, Orthodox; Irving Lehman, judge, Reform; Horace Stern, judge, Reform; Dr. Harry Friedenwald, physician, Zionist; Leon Huhner, lawyer, traditional Conservative. Figures on the submissions are in a letter from Samson Benderly to Julius Rosenwald, May 7, 1931, contest papers.

3. Kaplan journal, February 5, 1933.

4. Kaplan's characterization of himself is actually taken from his reaction to an article he read in *New Republic* about Woodrow Wilson. Kaplan journal, September 20, 1932; statement of loving Benderly, Kaplan journal, December 20, 1932.

5. Friedenwald opinions in letter to Benderly, February 9, 1933. Huhner in letter to Benderly, February 21, 1933. Isaacs opinion in letter to Huhner, March 1, 1933 (which Huhner apparently forwarded to Benderly). Lehman in letter to Benderly, March 9, 1933. On the sums awarded, Benderly to Elisha Friedman, December 18, 1933.

6. Kaplan journal, February 8, 1935.

7. The dedication might be translated as follows: "To the memory of Rabbi Israel Kaplan, my father and teacher, [a man] of pure knowledge and courageous spirit who became my eyes in my wanderings through the wilderness of doubt and confusion."

8. Most of this statement is taken directly from Rosenthal, but it has been altered in minor ways. See Henry Rosenthal, review of *Judaism as a Civilization* by Mordecai Kaplan, in *Proceedings of the Rabbinical Assembly of America — Thirty-fourth Annual Convention at Tannersville, New York, July 3–5, 1935* (New York: Rabbinical Assembly of America, 1935), pp. 88–89.

9. For the view that Kaplan and his followers were only engaged in "sociological theorizing," see Robert G. Goldy, *The Emergence of Jewish Theology in America* (Bloomington and Indianapolis: Indiana University Press, 1990), pp. 1–16. For the use of the term *ideology* in analyzing American Jewish thought, see Arnold Eisen, *The Chosen People in America: A Study in Jewish Religious Ideology* (Bloomington: Indiana University Press, 1983). Kaplan refers to God as the living universe in the journal, February 18, 1926.

10. Kaplan, *Judaism as a Civilization*, p. 390.

11. For Kaplan's use of the term *cosmic life urge*, see *Judaism as a Civilization*, p. 401.

12. The issue is a very complicated one, and the reader is referred to Eisen, *The Chosen People in America*. Chosenness as harmful. See Kaplan, *Judaism as a Civilization*, p. 43.

13. De Sola Pool's remark is in a letter to the editor, *Jewish Forum*, October 1934, p. 290. The original article is Rabbi Aaron Rosmarin, "Wither the Jewish Theological Seminary," *Jewish Forum*, September 1934, pp. 239–47. The Sabbath being dropped is in Eisenstein, *Reconstructing Judaism* (New York: Reconstructionist Press, 1986).

14. Charles S. Liebman, "Reconstructionism in American Jewish Life," *The American Jewish Yearbook 1970*, ed. by Morris Fine and Milton Himmelfarb (New York and Philadelphia: American Jewish Committee and Jewish Publication Society, 1970), pp. 3–101. Liebman discusses Kaplan's audience.

15. Max Arzt, "Dr. Kaplan's Philosophy of Judaism," *Proceedings of the Rabbinical Assembly of America, Thirty-fifth Annual Convention at Rockaway Park, N.Y. May 13–15, 1935* (New York: Rabbinical Assembly of America, 1939), p. 206.

16. I am extremely grateful to Rabbi Abraham Karp, who allowed me to peruse Hymanson's annotated copy of *Judaism as a Civilization* in his possession. The comment by Hyamson is on page 317.

17. The reader who wants an answer to this question should study Kaplan's *The Meaning of God in Modern Jewish Religion* (New York: Berman's Jewish House, 1937), especially chapter 7, "God as Felt Presence."

18. Irving Howe, *A Margin of Hope: An Intellectual Biography* (New York: Harcourt Brace Jovanovich, 1982), p. 53.

19. On the degradation of the middle class, see Kaplan journal, March 24, 1933; July 25, 1934. See Rebecca Trachtenberg Alpert, "The Quest for Economic Justice: Kaplan's Response to the Challenge of Communism, 1929–1940," *The American Judaism of Mordecai Kaplan*, pp. 385–400.

20. Kaplan journal, April 21, 1935.

21. Harriet Feiner, "Kaplan's Influence on Jewish Social Work," *The American Judaism of Mordecai Kaplan*, pp. 357–69. The students remarks are from a letter to Harriet Finer from A. Cohen, April 4, 1987. The letter is quoted in Feiner's essay, p. 361. Kaplan mentions the influence of the School of Social work in the preface to *Judaism as a Civilization*, xiii. The quotation from Kaplan about a larger context is in Feiner, p. 363, and appeared originally in "Jewish Philanthropy; Traditional and Modern," *Intelligent Philanthropy*, ed. by Ellsworth Fire, Ferris Laune, and Arthur J. Todd (Chicago: University of Chicago Press, 1930), pp. 77–78.

22. Unless otherwise noted, the family account has been drawn from interviews with Kaplan himself, his four daughters and their spouses, and his grandchildren. Statement appreciating Lena Kaplan is in Kaplan journal, January 11, 1931. The text for "I Love to Lean on Lena" is found in the Kaplan journal, June 4, 1933.

23. Judith was born in 1909, sisters coming a few years apart. Hadassah was named after the organization; whereas Selma was named for Solomon Schechter, who died a short time

before she was born. Kaplan's daughters' married names are Judith Eisenstein, Hadassah Musher, Naomi Wenner, and Selma Goldman.

24. Judith K. Eisenstein's published works include *Heritage of Music: The Music of the Jewish People* (New York: Union of American Hebrew Congregations, 1972) and *The Gateway to Jewish Song* (New York: Behrman's Jewish Book House, 1939).

25. Kaplan journal, August 19, 1934. In his later life, Kaplan became increasingly impatient with the *Halakhah*.

26. Judith Kaplan Eisenstein was good enough to allow me to read her recently written memoir and the diary she wrote as a youngster. We have also spoken many times.

27. The original events appear in Kaplan journal, December 7 and 10, 1922. Judith also showed me her childhood diary, indicating the place where the pages were torn out.

28. M. M. K. to Judith K. Eisenstein, July 30, 1926, Reconstructionist Rabbinical College.

29. Kaplan journal, April 13, 1929.

30. Sigmund Freud to Lou Andreas-Salome, March 13, 1922, in *Sigmund Freud and Lou Andreas-Salome Letters*, ed. by Ernst Pfeiffer (New York: Harcourt Brace Jovanovich, 1972), p. 113, as quoted in Elizabeth Young-Bruehl, *Anna Freud: A Biography* (New York: Summit Books, 1988), p. 117. See chapter in Young-Bruehl, "Being Analyzed," for theories about Anna Freud's dreams. Anna Freud's statement after the onset of his illness, Anna Freud to Lou Andreas-Salome, August 29, 1923, as quoted in Young-Bruehl, p. 118.

31. Joan Dash, *Summoned to Jerusalem: The Life of Henrietta Szold* (New York: Harper and Row, 1979), p. 32.

32. See Eisenstein's autobiography, *Reconstructing Judaism: An Autobiography* (New York: Reconstructionist Press, 1986), especially the chapter entitled "Judith and Judaism as a Civilization."

33. *What is Torah? A Cantata for Unison Chorus and Piano*, words by Ira Eisenstein, music by Judith Kaplan Eisenstein (New York: Jewish Reconstructionist Foundation, 1943); and *Our Bialik: A Cantata for Unison Chorus and Piano*, words by Ira Eisenstein, music by Judith Kaplan Eisenstein (New York: Jewish Reconstructionist Foundation, 1945).

34. According to Eisenstein, Kaplan in previous years had offered the position to Milton Steinberg and Henry Fisher, another Seminary graduate. There is also evidence that in the 1920s he offered it to Max Kadushin. They all turned him down. See Eisenstein's account in *Reconstructing Judaism: An Autobiography*, p. 95. Kaplan's remark is in Kaplan journal, May 14, 1930.

35. See Eisenstein, *Reconstructing Judaism*, pp. 91–102. Kaplan's comment in Kaplan journal, June 2, 1931.

36. Riv-Ellen Prell, *Prayer and Community: The Havurah in American Judaism* (Detroit: Wayne State University Press, 1989).

37. The analysis in this paragraph is found in the Kaplan journal, April 21, 1933.

38. My feeling is that the burning of the book was not intentional but was done by someone standing in the back of the large room. I do not have solid evidence for this and the details of the *herem* have never been investigated.

39. A complete bibliography of Kaplan's writings may be found in *The American Judaism of Mordecai Kaplan*, 415–452.

40. This organization is now called the Federation of Reconstructionist Congregations and Havurot.

CONCLUSION

1. Maurice Karpf to Alexander Dushkin, March 17, 1932, Dushkin papers, Hebrew University. Karpf certainly had Ahad Ha-Am's typology in mind here rather than the one we

sketched above. For Ahad Ha-Am, the priest was the administrator and the enabler of ritual, the functionary who kept the religious establishment going.

2. Neil Gilman, "The Changing Paradigm of the Conservative Movement," *Conservative Judaism* 43 (Winter 1991): 5.

3. Abraham Cohen to Harriet Feiner, April 4, 1987, as it appears in Harriet Feiner, "Kaplan's Influence on Jewish Social Work," *The American Judaism of Mordecai Kaplan*, p. 361.

4. Kaplan journal, October 29, 1934.

5. Ibid.

6. Kaplan, *Judaism as a Civilization*, p. 245.

7. Kaplan journal, September 23, 1934.

INDEX

Achavah Club, 106–7

Adler, Cyrus: archaeology lectures, 46; on denominationalism, 128–29, 206; opposition to World War I Jewish congress, 139, 140; relationship with Kaplan, 93, 205–8, 271; response to Kaplan's resignation, 273, 274–75; on social sciences, 218; traditionalism, 205–6

Adler, Felix, 53, 58, 79–81, 351; sense of transcendent, 82–83

Agudath Ha-Rabbonim. See Orthodox Rabbinical Union; Union of Orthodox Rabbis

Agudath Jeshurun – A Union for Promoting Traditional Judaism in America. *See* United Synagogue

Aguinaldo, Emilio, 31

Agus, Jacob, 381 n.22

Ahad Ha-Am (Asher Ginzberg), 55, 107, 189, 309–12, 421 n.1; centrality of Zion, 311–12; concept of God, 310–11; on creative genius of Jewish people, 309–10; on historical and archaeological truth, 249–50; "Moses idea," 311; on reinterpretation of scriptures, 241

Akiba, R., 173

American Hebrew: on anti-Kaplan circular, 69; on English as language of instruction, 48; on Felix Adler, 79; on *Kol Nidre* controversy, 289; on Pittsburgh Platform, 38; on Russian pogroms, 63; on Young Israel, 137

American Jewish Committee, 139

American Jewish Yearbook, 103

Arnold, Matthew: *Literature and Dogma*, 83; "the not ourselves," 84

Aronson, Rebecca, 392 n.56

Arzt, Max, 257, 276; on *Judaism as a Civilization*, 344–45; on the *Mitzvot*, 345

Asher, Joseph Mayer, 66, 106

Association of American Orthodox Hebrew Congregations, 29

Bagehot, William: *Physics and Politics*, 228

Balfour, Lord, 327, 328

Balfour Declaration, 169, 317

Baum, Abba, 65

Bavli, Hillel, 114, 115

Beecher, Henry Ward, 291

Benderly, Samson, 113, 258; *Achavah* Club, 106; "Benderly boys," 121, 392 n.56; and Central Jewish Institute, 199; denominationalism, 271; and Hebrew

Benderly, Samson (*cont.*)
 Free School for Poor and Orphaned
 Children, 120; philosophy of educa-
 tion, 122, 123–24; relationship with
 Kaplan, 120; and Teachers' Institute,
 124; on teaching Hebrew in Hebrew
 (*Ivrit Be-Ivrit*), 114, 120; in
 Weizmann-Brandeis conflict, 318,
 319; and writing contest, 339
Bentham, Jeremy: utilitarianism, 85
Bentwich, Norman, 293
Berkson, Isaac, 121, 392 n.56; and Central
 Jewish Institute, 199, 400 n.42
Berlin, Naphtali Zvi Judah (*Netziv*), 21–22;
 Ha'amek Davar, 22
Bet-Din (rabbinical court), 259–60
Bialik, Chaim Nahman, 327, 328
Birnbaum, Ben H., 392 n.56
Blue Book, 262, 410 n.15
Blumenthal, Joseph, 49, 50
Bragin, Joseph, 234
Brandeis, Louis, 308; Americanization of
 Zionism, 317; and Balfour declaration,
 317; and *Keren Hayesod*, 318; vs. Weiz-
 mann, 317–20; and World War I Jew-
 ish congress, 139; and World Zionist
 Organization, 318
Brickner, Barnett, 293, 335, 392 n.56
British Mandate, 166
Brush, Louis, 213
Buber, Martin, 342
Buber, Solomon, 49
Bublick, Gedaliah, 106
Bultmann, Rudolf: demythology, 220–21;
 The Theology of the New Testament, 221
Bureau of Jewish Education. See *Kehillah*
Butler, Nicholas Murray, 53–54, 201
Butler, Samuel: *The Way of All Flesh*, 86–87,
 385 n.28

Cahan, Abraham, 32, 377 n.20
Carlsbad (Czechoslovakia), 323
Catholic Israel (*K'lal Yisrael*), 40, 128
Central Jewish Institute, 199–202, 400 n.42
Chertoff, Paul, 114, 115; and Society for
 Jewish Renascence, 184, 185, 187
Chipkin, Israel, 111, 115, 259, 392 n.56
City College of New York, 377 n.23
Cohen, Joseph H., 65, 157, 158, 194, 196,
 214
Cohen, Morris Raphael, 33, 36, 377 n.21,
 377 n.24

Cohen, Mortimer, 236
Collective consciousness, 149–53
Columbia University, 52–53; joint program
 with Teachers' Institute, 112–13, 390
 n. 36; Teachers' College, 53
Conservative Judaism, 276; English language emphasis, 48; Historical School,
 37, 38, 39; on *Judaism as a Civilization*,
 344–45; self-definition problems, 127;
 turning point in histoy, 278
Cronson, Bernard, 118

Darwin, Charles, 53–54, 82
Davidson, Israel, 102, 224
Davis, Moshe: on Conservative Judaism,
 127–28
De Hass, Jacob, 139, 170, 312
Dewey, John, 81, 313; comparison with
 Kaplan, 385 n.20; question of influ-
 ence on Kaplan, 61, 145, 395 n.34
Dinin, Samuel, 114, 115, 230
Drachman, Bernard, 62; and Jewish Theo-
 logical Seminary, 40, 42, 101, 102, 378
 n.33, 386 n.4; on "Kaplanism," 190
Dropsie College, 128
Dubnov, Simon, 312, 314, 316
Durkheim, Emile, 55, 56–57; on collective
 consciousness, 150; influence on
 Kaplan, 381 n.22
Dushkin, Alexander, 121, 228, 335, 339,
 392 n.56, 392 n.63

Ehrlich, Arnold B., 379 n.41, 407 n.16; bib-
 lical criticism, 243–44; influence on
 Kaplan, 45–46, 89, 242–43, 379 n.40;
 *Mikra Kiphshuto: The Bible according to
 Its Literal Meaning*, 243
Eisen, Arnold, 345
Eisenstein, Ann, 351–52
Eisenstein, Ira, 29, 289; on Kaplan as a
 teacher, 235–36; marriage to Judith
 Kaplan, 355–56; *The New Haggadah*,
 360–61; Reconstructionist Rabbinical
 College, 362–63; relationship with
 Kaplan, 356; and Society for the Ad-
 vancement of Judaism, 356–58
Eisenstein, Judah David, 29, 71, 75, 235,
 376 n.15; on Conservative Judaism,
 48; defense of *Kol Nidre*, 289–90
Eisenstein, Judith Kaplan, 29, 113, 165,
 166, 397 n.18, 419 n.23; bas mitzvah,
 301–2, 415 n.31; professional achieve-